D0523336

PHP Objects, Patterns, and Practice

Third Edition

Matt Zandstra

Apress®

PHP Objects, Patterns, and Practice, Third Edition

Copyright © 2010 by Matt Zandstra

All rights reserved. No part of this work may be reproduced or transmitted in any form or by any means, electronic or mechanical, including photocopying, recording, or by any information storage or retrieval system, without the prior written permission of the copyright owner and the publisher.

ISBN-13 (pbk): 978-1-4302-2925-4

ISBN-13 (electronic): 978-1-4302-2926-1

Printed and bound in the United States of America (POD)

Trademarked names may appear in this book. Rather than use a trademark symbol with every occurrence of a trademarked name, we use the names only in an editorial fashion and to the benefit of the trademark owner, with no intention of infringement of the trademark.

President and Publisher: Paul Manning
Lead Editor: Michelle Lowman, Matt Wade
Technical Reviewer: Wes Hunt
Editorial Board: Steve Anglin, Mark Beckner, Ewan Buckingham, Gary Cornell, Jonathan Gennick, Jonathan Hassell, Michelle Lowman, Matthew Moodie, Jeff Olson, Jeffrey Pepper, Frank Pohlmann, Douglas Pundick, Ben Renow-Clarke, Dominic Shakeshaft, Matt Wade, Tom Welsh
Coordinating Editor: Jim Markham
Copy Editor: Tracy Brown Collins
Compositor: MacPS, LLC
Indexer: Toma Mulligan
Artist: April Milne
Cover Designer: Anna Ischenko

Distributed to the book trade worldwide by Springer Science+Business Media, LLC., 233 Spring Street, 6th Floor, New York, NY 10013. Phone 1-800-SPRINGER, fax 201-348-4505, e-mail orders-ny@springer-sbm.com, or visit www.springeronline.com.

For information on translations, please e-mail rights@apress.com, or visit www.apress.com.

Apress and friends of ED books may be purchased in bulk for academic, corporate, or promotional use. eBook versions and licenses are also available for most titles. For more information, reference our Special Bulk Sales–eBook Licensing web page at www.apress.com/info/bulksales.

The information in this book is distributed on an "as is" basis, without warranty. Although every precaution has been taken in the preparation of this work, neither the author(s) nor Apress shall have any liability to any person or entity with respect to any loss or damage caused or alleged to be caused directly or indirectly by the information contained in this work.

The source code for this book is available to readers at www.apress.com. You will need to answer questions pertaining to this book in order to successfully download the code.

Contents at a Glance

Contents

About the Author

Matt Zandstra has worked as a web programmer, consultant, and writer for over a decade. He is a senior developer at Yahoo, and a freelance coder and writer. Matt is the author of *Teach Yourself PHP in 24 Hours* (SAMS) and a contributor to *DHTML Unleashed* (SAMS). He has written articles for *Linux Magazine*, Zend.com, IBM DeveloperWorks, and *php|architect Magazine*, among others. He works primarily with PHP and Java, designing and building web and command-line applications.

Matt lives in Liverpool with his wife, Louise, and two children, Holly and Jake.

About the Technical Reviewer

 **Wes Hunt** is a web-application developer and consultant at 4th Dimension Development, which builds web solutions for organizations from small to the enterprise level. For over a decade, he has used Java and PHP to deliver everything plus the kitchen sink for clients. His latest passion is leveraging Flex with a PHP back-end to produce RIAs for clients. Wes uses development patterns and best practices in order to spend more time enjoying the outdoors near his home in Montana.

Acknowledgments

When you first have an idea for a book (in my case, while drinking good coffee in a Brighton cafe), it is the subject matter alone that grips you. In the enthusiasm of the moment, it is easy to forget the scale of the undertaking. I soon rediscovered the sheer hard work a book demands, and I learned once again that it's not something you can do alone. At every stage of this book's development, I have benefited from enormous support.

In fact, my thanks must predate the book's conception. The themes of this book first saw the light of day in a talk I gave for a Brighton initiative called Skillswap (`www.skillswap.org`) run by Andy Budd. It was Andy's invitation to speak that first planted the seeds of the idea in my mind. For that, I still owe Andy a pint and much thanks.

By chance, attending that meeting was Jessey White-Cinis, another Apress author, who put me in touch with Martin Streicher, who commissioned the book for Apress straightaway.

My thanks go out to both Jessey and Martin for seeing potential in the slightest of beginnings.

Once again the Apress team has provided enormous support in the face of a very tight deadline, and my tendency to go quiet as I moved with my family to a new continent in the middle of the project.

Thanks to Steven Metsker for his kind permission to re-implement in PHP a brutally simplified version of the parser API he presented in his book Building Parsers in Java.

Writing to a deadline is not conducive to family life, and so I must send my thanks and love to my wife, Louise, and to our children, Holly and Jake. I have missed you all.

Since the publication of the first edition, I have been lucky to receive much enthusiastic and constructive feedback from readers. I'm sorry that I haven't been able to reply to everyone individually, but I'd like to take this opportunity to thank all correspondents for your messages.

The soundtrack to the writing of the first edition was provided by John Peel. John was a broadcaster who waged a 40-year war on the bland and mass-produced in music simply by championing everything original and eclectic he could lay his hands on. John died suddenly in October 2004, leaving listeners around the world bereft. He had an extraordinary impact on many lives, and I would like to add my thanks here.

Introduction to the Third Edition

When I first had the idea for *PHP Objects, Patterns, and Practice*, I felt I was swimming against the tide. Many pattern implementations in PHP felt like glorified workarounds due to limitations in the language. These days, though, it can be hard to keep up with pace of innovation in PHP objects, design, and project practice.

If that's a problem, well, it's the kind you want to have. Especially if you have the tools at hand to navigate the risks and opportunities that present themselves.

PHP continues to tick items off the object-oriented developer's wish list. Since the last edition of this book, we have seen namespaces make it into the language, late static binding, anonymous functions, and closures (if those don't yet mean anything to you, don't worry, they're all covered by this book). PHP is an active language, constantly evolving to meet the needs of its users.

For a developer, this presents some interesting challenges. Not least, the tension between a stable codebase and the desire to take advantage of the goodies that every new release brings. With a good suite of tests, preferably run automatically, tools for collaboration, and an easily installed system, you can improve the design of your code, play with new features, and be fairly sure that you're not breaking stuff.

And that's where this book comes in, I hope. I want to explore what's exciting, both in the language and in the wider world of object-oriented design. At the same time, I want to take in the tools and practices you can use to safeguard your project from the hordes of bugs that lurk beyond sight whenever you make a change.

As well as new language features, this edition benefits from coverage of web testing with Selenium, and the ultimate tool of tools: a Continuous Integration server that runs tests, builds your system, and applies diagnostic tools to your project.

How real is a web application? It exists as lines of code, of course, bits stored on a computer. It exists in its execution on a server. But really, for the developer, an application first lives in the imagination. It is a structure made up of parts that interlock more or less elegantly. Then, if we're lucky, it is realized and deployed, and it really comes alive at the moment someone uses it. There, right there, is where the magic of coding lives.

That's what this book is really about. It's about taking an idea and shaping it, and the pleasure to be found in the process. It's about the shapes of a system in your imagination, and the satisfaction when these shapes are expressed in code. And then again when the system actually works. It's about the freedom that tests give you to take risks, and the risks that your imagination inspires you to take. It's the moment that something you wrote becomes real in the eyes of another.

■ ■ ■

PART 1

Introduction

CHAPTER 1

■ ■ ■

PHP: Design and Management

When PHP 5 was released early in 2004, among the most important features it introduced was enhanced support for object-oriented programming. This stimulated much interest in objects and design within the PHP community. In fact, this was an intensification of a process that began when version 4 first made object-oriented programming with PHP a serious reality.

In this chapter, I look at some of the needs that coding with objects can address. I very briefly summarize the evolution of patterns and related practices in the Java world. I look at signs that indicate a similar process is occurring among PHP coders.

I also outline the topics covered by this book.

I will look at

- *The evolution of disaster*: A project goes bad.

- *Design and PHP*: How object-oriented design techniques are taking root in the PHP community.

- *This book*: Objects. Patterns. Practice.

The Problem

The problem is that PHP is just too easy. It tempts you to try out your ideas, and flatters you with good results. You write much of your code straight into your web pages, because PHP is designed to support that. You add utility functions (such as database access code) to files that can be included from page to page, and before you know it you have a working web application.

You are well on the road to ruin. You don't realize this, of course, because your site looks fantastic. It performs well, your clients are happy, and your users are spending money.

Trouble strikes when you go back to the code to begin a new phase. Now you have a larger team, some more users, a bigger budget. Yet without warning, things begin to go wrong. It's as if your project has been poisoned.

Your new programmer is struggling to understand code that is second nature to you, though perhaps a little byzantine in its twists and turns. She is taking longer than you expected to reach full strength as a team member.

A simple change, estimated at a day, takes three days when you discover that you must update 20 or more web pages as a result.

One of your coders saves his version of a file over major changes you made to the same code some time earlier. The loss is not discovered for three days, by which time you have amended your own local copy. It takes a day to sort out the mess, holding up a third developer who was also working on the file.

Because of the application's popularity, you need to shift the code to a new server. The project has to be installed by hand, and you discover that file paths, database names, and passwords are hard-coded into many source files. You halt work during the move because you don't want to overwrite the configuration changes the migration requires. The estimated two hours becomes eight as it is revealed that someone did something clever involving the Apache module ModRewrite, and the application now requires this to operate properly.

You finally launch phase 2. All is well for a day and a half. The first bug report comes in as you are about to leave the office. The client phones minutes later to complain. Her report is similar to the first, but a little more scrutiny reveals that it is a different bug causing similar behavior. You remember the simple change back at the start of the phase that necessitated extensive modifications throughout the rest of the project.

You realize that not all the required modifications are in place. This is either because they were omitted to start with or because the files in question were overwritten in merge collisions. You hurriedly make the modifications needed to fix the bugs. You're in too much of a hurry to test the changes, but they are a simple matter of copy and paste, so what can go wrong?

The next morning you arrive at the office to find that a shopping basket module has been down all night. The last-minute changes you made omitted a leading quotation mark, rendering the code unusable. Of course, while you were asleep, potential customers in other time zones were wide awake and ready to spend money at your store. You fix the problem, mollify the client, and gather the team for another day's firefighting.

This everyday tale of coding folk may seem a little over the top, but I have seen all these things happen over and over again. Many PHP projects start their life small and evolve into monsters.

Because the presentation layer also contains application logic, duplication creeps in early as database queries, authentication checks, form processing, and more are copied from page to page. Every time a change is required to one of these blocks of code, it must be made everywhere the code is found, or bugs will surely follow.

Lack of documentation makes the code hard to read, and lack of testing allows obscure bugs to go undiscovered until deployment. The changing nature of a client's business often means that code evolves away from its original purpose until it is performing tasks for which it is fundamentally unsuited. Because such code has often evolved as a seething intermingled lump, it is hard, if not impossible, to switch out and rewrite parts of it to suit the new purpose.

Now, none of this is bad news if you are a freelance PHP consultant. Assessing and fixing a system like this can fund expensive espresso drinks and DVD box sets for six months or more. More seriously, though, problems of this sort can mean the difference between a business's success or failure.

PHP and Other Languages

PHP's phenomenal popularity meant that its boundaries were tested early and hard. As you will see in the next chapter, PHP started life as a set of macros for managing personal home pages. With the advent of PHP 3 and, to a greater extent, PHP 4, the language rapidly became the successful power behind large enterprise Web sites. In many ways, though, the legacy of PHP's beginnings carried through into script design and project management. In some quarters, PHP retained an unfair reputation as a hobbyist language, best suited for presentation tasks.

About this time (around the turn of the millennium), new ideas were gaining currency in other coding communities. An interest in object-oriented design galvanized the Java community. You may think that this is a redundancy, since Java is an object-oriented language. Java provides a grain that is easier to work with than against, of course, but using classes and objects does not in itself make a particular design approach.

The concept of the design pattern, as a way of describing a problem together with the essence of its solution, was first discussed in the '70s. Perhaps aptly, the idea originated in the field of architecture, and not computer science. By the early '90s, object-oriented programmers were using the same technique to name and describe problems of software design. The seminal book on design patterns, *Design Patterns: Elements of Reusable Object-Oriented Software*, by the affectionately nicknamed *Gang of Four*, was published in 1995, and is still indispensable today. The patterns it contains are a required first step for anyone starting out in this field, which is why most of the patterns in this book are drawn from it.

The Java language itself deployed many core patterns in its API, but it wasn't until the late '90s that design patterns seeped into the consciousness of the coding community at large. Patterns quickly infected the computer sections of High Street bookstores, and the first flame wars began on mailing lists and forums.

Whether you think that patterns are a powerful way of communicating craft knowledge or largely hot air (and, given the title of this book, you can probably guess where I stand on that issue), it is hard to deny that the emphasis on software design they have encouraged is beneficial in itself.

Related topics also grew in prominence. Among them was eXtreme Programming (XP), championed by Kent Beck. XP is an approach to projects that encourages flexible, design-oriented, highly focused planning and execution.

Prominent among XP's principles is an insistence that testing is crucial to a project's success. Tests should be automated, run often, and preferably designed before their target code is written.

XP also dictates that projects should be broken down into small (very small) iterations. Both code and requirements should be scrutinized at all times. Architecture and design should be a shared and constant issue, leading to the frequent revision of code.

If XP is the militant wing of the design movement, then the moderate tendency is well represented by one of the best books about programming I have ever read: *The Pragmatic Programmer* by Andrew Hunt and David Thomas, which was published in 2000.

XP is deemed a tad cultish by some, but it grew out of two decades of object-oriented practice at the highest level and its principles were widely cannibalized. In particular, code revision, known as refactoring, was taken up as a powerful adjunct to patterns. Refactoring has evolved since the '80s, but it was codified in Martin Fowler's catalog of refactorings, *Refactoring: Improving the Design of Existing Code*, which was published in 1999 and defined the field.

Testing too became a hot issue with the rise to prominence of XP and patterns. The importance of automated tests was further underlined by the release of the powerful JUnit test platform, which became a key weapon in the Java programmer's armory. A landmark article on the subject, "Test Infected: Programmers Love Writing Tests" by Kent Beck and Erich Gamma (`http://junit.sourceforge.net/doc/testinfected/testing.htm`), gives an excellent introduction to the topic and remains hugely influential.

PHP 4 was released at about this time, bringing with it improvements in efficiency and, crucially, enhanced support for objects. These enhancements made fully object-oriented projects a possibility. Programmers embraced this feature, somewhat to the surprise of Zend founders Zeev Suraski and Andi Gutmans, who had joined Rasmus Lerdorf to manage PHP development. As you shall see in the next chapter, PHP's object support was by no means perfect, but with discipline and careful use of syntax, one could really think in objects and PHP at the same time.

Nevertheless, design disasters like the one depicted at the start of this chapter remained common. Design culture was some way off, and almost nonexistent in books about PHP. Online, though, the interest was clear. Leon Atkinson wrote a piece about PHP and patterns for Zend in 2001 , and Harry Fuecks launched his journal at www.phppatterns.com (now largely mothballed, it seems) in 2002. Pattern-based framework projects such as BinaryCloud began to emerge, as well as tools for automated testing and documentation.

The release of the first PHP 5 beta in 2003 ensured the future of PHP as a language for object-oriented programming. The Zend 2 Engine provided greatly improved object support. Equally important, it sent a signal that objects and object-oriented design were now central to the PHP project.

Over the years, PHP 5 has continued to evolve and improve, incorporating important new features such as namespaces and closures. During this time, it has secured its reputation as the best choice for server side web programming.

About This Book

This book does not attempt to break new ground in the field of object-oriented design; in that respect it perches precariously upon the shoulders of giants. Instead, I examine, in the context of PHP, some well-established design principles and some key patterns (particularly those inscribed in *Design Patterns*, the classic Gang of Four book). Finally, I move beyond the strict limits of code to look at tools and techniques that can help to ensure the success of a project. Aside from this introduction and a brief conclusion, the book is divided into three main parts: objects, patterns, and practice.

Objects

I begin Part 2 with a quick look at the history of PHP and objects, charting their shift from afterthought in PHP 3 to core feature in PHP 5.

You can still be an experienced and successful PHP programmer with little or no knowledge of objects. For this reason, I start from first principles to explain objects, classes, and inheritance. Even at this early stage, I look at some of the object enhancements that PHP 5 introduced.

The basics established, I delve deeper into our topic, examining PHP's more advanced object-oriented features. I also devote a chapter to the tools that PHP provides to help you work with objects and classes.

It is not enough, though, to know how to declare a class, and to use it to instantiate an object. You must first choose the right participants for your system and decide the best ways for them to interact. These choices are much harder to describe and to learn than the bald facts about object tools and syntax. I finish Part 2 with an introduction to object-oriented design with PHP.

Patterns

A pattern describes a problem in software design and provides the kernel of a solution. "Solution" here does not mean the kind of cut-and-paste code you might find in a cookbook (excellent though cookbooks are as resources for the programmer). Instead, a design pattern describes an approach that can be taken to solve a problem. A sample implementation may be given, but it is less important than the concept it serves to illustrate.

Part 3 begins by defining design patterns and describing their structure. I also look at some of the reasons behind their popularity.

Patterns tend to promote and follow certain core design principles. An understanding of these can help in analyzing a pattern's motivation, and can usefully be applied to all programming. I discuss some of these principles. I also examine the Unified Modeling Language (UML), a platform-independent way of describing classes and their interactions.

Although this book is not a pattern catalog, I examine some of the most famous and useful patterns. I describe the problem that each pattern addresses, analyze the solution, and present an implementation example in PHP.

Practice

Even a beautifully balanced architecture will fail if it is not managed correctly. In Part 4, I look at the tools available to help you create a framework that ensures the success of your project. If the rest of the book is about the practice of design and programming, Part 4 is about the practice of managing your code. The tools I examine can form a support structure for a project, helping to track bugs as they occur, promoting collaboration among programmers, and providing ease of installation and clarity of code.

I have already discussed the power of the automated test. I kick off Part 4 with an introductory chapter that gives an overview of problems and solutions in this area.

Many programmers are guilty of giving in to the impulse to do everything themselves. The PHP community maintains PEAR, a repository of quality-controlled packages that can be stitched into projects with ease. I look at the trade-offs between implementing a feature yourself and deploying a PEAR package.

While I'm on the topic of PEAR, I look at the installation mechanism that makes the deployment of a package as simple as a single command. Best suited for stand-alone packages, this mechanism can be used to automate the installation of your own code. I show you how to do it.

Documentation can be a chore, and along with testing, it is probably the easiest part of a project to jettison when deadlines loom. I argue that this is probably a mistake, and show you PHPDocumentor, a tool that helps you turn comments in your code into a set of hyperlinked HTML documents that describe every element of your API.

Almost every tool or technique discussed in this book directly concerns or is deployed using PHP. The one exception to this rule is Subversion. Subversion is a version control system that enables many programmers to work together on the same codebase without overwriting one another's work. It lets you grab snapshots of your project at any stage in development, see who has made which changes, and split the project into mergeable branches. Subversion will save your project one day.

Two facts seem inevitable. First, bugs often recur in the same region of code, making some work days an exercise in déjà vu. Second, often improvements break as much as, or more than, they fix. Automated testing can address both of these issues, providing an early warning system for problems in your code. I introduce PHPUnit, a powerful implementation of the so-called xUnit test platform designed first for Smalltalk but ported now to many languages, notably Java. I look in particular at PHPUnit's features and more generally at the benefits, and some of the costs, of testing.

PEAR provides a build tool that is ideal for installing self-enclosed packages. For a complete application, however, greater flexibility is required. Applications are messy. They may need files to be installed in nonstandard locations, or want to set up databases, or need to patch server configuration. In short, applications need *stuff* to be done during installation. Phing is a faithful port of a Java tool called Ant. Phing and Ant interpret a build file and process your source files in any way you tell them to. This usually means copying them from a source directory to various target locations around your system, but as your needs get more complex, Phing scales effortlessly to meet them.

Testing and build are all very well, but you have to install and run your tests, and keep on doing so in order to reap the benefits. It's easy to become complacent and let things slide if you don't automate your builds and tests. I look at some tools and techniques that are lumped together in the category "continuous integration" that will help you do just that.

What's New in the Third Edition

PHP is a living language, and as such it's under constant review and development. This new edition has been reviewed and thoroughly updated to take account of changes and new opportunities. I cover new features such as closures, for example. The second edition examined an experimental version of namespaces, which has since been rendered obsolete by the release of PHP 5.3, with its own namespace support. I have, of course, updated this edition to address this.

I have updated the chapter on version control to cover Subversion rather than CVS. This reflects the general migration to the newer platform I have perceived since this book was first published. I also include a new chapter on continuous integration, both a practice and a set of tools that allows developers to automate and monitor their build and test strategies..

Summary

This is a book about object-oriented design and programming. It is also about tools for managing a PHP codebase from collaboration through to deployment.

These two themes address the same problem from different but complementary angles. The aim is to build systems that achieve their objectives and lend themselves well to collaborative development.

A secondary goals lies in the aesthetics of software systems. As programmers, we build machines that have shape and action. We invest many hours of our working day, and many days of our lives, writing these shapes into being. We want the tools we build, whether individual classes and objects, software components, or end products, to form an elegant whole. The process of version control, testing, documentation, and build does more than support this objective, it is part of the shape we want to achieve. Just as we want clean and clever code, we want a codebase that is designed well for developers and users alike. The mechanics of sharing, reading, and deploying the project should be as important as the code itself.

PART 2

Objects

CHAPTER 2

■ ■ ■

PHP and Objects

Objects were not always a key part of the PHP project. In fact, they have been described as an afterthought by PHP's designers.

As afterthoughts go, this one has proved remarkably resilient. In this chapter, I introduce coverage of objects by summarizing the development of PHP's object-oriented features.

We will look at

- *PHP/FI 2.0*: PHP, but not as we know it.

- *PHP 3*: Objects make their first appearance.

- *PHP 4*: Object-oriented programming grows up.

- *PHP 5*: Objects at the heart of the language.

- *PHP 6*: A glimpse of the future

The Accidental Success of PHP Objects

With so many object-oriented PHP libraries and applications in circulation, to say nothing of PHP 5's extensive object enhancements, the rise of the object in PHP may seem like the culmination of a natural and inevitable process. In fact, nothing could be further from the truth.

In the Beginning: PHP/FI

The genesis of PHP as we know it today lies with two tools developed by Rasmus Lerdorf using Perl. PHP stood for Personal Homepage Tools. FI stood for Form Interpreter. Together, they comprised macros for sending SQL statements to databases, processing forms, and flow control.

These tools were rewritten in C and combined under the name PHP/FI 2.0. The language at this stage looked different from the syntax we recognize today, but not *that* different. There was support for variables, associative arrays, and functions. Objects, though, were not even on the horizon.

Syntactic Sugar: PHP 3

In fact, even as PHP 3 was in the planning stage, objects were off the agenda. As today, the principal architects of PHP 3 were Zeev Suraski and Andi Gutmans. PHP 3 was a complete rewrite of PHP/FI 2.0, but objects were not deemed a necessary part of the new syntax.

According to Zeev Suraski, support for classes was added almost as an afterthought (on 27 August 1997, to be precise). Classes and objects were actually just another way to define and access associative arrays.

Of course, the addition of methods and inheritance made classes much more than glorified associative arrays, but there were still severe limitations as to what you could do with your classes. In particular, you could not access a parent class's overridden methods (don't worry if you don't know what this means yet; I will explain later). Another disadvantage that I will examine in the next section was the less than optimal way that objects were passed around in PHP scripts.

That objects were a marginal issue at this time is underlined by their lack of prominence in official documentation. The manual devoted one sentence and a code example to objects. The example did not illustrate inheritance or properties.

PHP 4 and the Quiet Revolution

If PHP 4 was yet another ground-breaking step for the language, most of the core changes took place beneath the surface. The Zend Engine (its name derived from **Zee**v and **And**i) was written from scratch to power the language. The Zend Engine is one of the main components that drive PHP. Any PHP function you might care to call is in fact part of the high level extensions layer. These do the busy work they were named for, like talking to database APIs or juggling strings for you. Beneath that the Zend Engine manages memory, delegates control to other components, and translates the familiar PHP syntax you work with every day into runnable bytecode. It is the Zend Engine we have to thank for core language features like classes.

From our *objecti*ve perspective, the fact that PHP 4 made it possible to override parent methods and access them from child classes was a major benefit.

A major drawback remained, however. Assigning an object to a variable, passing it to a function, or returning it from a method, resulted in a copy being made. So an assignment like this

```
$my_obj = new User('bob');
$other = $my_obj;
```

resulted in the existence of two User objects, rather than two references to the same User object. In most object-oriented languages you would expect assignment by reference, rather than by value as here. This means that you pass and assign handles that point to objects rather than copy the objects themselves. The default pass-by-value behavior resulted in many obscure bugs as programmers unwittingly modified objects in one part of a script, expecting the changes to be seen via references elsewhere. Throughout this book, you will see many examples in which I maintain multiple references to the same object.

Luckily, there was a way of enforcing pass-by-reference, but it meant remembering to use a clumsy construction.

Assign by reference as follows:

```
$other =& $my_obj;
// $other and $my_obj point to same object
```

Pass by reference as follows:

```
function setSchool( & $school ) {
    // $school is now a reference to not a copy of passed object
}
```

And return by reference as follows:

```
function & getSchool( ) {
    // returning a reference not a copy
    return $this->school;
}
```

Although this worked fine, it was easy to forget to add the ampersand, and it was all too easy for bugs to creep into object-oriented code. These were particularly hard to track down, because they rarely caused any reported errors, just plausible but broken behavior.

Coverage of syntax in general, and objects in particular, was extended in the PHP manual, and object-oriented coding began to bubble up to the mainstream. Objects in PHP were not uncontroversial (then, as now, no doubt), and threads like "Do I need objects?" were common flame-bait in mailing lists. Indeed, the Zend site played host to articles that encouraged object-oriented programming side by side with others that sounded a warning note.

Pass-by-reference issues and controversy notwithstanding, many coders just got on and peppered their code with ampersand characters. Object-oriented PHP grew in popularity. As Zeev Suraski wrote in an article for DevX.com (http://www.devx.com/webdev/Article/10007/0/page/1):

> One of the biggest twists in PHP's history was that despite the very limited functionality, and despite a host of problems and limitations, object-oriented programming in PHP thrived and became the most popular paradigm for the growing numbers of off-the-shelf PHP applications. This trend, which was mostly unexpected, caught PHP in a suboptimal situation. It became apparent that objects were not behaving like objects in other OO languages, and were instead behaving like [associative] arrays.

As noted in the previous chapter, interest in object-oriented design became obvious in sites and articles online. PHP's official software repository, PEAR, itself embraced object-oriented programming. Some of the best examples of deployed object-oriented design patterns are to be found in the packages that PEAR makes available to extend PHP's functionality.

With hindsight, it's easy to think of PHP's adoption of object-oriented support as a reluctant capitulation to an inevitable force. It's important to remember that, although object-oriented programming has been around since the sixties, it really gained ground in the mid-nineties. Java, the great popularizer, was not released until 1995. A superset of C, a procedural language, C++ has been around since 1979. After a long evolution, it arguably made the leap to the big time during the nineties. Perl 5 was released in 1994, another revolution within a formerly procedural language that made it possible for its users to think in objects (although some argue that Perl's object-oriented support still feels like something of an afterthought). For a small procedural language, PHP developed its object support remarkably fast, showing a real responsiveness to the requirements of its users.

Change Embraced: PHP 5

PHP 5 represented an explicit endorsement of objects and object-oriented programming. That is not to say that objects are now the only way to work with PHP (this book does not say that either, by the way). Objects, are, however, now recognized as a powerful and important means for developing enterprise systems, and PHP fully supports them in its core design.

Objects have moved from afterthought to language driver. Perhaps the most important change is the default pass-by-reference behavior in place of the evils of object copying. This is only the beginning though. Throughout this book, and particularly this part of it, we will encounter many more changes that extend and enhance PHP's object support, including argument hinting, private and protected methods and properties, the static keyword, namespaces, and exceptions, among many others.

PHP remains a language that supports object-oriented development, rather than an object-oriented language. Its support for objects, however, is now well enough developed to justify books like this one that concentrate on design from an exclusively object-oriented point of view.

Into the Future

As I write this, PHP 6 is still some way off, but it is under active development. It will be built on an entirely new generation of the Zend Engine (ZE3), and will provide built-in support for Unicode sting handling, which will make the language better able to support internationalization. This means you will be able to use all PHP's string functions without worrying about whether they can work with the current character set. In the past, developers had to use multibyte equivalents for many common functions—a frustrating and error-prone task. As internationalization becomes more and more important, this core feature is fast becoming essential in any serious programming language..

In some ways the future is already here. A feature that was slated for PHP 6 has now found its way into PHP 5 (as of PHP 5.3): support for namespaces. Namespaces let you create a naming scope for classes and functions so that you are less likely to run into duplicate names as you include libraries and expand your system. They also rescue you from ugly but necessary naming conventions like this:

```
class megaquiz_util_Conf {
}
```

Class names like this are one way of preventing clashes between packages, but they can make for tortuous code.

At the time of this writing, it looks like support for hinted return types is once again slated for PHP 6. This will allow you to declare in a method or function's declaration the object type it returns. This commitment will then be enforced by the PHP engine. Hinted return types will further improve PHP's support for pattern principles (principles such as "code to an interface, not an implementation"). I hope to revise this book to cover that feature!

Advocacy and Agnosticism: The Object Debate

Objects and object-oriented design seem to stir passions on both sides of the enthusiasm divide. Many excellent programmers have produced excellent code for years without using objects, and PHP continues to be a superb platform for procedural web programming.

This book naturally displays an object-oriented bias throughout, a bias that reflects my object-infected outlook. Because this book *is* a celebration of objects, and an introduction to object-oriented design, it is inevitable that the emphasis is unashamedly object oriented. Nothing in this book is intended, however, to suggest that objects are the one true path to coding success with PHP.

As you read, it is worth bearing in mind the famous Perl motto, "There's more than one way to do it." This is especially true of smaller scripts, where quickly getting a working example up and running is more important than building a structure that will scale well into a larger system (scratch projects of this sort are known as "spikes" in the eXtreme Programming world).

Code is a flexible medium. The trick is to know when your quick proof of concept is becoming the root of a larger development, and to call a halt before your design decisions are made for you by sheer weight of code. Now that you have decided to take a design-oriented approach to your growing project, there are plenty of books that will provide examples of procedural design for many different kinds of projects. This book offers some thoughts about designing with objects. I hope that it provides a valuable starting point.

Summary

This short chapter placed objects in their context in the PHP language. The future for PHP is very much bound up with object-oriented design. In the next few chapters, I take a snapshot of PHP's current support for object features, and introduce some design issues.

CHAPTER 3

∎∎∎

Object Basics

Objects and classes lie at the heart of this book, and since the introduction of PHP 5, they lie at the heart of PHP too. In this chapter, I lay down the groundwork for more in-depth work with objects and design by examining PHP's core object-oriented features.

PHP 5 brought with it a radical advance in object-oriented support, so if you are already familiar with PHP 4, you will probably find something new here. If you are new to object-oriented programming, you should read this chapter carefully.

This chapter will cover

- *Classes and objects*: Declaring classes and instantiating objects

- *Constructor methods*: Automating the setup of your objects

- *Primitive and class types*: Why type matters

- *Inheritance*: Why we need inheritance and how to use it

- *Visibility*: Streamlining your object interfaces and protecting your methods and properties from meddling

Classes and Objects

The first barrier to understanding object-oriented programming is the strange and wonderful relationship between the class and the object. For many people it is this relationship that represents the first moment of revelation, the first flash of object-oriented excitement. So let's not skimp on the basics.

A First Class

Classes are often described in terms of objects. This is interesting, because objects are often described in terms of classes. This circularity can make the first steps in object-oriented programming hard going. Since classes define objects, we should begin by defining a class.

In short, a class is a code template used to generate objects. You declare a class with the class keyword and an arbitrary class name. Class names can be any combination of numbers and letters, although they must not begin with a number. The code associated with a class must be enclosed within braces. Let's combine these elements to build a class.

```
class ShopProduct {
    // class body
}
```

The ShopProduct class in the example is already a legal class, although it is not terribly useful yet. I have done something quite significant, however. I have defined a type; that is, I have created a category of data that I can use in my scripts. The power of this should become clearer as you work through the chapter.

A First Object (or Two)

If a class is a template for generating objects, it follows that an object is data that has been structured according to the template defined in a class. An object is said to be an instance of its class. It is of the type defined by the class.

I use the ShopProduct class as a mold for generating ShopProduct objects. To do this, I need the new operator. The new operator is used in conjunction with the name of a class, like this:

```
$product1 = new ShopProduct();
$product2 = new ShopProduct();
```

The new operator is invoked with a class name as its only operand and generates an instance of that class; in our example, it generates a ShopProduct object.

I have used the ShopProduct class as a template to generate two ShopProduct objects. Although they are functionally identical (that is, empty), $product1 and $product2 are different objects of the same type generated from a single class.

If you are still confused, try this analogy. Think of a class as a cast in a machine that makes plastic ducks. Our objects are the ducks that this machine generates. The type of thing generated is determined by the mold from which it is pressed. The ducks look identical in every way, but they are distinct entities. In other words, they are different instances of the same type. The ducks may even have their own serial numbers to prove their identities. Every object that is created in a PHP script is also given its own unique identifier (unique for the life of the object), that is, PHP reuses identifiers, even within a process. I can demonstrate this by printing out the $product1 and $product2 objects:

```
var_dump($product1);
var_dump($product2);
```

Executing these functions produces the following output:

```
object(ShopProduct)#1 (0) {
}
object(ShopProduct)#2 (0) {
}
```

▓**Note** In PHP 4 and PHP 5 (up to version 5.1), you can print an object directly. This casts the object to a string containing the object's ID. From PHP 5.2 onwards the language no longer supported this magic, and any attempt to treat an object as a string now causes an error unless a method called __toString() is defined in the object's class. I look at methods later in this chapter, and I cover __toString() in Chapter 4, "Advanced Features."

By passing our objects to var_dump(), I extract useful information including, after the hash sign, each object's internal identifier.

In order to make these objects more interesting, I can amend the ShopProduct class to support special data fields called properties.

Setting Properties in a Class

Classes can define special variables called properties. A property, also known as a member variable, holds data that can vary from object to object. So in the case of ShopProduct objects you may wish to manipulate title and price fields, for example.

A property in a class looks similar to a standard variable except that you must precede your declaration and assignment with a visibility keyword. This can be public, protected, or private, and it determines the scope from which the property can be accessed.

▨**Note** Scope refers to the function or class context in which a variable has meaning (it refers in the same way to methods, which I will cover later in this chapter). So a variable defined in a function exists in local scope, and a variable defined outside of the function exists in global scope. As a rule of thumb, it is not possible to access data defined in a scope that is more local than the current. So if you define a variable inside a function, you cannot later access it from outside that function. Objects are more permeable than this, in that some object variables can sometimes be accessed from other contexts. Which variables can be accessed and from what context is determined by the public, protected, and private keywords, as you shall see.

I will return to these keywords and the issue of visibility later in this chapter. For now, I will declare some properties using the public keyword:

```
class ShopProduct {
    public $title               = "default product";
    public $producerMainName    = "main name";
    public $producerFirstName   = "first name";
    public $price               = 0;
}
```

As you can see, I set up four properties, assigning a default value to each of them. Any objects that I instantiate from the ShopProduct class will now be prepopulated with default data. The public keyword in each property declaration ensures that I can access the property from outside of the object context.

▨**Note** The visibility keywords public, private, and protected were introduced in PHP 5. If you are running PHP 4, these examples will not work for you. In PHP 4, all properties were declared with the var keyword, which is identical in effect to using public. For the sake of backward compatibility, PHP 5 accepts var in place of public for properties.

You can access property variables on an object-by-object basis using the characters '->' in conjunction with an object variable and property name, like this:

```
$product1 = new ShopProduct();
print $product1->title;
```

---

default product

Because the properties are defined as public, you can assign values to them just as you can read them, replacing any default value set in the class:

```
$product1 = new ShopProduct();
$product2 = new ShopProduct();
$product1->title="My Antonia";
$product2->title="Catch 22";
```

By declaring and setting the $title property in the ShopProduct class, I ensure that all ShopProduct objects have this property when first created. This means that code that uses this class can work with ShopProduct objects on that assumption. Because I can reset it, though, the value of $title may vary from object to object.

■**Note** Code that uses a class, function, or method is often described as the class's, function's, or method's client or as client code. You will see this term frequently in the coming chapters.

In fact, PHP does not force us to declare all our properties in the class. You could add properties dynamically to an object, like this:

```
$product1->arbitraryAddition = "treehouse";
```

However, this method of assigning properties to objects is not considered good practice in object-oriented programming and is almost never used.

Why is it bad practice to set properties dynamically? When you create a class you define a type. You inform the world that your class (and any object instantiated from it) consists of a particular set of fields and functions. If your ShopProduct class defines a $title property, then any code that works with ShopProduct objects can proceed on the assumption that a $title property will be available. There can be no guarantees about properties that have been dynamically set, though.

My objects are still cumbersome at this stage. When I need to work with an object's properties, I must currently do so from outside the object. I reach in to set and get property information. Setting multiple properties on multiple objects will soon become a chore:

```
$product1 = new ShopProduct();
$product1->title = "My Antonia";
$product1->producerMainName  = "Cather";
$product1->producerFirstName = "Willa";
$product1->price = 5.99;
```

I work once again with the ShopProduct class, overriding all the default property values one by one until I have set all product details. Now that I have set some data I can also access it:

```
print "author: {$product1->producerFirstName} "
            ."{$product1->producerMainName}\n";
```

This outputs

```
author: Willa Cather
```

There are a number of problems with this approach to setting property values. Because PHP lets you set properties dynamically, you will not get warned if you misspell or forget a property name. For example, I might mistakenly type the line

```
$product1->producerMainName  = "Cather";
```

as

```
$product1->producerSecondName  = "Cather";
```

As far as the PHP engine is concerned, this code is perfectly legal, and I would not be warned. When I come to print the author's name, though, I will get unexpected results.

Another problem is that my class is altogether too relaxed. I am not forced to set a title, or a price, or producer names. Client code can be sure that these properties exist but is likely to be confronted with default values as often as not. Ideally, I would like to encourage anyone who instantiates a ShopProduct object to set meaningful property values.

Finally, I have to jump through hoops to do something that I will probably want to do quite often. Printing the full author name is a tiresome process:

```
print "author: {$product1->producerFirstName} "
            ."{$product1->producerMainName}\n";
```

It would be nice to have the object handle such drudgery on my behalf.

All of these problems can be addressed by giving the ShopProduct object its own set of functions that can be used to manipulate property data from within the object context.

Working with Methods

Just as properties allow your objects to store data, methods allow your objects to perform tasks. Methods are special functions declared within a class. As you might expect, a method declaration resembles a function declaration. The function keyword precedes a method name, followed by an optional list of argument variables in parentheses. The method body is enclosed by braces:

```
public function myMethod( $argument, $another ) {
    // ...
}
```

Unlike functions, methods must be declared in the body of a class. They can also accept a number of qualifiers, including a visibility keyword. Like properties, methods can be declared public, protected, or private. By declaring a method public, you ensure that it can be invoked from outside of the current object. If you omit the visibility keyword in your method declaration, the method will be declared public implicitly. I will return to method modifiers later in the chapter.

■**Note** PHP 4 does not recognize visibility keywords for methods or properties. Adding `public`, `protected`, or `private` to a method declaration will cause a fatal error. All methods in PHP 4 are implicitly public.

In most circumstances, you will invoke a method using an object variable in conjunction with -> and the method name. You must use parentheses in your method call as you would if you were calling a function (even if you are not passing any arguments to the method).

```
class ShopProduct {
    public $title              = "default product";
    public $producerMainName   = "main name";
    public $producerFirstName  = "first name";
    public $price              = 0;

    function getProducer() {
        return "{$this->producerFirstName}".
            " {$this->producerMainName}";
    }
}

$product1 = new ShopProduct();
$product1->title = "My Antonia";
$product1->producerMainName  = "Cather";
$product1->producerFirstName = "Willa";
$product1->price = 5.99;


print "author: {$product1->getProducer()}\n";
```

This outputs the following:

```
author: Willa Cather
```

I add the getProducer() method to the ShopProduct class. Notice that I do not include a visibility keyword. This means that getProducer() is a public method and can be called from outside the class.

I introduce a feature in this method. The $this pseudo-variable is the mechanism by which a class can refer to an object instance. If you find this concept hard to swallow, try replacing $this with "the current instance." So the statement

```
$this->producerFirstName
```

translates to

```
the $producerFirstName property of the current instance
```

So getProducer() combines and returns the $producerFirstName and $producerMainName properties, saving me from the chore of performing this task every time I need to quote the full producer name.

This has improved the class a little. I am still stuck with a great deal of unwanted flexibility, though. I rely on the client coder to change a ShopProduct object's properties from their default values. This is problematic in two ways. First, it takes five lines to properly initialize a ShopProduct object, and no coder will thank you for that. Second, I have no way of ensuring that any of the properties are set when a ShopProduct object is initialized. What I need is a method that is called automatically when an object is instantiated from a class.

Creating a Constructor Method

A constructor method is invoked when an object is created. You can use it to set things up, ensuring that essential properties are set, and any necessary preliminary work is completed. In versions previous to PHP 5, constructor methods took on the name of the class that enclosed them. So the ShopProduct class would use a ShopProduct() method as its constructor. Although this still works, as of PHP 5, you should name your constructor method __construct(). Note that the method name begins with two underscore characters. You will see this naming convention for many other special methods in PHP classes. Here I define a constructor for the ShopProduct class:

```
class ShopProduct {
    public $title;
    public $producerMainName;
    public $producerFirstName;
    public $price = 0;


    function __construct( $title,
                          $firstName, $mainName, $price ) {
        $this->title             = $title;
        $this->producerFirstName = $firstName;
        $this->producerMainName  = $mainName;
        $this->price             = $price;
    }

    function getProducer() {
        return "{$this->producerFirstName}".
            " {$this->producerMainName}";
    }

}
```

Once again, I gather functionality into the class, saving effort and duplication in the code that uses it. The __construct() method is invoked when an object is created using the new operator.

```
$product1 = new ShopProduct( "My Antonia",
                             "Willa", "Cather", 5.99 );
print "author: {$product1->getProducer()}\n";
```

This produces

```
author: Willa Cather
```

Any arguments supplied are passed to the constructor. So in my example I pass the title, the first name, the main name, and the product price to the constructor. The constructor method uses the pseudo-variable $this to assign values to each of the object's properties.

■**Note** PHP 4 does not recognize the __construct() method as a constructor. If you are using PHP 4, you can create a constructor by declaring a method with the same name as the class that contains it. So for a class called ShopProduct, you would declare a constructor using a method named shopProduct().

PHP still honors this naming scheme, but unless you are writing for backward compatibility, it is better to use __construct() when you name your constructor methods.

A ShopProduct object is now easier to instantiate and safer to use. Instantiation and setup are completed in a single statement. Any code that uses a ShopProduct object can be reasonably sure that all its properties are initialized.

This predictability is an important aspect of object-oriented programming. You should design your classes so that users of objects can be sure of their features. By the same token, when you use an object, you should be sure of its type. In the next section, I examine a mechanism that you can use to enforce object types in method declarations.

Arguments and Types

Type determines the way that data can be managed in your scripts. You use the string type to display character data, for example, and manipulate such data with string functions. Integers are used in mathematical expressions; Booleans are used in test expressions, and so on. These categories are known as primitive types. On a higher level, though, a class defines a type. A ShopProduct object, therefore, belongs to the primitive type object, but it also belongs to the ShopProduct class type. In this section, I will look at types of both kinds in relation to class methods.

Method and function definitions do not necessarily require that an argument should be of a particular type. This is both a curse and a blessing. The fact that an argument can be of any type offers you flexibility. You can build methods that respond intelligently to different data types, tailoring functionality to changing circumstances. This flexibility can also cause ambiguity to creep into code when a method body expects an argument to hold one type but gets another.

Primitive Types

PHP is a loosely typed language. This means that there is no necessity for a variable to be declared to hold a particular data type. The variable $number could hold the value 2 and the string "two" within the same scope. In strongly typed languages, such as C or Java, you must declare the type of a variable before assigning a value to it, and, of course, the value must be of the specified type.

This does not mean that PHP has no concept of type. Every value that can be assigned to a variable has a type. You can determine the type of a variable's value using one of PHP's type-checking functions. Table 3-1 lists the primitive types recognized in PHP and their corresponding test functions. Each function accepts a variable or value and returns true if this argument is of the relevant type.

Table 3-1. *Primitive Types and Checking Functions in PHP*

Type Checking Function	Type	Description
is_bool()	Boolean	One of the two special values true or false
is_integer()	Integer	A whole number
is_double()	Double	A floating point number (a number with a decimal point)
is_string()	String	Character data
is_object()	Object	An object
is_array()	Array	An array
is_resource()	Resource	A handle for identifying and working with external resources such as databases or files
is_null()	Null	An unassigned value

Checking the type of a variable can be particularly important when you work with method and function arguments.

Primitive Types Matter: An Example

You need to keep a close eye on type in your code. Here's an example of one of the many type-related problems that you could encounter.

Imagine that you are extracting configuration settings from an XML file. The <resolvedomains> XML element tells your application whether it should attempt to resolve IP addresses to domain names, a useful but relatively expensive process in terms of time. Here is some sample XML:

```
<settings>
    <resolvedomains>false</resolvedomains>
</settings>
```

The string "false" is extracted by your application and passed as a flag to a method called outputAddresses(), which displays IP address data. Here is outputAddresses():

```
class AddressManager {
    private $addresses = array( "209.131.36.159", "74.125.19.106" );


    function outputAddresses( $resolve ) {
        foreach ( $this->addresses as $address ) {
            print $address;
            if ( $resolve ) {
                print " (".gethostbyaddr( $address ).")";
            }
            print "\n";
        }
    }
}
```

As you can see, the outputAddresses() method loops through an array of IP addresses, printing each one. If the $resolve argument variable itself resolves to true, the method outputs the domain name as well as the IP address.

Let's examine some code that might invoke this method:

```
$settings = simplexml_load_file("settings.xml");
$manager = new AddressManager();
$manager->outputAddresses( (string)$settings->resolvedomains );
```

The code fragment uses the SimpleXML API (which was introduced with PHP 5) to acquire a value for the resolvedomains element. In this example, I know that this value is the element text "false", and I cast it to a string as the SimpleXML documentation suggests I should.

This code will not behave as you might expect. In passing the string "false" to the outputAddresses() method, I misunderstand the implicit assumption the method makes about the argument. The method is expecting a Boolean value (that is true or false). The string "false" will, in fact, resolve to true in a test. This is because PHP will helpfully cast a nonempty string value to the Boolean true for you in a test context. So

```
if ( "false" ) {
    // ...
}
```

is equivalent to

```
if ( true ) {
    // ...
}
```

There are a number of approaches you might take to fix this.

You could make the outputAddresses() method more forgiving so that it recognizes a string and applies some basic rules to convert it to a Boolean equivalent.

```
// class AddressManager...
    function outputAddresses( $resolve ) {
        if ( is_string( $resolve ) ) {
            $resolve =
                ( preg_match("/false|no|off/i", $resolve ) )?
                    false:true;
        }
        // ...
    }
```

You could leave the outputAddresses() method as it is and include a comment containing clear instructions that the $resolve argument should contain a Boolean value. This approach essentially tells the coder to read the small print or reap the consequences.

```
/**
 * Outputs the list of addresses.
 * If $resolve is true then each address will be resolved
 * @param    $resolve    Boolean    Resolve the address?
 */
function outputAddresses( $resolve ) {
    // ...
}
```

Finally, you could make outputAddresses() strict about the type of data it is prepared to find in the $resolve argument.

```
function outputAddresses( $resolve ) {
    if ( ! is_bool( $resolve ) ) {
        die( "outputAddress() requires a Boolean argument\n" );
    }
    //...
}
```

This approach forces client code to provide the correct data type in the $resolve argument. Converting a string argument on the client's behalf would be friendly but would probably present other problems. In providing a conversion mechanism, you second-guess the context and intent of the client. By enforcing the Boolean data type, on the other hand, you leave the client to decide whether to map strings to Boolean values and which word will map to which value. The outputAddresses() method, meanwhile, concentrates on the task it is designed to perform. This emphasis on performing a specific task in deliberate ignorance of the wider context is an important principle in object-oriented programming, and I will return to it frequently throughout the book.

In fact, your strategies for dealing with argument types will depend on the seriousness of any potential bugs. PHP casts most primitive values for you depending on context. Numbers in strings are converted to their integer or floating point equivalents when used in a mathematical expression, for example. So your code might be naturally forgiving of type errors. If you expect one of your method arguments to be an array, however, you may need to be more careful. Passing a nonarray value to one of PHP's array functions will not produce a useful result and could cause a cascade of errors in your method.

It is likely, therefore, that you will strike a balance among testing for type, converting from one type to another, and relying on good, clear documentation (you should provide the documentation whatever else you decide to do).

However you address problems of this kind, you can be sure of one thing—type matters. The fact that PHP is loosely typed makes it all the more important. You cannot rely on a compiler to prevent type-related bugs; you must consider the potential impact of unexpected types when they find their way into your arguments. You cannot afford to trust client coders to read your thoughts, and you should always consider how your methods will deal with incoming garbage.

Taking the Hint: Object Types

Just as an argument variable can contain any primitive type, by default it can contain an object of any type. This flexibility has its uses but can present problems in the context of a method definition.

Imagine a method designed to work with a ShopProduct object:

```
class ShopProductWriter {
    public function write( $shopProduct ) {
        $str = "{$shopProduct->title}: " .
                $shopProduct->getProducer() .
                " ({$shopProduct->price})\n";
        print $str;
    }
}
```

You can test this class like this:

```
$product1 = new ShopProduct( "My Antonia", "Willa", "Cather", 5.99 );
$writer = new ShopProductWriter();
$writer->write( $product1 );
```

This outputs

My Antonia: Willa Cather (5.99)

The ShopProductWriter class contains a single method, write(). The write() method accepts a ShopProduct object and uses its properties and methods to construct and print a summary string. I used the name of the argument variable, $shopProduct, as a signal that the method expects a ShopProduct object, but I did not enforce this. That means I could be passed an unexpected object or primitive type and be none the wiser until I begin trying to work with the $shopProduct argument. By that time, my code may already have acted on the assumption that it has been passed a genuine ShopProduct object.

You might wonder why I didn't add the write() method directly to ShopProduct. The reason lies with areas of responsibility. The ShopProduct class is responsible for managing product data; the ShopProductWriter is responsible for writing it. You will begin to see why this division of labor can be useful as you read this chapter.

To address this problem, PHP 5 introduced class type hints. To add a type hint to a method argument, you simply place a class name in front of the method argument you need to constrain. So I can amend the write() method thus:

```
public function write( ShopProduct $shopProduct ) {
    // ...
}
```

Now the write() method will only accept the $shopProduct argument if it contains an object of type ShopProduct. Let's try to call write() with a dodgy object:

```
class Wrong { }
$writer = new ShopProductWriter();
$writer->write( new Wrong() );
```

Because the write() method contains a class type hint, passing it a Wrong object causes a fatal error.

PHP Catchable fatal error: Argument 1 passed to ShopProductWriter::write() must be an instance of ShopProduct, instance of Wrong given ...

This saves me from having to test the type of the argument before I work with it. It also makes the method signature much clearer for the client coder. She can see the requirements of the write() method at a glance. She does not have to worry about some obscure bug arising from a type error, because the hint is rigidly enforced.

Even though this automated type checking is a great way of preventing bugs, it is important to understand that hints are checked at runtime. This means that a class hint will only report an error at the moment that an unwanted object is passed to the method. If a call to write() is buried in a conditional clause that only runs on Christmas morning, you may find yourself working the holiday if you haven't checked your code carefully.

Type hinting cannot be used to enforce primitives like strings and integers in your arguments. For these, you must fall back on type checking functions such as is_int() in the body of your methods. You can, however, enforce array arguments:

```
function setArray( array $storearray ) {
    $this->array = $storearray;
}
```

Support for array hinting was added to the language with version 5.1. Support for null default values in hinted arguments was another late addition. This means that you can demand either a particular type or a null value in an argument. Here's how:

```
function setWriter( ObjectWriter $objwriter=null ) {
    $this->writer = $objwriter;
}
```

So far, I have discussed types and classes as if they were synonymous. There is a key difference, however. When you define a class you also define a type, but a type can describe an entire family of classes. The mechanism by which different classes can be grouped together under a type is called inheritance. I discuss inheritance in the next section.

Inheritance

Inheritance is the means by which one or more classes can be derived from a base class.

A class that inherits from another is said to be a subclass of it. This relationship is often described in terms of parents and children. A child class is derived from and inherits characteristics from the parent. These characteristics consist of both properties and methods. The child class will typically add new functionality to that provided by its parent (also known as a superclass); for this reason, a child class is said to extend its parent.

Before I dive into the syntax of inheritance, I'll examine the problems it can help you to solve.

The Inheritance Problem

Look again at the ShopProduct class. At the moment, it is nicely generic. It can handle all sorts of products.

```
$product1 = new ShopProduct( "My Antonia", "Willa", "Cather", 5.99 );
$product2 = new ShopProduct( "Exile on Coldharbour Lane",
                             "The", "Alabama 3", 10.99 );
print "author: ".$product1->getProducer()."\n";
print "artist: ".$product2->getProducer()."\n";
```

Here's the output:

```
author: Willa Cather
artist: The Alabama 3
```

Separating the producer name into two parts works well with both books and CDs. I want to be able to sort on "Alabama 3" and "Cather", not on "The" and "Willa". Laziness is an excellent design strategy, so there is no need to worry about using ShopProduct for more than one kind of product at this stage.

If I add some new requirements to my example, however, things rapidly become more complicated. Imagine, for example, that you need to represent data specific to books and CDs. For CDs, you must store the total playing time; for books, the total number of pages. There could be any number of other differences, but these will serve to illustrate the issue.

How can I extend my example to accommodate these changes? Two options immediately present themselves. First, I could throw all the data into the ShopProduct class. Second, I could split ShopProduct into two separate classes.

Let's examine the first approach. Here, I combine CD- and book-related data in a single class:

```
class ShopProduct {
    public $numPages;
    public $playLength;
    public $title;
    public $producerMainName;
    public $producerFirstName;
    public $price;

    function __construct(    $title, $firstName,
                             $mainName, $price,
                             $numPages=0, $playLength=0 ) {
        $this->title             = $title;
        $this->producerFirstName = $firstName;
        $this->producerMainName  = $mainName;
        $this->price             = $price;
        $this->numPages          = $numPages;
        $this->playLength        = $playLength;
    }

    function getNumberOfPages() {
        return $this->numPages;
    }

    function getPlayLength() {
        return $this->playLength;
    }

    function getProducer() {
        return "{$this->producerFirstName}".
               " {$this->producerMainName}";
    }
}
```

I have provided method access to the $numPages and $playLength properties to illustrate the divergent forces at work here. An object instantiated from this class will include a redundant method and, for a CD, must be instantiated using an unnecessary constructor argument: a CD will store information and functionality relating to book pages, and a book will support play-length data. This is probably something you could live with right now. But what would happen if I added more product types, each with its own methods, and then added more methods for each type? Our class would become increasingly complex and hard to manage.

So forcing fields that don't belong together into a single class leads to bloated objects with redundant properties and methods.

The problem doesn't end with data, either. I run into difficulties with functionality as well. Consider a method that summarizes a product. The sales department has requested a clear summary line for use in invoices. They want me to include the playing time for CDs and a page count for books, so I will be forced to provide different implementations for each type. I could try using a flag to keep track of the object's format. Here's an example:

```
    function getSummaryLine() {
        $base  = "{$this->title} ( {$this->producerMainName}, ";
        $base .= "{$this->producerFirstName} )";
        if ( $this->type == 'book' ) {
            $base .= ": page count - {$this->numPages}";
        } else if ( $this->type == 'cd' ) {
            $base .= ": playing time - {$this->playLength}";
        }
        return $base;
    }
}
```

In order to set the $type property, I could test the $numPages argument to the constructor. Still, once again, the ShopProduct class has become more complex than necessary. As I add more differences to my formats, or add new formats, these functional differences will become even harder to manage. Perhaps I should try another approach to this problem.

Since ShopProduct is beginning to feel like two classes in one, I could accept this and create two types rather than one. Here's how I might do it:

```
class CdProduct {
    public $playLength;
    public $title;
    public $producerMainName;
    public $producerFirstName;
    public $price;

    function __construct(   $title, $firstName,
                            $mainName, $price,
                            $playLength ) {
        $this->title             = $title;
        $this->producerFirstName = $firstName;
        $this->producerMainName  = $mainName;
        $this->price             = $price;
        $this->playLength        = $playLength;

    }

    function getPlayLength() {
        return $this->playLength;
    }

    function getSummaryLine() {
        $base  = "{$this->title} ( {$this->producerMainName}, ";
        $base .= "{$this->producerFirstName} )";
        $base .= ": playing time - {$this->playLength}";
        return $base;
    }

    function getProducer() {
        return "{$this->producerFirstName}".
               " {$this->producerMainName}";
    }
}

class BookProduct {
```

```
    public $numPages;
    public $title;
    public $producerMainName;
    public $producerFirstName;
    public $price;

    function __construct(   $title, $firstName,
                            $mainName, $price,
                            $numPages ) {
        $this->title             = $title;
        $this->producerFirstName = $firstName;
        $this->producerMainName  = $mainName;
        $this->price             = $price;
        $this->numPages          = $numPages;
    }

    function getNumberOfPages() {
        return $this->numPages;
    }

    function getSummaryLine() {
        $base  = "{$this->title} ( {$this->producerMainName}, ";
        $base .= "{$this->producerFirstName} )";
        $base .= ": page count - {$this->numPages}";
        return $base;
    }

    function getProducer() {
        return "{$this->producerFirstName}".
            " {$this->producerMainName}";
    }
}
```

I have addressed the complexity issue, but at a cost. I can now create a getSummaryLine() method for each format without having to test a flag. Neither class maintains fields or methods that are not relevant to it.

The cost lies in duplication. The getProducerName() method is exactly the same in each class. Each constructor sets a number of identical properties in the same way. This is another unpleasant odor you should train yourself to sniff out.

If I need the getProducer() methods to behave identically for each class, any changes I make to one implementation will need to be made for the other. Without care, the classes will soon slip out of synchronization.

Even if I am confident that I can maintain the duplication, my worries are not over. I now have two types rather than one.

Remember the ShopProductWriter class? Its write() method is designed to work with a single type: ShopProduct. How can I amend this to work as before? I could remove the class type hint from the method declaration, but then I must trust to luck that write() is passed an object of the correct type. I could add my own type checking code to the body of the method:

```
class ShopProductWriter {
    public function write( $shopProduct ) {
        if ( ! ( $shopProduct instanceof CdProduct )  &&
             ! ( $shopProduct instanceof BookProduct ) ) {
            die( "wrong type supplied" );
```

```
        }
        $str    = "{$shopProduct->title}: " .
                $shopProduct->getProducer() .
                " ({$shopProduct->price})\n";
        print $str;
    }
}
```

Notice the `instanceof` operator in the example; `instanceof` resolves to `true` if the object in the left-hand operand is of the type represented by the right-hand operand.

Once again, I have been forced to include a new layer of complexity. Not only do I have to test the `$shopProduct` argument against two types in the `write()` method but I have to trust that each type will continue to support the same fields and methods as the other. It was all much neater when I simply demanded a single type because I could use class type hinting, and because I could be confident that the `ShopProduct` class supported a particular interface.

The CD and book aspects of the `ShopProduct` class don't work well together but can't live apart, it seems. I want to work with books and CDs as a single type while providing a separate implementation for each format. I want to provide common functionality in one place to avoid duplication but allow each format to handle some method calls differently. I need to use inheritance.

Working with Inheritance

The first step in building an inheritance tree is to find the elements of the base class that don't fit together or that need to be handled differently.

I know that the `getPlayLength()` and `getNumberOfPages()` methods do not belong together. I also know that I need to create different implementations for the `getSummaryLine()` method. Let's use these differences as the basis for two derived classes:

```
class ShopProduct {
    public $numPages;
    public $playLength;
    public $title;
    public $producerMainName;
    public $producerFirstName;
    public $price;

    function __construct(    $title, $firstName,
                            $mainName, $price,
                            $numPages=0, $playLength=0 ) {
        $this->title            = $title;
        $this->producerFirstName = $firstName;
        $this->producerMainName  = $mainName;
        $this->price             = $price;
        $this->numPages          = $numPages;
        $this->playLength        = $playLength;
    }

    function getProducer() {
        return "{$this->producerFirstName}".
            " {$this->producerMainName}";
    }

    function getSummaryLine() {
```

```
            $base   = "$this->title ( {$this->producerMainName}, ";
            $base  .= "{$this->producerFirstName} )";
            return $base;
        }
}

class CdProduct extends ShopProduct {
    function getPlayLength() {
        return $this->playLength;
    }

    function getSummaryLine() {
        $base   = "{$this->title} ( {$this->producerMainName}, ";
        $base  .= "{$this->producerFirstName} )";
        $base  .= ": playing time - {$this->playLength}";
        return $base;
    }
}

class BookProduct extends ShopProduct {
    function getNumberOfPages() {
        return $this->numPages;
    }

    function getSummaryLine() {
        $base   = "{$this->title} ( {$this->producerMainName}, ";
        $base  .= "{$this->producerFirstName} )";
        $base  .= ": page count - {$this->numPages}";
        return $base;
    }
}
```

To create a child class, you must use the extends keyword in the class declaration. In the example, I created two new classes, BookProduct and CdProduct. Both extend the ShopProduct class.

Because the derived classes do not define constructors, the parent class's constructor is automatically invoked when they are instantiated. The child classes inherit access to all the parent's public and protected methods (though not to private methods or properties). This means that you can call the getProducer() method on an object instantiated from the CdProduct class, even though getProducer() is defined in the ShopProduct class.

```
$product2 =   new CdProduct(    "Exile on Coldharbour Lane",
                                "The", "Alabama 3",
                                10.99, null, 60.33 );
print "artist: {$product2->getProducer()}\n";
```

So both the child classes inherit the behavior of the common parent. You can treat a BookProduct object as if it were a ShopProduct object. You can pass a BookProduct or CdProduct object to the ShopProductWriter class's write() method and all will work as expected.

Notice that both the CdProduct and BookProduct classes override the getSummaryLine() method, providing their own implementation. Derived classes can extend but also alter the functionality of their parents.

The super class's implementation of this method might seem redundant, because it is overridden by both its children. Nevertheless it provides basic functionality that new child classes might use. The method's presence also provides a guarantee to client code that all ShopProduct objects will provide a getSummaryLine() method. Later on you will see how it is possible to make this promise in a base class without providing any implementation at all. Each child ShopProduct class inherits its parent's properties. Both BookProduct and CdProduct access the $title property in their versions of getSummaryLine().

Inheritance can be a difficult concept to grasp at first. By defining a class that extends another, you ensure that an object instantiated from it is defined by the characteristics of first the child and then the parent class. Another way of thinking about this is in terms of searching. When I invoke $product2->getProducer(), there is no such method to be found in the CdProduct class, and the invocation falls through to the default implementation in ShopProduct. When I invoke $product2->getSummaryLine(), on the other hand, the getSummaryLine() method is found in CdProduct and invoked.

The same is true of property accesses. When I access $title in the BookProduct class's getSummaryLine() method, the property is not found in the BookProduct class. It is acquired instead from the parent class, from ShopProduct. The $title property applies equally to both subclasses, and therefore, it belongs in the superclass.

A quick look at the ShopProduct constructor, however, shows that I am still managing data in the base class that should be handled by its children. The BookProduct class should handle the $numPages argument and property, and the CdProduct class should handle the $playLength argument and property. To make this work, I will define constructor methods in each of the child classes.

Constructors and Inheritance

When you define a constructor in a child class, you become responsible for passing any arguments on to the parent. If you fail to do this, you can end up with a partially constructed object.

To invoke a method in a parent class, you must first find a way of referring to the class itself: a handle. PHP provides us with the parent keyword for this purpose.

To refer to a method in the context of a class rather than an object you use :: rather than ->. So

```
parent::__construct()
```

means "Invoke the __construct() method of the parent class." Here I amend my example so that each class handles only the data that is appropriate to it:

```
class ShopProduct {
    public $title;
    public $producerMainName;
    public $producerFirstName;
    public $price;

    function __construct(  $title, $firstName,
                           $mainName, $price ) {
        $this->title            = $title;
        $this->producerFirstName = $firstName;
        $this->producerMainName  = $mainName;
        $this->price            = $price;
    }

    function getProducer() {
        return "{$this->producerFirstName}".
            " {$this->producerMainName}";
    }

      function getSummaryLine() {
        $base  = "{$this->title} ( {$this->producerMainName}, ";
```

```php
        $base .= "{$this->producerFirstName} )";
        return $base;
    }
}

class CdProduct extends ShopProduct {
    public $playLength;

    function __construct(   $title, $firstName,
                            $mainName, $price, $playLength ) {
        parent::__construct(    $title, $firstName,
                                $mainName, $price );
        $this->playLength = $playLength;
    }

    function getPlayLength() {
        return $this->playLength;
    }

    function getSummaryLine() {
        $base  = "{$this->title} ( {$this->producerMainName}, ";
        $base .= "{$this->producerFirstName} )";
        $base .= ": playing time - {$this->playLength}";
        return $base;
    }
}

class BookProduct extends ShopProduct {
    public $numPages;

    function __construct(   $title, $firstName,
                            $mainName, $price, $numPages ) {
        parent::__construct(    $title, $firstName,
                                $mainName, $price );
        $this->numPages = $numPages;
    }

    function getNumberOfPages() {
        return $this->numPages;
    }

    function getSummaryLine() {
        $base  = "$this->title ( $this->producerMainName, ";
        $base .= "$this->producerFirstName )";
        $base .= ": page count - $this->numPages";
        return $base;
    }
}
```

Each child class invokes the constructor of its parent before setting its own properties. The base class now knows only about its own data. Child classes are generally specializations of their parents. As a rule of thumb, you should avoid giving parent classes any special knowledge about their children.

Note Prior to PHP 5, constructors took on the name of the enclosing class. The new unified constructors use the name __construct(). Using the old syntax, a call to a parent constructor would tie you to that particular class: parent::ShopProduct();

This could cause problems if the class hierarchy changed. Many bugs result from programmers changing the immediate parent of a class but forgetting to update the constructor. Using the unified constructor, a call to the parent constructor, parent::__construct(), invokes the immediate parent, no matter what changes are made in the hierarchy. Of course, you still need to ensure that the correct arguments are passed to an inserted parent!

Invoking an Overridden Method

The parent keyword can be used with any method that overrides its counterpart in a parent class. When you override a method, you may not wish to obliterate the functionality of the parent but rather extend it. You can achieve this by calling the parent class's method in the current object's context. If you look again at the getSummaryLine() method implementations, you will see that they duplicate a lot of code. It would be better to use rather than reproduce the functionality already developed in the ShopProduct class.

```
// ShopProduct class...
    function getSummaryLine() {
        $base  = "{$this->title} ( {$this->producerMainName}, ";
        $base .= "{$this->producerFirstName} )";
        return $base;
    }

// BookProduct class...
    function getSummaryLine() {
        $base = parent::getSummaryLine();
        $base .= ": page count - {$this->numPages}";
        return $base;
    }
```

I set up the core functionality for the getSummaryLine() method in the ShopProduct base class. Rather than reproduce this in the CdProduct and BookProduct subclasses, I simply call the parent method before proceeding to add more data to the summary string.

Now that you have seen the basics of inheritance, I will reexamine property and method visibility in light of the full picture.

Public, Private, and Protected: Managing Access to Your Classes

So far, I have declared all properties public, implicitly or otherwise. Public access is the default setting for methods and for properties if you use the old var keyword in your property declaration.

Elements in your classes can be declared public, private, or protected:

- Public properties and methods can be accessed from any context.

- A private method or property can only be accessed from within the enclosing class. Even subclasses have no access.

- A protected method or property can only be accessed from within either the enclosing class or from a subclass. No external code is granted access.

So how is this useful to us? Visibility keywords allow you to expose only those aspects of a class that are required by a client. This sets a clear interface for your object.

By preventing a client from accessing certain properties, access control can also help prevent bugs in your code. Imagine, for example, that you want to allow ShopProduct objects to support a discount. You could add a $discount property and a setDiscount() method.

```
// ShopProduct class
    public $discount = 0;
// ...
    function setDiscount( $num ) {
        $this->discount=$num;
    }
```

Armed with a mechanism for setting a discount, you can create a getPrice() method that takes account of the discount that has been applied.

```
// ShopProduct class
    function getPrice() {
        return ($this->price - $this->discount);
    }
```

At this point, you have a problem. You only want to expose the adjusted price to the world, but a client can easily bypass the getPrice() method and access the $price property:

```
print "The price is {$product1->price}\n";
```

This will print the raw price and not the discount-adjusted price you wish to present. You can put a stop to this straight away by making the $price property private. This will prevent direct access, forcing clients to use the getPrice() method. Any attempt from outside the ShopProduct class to access the $price property will fail. As far as the wider world is concerned, this property has ceased to exist.

Setting properties to private can be an overzealous strategy. A private property cannot be accessed by a child class. Imagine that our business rules state that books alone should be ineligible for discounts. You could override the getPrice() method so that it returns the $price property, applying no discount.

```
// BookProduct class
    function getPrice() {
        return $this->price;
    }
```

Since the private $price property is declared in the ShopProduct class and not BookProduct, the attempt to access it here will fail. The solution to this problem is to declare $price protected, thereby granting access to descendent classes. Remember that a protected property or method cannot be accessed from outside the class hierarchy in which it was declared. It can only be accessed from within its originating class or from within children of the originating class.

As a general rule, err on the side of privacy. Make properties private or protected at first and relax your restriction only as needed. Many (if not most) methods in your classes will be public, but once again, if in doubt, lock it down. A method that provides local functionality for other methods in your class has no relevance to your class's users. Make it private or protected.

Accessor Methods

Even when client programmers need to work with values held by your class, it is often a good idea to deny direct access to properties, providing methods instead that relay the needed values. Such methods are known as accessors or getters and setters.

You have already seen one benefit afforded by accessor methods. You can use an accessor to filter a property value according to circumstances, as was illustrated with the getPrice() method.

You can also use a setter method to enforce a property type. You have seen that class type hints can be used to constrain method arguments, but you have no direct control over property types. Remember the ShopProductWriter class that uses a ShopProduct object to output list data? I can develop this further so that it writes any number of ShopProduct objects at one time:

```
class ShopProductWriter {
    public $products = array();

    public function addProduct( ShopProduct $shopProduct ) {
        $this->products[] = $shopProduct;
    }

    public function write() {
        $str =  "";
        foreach ( $this->products as $shopProduct ) {
            $str .= "{$shopProduct->title}: ";
            $str .= $shopProduct->getProducer();
            $str .= " ({$shopProduct->getPrice()})\n";
        }
        print $str;
    }
}
```

The ShopProductWriter class is now much more useful. It can hold many ShopProduct objects and write data for them all in one go. I must trust my client coders to respect the intentions of the class, though. Despite the fact that I have provided an addProduct() method, I have not prevented programmers from manipulating the $products property directly. Not only could someone add the wrong kind of object to the $products array property, but he could even overwrite the entire array and replace it with a primitive value. I can prevent this by making the $products property private:

```
class ShopProductWriter {
    private $products = array();
//...
```

It's now impossible for external code to damage the $products property. All access must be via the addProduct() method, and the class type hint I use in the method declaration ensures that only ShopProduct objects can be added to the array property.

The ShopProduct Classes

Let's close this chapter by amending the ShopProduct class and its children to lock down access control:

```
class ShopProduct {
    private $title;
    private $producerMainName;
    private $producerFirstName;
    protected $price;
```

```php
    private $discount = 0;

    public function __construct(    $title, $firstName,
                            $mainName, $price ) {
        $this->title            = $title;
        $this->producerFirstName = $firstName;
        $this->producerMainName  = $mainName;
        $this->price            = $price;
    }

    public function getProducerFirstName() {
        return $this->producerFirstName;
    }

    public function getProducerMainName() {
        return $this->producerMainName;
    }

    public function setDiscount( $num ) {
        $this->discount=$num;
    }

    public function getDiscount() {
        return $this->discount;
    }

    public function getTitle() {
        return $this->title;
    }

    public function getPrice() {
        return ($this->price - $this->discount);
    }

    public function getProducer() {
        return "{$this->producerFirstName}".
                " {$this->producerMainName}";
    }

    public function getSummaryLine() {
        $base  = "{$this->title} ( {$this->producerMainName}, ";
        $base .= "{$this->producerFirstName} )";
        return $base;
    }
}

class CdProduct extends ShopProduct {
    private $playLength = 0;

    public function __construct(    $title, $firstName,
                            $mainName, $price, $playLength ) {
        parent::__construct(    $title, $firstName,
                            $mainName, $price );
```

```
            $this->playLength = $playLength;
        }

        public function getPlayLength() {
            return $this->playLength;
        }

        public function getSummaryLine() {
            $base = parent::getSummaryLine();
            $base .= ": playing time - {$this->playLength}";
            return $base;
        }

    }

    class BookProduct extends ShopProduct {
        private $numPages = 0;

        public function __construct(    $title, $firstName,
                                    $mainName, $price, $numPages ) {
            parent::__construct(    $title, $firstName,
                                    $mainName, $price );
            $this->numPages = $numPages;
        }

        public function getNumberOfPages() {
            return $this->numPages;
        }

        public function getSummaryLine() {
            $base = parent::getSummaryLine();
            $base .= ": page count - {$this->numPages}";
            return $base;
        }

        public function getPrice() {
            return $this->price;
        }
    }
```

There is nothing substantially new in this version of the *ShopProduct* family. I made all methods explicitly public, and all properties are either private or protected. I added a number of accessor methods to round things off.

Summary

This chapter covered a lot of ground, taking a class from an empty implementation through to a fully featured inheritance hierarchy. You took in some design issues, particularly with regard to type and inheritance. You saw PHP's support for visibility and explored some of its uses. In the next chapter, I will show you more of PHP's object-oriented features.

CHAPTER 4

■ ■ ■

Advanced Features

You have already seen how class type hinting and access control give you more control over a class's interface. In this chapter, I will delve deeper into PHP's object-oriented features.

This chapter will cover

- *Static methods and properties*: Accessing data and functionality through classes rather than objects

- *Abstract classes and interfaces*: Separating design from implementation

- *Error handling*: Introducing exceptions

- *Final classes and methods*: Limiting inheritance

- *Interceptor methods*: Automating delegation

- *Destructor methods*: Cleaning up after your objects

- *Cloning objects*: Making object copies

- *Resolving objects to strings*: Creating a summary method

- *Callbacks*: Adding functionality to components with anonymous functions

Static Methods and Properties

All the examples in the previous chapter worked with objects. I characterized classes as templates from which objects are produced, and objects as active components, the things whose methods you invoke and whose properties you access. I implied that, in object-oriented programming, the real work is done by instances of classes. Classes, after all, are merely templates for objects.

In fact, it is not that simple. You can access both methods and properties in the context of a class rather than that of an object. Such methods and properties are "static" and must be declared as such by using the static keyword.

```
class StaticExample {
    static public $aNum = 0;
    static public function sayHello() {
        print "hello";
    }
}
```

▓**Note** The static keyword was introduced with PHP 5. It cannot be used in PHP 4 scripts.

Static methods are functions with class scope. They cannot themselves access any normal properties in the class, because these would belong to an object, but they can access static properties. If you change a static property, all instances of that class are able to access the new value.

Because you access a static element via a class and not an instance, you do not need a variable that references an object. Instead, you use the class name in conjunction with ::.

```
print StaticExample::$aNum;
StaticExample::sayHello();
```

This syntax should be familiar from the previous chapter. I used :: in conjunction with parent to access an overridden method. Now, as then, I am accessing class rather than object data. Class code can use the parent keyword to access a superclass without using its class name. To access a static method or property from within the same class (rather than from a child), I would use the self keyword. self is to classes what the $this pseudo-variable is to objects. So from outside the StaticExample class, I access the $aNum property using its class name:

```
StaticExample::$aNum;
```

From within the StaticExample class I can use the self keyword:

```
class StaticExample {
    static public $aNum = 0;
    static public function sayHello() {
        self::$aNum++;
        print "hello (".self::$aNum.")\n";
    }
}
```

▓**Note** Making a method call using parent is the only circumstance in which you should use a static reference to a nonstatic method.

Unless you are accessing an overridden method, you should only ever use :: to access a method or property that has been explicitly declared static.

In documentation, however, you will often see static syntax used to refer to a method or property. This does not mean that the item in question is necessarily static, just that it belongs to a certain class. The write() method of the ShopProductWriter class might be referred to as ShopProductWriter::write(), for example, even though the write() method is not static. You will see this syntax here when that level of specificity is appropriate.

By definition, static methods are not invoked in the context of an object. For this reason, static methods and properties are often referred to as class variables and properties. A consequence of this is you cannot use the $this pseudo-variable inside a static method.

So, why would you use a static method or property? Static elements have a number of characteristics that can be useful. First, they are available from anywhere in your script (assuming that you have access to the class). This means you can access functionality without needing to pass an instance of the class from object to object or, worse, storing an instance in a global variable. Second, a static property is available to every instance of a class, so you can set values that you want to be available to all members of a type. Finally, the fact that you don't need an instance to access a static property or method can save you from instantiating an object purely to get at a simple function.

To illustrate this I will build a static method for the ShopProduct class that automates the instantiation of ShopProduct objects. Using SQLite, I might define a products table like this:

```
CREATE TABLE products (
                    id INTEGER PRIMARY KEY AUTOINCREMENT,
                    type TEXT,
                    firstname TEXT,
                    mainname TEXT,
                    title TEXT,
                    price float,
                    numpages int,
                    playlength int,
                    discount int )
```

Now to build a getInstance() method that accepts a row ID and PDO object, uses them to acquire a database row, and then returns a ShopProduct object. I can add these methods to the ShopProduct class I created in the previous chapter. As you probably know, *PDO* stands for *PHP Data Object*. The PDO class provides a common interface to different database applications.

```
// ShopProduct class...
    private $id = 0;
    // ...
    public function setID( $id ) {
        $this->id = $id;
    }
    // ...
    public static function getInstance( $id, PDO $pdo ) {
$stmt = $pdo->prepare("select * from products where id=?");

        $result = $stmt->execute( array( $id ) );

        $row = $stmt->fetch( );

        if ( empty( $row ) ) { return null; }

        if ( $row['type'] == "book" ) {
            $product = new BookProduct(
                                    $row['title'],
                                    $row['firstname'],
                                    $row['mainname'],
                                    $row['price'],
                                    $row['numpages'] );
        } else if ( $row['type'] == "cd" ) {
            $product = new CdProduct(
                                    $row['title'],
                                    $row['firstname'],
                                    $row['mainname'],
                                    $row['price'],
```

```
                                        $row['playlength'] );
        } else {
            $product = new ShopProduct(
                                    $row['title'],
                                    $row['firstname'],
                                    $row['mainname'],
                                    $row['price'] );
        }
        $product->setId(            $row['id'] );
        $product->setDiscount(      $row['discount'] );
        return $product;
    }
//...
```

As you can see, the getInstance() method returns a ShopProduct object and, based on a type flag, is smart enough to work out the precise specialization it should instantiate. I have omitted any error handling to keep the example compact. In a real-world version of this, for example, I would not be so trusting as to assume that the provided PDO object was initialized to talk to the correct database. In fact, I probably wrap the PDO with a class that would guarantee this behavior. You can read more about object-oriented coding and databases in Chapter 13.

This method is more useful in a class context than an object context. It lets us convert raw data from the database into an object easily without requiring that I have a ShopProduct object to start with. The method does not use any instance properties or methods, so there is no reason why it should not be declared static. Given a valid PDO object, I can invoke the method from anywhere in an application:

```
$dsn = "sqlite://home/bob/projects/products.db";
$pdo = new PDO( $dsn, null, null );
$pdo->setAttribute(PDO::ATTR_ERRMODE, PDO::ERRMODE_EXCEPTION);
$obj = ShopProduct::getInstance( 1, $pdo );
```

Methods like this act as "factories" in that they take raw materials (such as row data, for example, or configuration information) and use them to produce objects. The term *factory* is applied to code designed to generate object instances. You will encounter factory examples again in future chapters.

Constant Properties

Some properties should not be changed. The Answer to Life, the Universe, and Everything is 42, and you want it to stay that way. Error and status flags will often be hard-coded into your classes. Although they should be publicly and statically available, client code should not be able to change them.

PHP 5 allows us to define constant properties within a class. Like global constants, class constants cannot be changed once they are set. A constant property is declared with the const keyword. Constants are not prefixed with a dollar sign like regular properties. By convention, they are often named using only uppercase characters, like this:

```
class ShopProduct {
    const AVAILABLE      = 0;
    const OUT_OF_STOCK   = 1;
    // ...
```

Constant properties can contain only primitive values. You cannot assign an object to a constant. Like static properties, constant properties are accessed via the class and not an instance. Just as you define a constant without a dollar sign, no leading symbol is required when you refer to one:

```
print ShopProduct::AVAILABLE;
```

Attempting to set a value on a constant once it has been declared will cause a parse error.

You should use constants when your property needs to be available across all instances of a class, and when the property value needs to be fixed and unchanging.

Abstract Classes

The introduction of abstract classes was one of the major changes ushered in with PHP 5. Its inclusion in the list of new features was another sign of PHP's extended commitment to object-oriented design.

An abstract class cannot be instantiated. Instead it defines (and, optionally, partially implements) the interface for any class that might extend it.

You define an abstract class with the abstract keyword. Here I redefine the ShopProductWriter class I created in the previous chapter, this time as an abstract class.

```
abstract class ShopProductWriter {
    protected $products = array();

    public function addProduct( ShopProduct $shopProduct ) {
        $this->products[]=$shopProduct;
    }
}
```

You can create methods and properties as normal, but any attempt to instantiate an abstract object will cause an error like this:

```
$writer = new ShopProductWriter();
// output:
// Fatal error: Cannot instantiate abstract class
// shopproductwriter ...
```

In most cases, an abstract class will contain at least one abstract method. These are declared, once again, with the abstract keyword. An abstract method cannot have an implementation. You declare it in the normal way, but end the declaration with a semicolon rather than a method body. Here I add an abstract write() method to the ShopProductWriter class:

```
abstract class ShopProductWriter {
    protected $products = array();

    public function addProduct( ShopProduct $shopProduct ) {
        $this->products[]=$shopProduct;
    }

    abstract public function write();
}
```

In creating an abstract method, you ensure that an implementation will be available in all concrete child classes, but you leave the details of that implementation undefined.

If I were to create a class derived from ShopProductWriter that does not implement the write() method like this:

```
class ErroredWriter extends ShopProductWriter{}
```

I would face the following error:

```
PHP Fatal error:  Class ErroredWriter contains 1 abstract method and
must therefore be declared abstract or implement the remaining methods
 (ShopProductWriter::write) in...
```

So any class that extends an abstract class must implement all abstract methods or itself be declared abstract. An extending class is responsible for more than simply implementing an abstract method. In doing so, it must reproduce the method signature. This means that the access control of the implementing method cannot be stricter than that of the abstract method. The implementing method should also require the same number of arguments as the abstract method, reproducing any class type hinting.

Here are two implementations of ShopProductWriter():

```php
class XmlProductWriter extends ShopProductWriter{
    public function write() {
        $str = '<?xml version="1.0" encoding="UTF-8"?>'."\n";
        $str .= "<products>\n";
        foreach ( $this->products as $shopProduct ) {
            $str .= "\t<product title=\"{$shopProduct->getTitle()}\">\n";
            $str .= "\t\t<summary>\n";
            $str .= "\t\t{$shopProduct->getSummaryLine()}\n";
            $str .= "\t\t</summary>\n";
            $str .= "\t</product>\n";
        }
        $str .= "</products>\n";
        print $str;
    }
}

class TextProductWriter extends ShopProductWriter{
    public function write() {
        $str = "PRODUCTS:\n";
        foreach ( $this->products as $shopProduct ) {
            $str .= $shopProduct->getSummaryLine()."\n";
        }
        print $str;
    }
}
```

I create two classes, each with its own implementation of the write() method. The first outputs XML and the second outputs text. A method that requires a ShopProductWriter object will not know which of these two classes it is receiving but can be absolutely certain that a write() method is implemented. Note that I don't test the type of $products before treating it as an array. This is because this property is initialized as an empty array in the ShopProductWriter.

Abstract classes were often approximated in PHP 4 by creating methods that contain warnings or even die() statements. This forces a derived class to implement the abstract methods or risk having them invoked.

```php
class AbstractClass {
    function abstractFunction() {
        die( "AbstractClass::abstractFunction() is abstract\n" );
    }
}
```

The problem here is that the abstract nature of the base class is only tested when an abstract method is invoked. In PHP 5, abstract classes are tested when they are parsed, which is much safer.

Interfaces

While abstract classes let you provide some measure of implementation, interfaces are pure templates. An interface can only define functionality; it can never implement it. An interface is declared with the `interface` keyword. It can contain properties and method declarations, but not method bodies.

Here's an interface:

```
interface Chargeable {
    public function getPrice();
}
```

As you can see, an interface looks very much like a class. Any class that incorporates this interface commits to implementing all the methods it defines or it must be declared abstract.

A class can implement an interface using the `implements` keyword in its declaration. Once you have done this, the process of implementing an interface is the same as extending an abstract class that contains only abstract methods. Now to make the ShopProduct class implement Chargeable.

```
class ShopProduct implements Chargeable {
    // ...
    public function getPrice() {
        return ( $this->price - $this->discount );
    }
    // ...
```

ShopProduct already had a getPrice() method, so why might it be useful to implement the Chargeable interface? Once again, the answer has to do with types. An implementing class takes on the type of the class it extends and the interface that it implements.

This means that the CdProduct class belongs to

```
CdProduct
ShopProduct
Chargeable
```

This can be exploited by client code. To know an object's type is to know its capabilities. So the method

```
public function cdInfo( CdProduct $prod ) {
    // ...
}
```

knows that the $prod object has a getPlayLength() method in addition to all the methods defined in the ShopProduct class and Chargeable interface.

Passed the same object, the method

```
public function addProduct( ShopProduct $prod ) {
    // ..
}
```

knows that $prod supports all the methods in ShopProduct, but without further testing, it will know nothing of the getPlayLength() method.

Once again, passed the same CdProduct object, the method

```
public function addChargeableItem( Chargeable $item ) {
```

```
    //...
}
```

knows nothing at all of the ShopProduct or CdProduct types. This method is only concerned with whether the $item argument contains a getPrice() method.

Because any class can implement an interface (in fact, a class can implement any number of interfaces), interfaces effectively join types that are otherwise unrelated. I might define an entirely new class that implements Chargeable:

```
class Shipping implements Chargeable {
    public function getPrice() {
        //...
    }
}
```

I can pass a Shipping object to the addChargeableItem() method just as I can pass it a ShopProduct object.

The important thing to a client working with a Chargeable object is that it can call a getPrice() method. Any other available methods are associated with other types, whether through the object's own class, a superclass, or another interface. These are irrelevant to the client.

A class can both extend a superclass and implement any number of interfaces. The extends clause should precede the implements clause:

```
class Consultancy extends TimedService implements Bookable, Chargeable {
    // ...
}
```

Notice that the Consultancy class implements more than one interface. Multiple interfaces follow the implements keyword in a comma-separated list.

PHP only supports inheritance from a single parent, so the extends keyword can precede a single class name only.

Late Static Bindings: The `static` Keyword

Now that you've seen abstract classes and interfaces, it's time to return briefly to static methods. You saw that a static method can be used as factory, a way of generating instances of the containing class. If you're as lazy a coder as me, you might chafe at the duplication in an example like this:

```
abstract class DomainObject {
}


class User extends DomainObject {
    public static function create() {
        return new User();
    }
}


class Document extends DomainObject {
    public static function create() {
        return new Document();
    }
}
```

I create a super class named DomainObject. In a real-world project, of course, this would contain functionality common to its extending classes. Then I create two child classes, User and Document. I would like my concrete classes to have static create() methods.

▓Note Why would I use a static factory method when a constructor performs the work of creating an object already? In chapter 12, I'll describe a pattern called Identity Map. An Identity Map component generates and manages a new object only if an object with the same distinguishing characteristics is not already under management. If the target object already exists, it is returned. A factory method like create() would make a good client for a component of this sort.

This code works fine, but it has an annoying amount of duplication. I don't want to have to create boilerplate code like this for every DomainObject child class that I create. How about I push the create() method up to the super class?

```
abstract class DomainObject {
    public static function create() {
        return new self();
    }
}

class User extends DomainObject {
}

class Document extends DomainObject {
}
Document::create();
```

Well, that *looks* neat. I now have common code in one place, and I've used self as a reference to the class. But I have made an assumption about the self keyword. In fact, it does not act for classes exactly the same way that $this does for objects. self does not refer to the calling context; it refers to the context of resolution. So if I run the previous example I get this:

```
PHP Fatal error:  Cannot instantiate abstract class DomainObject in ....
```

So self resolves to DomainObject, the place where create() is defined, and not to Document, the class on which it was called. Until PHP 5.3 this was a serious limitation, which spawned many rather clumsy workarounds. PHP 5.3 introduced a concept called *late static bindings*. The most obvious manifestation of this feature is a new keyword: static. static is similar to self, except that it refers to the *invoked* rather than the *containing* class. In this case it means that calling Document::create() results in a new Document object and not a doomed attempt to instantiate a DomainObject object.

So now I can take advantage of my inheritance relationship in a static context.

```
abstract class DomainObject {
    public static function create() {
        return new static();
    }
```

```
}

class User extends DomainObject {
}

class Document extends DomainObject {
}

print_r(Document::create());
```

```
Document Object
(
)
```

The static keyword can be used for more than just instantiation. Like self and parent, it can be used as an identifier for static method calls, even from a non-static context. Let's say I want to include the concept of a group for my DomainObjects. By default, all classes fall into category 'default', but I'd like to be able override this for some branches of my inheritance hierarchy:

```
abstract class DomainObject {
    private $group;
    public function __construct() {
        $this->group = static::getGroup();
    }

    public static function create() {
        return new static();
    }

    static function getGroup() {
        return "default";
    }
}

class User extends DomainObject {
}

class Document extends DomainObject {
    static function getGroup() {
        return "document";
    }
}

class SpreadSheet extends Document {
}

print_r(User::create());
print_r(SpreadSheet::create());
```

I introduced a constructor to the DomainObject class. It uses the static keyword to invoke a static method: getGroup(). DomainObject provides the default implementation, but Document overrides it. I also created a new class SpreadSheet that extends Document. Here's the output:

```
User Object
(
    [group:DomainObject:private] => default
)
SpreadSheet Object
(
    [group:DomainObject:private] => document
)
```

For the User class, not much clever needs to happen. The DomainObject constructor calls getGroup(), and finds locally. In the case of SpreadSheet, though, the search begins at the invoked class, SpreadSheet itself. It provides no implementation, so the getGroup() method in the Document class is invoked. Before PHP 5.3 and late static binding, I would have been stuck with the self keyword here, which would only look for getGroup() in the DomainObject class.

Handling Errors

Things go wrong. Files are misplaced, database servers are left uninitialized, URLs are changed, XML files are mangled, permissions are poorly set, disk quotas are exceeded. The list goes on and on. In the fight to anticipate every problem, a simple method can sometimes sink under the weight of its own error-handling code.

Here is a simple Conf class that stores, retrieves, and sets data in an XML configuration file:

```
class Conf {
    private $file;
    private $xml;
    private $lastmatch;

    function __construct( $file ) {
        $this->file = $file;
        $this->xml = simplexml_load_file($file);
    }

    function write() {
        file_put_contents( $this->file, $this->xml->asXML() );
    }

    function get( $str ) {
        $matches = $this->xml->xpath("/conf/item[@name=\"$str\"]");
        if ( count( $matches ) ) {
            $this->lastmatch = $matches[0];
            return (string)$matches[0];
        }
        return null;
    }

    function set( $key, $value ) {
        if ( ! is_null( $this->get( $key ) ) ) {
            $this->lastmatch[0]=$value;
            return;
```

```
        }
        $conf = $this->xml->conf;
        $this->xml->addChild('item', $value)->addAttribute( 'name', $key );
    }
}
```

The Conf class uses the SimpleXml extension to access name value pairs. Here's the kind of format with which it is designed to work:

```
<?xml version="1.0"?>
<conf>
    <item name="user">bob</item>
    <item name="pass">newpass</item>
    <item name="host">localhost</item>
</conf>
```

The Conf class's constructor accepts a file path, which it passes to simplexml_load_file(). It stores the resulting SimpleXmlElement object in a property called $xml. The get() method uses XPath to locate an item element with the given name attribute, returning its value. set() either changes the value of an existing item or creates a new one. Finally, the write() method saves the new configuration data back to the file.

Like much example code, the Conf class is highly simplified. In particular, it has no strategy for handling nonexistent or unwriteable configurations. It is also optimistic in outlook. It assumes that the XML document will be well-formed and contain the expected elements.

Testing for these error conditions is relatively trivial, but I must still decide how to respond to them should they arise. You generally have two options:

First, I could end execution. This is simple but drastic. My humble class would then takes responsibility for bringing an entire script crashing down around it. Although methods like __construct() and write() are well placed to detect errors, they do not have the information to decide how to handle them.

Rather than handle the error in my class, then, I could return an error flag of some kind. This could be a Boolean or an integer value such as 0 or -1. Some classes will also set an error string or flag so that the client code can request more information after a failure.

Many PEAR packages combine these two approaches by returning an error object (an instance of PEAR_Error), which acts both as notification that an error has occurred and contains the error message within it. This approach is now deprecated, but plenty of classes have not been upgraded, not least because client code often depends upon the old behavior.

The problem here is that you pollute your return value. PHP does not enforce a unified return value. At the time of this writing, there is no support for return class type hinting in PHP, so there is nothing to prevent you from returning an error flag instead of the promised object or primitive. When you do this, you have to rely on the client coder to test for the return type every time your error-prone method is called. This can be risky. Trust no one!

When you return an error value to the calling code, there is no guarantee that the client will be any better equipped than your method to decide how to handle the error. If this is the case then the problem begins all over again. The client method will have to determine how to respond to the error condition, maybe even implementing a different error reporting strategy.

Exceptions

PHP 5 introduced exceptions to PHP, a radically different way of handling error conditions. Different for PHP, that is. You will find them hauntingly familiar if you have Java or C++ experience. Exceptions address all of the issues that I have raised so far in this section.

An exception is a special object instantiated from the built-in Exception class (or from a derived class). Objects of type Exception are designed to hold and report error information.

The Exception class constructor accepts two optional arguments, a message string and an error code. The class provides some useful methods for analyzing error conditions. These are described in Table 4–1.

Table 4–1. *The Exception Class's Public Methods*

Method	Description
getMessage()	Get the message string that was passed to the constructor.
getCode()	Get the code integer that was passed to the constructor.
getFile()	Get the file in which the exception was generated.
getLine()	Get the line number at which the exception was generated.
getPrevious()	Get a nested Exception object.
getTrace()	Get a multidimensional array tracing the method calls that led to the exception, including method, class, file, and argument data.
getTraceAsString()	Get a string version of the data returned by getTrace().
__toString()	Called automatically when the Exception object is used in string context. Returns a string describing the exception details.

The Exception class is fantastically useful for providing error notification and debugging information (the getTrace() and getTraceAsString() methods are particularly helpful in this regard). In fact, it is almost identical to the PEAR_Error class that was discussed earlier. There is much more to an exception than the information it holds, though.

Throwing an Exception

The throw keyword is used in conjunction with an Exception object. It halts execution of the current method and passes responsibility for handling the error back to the calling code. Here I amend the __construct() method to use the throw statement:

```
function __construct( $file ) {
    $this->file = $file;
    if ( ! file_exists( $file ) ) {
        throw new Exception( "file '$file' does not exist" );
    }
    $this->xml = simplexml_load_file($file);
}
```

The write() method can use a similar construct:

```
function write() {
    if ( ! is_writeable( $this->file ) ) {
```

```
        throw new Exception("file '{$this->file}' is not writeable");
    }
    file_put_contents( $this->file, $this->xml->asXML() );
}
```

The __construct() and write() methods can now check diligently for file errors as they do their work, but let code more fitted for the purpose decide how to respond to any errors detected.

So how does client code know how to handle an exception when thrown? When you invoke a method that may throw an exception, you can wrap your call in a try clause. A try clause is made up of the try keyword followed by braces. The try clause must be followed by at least one catch clause in which you can handle any error, like this:

```
try {
    $conf = new Conf( dirname(__FILE__)."/conf01.xml" );
    print "user: ".$conf->get('user')."\n";
    print "host: ".$conf->get('host')."\n";
    $conf->set("pass", "newpass");
    $conf->write();
} catch ( Exception $e ) {
    die( $e->__toString() );
}
```

As you can see, the catch clause superficially resembles a method declaration. When an exception is thrown, the catch clause in the invoking scope is called. The Exception object is automatically passed in as the argument variable.

Just as execution is halted within the throwing method when an exception is thrown, so it is within the try clause—control passes directly to the catch clause.

Subclassing Exception

You can create classes that extend the Exception class as you would with any user-defined class. There are two reasons why you might want to do this. First, you can extend the class's functionality. Second, the fact that a derived class defines a new class type can aid error handling in itself.

You can, in fact, define as many catch clauses as you need for a try statement. The particular catch clause invoked will depend upon the type of the thrown exception and the class type hint in the argument list. Here are some simple classes that extend Exception:

```
class XmlException extends Exception {
    private $error;

    function __construct( LibXmlError $error ) {
        $shortfile = basename( $error->file );
        $msg = "[{$shortfile}, line {$error->line}, col {$error->column}] ➥
{$error->message}";
        $this->error = $error;
        parent::__construct( $msg, $error->code );
    }

    function getLibXmlError() {
        return $this->error;
    }
}

class FileException extends Exception { }
```

```
class ConfException extends Exception { }
```

The LibXmlError class is generated behind the scenes when SimpleXml encounters a broken XML file. It has message and code properties, and resembles the Exception class. I take advantage of this similarity and use the LibXmlError object in the XmlException class. The FileException and ConfException classes do nothing more than subclass Exception. I can now use these classes in my code and amend both __construct() and write():

```
// Conf class...
    function __construct( $file ) {
        $this->file = $file;
        if ( ! file_exists( $file ) ) {
            throw new FileException( "file '$file' does not exist" );
        }
        $this->xml = simplexml_load_file($file, null, LIBXML_NOERROR );
        if ( ! is_object( $this->xml ) ) {
            throw new XmlException( libxml_get_last_error() );
        }
        print gettype( $this->xml );
        $matches = $this->xml->xpath("/conf");
        if ( ! count( $matches ) ) {
            throw new ConfException( "could not find root element: conf" );
        }
    }

    function write() {

        if ( ! is_writeable( $this->file ) ) {
            throw new FileException("file '{$this->file}' is not writeable");
        }
        file_put_contents( $this->file, $this->xml->asXML() );
    }
```

__construct() throws either an XmlException, a FileException, or a ConfException, depending on the kind of error it encounters. Note that I pass the option flag LIBXML_NOERROR to simplexml_load_file(). This suppresses warnings, leaving me free to handle them with my XmlException class after the fact. If I encounter a malformed XML file, I know that an error has occurred because simplexml_load_file() won't have returned an object. I can then access the error using libxml_get_last_error().

The write() method throws a FileException if the $file property points to an unwriteable entity.

So, I have established that __construct() might throw one of three possible exceptions. How can I take advantage of this? Here's some code that instantiates a Conf() object:

```
class Runner {
    static function init() {
        try {
            $conf = new Conf( dirname(__FILE__)."/conf01.xml" );
            print "user: ".$conf->get('user')."\n";
            print "host: ".$conf->get('host')."\n";
            $conf->set("pass", "newpass");
            $conf->write();
        } catch ( FileException $e ) {
            // permissions issue or non-existent file
        } catch ( XmlException $e ) {
```

```
        // broken xml
    } catch ( ConfException $e ) {
        // wrong kind of XML file
    } catch ( Exception $e ) {
        // backstop: should not be called
    }
  }
}
```

I provide a catch clause for each class type. The clause invoked depends on the exception type thrown. The first to match will be executed, so remember to place the most generic type at the end and the most specialized at the start. For example, if you were to place the catch clause for Exception ahead of the clause for XmlException and ConfException, neither of these would ever be invoked. This is because both of these classes belong to the Exception type, and would therefore match the first clause.

The first catch clause (FileException) is invoked if there is a problem with the configuration file (if the file is non-existent or unwriteable). The second clause (XmlException) is invoked if an error occurs in parsing the XML file (if an element is not closed, for example). The third clause (ConfException) is invoked if a valid XML file does not contain the expected root conf element. The final clause (Exception) should not be reached, because my methods only generate the three exceptions, which are explicitly handled. It is often a good idea to have a "backstop" clause like this, in case you add new exceptions to the code during development.

The benefit of these fine-grained catch clauses is that they allow you to apply different recovery or failure mechanisms to different errors. For example, you may decide to end execution, log the error and continue, or explicitly rethrow an error:

```
    try {
        //...
    } catch ( FileException $e ) {
        throw $e;
    }
```

Another trick you can play here is to throw a new exception that wraps the current one. This allows you to stake a claim to the error, to add your own contextual information, while retaining the data encapsulated by the exception you have caught. You can read more about this technique in Chapter 15.

So what happens if an exception is not caught by client code? It is implicitly rethrown, and the client's own calling code is given the opportunity to catch it. This process continues either until the exception is caught or until it can no longer be thrown. At this point, a fatal error occurs. Here's what would happen if I did not catch one of the exceptions in my example:

```
PHP Fatal error:  Uncaught exception 'FileException' with message
'file 'nonexistent/not_there.xml' does not exist' in ...
```

So when you throw an exception, you force the client to take responsibility for handling it. This is not an abdication of responsibility. An exception should be thrown when a method has detected an error but does not have the contextual information to be able to handle it intelligently. The write() method in my example knows when the attempt to write will fail, and it knows why, but it does not know what to do about it. This is as it should be. If I were to make the Conf class more knowledgeable than it currently is, it would lose focus and become less reusable.

Final Classes and Methods

Inheritance allows for enormous flexibility within a class hierarchy. You can override a class or method so that a call in a client method will achieve radically different effects according to which class instance it has been passed. Sometimes, though, a class or method should remain fixed and unchanging. If you have achieved the definitive functionality for your class or method, and you feel that overriding it can only damage the ultimate perfection of your work, you may need the final keyword.

final puts a stop to inheritance. A final class cannot be subclassed. Less drastically, a final method cannot be overridden.

Here's a final class:

```
final class Checkout {
    // ...
}
```

Here's an attempt to subclass the Checkout class:

```
class IllegalCheckout extends Checkout {
    // ...
}
```

This produces an error:

```
PHP Fatal error:  Class IllegalCheckout may not inherit from
final class (Checkout) in ...
```

I could relax matters somewhat by declaring a method in Checkout final, rather than the whole class. The final keyword should be placed in front of any other modifiers such as protected or static, like this:

```
class Checkout {
    final function totalize() {
        // calculate bill
    }
}
```

I can now subclass Checkout, but any attempt to override totalize() will cause a fatal error:

```
class IllegalCheckout extends Checkout {
    final function totalize() {
        // change bill calculation
    }
}
```

```
// Fatal error: Cannot override final method
// checkout::totalize() in ...
```

Good object-oriented code tends to emphasize the well-defined interface. Behind the interface, though, implementations will often vary. Different classes or combinations of classes conform to common interfaces but behave differently in different circumstances. By declaring a class or method final, you limit this flexibility. There will be times when this is desirable, and you will see some of them later in the book, but you should think carefully before declaring something final. Are there really no circumstances in which overriding would be useful? You could always change your mind later on, of course, but this might not be so easy if you are distributing a library for others to use. Use final with care.

Working with Interceptors

PHP provides built-in interceptor methods, which can intercept messages sent to undefined methods and properties. This is also known as *overloading*, but since that term means something quite different in Java and C++, I think it is better to talk in terms of interception.

PHP 5 supports three built-in interceptor methods. Like __construct(), these are invoked for you when the right conditions are met. Table 4–2 describes the methods.

Table 4–2. *The Interceptor Methods*

Method	Description
__get($property)	Invoked when an undefined property is accessed
__set($property, $value)	Invoked when a value is assigned to an undefined property
__isset($property)	Invoked when isset() is called on an undefined property
__unset($property)	Invoked when unset() is called on an undefined property
__call($method, $arg_array)	Invoked when an undefined method is called

The __get() and __set() methods are designed for working with properties that have not been declared in a class (or its parents).

__get() is invoked when client code attempts to read an undeclared property. It is called automatically with a single string argument containing the name of the property that the client is attempting to access. Whatever you return from the __get() method will be sent back to the client as if the target property exists with that value. Here's a quick example:

```
class Person {
    function __get( $property ) {
        $method = "get{$property}";
        if ( method_exists( $this, $method ) ) {
            return $this->$method();
        }
    }

    function getName() {
        return "Bob";
    }

    function getAge() {
        return 44;
    }
}
```

When a client attempts to access an undefined property, the __get() method is invoked. I have implemented __get() to take the property name and construct a new string, prepending the word "get". I pass this string to a function called method_exists(), which accepts an object and a method name and tests for method existence. If the method does exist, I invoke it and pass its return value to the client. So if the client requests a $name property:

```
$p = new Person();
print $p->name;
```

the getName() method is invoked behind the scenes.

Bob

If the method does not exist, I do nothing. The property that the user is attempting to access will resolve to NULL.

The __isset() method works in a similar way to __get(). It is invoked after the client calls isset() on an undefined property. Here's how I might extend Person:

```
function __isset( $property ) {
    $method = "get{$property}";
    return ( method_exists( $this, $method ) );
}
```

Now a cautious user can test a property before working with it:

```
if ( isset( $p->name ) ) {
    print $p->name;
}
```

The __set() method is invoked when client code attempts to assign to an undefined property. It is passed two arguments: the name of the property, and the value the client is attempting to set. You can then decide how to work with these arguments. Here I further amend the Person class:

```
class Person {
    private $_name;
    private $_age;

    function __set( $property, $value ) {
        $method = "set{$property}";
        if ( method_exists( $this, $method ) ) {
            return $this->$method( $value );
        }
    }

    function setName( $name ) {
        $this->_name = $name;
        if ( ! is_null( $name ) ) {
            $this->_name = strtoupper($this->_name);
        }
    }

    function setAge( $age ) {
        $this->_age =  strtoupper($age);
    }
```

```
}
```

In this example I work with "setter" methods rather than "getters." If a user attempts to assign to an undefined property, the __set() method is invoked with the property name and the assigned value. I test for the existence of the appropriate method, and invoke it if it exists. In this way I can filter the assigned value.

▓**Note** Remember that methods and properties in PHP documentation are frequently spoken of in static terms in order to identify them with their classes. So you might talk about the Person::$name property, even though the property is not declared static and would in fact be accessed via an object.

So if I create a Person object and then attempt to set a property called Person::$name, the __set() method is invoked, because this class does not define a $name property. The method is passed the string "name" and the value that the client assigned. How the value is then used depends upon the implementation of __set(). In this example, I construct a method name out of the property argument combined with the string "set". The setName() method is found and duly invoked. This transforms the incoming value and stores it in a real property.

```
$p = new Person();
$p->name = "bob";
// the $_name property becomes 'BOB'
```

As you might expect, __unset() mirrors __set(). When unset() is called on an undefined property, __unset() is invoked with the name of the property. You can then do what you like with the information. This example passes null to a method resolved using the same technique as you saw used by __set().

```
    function __unset( $property ) {
        $method = "set{$property}";
        if ( method_exists( $this, $method ) ) {
            $this->$method( null );
        }
    }
```

The __call() method is probably the most useful of all the interceptor methods. It is invoked when an undefined method is called by client code. __call() is invoked with the method name and an array holding all arguments passed by the client. Any value that you return from the __call() method is returned to the client as if it were returned by the method invoked.

The __call() method can be useful for delegation. Delegation is the mechanism by which one object passes method invocations on to a second. It is similar to inheritance, in that a child class passes on a method call to its parent implementation. With inheritance the relationship between child and parent is fixed, so the ability to switch the receiving object at runtime means that delegation can be more flexible than inheritance. An example clarify things a little. Here is a simple class for formatting information from the Person class:

```
class PersonWriter {

    function writeName( Person $p ) {
        print $p->getName()."\n";
    }
```

```
    function writeAge( Person $p ) {
        print $p->getAge()."\n";
    }
}
```

I could, of course, subclass this to output Person data in various ways. Here is an implementation of the Person class that uses both a PersonWriter object and the __call() method:

```
class Person {
    private $writer;

    function __construct( PersonWriter $writer ) {
        $this->writer = $writer;
    }

    function __call( $methodname, $args ) {
        if ( method_exists( $this->writer, $methodname ) ) {
            return $this->writer->$methodname( $this );
        }
    }

    function getName()  { return "Bob"; }
    function getAge() { return 44; }
}
```

The Person class here demands a PersonWriter object as a constructor argument and stores it in a property variable. In the __call() method, I use the provided $methodname argument, testing for a method of the same name in the PersonWriter object I have stored. If I encounter such a method, I delegate the method call to the PersonWriter object, passing my current instance to it (in the $this pseudo-variable). So if the client makes this call to Person:

```
$person = new Person( new PersonWriter() );
$person->writeName();
```

the __call() method is invoked. I find a method called writeName() in my PersonWriter object and invoke it. This saves me from manually invoking the delegated method like this:

```
function writeName() {
    $this->writer->writeName( $this );
}
```

The Person class has magically gained two new methods. Although automated delegation can save a lot of legwork, there can be a cost in clarity. If you rely too much on delegation, you present the world with a dynamic interface that resists reflection (the runtime examination of class facets) and is not always clear to the client coder at first glance. This is because the logic that governs the interaction between a delegating class and its target can be obscure—buried away in methods like __call() rather than signaled up front by inheritance relationships or method type hints, as is the case for similar relationships. The interceptor methods have their place, but they should be used with care, and classes that rely on them should document this fact very clearly.

I will return to the topics of delegation and reflection later in the book.

Defining Destructor Methods

You have seen that the __construct() method is automatically invoked when an object is instantiated. PHP 5 also introduced the __destruct() method. This is invoked just before an object is garbage-collected; that is, before it is expunged from memory. You can use this method to perform any final cleaning up that might be necessary.

Imagine, for example, a class that saves itself to a database when so ordered. I could use the __destruct() method to ensure that an instance saves its data when it is deleted.

```
class Person {
    private $name;
    private $age;
    private $id;

    function __construct( $name, $age ) {
        $this->name = $name;
        $this->age  = $age;
    }

    function setId( $id ) {
        $this->id = $id;
    }

    function __destruct() {
        if ( ! empty( $this->id ) ) {
            // save Person data
            print "saving person\n";
        }
    }
}
```

The __destruct() method is invoked whenever a Person object is removed from memory. This will happen either when you call the unset() function with the object in question or when no further references to the object exist in the process. So if I create and destroy a Person object, you can see the __destruct() method come into play.

```
$person = new Person( "bob", 44 );
$person->setId( 343 );
unset( $person );
// output:
// saving person
```

Although tricks like this are fun, it's worth sounding a note of caution. __call(), __destruct(), and their colleagues are sometimes called *magic methods*. As you will know if you have ever read a fantasy novel, magic is not always a good thing. Magic is arbitrary and unexpected. Magic bends the rules. Magic incurs hidden costs.

In the case of __destruct(), for example, you can end up saddling clients with unwelcome surprises. Think about the Person class—it performs a database write in its __destruct() method. Now imagine a novice developer idly putting the Person class through its paces. He doesn't spot the __destruct() method and he sets about instantiating a set of Person objects. Passing values to the constructor, he assigns the CEO's secret and faintly obscene nickname to the $name property, and sets $age at 150. He runs his test script a few times, trying out colorful name and age combinations.

The next morning, his manager asks him to step into a meeting room to explain why the database contains insulting Person data. The moral? Do not trust magic.

Copying Objects with __clone()

In PHP 4, copying an object was a simple matter of assigning from one variable to another.

```
class CopyMe {}
$first = new CopyMe();
$second = $first;
// PHP 4: $second and $first are 2 distinct objects
// PHP 5 plus: $second and $first refer to one object
```

This "simple matter" was a source of many bugs, as object copies were accidentally spawned when variables were assigned, methods were called, and objects were returned. This was made worse by the fact that there was no way of testing two variables to see whether they referred to the same object. Equivalence tests would tell you whether all fields were the same (==) or whether both variables were objects (===), but not whether they pointed to the same object.

In PHP, objects are always assigned and passed around by reference. This means that when my previous example is run with PHP 5, $first and $second contain references to the same object instead of two copies. While this is generally what you want when working with objects, there will be occasions when you need to get a copy of an object rather than a reference to an object.

PHP provides the clone keyword for just this purpose. clone operates on an object instance, producing a by-value copy.

```
class CopyMe {}
$first  = new CopyMe();
$second = clone $first;
// PHP 5 plus: $second and $first are 2 distinct objects
```

The issues surrounding object copying only start here. Consider the Person class that I implemented in the previous section. A default copy of a Person object would contain the identifier (the $id property), which in a full implementation I would use to locate the correct row in a database. If I allow this property to be copied, a client coder can end up with two distinct objects referencing the same data source, which is probably not what she wanted when she made her copy. An update in one object will affect the other, and vice versa.

Luckily you can control what is copied when clone is invoked on an object. You do this by implementing a special method called __clone() (note the leading two underscores that are characteristic of built-in methods). __clone() is called automatically when the clone keyword is invoked on an object.

When you implement __clone(), it is important to understand the context in which the method runs. __clone() is run on the *copied* object and not the original. Here I add __clone() to yet another version of the Person class:

```
class Person {
    private $name;
    private $age;
    private $id;

    function __construct( $name, $age ) {
        $this->name = $name;
        $this->age  = $age;
    }

    function setId( $id ) {
        $this->id = $id;
    }
```

```
    function __clone() {

        $this->id    = 0;
    }
}
```

When clone is invoked on a Person object, a new shallow copy is made, and *its* __clone() method is invoked. This means that anything I do in __clone() overwrites the default copy I already made. In this case, I ensure that the copied object's $id property is set to zero.

```
$person = new Person( "bob", 44 );
$person->setId( 343 );
$person2 = clone $person;
// $person2 :
//      name: bob
//      age: 44
//      id: 0.
```

A shallow copy ensures that primitive properties are copied from the old object to the new. Object properties, though, are copied by reference, which may not be what you want or expect when cloning an object. Say that I give the Person object an Account object property. This object holds a balance that I want copied to the cloned object. What I don't want, though, is for both Person objects to hold references to the *same* account.

```
class Account {
    public $balance;
    function __construct( $balance ) {
        $this->balance = $balance;
    }
}

class Person {
    private $name;
    private $age;
    private $id;
    public $account;

    function __construct( $name, $age, Account $account ) {
        $this->name = $name;
        $this->age  = $age;
        $this->account = $account;
    }

    function setId( $id ) {
        $this->id = $id;
    }

    function __clone() {
        $this->id    = 0;
    }
}

$person = new Person( "bob", 44, new Account( 200 ) );
$person->setId( 343 );
```

```
$person2 = clone $person;

// give $person some money
$person->account->balance += 10;
// $person2 sees the credit too
print $person2->account->balance;
```

This gives the output:

```
210
```

$person holds a reference to an Account object that I have kept publicly accessible for the sake of brevity (as you know, I would usually restrict access to a property, providing an accessor method if necessary). When the clone is created, it holds a reference to the same Account object that $person references. I demonstrate this by adding to the $person object's Account and confirming the increased balance via $person2.

If I do not want an object property to be shared after a clone operation then it is up to me to clone it explicitly in the __clone() method:

```
function __clone() {
    $this->id    = 0;
    $this->account = clone $this->account;
}
```

Defining String Values for Your Objects

Another Java-inspired feature introduced by PHP 5 was the __toString() method. Before PHP 5.2, when you printed an object, it would resolve to a string like this:

```
class StringThing {}
$st = new StringThing();
print $st;
```

```
Object id #1
```

Since PHP 5.2, this code will produce an error like this:

```
PHP Catchable fatal error:  Object of class StringThing could not be
converted to string in ...
```

By implementing a __toString() method, you can control how your objects represent themselves when printed. __toString() should be written to return a string value. The method is invoked automatically when your object is passed to print or echo, and its return value is substituted. Here I add a __toString() version to a minimal Person class:

```
class Person {
    function getName()  { return "Bob"; }
```

```
    function getAge() { return 44; }
    function __toString() {
        $desc = $this->getName();
        $desc .= " (age ".$this->getAge().")";
        return $desc;
    }
}
```

Now when I print a Person object, the object will resolve to this:

```
$person = new Person();
print $person;
```

```
Bob (age 44)
```

The __toString() method is particularly useful for logging and error reporting, and for classes whose main task is to convey information. The Exception class, for example, summarizes exception data in its __toString() method.

Callbacks, Anonymous Functions and Closures

Although not strictly an object-oriented feature, anonymous functions are useful enough to mention here, because may encounter them in object-oriented applications that utilize callbacks. What's more, there have been some pretty interesting recent developments in this area.

To kick things off, here are a couple of classes:

```
class Product {
    public $name;
    public $price;

    function __construct( $name, $price ) {
        $this->name = $name;
        $this->price = $price;
    }
}

class ProcessSale {
    private $callbacks;

    function registerCallback( $callback ) {
        if ( ! is_callable( $callback ) ) {
            throw new Exception( "callback not callable" );
        }
        $this->callbacks[] = $callback;
    }

    function sale( $product ) {
        print "{$product->name}: processing \n";
        foreach ( $this->callbacks as $callback ) {
            call_user_func( $callback, $product );
        }
```

```
        }
}
```

This code is designed to run my various callbacks. It consists of two classes. `Product` simply stores `$name` and `$price` properties. I've made these public for the purposes of brevity. Remember, in the real world you'd probably want to make your properties private or protected and provide accessor methods. `ProcessSale` consists of two methods: `registerCallback()` accepts an unhinted scalar, tests it, and adds it to a callback array. The test, a built-in function called `is_callable()`, ensures that whatever I've been given can be invoked by a function such as `call_user_func()` or `array_walk()`.

The `sale()` method accepts a `Product` object, outputs a message about it, and then loops through the `$callback` array property. It passes each element to `call_user_func()` which calls the code, passing it a reference to the product. All the following examples will work with the framework.

Why are callbacks useful? They allow you to plug functionality into a component at runtime that is not directly related to that component's core task. By making a component callback aware, you give others the power to extend your code in contexts you don't yet know about.

Imagine, for example, that a future user of `ProcessSale` wants to create a log of sales. If the user has access to the class she might add logging code directly to the `sale()` method. This isn't always a good idea though. If she is not the maintainer of the package, which provides `ProcessSale`, then her amendments will be overwritten next time the package is upgraded. Even if she is the maintainer of the component, adding many incidental tasks to the `sale()` method will begin to overwhelm its core responsibility, and potentially make it less usable across projects. I will return to these themes in the next section.

Luckily, though, I made ProcessSale callback-aware. Here I create a callback that simulates logging:

```
$logger = create_function( '$product',
                        'print "    logging ({$product->name})\n";' );

$processor = new ProcessSale();
$processor->registerCallback( $logger );

$processor->sale( new Product( "shoes", 6 ) );
print "\n";
$processor->sale( new Product( "coffee", 6 ) );
```

I use `create_function()` to build my callback. As you can see, it accepts two string arguments. Firstly, a list of parameters, and secondly the function body. The result is often called an anonymous function since it's not named in the manner of a standard function. Instead, it can be stored in a variable and passed to functions and methods as a parameter. That's just what I do, storing the function in the `$logger` variable and passing it to `ProcessSale::registerCallback()`. Finally I create a couple of products and pass them to the `sale()` method. You have already seen what happens there. The sale is processed (in reality a simple message is printed about the product), and any callbacks are executed. Here is the code in action:

```
shoes: processing
    logging (shoes)

coffee: processing
    logging (coffee)
```

Look again at that create_function() example. See how ugly it is? Placing code designed to be executed inside a string is always a pain. You need to escape variables and quotation marks, and, if the callback grows to any size, it can be very hard to read indeed. Wouldn't it be neater if there were a more elegant way of creating anonymous functions? Well since PHP 5.3 there is a much better way of doing it. You can simply declare and assign a function in one statement. Here's the previous example using the new syntax:

```
$logger2 = function( $product ) {
    print "    logging ({$product->name})\n";
};

$processor = new ProcessSale();
$processor->registerCallback( $logger2 );

$processor->sale( new Product( "shoes", 6 ) );
print "\n";
$processor->sale( new Product( "coffee", 6 ) );
```

The only difference here lies in the creation of the anonymous variable. As you can see, it's a lot neater. I simply use the function keyword inline, and without a function name. Note that because this is an inline statement, a semi-colon is required at the end of the code block. Of course if you want your code to run on older versions of PHP, you may be stuck with create_function() for a while yet. The output here is the same as that of the previous example.

Of course, callbacks needn't be anonymous. You can use the name of a function, or even an object reference and a method, as a callback. Here I do just that:

```
class Mailer {
    function doMail( $product ) {
        print "    mailing ({$product->name})\n";
    }
}

$processor = new ProcessSale();
$processor->registerCallback( array( new Mailer(), "doMail" ) );

$processor->sale( new Product( "shoes", 6 ) );
print "\n";
$processor->sale( new Product( "coffee", 6 ) );
```

I create a class: Mailer. Its single method, doMail(), accepts a $product object, and outputs a message about it. When I call registerCallback() I pass it an array. The first element is a $mailer object, and the second is a string that matches the name of the method I want invoked. Remember that registerCallback() checks its argument for callability. is_callable() is smart enough to test arrays of this sort. A valid callback in array form should have an object as its first element, and the name of a method as its second element. I pass that test here, and here is my output:

```
shoes: processing
    mailing (shoes)

coffee: processing
    mailing (coffee)
```

Of course you can have a method return an anonymous function. Something like this:

```
class Totalizer {
    static function warnAmount() {
        return function( $product ) {
            if ( $product->price > 5 ) {
                print "    reached high price: {$product->price}\n";
            }
        };
    }
}

$processor = new ProcessSale();
$processor->registerCallback( Totalizer::warnAmount() );
...
```

Apart from the convenience of using the warnAmount() method as a factory for the anonymous function, I have not added much of interest here. But this structure allows me to do much more than just generate an anonymous function. It allows me to take advantage of closures. The new style anonymous functions can reference variables declared in the anonymous functions parent scope. This is a hard concept to grasp at times. It's as if the anonymous function continues to remember the context in which it was created. Imagine that I want Totalizer::warnAmount() to do two things. First of all, I'd like it to accept an arbitrary target amount. Second, I want it to keep a tally of prices as products are sold. When the total exceeds the target amount, the function will perform an action (in this case, as you might have guessed, it will simply write a message).

I can make my anonymous function track variables from its wider scope with a use clause:

```
class Totalizer {
    static function warnAmount( $amt ) {
        $count=0;
        return function( $product ) use ( $amt, &$count ) {
            $count += $product->price;
            print "    count: $count\n";
            if ( $count > $amt ) {
                print "    high price reached: {$count}\n";
            }
        };
    }
}

$processor = new ProcessSale();
$processor->registerCallback( Totalizer::warnAmount( 8) );

$processor->sale( new Product( "shoes", 6 ) );
print "\n";
$processor->sale( new Product( "coffee", 6 ) );
```

The anonymous function returned by Totalizer::warnAmount() specifies two variables in its use clause. The first is $amt. This is the argument that warnAmount() accepted. The second closure variable is $count. $count is declared in the body of warnAmount() and set initially to zero. Notice that I prepend an ampersand to the $count variable in the use clause. This means the variable will be accessed by reference rather than by value in the anonymous function. In the body of the anonymous function, I increment $count by the product's value, and then test the new total against $amt. If the target value has been reached, I output a notification.

Here is the code in action:

```
shoes: processing
    count: 6

coffee: processing
    count: 12

    high price reached: 12
```

This demonstrates that the callback is keeping track of $count between invocations. Both $count and $amt remain associated with the function because they were present to the context of its declaration, and because they were specified in its use clause.

Summary

In this chapter, we came to grips with PHP's advanced object-oriented features. Some of these will become familiar as you work through the book. In particular, I will return frequently to abstract classes, exceptions, and static methods.

In the next chapter, I take a step back from built-in object features and look at classes and functions designed to help you work with objects.

CHAPTER 5

Object Tools

As we have seen, PHP supports object-oriented programming through language constructs such as classes and methods. The language also provides wider support through functions and classes designed to help you work with objects.

In this chapter, We will look at some tools and techniques that you can use to organize, test, and manipulate objects and classes.

This chapter will cover

- Packages: Organizing your code into logical categories

- .Namespaces: Since PHP 5.3 you can encapsulate your code elements in discrete compartments .

- Include paths: Setting central accessible locations for your library code.

- Class and object functions: Functions for testing objects, classes, properties, and methods.

- The Reflection API: A powerful suite of built-in classes that provide unprecedented access to class information at runtime.

PHP and Packages

A package is a set of related classes, usually grouped together in some way. Packages can be used to separate parts of a system from one another. Some programming languages formally recognize packages and provide them with distinct namespaces. PHP has no native concept of a package, but as of PHP 5.3, it does understand namespaces. I'll look at this feature in the next section.

Since we will probably all have to work with older code for a while yet, I'll go on to look at the old way of organizing classes into package-like structures.

PHP Packages and Namespaces

Although PHP does not intrinsically support the concept of a package, developers have traditionally used both naming schemes and the filesystem to organize their code into package-like structures. Later on I will cover the way that you can use files and directories to organize your code. First though, I'll look at naming schemes, and a new, but related, feature: namespace support.

Up until PHP 5.3, developers were forced to name their files in a global context. In other words, if you named a class ShoppingBasket, it would become instantly available across your system. This caused two major problems. First, and most damaging, was the possibility of naming collisions. You might think that this is unlikely. After all, all you have to do is remember to give all your classes unique names, right? The trouble is, we all rely increasingly on library code. This is a good thing, of course, because it promotes code reuse. But what if your project does this:

```
// my.php

require_once "useful/Outputter1.php"
class Outputter {
    // output data
}
```

and the included file does this:

```
// useful/Outputter1.php
class Outputter {
    //
}
```

Well you can guess, right? This happens:

```
Fatal error: Cannot redeclare class Outputter in ../useful/Outputter1.php on line 3
```

Of course, as you'll see there was a conventional workaround to this. The answer was to prepend package names to class names, so that class names are guaranteed unique.

```
// my.php

require_once "useful/Outputter2.php";
class my_Outputter {
    // output data
}
```

```
// useful/Outputter2.php

class useful_Outputter {
    //
}
```

The problem here was that as projects got more involved, class names grew longer and longer. It was not an enormous problem, but it resulted in issues with code readability, and made it harder to hold classnames in your head while you worked. Many cumulative coding hours were lost to typos.

We'll all be stuck with this convention for years to come, because most of us will be maintaining legacy code in one form or other for a long time. For that reason, I'll return to the old way of handling packages later in this chapter.

Namespaces to the Rescue

Namespaces have been a wish-list feature for a long time now. The previous edition of this book included a proposed implementation that made it into the PHP 6 development code. The developer mailing lists have been lit up periodically by debates about the merits of the feature.

With PHP 5.3 the debates are academic. Namespaces are part of the language, and they're here to stay.

So, what are they? In essence a namespace is a bucket in which you can place your classes, functions and variables. Within a namespace you can access these items without qualification. From outside, you must either import the namespace, or reference it, in order to access the items it contains.

Confused? An example should help. Here I rewrite the previous example using namespaces:

```
namespace my;
require_once "useful/Outputter3.php";

class Outputter {
    // output data
}

// useful/Outputter3.php
namespace useful;

class Outputter {
    //
}
```

Notice the `namespace` keyword. As you might expect that establishes a namespace. If you are using this feature, then the namespace declaration must be the first statement in its file. I have created two namespaces: `my` and `useful`. Typically, though, you'll want to have deeper namespaces. You'll start with an organization or project identifier. Then you'll want to further qualify this by package. PHP lets you declare nested namespaces. To do this you simply use a backslash character to divide each level.

```
namespace com\getinstance\util;

class Debug {
    static function helloWorld() {
        print "hello from Debug\n";
    }
}
```

If I were to provide a code repository, I might use one of my domains: getinstance.com. I might then use this domain name as my namespace. This is a trick that Java developers typically use for their package names. They invert domain names so that they run from the most generic to the most specific. Once I've identified my repository, I might go on to define packages. In this case I use `util`.

So how would I call the method? In fact it depends where you're doing the calling from. If you are calling the method from within the namespace, you can go ahead and call the method directly:

```
Debug::helloWorld();
```

This is known as an unqualified name. Because I'm already in the `com\getinstance\util` namespace, I don't have to prepend any kind of path to the class name. If I were accessing the class from outside of a namespaced context I could do this:

```
com\getinstance\util\Debug::helloWorld();
```

What output would I get from the following code?

```
namespace main;


com\getinstance\util\Debug::helloWorld();
```

That's a trick question. In fact this is my output:

```
PHP Fatal error:  Class 'main\com\getinstance\util\Debug' not found in .../listing5.04.php o
n line 12
```

That's because I'm using a relative namespace here. PHP is looking below the namespace main for com\getinstance\util and not finding it. Just as you can make absolute URLs and filepaths by starting off with a separator so you can with namespaces. This version of the example fixes the previous error:

```
namespace main;

\com\getinstance\util\Debug::helloWorld();
```

That leading backslash tells PHP to begin its search at the root, and not from the current namespace.

But aren't namespaces supposed to help you cut down on typing? The Debug class declaration is shorter, certainly, but those calls are just as wordy as they would have been with the old naming convention. You can get round this with the use keyword. This allows you to alias other namespaces within the current namespace. Here's an example:

```
namespace main;
use com\getinstance\util;
util\Debug::helloWorld();
```

The com\getinstance\util namespace is imported and implicitly aliased to util. Notice that I didn't begin with a leading backslash character. The argument to use is searched from global space and not from the current namespace. If I don't want to reference a namespace at all, I can import the Debug class itself:

```
namespace main;
use com\getinstance\util\Debug;
Debug::helloWorld();
```

But what would happen if I already had a Debug class in the main namespace? I think you can guess. Here's the code and some output.

```
namespace main;
use com\getinstance\util\Debug;
class Debug {
    static function helloWorld() {
        print "hello from main\Debug";
    }
}

Debug::helloWorld();
```

```
PHP Fatal error:  Cannot declare class main\Debug because the name is already in use in .../
listing5.08.php on line 13
```

So I seem to have come full circle, arriving back at class name collisions. Luckily there's an answer for this problem. I can make my alias explicit:

```
namespace main;
```

```
use com\getinstance\util\Debug as uDebug;

class Debug {
    static function helloWorld() {
        print "hello from main\Debug";
    }
}

uDebug::helloWorld();
```

By using the as clause to use, I am able to change the Debug alias to uDebug.

If you are writing code in a namespace and you want to access a class that resides in global (non-namespaced) space, you can simply precede the name with a backslash. Here's a method declared in global space:

```
// global.php: no namespace

class Lister {
    public static function helloWorld() {
        print "hello from global\n";
    }
}
```

And here's some namespaced code that references the class:

```
namespace com\getinstance\util;
require_once 'global.php';
class Lister {
    public static function helloWorld() {
        print "hello from ".__NAMESPACE__."\n";
    }
}

Lister::helloWorld();  // access local
\Lister::helloWorld(); // access global
```

The namespaced code declares its own Lister class. An unqualified name accesses the local version. A name qualified with a single backslash will access a class in global space.

Here's the output from the previous fragment.

```
hello from com\getinstance\util
hello from global
```

It's worth showing, because it demonstrates the operation of the __NAMESPACE__ constant. This will output the current namespace, and is useful in debugging.

You can declare more than one namespace in the same file using the syntax you have already seen. You can also use an alternative syntax that uses braces with the namespace keyword.

```
namespace com\getinstance\util {
    class Debug {
        static function helloWorld() {
            print "hello from Debug\n";
```

```
            }
        }
}

namespace main {
    \com\getinstance\util\Debug::helloWorld();
}
```

If you must combine multiple namespaces in the same file, then this is the recommended practice. Usually, however, it's considered best practice to define namespaces on a per-file basis.

One feature that the braces syntax offers is the ability to switch to global space within a file. Earlier on I used require_once to acquire code from global space. In fact, I could have just used the alternative namespace syntax and kept everything on file.

```
namespace {
    class Lister {
        //...
    }
}

namespace com\getinstance\util {
    class Lister {
        //...
    }

    Lister::helloWorld();  // access local
    \Lister::helloWorld(); // access global
}
```

I step into global space by opening a namespace block without specifying a name.

■**Note** You can't use both the brace and line namespace syntaxes in the same file. You must choose one and stick to it throughout.

Using the File System to Simulate Packages

Whichever version of PHP you use, you should organize classes using the file system, which affords a kind of package structure. For example, you might create util and business directories and include class files with the require_once() statement, like this:

```
require_once('business/Customer.php');
require_once('util/WebTools.php');
```

You could also use include_once() with the same effect. The only difference between the include() and require() statements lies in their handling of errors. A file invoked using require() will bring down your entire process when you meet an error. The same error encountered via a call to include() will merely generate a warning and end execution of the included file, leaving the calling code to continue. This makes require() and require_once() the safe choice for including library files and include() and include_once() useful for operations like templating.

■**Note** require() and require_once() are actually statements, not functions. This means that you can omit the brackets when using them. Personally, I prefer to use brackets anyway, but if you follow suit, be prepared to be bored by pedants eager to explain your mistake.

Figure 5–1 shows the util and business packages from the point of view of the Nautilus file manager.

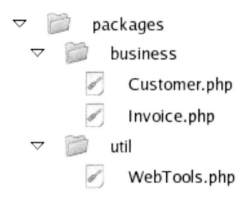

Figure 5–1. *PHP packages organized using the file system*

■**Note** require_once() accepts a path to a file and includes it evaluated in the current script. The function will only incorporate its target if it has not already been incorporated elsewhere. This one-shot approach is particularly useful when accessing library code, because it prevents the accidental redefinition of classes and functions. This can happen when the same file is included by different parts of your script in a single process using a function like require() or include().

It is customary to use require() and require_once() in preference to the similar include() and include_once() functions. This is because a fatal error encountered in a file accessed with the require() functions takes down the entire script. The same error encountered in a file accessed using the include() functions will cause the execution of the included file to cease but will only generate a warning in the calling script. The former, more drastic, behavior is safer.

There is an overhead associated with the use of require_once() when compared with require(). If you need to squeeze every last millisecond out of your system you may like to consider using require() instead. As is so often the case, this is a trade-off between efficiency and convenience.

As far as PHP is concerned, there is nothing special about this structure. You are simply placing library scripts in different directories. It does lend itself to clean organization, and can be used in parallel with either namespaces or a naming convention.

Naming the PEAR Way

Even if you upgraded to PHP 5.3 the moment it became available, you probably won't always get to use namespaces. Often employers, clients, and hosting companies are slow to upgrade, often for good reasons. And even if your project does run on the latest version of PHP, you may find that you're working on legacy code. If you're given time to recode your project for namespaces, that's great. Most of us won't get that luxury.

So, without using the new namespace support, how should you address the danger of name clashes? I have already touched on one answer, which is to use the naming convention common to PEAR packages.

■**Note** PEAR stands for the PHP Extension and Application Repository. It is an officially maintained archive of packages and tools that add to PHP's functionality. Core PEAR packages are included in the PHP distribution, and others can be added using a simple command line tool. You can browse the PEAR packages at `http://pear.php.net`. We will look at some other aspects of PEAR in Chapter 15.

PEAR uses the file system to define its packages as I have described. Every class is then named according to its package path, with each directory name separated by an underscore character.

For example, PEAR includes a package called XML, which has an RPC subpackage. The RPC package contains a file called `Server.php`. The class defined inside `Server.php` is not called `Server` as you might expect. Sooner or later that would clash with another `Server` class elsewhere in the PEAR project or in a user's code. Instead, the class is named `XML_RPC_Server`. This makes for unattractive class names. It does, however, make your code easy to read in that a class name always describes its own context.

Include Paths

When you organize your components, there are two perspectives that you must bear in mind. I have covered the first. That is, where files and directories are placed on the filesystem. But you must also consider the way that components access one another. I have glossed over the issue of include paths so far in this section. When you include a file, you could refer to it using a relative path from the current working directory or an absolute path on the file system.

The examples you have seen so far seem to suggest a relative path:

```
require_once('business/User.php');
```

But this would require that your current working directory contain the `business` directory, which would soon become impractical. Using relative paths for your library inclusions, you would be more likely to see tortuous `require_once()` statements:

```
require_once('../../projectlib/business/User.php');
```

You could use an absolute path, of course:

```
require_once('/home/john/projectlib/business/User.php');
```

Neither solution is ideal. By specifying paths in this much detail, you freeze the library file in place. In using an absolute path, you tie the library to a particular file system. Whenever you install the project on a new server, all require statements will need changing to account for a new file path.

By using a relative path, you fix the relationship between the script's working directory and the library. This can make libraries hard to relocate on the filesystem without editing require() statements and impractical to share among projects without making copies. In either case, you lose the package idea in all the additional directories. Is it the business package, or is it the projectlib/business package?

In order to make included libraries work well in your code, you need to decouple the invoking code from the library so that

business/User.php

can be referenced from anywhere on a system. You can do this by putting the package in one of the directories to which the include_path directive refers. include_path is usually set in PHP's central configuration file, php.ini. It defines a list of directories separated by colons on Unix-like systems and semicolons on Windows systems.

```
include_path = ".:/usr/local/lib/php-libraries"
```

If you're using Apache you can also set include_path in the server application's configuration file (usually called httpd.conf) or a per-directory Apache configuration file (usually called .htaccess) with this syntax:

```
php_value  include_path  value    .:/usr/local/lib/php-libraries
```

▓**Note** .htaccess files are particularly useful in web space provided by some hosting companies, which provide very limited access to the server environment.

When you use a filesystem function such as fopen() or require() with a nonabsolute path that does not exist relative to the current working directory, the directories in the include path are searched automatically, beginning with the first in the list (in the case of fopen() you must include a flag in its argument list to enable this feature). When the target file is encountered, the search ends, and the file function completes its task.

So by placing a package directory in an include directory, you need only refer to packages and files in your require() statements.

You may need to add a directory to the include_path so that you can maintain your own library directory. To do this, you can, of course, edit the php.ini file (remember that, for the PHP server module, you will need to restart your server for the changes to take effect).

If you do not have the privileges necessary to work with the php.ini file, you can set the include path from within your scripts using the set_include_path() function. set_include_path() accepts an include path (as it would appear in php.ini) and changes the include_path setting for the current process only. The php.ini file probably already defines a useful value for include_path, so rather than overwrite it, you can access it using the get_include_path() function and append your own directory. Here's how you can add a directory to the current include path:

```
set_include_path( get_include_path().":/home/john/phplib/");
```

If you are working on a Windows platform, you should use semicolons rather than colons to separate each directory path.

Autoload

In some circumstances, you may wish to organize your classes so that each sits in its own file. There is overhead to this approach (including a file comes with a cost), but this kind of organization can be very useful, especially if your system needs to expand to accommodate new classes at runtime (see the Command pattern in Chapters 11 and 12 for more on this kind of strategy). In such cases, each class file may bear a fixed relationship to the name of the class it contains, so you might define a ShopProduct class in a file named ShopProduct.php. Using the PEAR convention, on the other hand, you would name the file ShopProduct.php, but the class would be named according to its package address: business_ShopProduct, perhaps.

PHP 5 introduced the __autoload() interceptor function to help automate the inclusion of class files. __autoload() should be implemented by the coder as a function requiring a single argument. When the PHP engine encounters an attempt to instantiate an unknown class, it invokes the __autoload() function (if defined), passing it the class name as a string. It is up to the implementer to define a strategy for locating and including the missing class file.

Here's a simple __autoload() function:

```
function __autoload( $classname ) {
    include_once( "$classname.php" );
}

$product = new ShopProduct( 'The Darkening', 'Harry', 'Hunter', 12.99 );
```

Assuming that I have not already included a file that defines a class named ShopProduct, the instantiation of ShopProduct seems bound to fail. The PHP engine sees that I have defined an __autoload() function and passes it the string "ShopProduct". My implementation simply attempts to include the file ShopProduct.php. This will only work, of course, if the file is in the current working directory or in one of my include directories. I have no easy way here of handling packages. This is another circumstance in which the PEAR naming scheme can pay off.

```
function __autoload( $classname ) {
    $path = str_replace('_', DIRECTORY_SEPARATOR, $classname );
    require_once( "$path.php" );
}

$y = new business_ShopProduct();
```

As you can see, the __autoload() function transforms underscores in the supplied $classname to the DIRECTORY_SEPARATOR character (/ on Unix systems). I attempt to include the class file (business/shopProduct.php). If the class file exists, and the class it contains has been named correctly, the object should be instantiated without error. Of course, this does require the programmer to observe a naming convention that forbids the underscore character in a class name except where it divides up packages.

What about namespaces? It's just a matter of testing for the backslash character and adding a conversion if the character is present:

```
function __autoload( $classname ) {
    if ( preg_match( '/\\\\/', $classname ) ) {
        $path = str_replace('\\', DIRECTORY_SEPARATOR, $classname );
    } else {
        $path = str_replace('_', DIRECTORY_SEPARATOR, $classname );
    }
    require_once( "$path.php" );
}
```

Again, I make some assumptions about the location of class files and directories and their relationship to either namespaces or PEAR-style classnames. You might be concerned about the various ways in which we can call a class in a namespace, given the flexibility of importing and aliasing. After all, I could use an alias to call business\ShopProduct anything I want. Percy, for example. The good news is that the value that is passed to __autoload is always normalized to a fully qualified name, without a leading backslash.

Depending on the organization of your classes and files, the __autoload() function can be a useful way of managing your library inclusions.

Note . __autoload is a powerful tool, but it does have some limitations. In particular, you can only define it once in a process. If you need to change your autoload function dynamically you should look at the spl_autoload_register function (http://www.php.net/spl_autoload_register), which supports that functionality.

The Class and Object Functions

PHP provides a powerful set of functions for testing classes and objects. Why is this useful? After all, you probably wrote most of the classes you are using in your script.

In fact, you don't always know at runtime about the classes that you are using. You may have designed a system to work transparently with third-party bolt-on classes, for example. In this case, you will typically instantiate an object given only a class name. PHP allows you to use strings to refer to classes dynamically like this:

```
// Task.php

namespace tasks;

class Task {
    function doSpeak() {
        print "hello\n";
    }
}
```

```
// TaskRunner.php

$classname = "Task";

require_once( "tasks/{$classname}.php" );
$classname = "tasks\\$classname";
$myObj = new $classname();
$myObj->doSpeak();
```

This script might acquire the string I assign to $classname from a configuration file or by comparing a web request with the contents of a directory. You can then use the string to load a class file and instantiate an object. Notice that I've constructed a namespace qualification in this fragment.

Typically, you would do something like this when you want your system to be able to run user-created plug-ins. Before you do anything as risky as that in a real project, you would have to check that the class exists, that it has the methods you are expecting, and so on.

Some class functions have been superseded by the more powerful Reflection API, which I will examine later in the chapter. Their simplicity and ease of use make them a first port of call in some instances, however.

Looking for Classes

The class_exists() function accepts a string representing the class to check for and returns a Boolean true value if the class exists and false otherwise.

Using this function, I can make the previous fragment a little safer.

```
// TaskRunner.php
$classname = "Task";

$path = "tasks/{$classname}.php";
if ( ! file_exists( $path ) ) {
    throw new Exception( "No such file as {$path}" );
}

require_once( $path );
$qclassname = "tasks\\$classname";
if ( ! class_exists( $qclassname ) ) {
    throw new Exception( "No such class as $qclassname" );
}

$myObj = new $qclassname();
$myObj->doSpeak();
```

Of course, you can't be sure that the class in question does not require constructor arguments. For that level of safety, you would have to turn to the Reflection API, covered later in the chapter. Nevertheless, class_exists() does allow you to check that the class exists before you work with it.

■**Note** Remember, you should always be wary of any data provided by outside sources. Test it and treat it before using it in any way. In the case of a file path, you should escape or remove dots and directory separators to prevent an unscrupulous user from changing directories and including unexpected files.

You can also get an array of all classes defined in your script process using the get_declared_classes() function.

```
print_r( get_declared_classes() );
```

This will list user-defined and built-in classes. Remember that it only returns the classes declared at the time of the function call. You may run require() or require_once() later on and thereby add to the number of classes in your script.

Learning About an Object or Class

As you know, you can constrain the object types of method arguments using class type hinting. Even with this tool, we can't always be certain of an object's type. At the time of this writing, PHP does not allow you to constrain class type returned from a method or function, though this is apparently due for inclusion at a later date.

There are a number of basic tools available to check the type of an object. First of all, you can check the class of an object with the get_class() function. This accepts any object as an argument and returns its class name as a string.

```
$product = getProduct();
if ( get_class( $product ) == 'CdProduct' ) {
    print "\$product is a CdProduct object\n";
}
```

In the fragment I acquire *something* from the getProduct() function. To be absolutely certain that it is a CdProduct object, I use the get_class() method.

▨**Note** I covered the CdProduct and BookProduct classes in Chapter 3: Object Basics

---

Here's the getProduct() function:

```
function getProduct() {
    return new CdProduct(    "Exile on Coldharbour Lane",
                         "The", "Alabama 3", 10.99, 60.33 );
}
```

getProduct() simply instantiates and returns a CdProduct object. I will make good use of this function in this section.

The get_class() function is a very specific tool. You often want a more general confirmation of a class's type. You may want to know that an object belongs to the ShopProduct family, but you don't care whether its actual class is BookProduct or CdProduct. To this end, PHP provides the instanceof operator.

▨**Note** PHP 4 did not support instanceof. Instead, it provided the is_a() function which was deprecated in PHP 5.0 deprecated. As of PHP 5.3 it is_a() no longer deprecated.

The instanceof operator works with two operands, the object to test on the left of the keyword and the class or interface name on the right. It resolves to true if the object is an instance of the given type.

```
$product = getProduct();
if ( $product instanceof ShopProduct  ) {
    print "\$product is a ShopProduct object\n";
}
```

Learning About Methods

You can acquire a list of all the methods in a class using the get_class_methods() function. This requires a class name and returns an array containing the names of all the methods in the class.

```
print_r( get_class_methods( 'CdProduct' ) );
```

Assuming the CdProduct class exists, you might see something like this:

```
Array
(
    [0] => __construct
    [1] => getPlayLength
    [2] => getSummaryLine
    [3] => getProducerFirstName
    [4] => getProducerMainName
    [5] => setDiscount
    [6] => getDiscount
    [7] => getTitle
    [8] => getPrice
    [9] => getProducer
)
```

In the example, I pass a class name to get_class_methods() and dump the returned array with the print_r() function. I could alternatively have passed an *object* to get_class_methods() with the same result.

Unless you're running a very early version of PHP 5, only the names of public methods will be included in the returned list.

As you have seen, you can store a method name in a string variable and invoke it dynamically together with an object, like this:

```
$product = getProduct(); // acquire an object
$method = "getTitle";    // define a method name
print $product->$method();  // invoke the method
```

Of course, this can be dangerous. What happens if the method does not exist? As you might expect, your script will fail with an error. You have already encountered one way of testing that a method exists:

```
if ( in_array( $method, get_class_methods( $product ) ) ) {
    print $product->$method();  // invoke the method
}
```

I check that the method name exists in the array returned by get_class_methods() before invoking it. PHP provides more specialized tools for this purpose. You can check method names to some extent with the two functions is_callable() and method_exists(). is_callable() is the more sophisticated of the two functions. It accepts a string variable representing a function name as its first argument and returns true if the function exists and can be called. To apply the same test to a method, you should pass it an array in place of the function name. The array must contain an object or class name as its first element and the method name to check as its second element. The function will return true if the method exists in the class.

```
if ( is_callable( array( $product, $method) ) ) {
    print $product->$method(); // invoke the method
}
```

is_callable() optionally accepts a second argument, a Boolean. If you set this to true, the function will only check the syntax of the given method or function name and not its actual existence.

The method_exists() function requires an object (or a class name) and a method name, and returns true if the given method exists in the object's class.

```
if ( method_exists( $product, $method ) ) {
    print $product->$method();  // invoke the method
}
```

■Caution Remember that the fact that a method exists does not mean that it will be callable. method_exists() returns true for private and protected methods as well as for public ones.

Learning About Properties

Just as you can query the methods of a class, so can you query its fields. The get_class_vars() function requires a class name and returns an associative array. The returned array contains field names as its keys and field values as its values. Let's apply this test to the CdProduct object. For the purposes of illustration, we add a public property to the class: CdProduct::$coverUrl.

```
print_r( get_class_vars( 'CdProduct' ) );
```

Only the public property is shown:

```
Array
(
    [coverUrl] =>
)
```

Learning About Inheritance

The class functions also allow us to chart inheritance relationships. We can find the parent of a class, for example, with get_parent_class(). This function requires either an object or a class name, and it returns the name of the superclass, if any. If no such class exists, that is, if the class we are testing does not have a parent, then the function returns false.

```
print get_parent_class( 'CdProduct' );
```

As you might expect, this yields the parent class: ShopProduct.

We can also test whether a class is a descendent of another using the is_subclass_of() function. This requires a child object and the name of the parent class. The function returns true if the second argument is a superclass of the first argument.

```
$product = getProduct(); // acquire an object
if ( is_subclass_of( $product, 'ShopProduct' ) ) {
    print "CdProduct is a subclass of ShopProduct\n";
}
```

is_subclass_of() will tell you only about class inheritance relationships. It will not tell you that a class implements an interface. For that, you should use the instanceof operator. Or, you can use a function which is part of the SPL (Standard PHP Library).; class_implements() accepts a class name or an object reference, and returns an array of interface names.

```
if ( in_array( 'someInterface', class_implements( $product )) ) {
    print "CdProduct is an interface of someInterface\n";
}
```

Method Invocation

You have already encountered an example in which I used a string to invoke a method dynamically:

```
$product = getProduct(); // acquire an object
$method = "getTitle";    // define a method name
print $product->$method(); // invoke the method
```

PHP also provides the call_user_func() method to achieve the same end. call_user_func() can invoke either methods or functions. To invoke a function, it requires a single string as its first argument:

```
$returnVal = call_user_func("myFunction");
```

To invoke a method, it requires an array. The first element of this should be an object, and the second should be the name of the method to invoke:

```
$returnVal = call_user_func( array( $myObj, "methodName") );
```

You can pass any arguments that the target method or function requires in additional arguments to call_user_func(), like this:

```
$product = getProduct(); // acquire an object
call_user_func( array( $product, 'setDiscount' ), 20 );
```

This dynamic call is, of course, equivalent to

```
$product->setDiscount( 20 );
```

Because you can equally use a string directly in place of the method name, like this:

```
$method = "setDiscount";
$product->$method(20);
```

the call_user_func() method won't change your life greatly. Much more impressive, though, is the related call_user_func_array() function. This operates in the same way as call_user_func() as far as selecting the target method or function is concerned. Crucially, though, it accepts any arguments required by the target method as an array.

So why is this useful? Occasionally you are given arguments in array form. Unless you know in advance the number of arguments you are dealing with, it can be difficult to pass them on. In Chapter 4, I looked at the interceptor methods that can be used to create delegator classes. Here's a simple example of a __call() method:

```
function __call( $method, $args ) {
    if ( method_exists( $this->thirdpartyShop, $method ) ) {
        return $this->thirdpartyShop->$method( );
    }
}
```

As you have seen, the __call() method is invoked when an undefined method is called by client code. In this example, I maintain an object in a property called $thirdpartyShop. If I find a method in the stored object that matches the $method argument, I invoke it. I blithely assume that the target method does not require any arguments, which is where my problems begin. When I write the __call() method, I have no way of telling how large the $args array may be from invocation to invocation. If I pass $args directly to the delegate method, I will pass a single array argument, and not the separate arguments it may be expecting. call_user_func_array() solves the problem perfectly:

```
function __call( $method, $args ) {
    if ( method_exists( $this->thirdpartyShop, $method ) ) {
        return call_user_func_array(
                    array( $this->thirdpartyShop,
                    $method ), $args );
    }
}
```

The Reflection API

PHP's Reflection API is to PHP what the java.lang.reflect package is to Java. It consists of built-in classes for analyzing properties, methods, and classes. It's similar in some respects to existing object functions, such as get_class_vars(), but is more flexible and provides much greater detail. It's also designed to work with PHP's object-oriented features, such as access control, interfaces, and abstract classes, in a way that the older, more limited class functions are not.

Getting Started

The Reflection API can be used to examine more than just classes. For example, the ReflectionFunction class provides information about a given function, and ReflectionExtension yields insight about an extension compiled into the language. Table 5–1 lists some of the classes in the API.

Between them, the classes in the Reflection API provide unprecedented runtime access to information about the objects, functions, and extensions in your scripts.

Because of its power and reach, you should usually use the Reflection API in preference to the class and object functions. You will soon find it indispensable as a tool for testing classes. You might want to generate class diagrams or documentation, for example, or you might want to save object information to a database, examining an object's accessor (getter and setter) methods to extract field names. Building a framework that invokes methods in module classes according to a naming scheme is another use of Reflection.

Table 5–1. Some of the Classes in the Reflection API

Class	Description
Reflection	Provides a static export() method for summarizing class information
ReflectionClass	Class information and tools
ReflectionMethod	Class method information and tools

Class	Description
ReflectionParameter	Method argument information
ReflectionProperty	Class property information
ReflectionFunction	Function information and tools
ReflectionExtension	PHP extension information
ReflectionException	An error class

Time to Roll Up Your Sleeves

You have already encountered some functions for examining the attributes of classes. These are useful but often limited. Here's a tool that *is* up to the job. ReflectionClass provides methods that reveal information about every aspect of a given class, whether it's a user-defined or internal class. The constructor of ReflectionClass accepts a class name as its sole argument:

```
$prod_class = new ReflectionClass( 'CdProduct' );
Reflection::export( $prod_class );
```

Once you've created a ReflectionClass object, you can use the Reflection utility class to dump information about CdProduct. Reflection has a static export() method that formats and dumps the data managed by a Reflection object (that is, any instance of a class that implements the Reflector interface, to be pedantic). Here's an slightly amended extract from the output generated by a call to Reflection::export():

```
Class [ <user> class CdProduct extends ShopProduct ] {
  @@ fullshop.php 53-73
  - Constants [0] {
  }
  - Static properties [0] {
  }
  - Static methods [0] {
  }
  - Properties [2] {
    Property [ <default> private $playLength ]
    Property [ <default> protected $price ]
  }

  - Methods [10] {
    Method [ <user, overwrites ShopProduct, ctor> public method __construct ] {
      @@ fullshop.php 56 - 61

      - Parameters [5] {
        Parameter #0 [ <required> $title ]
```

```
        Parameter #1 [ <required> $firstName ]

        Parameter #2 [ <required> $mainName ]

        Parameter #3 [ <required> $price ]
        Parameter #4 [ <required> $playLength ]
      }
    }
    Method [ public method getPlayLength ] {
      @@ fullshop.php 63 - 65
    }

    Method [ <user, overwrites ShopProduct, prototype ShopProduct> public method
getSummaryLine ] {
      @@ fullshop.php 67 - 71
    }
  }
}
```

As you can see, Reflection::export() provides remarkable access to information about a class. Reflection::export() provides summary information about almost every aspect of CdProduct, including the access control status of properties and methods, the arguments required by every method, and the location of every method within the script document. Compare that with a more established debugging function. The var_dump() function is a general-purpose tool for summarizing data. You must instantiate an object before you can extract a summary, and even then, it provides nothing like the detail made available by Reflection::export().

```
$cd = new CdProduct("cd1", "bob", "bobbleson", 4, 50 );
var_dump( $cd );
```

Here's the output:

```
object(CdProduct)#1 (6) {
  ["playLength:private"]=>
  int(50)
  ["title:private"]=>
  string(3) "cd1"
  ["producerMainName:private"]=>
  string(9) "bobbleson"
  ["producerFirstName:private"]=>
  string(3) "bob"
  ["price:protected"]=>
  int(4)
  ["discount:private"]=>
  int(0)
}
```

var_dump() and its cousin print_r() are fantastically convenient tools for exposing the data in your scripts. For classes and functions, the Reflection API takes things to a whole new level, though.

Examining a Class

The Reflection ::export() method can provide a great deal of useful information for debugging, but we can use the API in more specialized ways. Let's work directly with the Reflection classes.

You've already seen how to instantiate a ReflectionClass object:

```
$prod_class = new ReflectionClass( 'CdProduct' );
```

Next, I will use the ReflectionClass object to investigate CdProduct within a script. What kind of class is it? Can an instance be created? Here's a function to answer these questions:

```
function classData( ReflectionClass $class ) {
  $details = "";
  $name = $class->getName();
  if ( $class->isUserDefined() ) {
    $details .= "$name is user defined\n";
  }
  if ( $class->isInternal() ) {
    $details .= "$name is built-in\n";
  }
  if ( $class->isInterface() ) {
    $details .= "$name is interface\n";
  }
  if ( $class->isAbstract() ) {
    $details .= "$name is an abstract class\n";
  }
  if ( $class->isFinal() ) {
    $details .= "$name is a final class\n";
  }
  if ( $class->isInstantiable() ) {
    $details .= "$name can be instantiated\n";
  } else {
    $details .= "$name can not be instantiated\n";
  }
  return $details;
}

$prod_class = new ReflectionClass( 'CdProduct' );
print classData( $prod_class );
```

I create a ReflectionClass object, assigning it to a variable called $prod_class by passing the CdProduct class name to ReflectionClass's constructor. $prod_class is then passed to a function called classData() that demonstrates some of the methods that can be used to query a class.

- The methods should be self-explanatory, but here's a brief description of each one: ReflectionClass::getName() returns the name of the class being examined.

- The ReflectionClass::isUserDefined() method returns true if the class has been declared in PHP code, and ReflectionClass::isInternal() yields true if the class is built-in.

- You can test whether a class is abstract with ReflectionClass::isAbstract() and whether it's an interface with ReflectionClass::isInterface().

- If you want to get an instance of the class, you can test the feasibility of that with ReflectionClass::isInstantiable().

You can even examine a user-defined class's source code. The ReflectionClass object provides access to its class's file name and to the start and finish lines of the class in the file.

Here's a quick-and-dirty method that uses ReflectionClass to access the source of a class:

```
class ReflectionUtil {
  static function getClassSource( ReflectionClass $class ) {
    $path = $class->getFileName();
    $lines = @file( $path );
    $from = $class->getStartLine();
    $to   = $class->getEndLine();
    $len  = $to-$from+1;
    return implode( array_slice( $lines, $from-1, $len ));
  }
}

print ReflectionUtil::getClassSource(
  new ReflectionClass( 'CdProduct' ) );
```

ReflectionUtil is a simple class with a single static method, ReflectionUtil::getClassSource(). That method takes a ReflectionClass object as its only argument and returns the referenced class's source code. ReflectionClass::getFileName() provides the path to the class's file as an absolute path, so the code should be able to go right ahead and open it. file() obtains an array of all the lines in the file. ReflectionClass::getStartLine() provides the class's start line; ReflectionClass::getEndLine() finds the final line. From there, it's simply a matter of using array_slice() to extract the lines of interest.

To keep things brief, this code omits error handling. In a real-world application, you'd want to check arguments and result codes.

Examining Methods

Just as ReflectionClass is used to examine a class, a ReflectionMethod object examines a method.

You can acquire a ReflectionMethod in two ways: you can get an array of ReflectionMethod objects from ReflectionClass::getMethods(), or if you need to work with a specific method, ReflectionClass::getMethod() accepts a method name and returns the relevant ReflectionMethod object.

Here, we use ReflectionClass::getMethods() to put the ReflectionMethod class through its paces:

```
$prod_class = new ReflectionClass( 'CdProduct' );
$methods = $prod_class->getMethods();

foreach ( $methods as $method ) {
  print methodData( $method );
  print "\n----\n";
}

function methodData( ReflectionMethod $method ) {
  $details = "";
  $name = $method->getName();
  if ( $method->isUserDefined() ) {
    $details .= "$name is user defined\n";
  }
  if ( $method->isInternal() ) {
    $details .= "$name is built-in\n";
```

```
   }
   if ( $method->isAbstract() ) {
     $details .= "$name is abstract\n";
   }
   if ( $method->isPublic() ) {
     $details .= "$name is public\n";
   }
   if ( $method->isProtected() ) {
     $details .= "$name is protected\n";
   }
   if ( $method->isPrivate() ) {
     $details .= "$name is private\n";
   }
   if ( $method->isStatic() ) {
     $details .= "$name is static\n";
   }
   if ( $method->isFinal() ) {
     $details .= "$name is final\n";
   }
   if ( $method->isConstructor() ) {
     $details .= "$name is the constructor\n";
   }
   if ( $method->returnsReference() ) {
     $details .= "$name returns a reference (as opposed to a value)\n";
   }
   return $details;
}
```

The code uses ReflectionClass::getMethods() to get an array of ReflectionMethod objects and then loops through the array, passing each object to methodData().

The names of the methods used in methodData() reflect their intent: the code checks whether the method is user-defined, built-in, abstract, public, protected, static, or final. You can also check whether the method is the constructor for its class and whether or not it returns a reference.

There's one caveat: ReflectionMethod::returnsReference() doesn't return true if the tested method simply returns an object, even though objects are passed and assigned by reference in PHP 5. Instead, ReflectionMethod::returnsReference() returns true only if the method in question has been explicitly declared to return a reference (by placing an ampersand character in front of the method name).

As you might expect, you can access a method's source code using a technique similar to the one used previously with ReflectionClass:

```
class ReflectionUtil {
  static function getMethodSource( ReflectionMethod $method ) {
    $path  = $method->getFileName();
    $lines = @file( $path );
    $from  = $method->getStartLine();
    $to    = $method->getEndLine();
    $len   = $to-$from+1;
    return implode( array_slice( $lines, $from-1, $len ));
  }
}

$class  = new ReflectionClass( 'CdProduct' );
$method = $class->getMethod( 'getSummaryLine' );
print ReflectionUtil::getMethodSource( $method );
```

Because ReflectionMethod provides us with getFileName(), getStartLine(), and getEndLine() methods, it's a simple matter to extract the method's source code.

Examining Method Arguments

Now that method signatures can constrain the types of object arguments, the ability to examine the arguments declared in a method signature becomes immensely useful. The Reflection API provides the ReflectionParameter class just for this purpose. To get a ReflectionParameter object, you need the help of a ReflectionMethod object. The ReflectionMethod::getParameters() method returns an array of ReflectionParameter objects.

ReflectionParameter can tell you the name of an argument, whether the variable is passed by reference (that is, with a preceding ampersand in the method declaration), and it can also tell you the class required by argument hinting and whether the method will accept a null value for the argument.

Here are some of ReflectionParameter's methods in action:

```
$prod_class = new ReflectionClass( 'CdProduct' );
$method = $prod_class->getMethod( "__construct" );
$params = $method->getParameters();

foreach ( $params as $param ) {
    print argData( $param )."\n";
}

function argData( ReflectionParameter $arg ) {
    $details = "";
    $declaringclass = $arg->getDeclaringClass();
    $name  = $arg->getName();
    $class = $arg->getClass();
    $position = $arg->getPosition();
    $details .= "\$$name has position $position\n";
    if ( ! empty( $class )  ) {
        $classname = $class->getName();
        $details .= "\$$name must be a $classname object\n";
    }

    if ( $arg->isPassedByReference() ) {
        $details .= "\$$name is passed by reference\n";
    }

    if ( $arg->isDefaultValueAvailable()  ) {
        $def = $arg->getDefaultValue();
        $details .= "\$$name has default: $def\n";
    }

    return $details;
}
```

Using the ReflectionClass::getMethod() method, the code acquires a ReflectionMethod object. It then uses ReflectionMethod::getParameters() to get an array of ReflectionParameter objects. The argData() function uses the ReflectionParameter object it was passed to acquire information about the argument.

First, it gets the argument's variable name with ReflectionParameter::getName(). The ReflectionParameter::getClass() method returns a ReflectionClass object if a hint's been provided.

The code checks whether the argument is a reference with isPassedByReference(), and finally looks for the availability of a default value, which it then adds to the return string.

Using the Reflection API

With the basics of the Reflection API under your belt, you can now put the API to work.

Imagine that you're creating a class that calls Module objects dynamically. That is, it can accept plug-ins written by third parties that can be slotted into the application without the need for any hard coding. To achieve this, you might define an execute() method in the Module interface or abstract base class, forcing all child classes to define an implementation. You could allow the users of your system to list Module classes in an external XML configuration file. Your system can use this information to aggregate a number of Module objects before calling execute() on each one.

What happens, however, if each Module requires *different* information to do its job? In that case, the XML file can provide property keys and values for each Module, and the creator of each Module can provide setter methods for each property name. Given that foundation, it's up to your code to ensure that the correct setter method is called for the correct property name.

Here's some groundwork for the Module interface and a couple of implementing classes:

```php
class Person {
    public $name;
    function __construct( $name ) {
        $this->name = $name;
    }
}

interface Module {
    function execute();
}

class FtpModule implements Module {
    function setHost( $host ) {
        print "FtpModule::setHost(): $host\n";
    }

    function setUser( $user ) {
        print "FtpModule::setUser(): $user\n";
    }

    function execute() {
        // do things
    }
}

class PersonModule implements Module {
    function setPerson( Person $person ) {
        print "PersonModule::setPerson(): {$person->name}\n";
    }

    function execute() {
        // do things
    }
}
```

Here, PersonModule and FtpModule both provide empty implementations of the execute() method. Each class also implements setter methods that do nothing but report that they were invoked. The system lays down the convention that all setter methods must expect a single argument: either a string or an object that can be instantiated with a single string argument. The PersonModule::setPerson() method expects a Person object, so I include a Person class in my example.

To work with PersonModule and FtpModule, the next step is to create a ModuleRunner class. It will use a multidimensional array indexed by module name to represent configuration information provided in the XML file. Here's that code:

```
class ModuleRunner {
    private $configData
            = array(
                    "PersonModule" => array( 'person'=>'bob' ),
                    "FtpModule"    => array( 'host'
                                            =>'example.com',
                                            'user'  =>'anon' )
            );
    private $modules = array();
// ...
}
```

The ModuleRunner::$configData property contains references to the two Module classes. For each module element, the code maintains a subarray containing a set of properties. ModuleRunner's init() method is responsible for creating the correct Module objects, as shown here:

```
class ModuleRunner {
  // ...

    function init() {
        $interface = new ReflectionClass('Module');
        foreach ( $this->configData as $modulename => $params ) {
            $module_class = new ReflectionClass( $modulename );
            if ( ! $module_class->isSubclassOf( $interface ) ) {
                throw new Exception( "unknown module type: $modulename" );
            }
            $module = $module_class->newInstance();
            foreach ( $module_class->getMethods() as $method ) {
                $this->handleMethod( $module, $method, $params );
                // we cover handleMethod() in a future listing!
            }
            array_push( $this->modules, $module );
        }
    }

  //...
}

$test = new ModuleRunner();
$test->init();
```

The init() method loops through the ModuleRunner::$configData array, and for each module element, it attempts to create a ReflectionClass object. An exception is generated when ReflectionClass's constructor is invoked with the name of a nonexistent class, so in a real-world context, I would include more error handling here. I use the ReflectionClass::isSubclassOf() method to ensure that the module class belongs to the Module type.

Before you can invoke the execute() method of each Module, an instance has to be created. That's the purpose of method::ReflectionClass::newInstance(). That method accepts any number of arguments, which it passes on to the relevant class's constructor method. If all's well, it returns an instance of the class (for production code, be sure to code defensively: check that the constructor method for each Module object doesn't require arguments before creating an instance).

ReflectionClass::getMethods() returns an array of all ReflectionMethod objects available for the class. For each element in the array, the code invokes the ModuleRunner::handleMethod() method; passes it a Module instance, the ReflectionMethod object, and an array of properties to associate with the Module. handleMethod() verifies; and invokes the Module object's setter methods.

```
class ModuleRunner {
  // ...
  function handleMethod( Module $module, ReflectionMethod $method, $params ) {
    $name = $method->getName();
    $args = $method->getParameters();

    if ( count( $args ) != 1 ||
        substr( $name, 0, 3 ) != "set" ) {
      return false;
    }

    $property = strtolower( substr( $name, 3 ));
    if ( ! isset( $params[$property] ) ) {
      return false;
    }

    $arg_class = $args[0]->getClass();
    if ( empty( $arg_class ) ) {
      $method->invoke( $module, $params[$property] );
    } else {
      $method->invoke( $module,
          $arg_class->newInstance( $params[$property] ) );
    }
  }
}
```

handleMethod() first checks that the method is a valid setter. In the code, a valid setter method must be named setXXXX() and must declare one and only one argument.

Assuming that the argument checks out, the code then extracts a property name from the method name by removing set from the beginning of the method name and converting the resulting substring to lowercase characters. That string is used to test the $params array argument. This array contains the user-supplied properties that are to be associated with the Module object. If the $params array doesn't contain the property, the code gives up and returns false.

If the property name extracted from the module method matches an element in the $params array, I can go ahead and invoke the correct setter method. To do that, the code must check the type of the first (and only) required argument of the setter method. The ReflectionParameter::getClass() method provides this information. If the method returns an empty value, the setter expects a primitive of some kind; otherwise, it expects an object.

To call the setter method, I need a new Reflection API method. ReflectionMethod::invoke() requires an object and any number of method arguments to pass on to the method it represents. ReflectionMethod::invoke() throws an exception if the provided object does not match its method. I call this method in one of two ways. If the setter method doesn't require an object argument, I call ReflectionMethod::invoke() with the user-supplied property string. If the method requires an object, I use the property string to instantiate an object of the correct type, which is then passed to the setter.

The example assumes that the required object can be instantiated with a single string argument to its constructor. It's best, of course, to check this before calling `ReflectionClass::newInstance()`.

By the time the `ModuleRunner::init()` method has run its course, the object has a store of `Module` objects, all primed with data. The class can now be given a method to loop through the `Module` objects, calling `execute()` on each one.

Summary

In this chapter, I covered some of the techniques and tools that you can use to manage your libraries and classes. I explored PHP's new namespace feature. You saw that we can combine include paths, namespaces, the PEAR class naming convention, and the file system to provide flexible organization for classes. We examined PHP's object and class functions, before taking things to the next level with the powerful Reflection API. Finally, we used the `Reflection` classes to build a simple example that illustrates one of the potential uses that Reflection has to offer.

■ ■ ■

CHAPTER 6

Objects and Design

Now that we have seen the mechanics of PHP's object support in some detail, in this chapter, we step back from the details and consider how best to use the tools that we have encountered. In this chapter, I introduce you to some of the issues surrounding objects and design. I will also look at the UML, a powerful graphical language for describing object-oriented systems.

This chapter will cover

- *Design basics*: What I mean by design, and how object-oriented design differs from procedural code

- *Class scope*: How to decide what to include in a class

- *Encapsulation*: Hiding implementation and data behind a class's interface

- *Polymorphism*: Using a common supertype to allow the transparent substitution of specialized subtypes at runtime

- *The UML*: Using diagrams to describe object-oriented architectures

Defining Code Design

One sense of code design concerns the definition of a system: the determination of a system's requirements, scope, and objectives. What does the system need to do? For whom does it need to do it? What are the outputs of the system? Do they meet the stated need? On a lower level, design can be taken to mean the process by which you define the participants of a system and organize their relationships. This chapter is concerned with the second sense: the definition and disposition of classes and objects.

So what is a participant? An object-oriented system is made up of classes. It is important to decide the nature of these players in your system. Classes are made up, in part, of methods, so in defining your classes, you must decide which methods belong together. As you will see, though, classes are often combined in inheritance relationships to conform to common interfaces. It is these interfaces, or types, that should be your first port of call in designing your system.

There are other relationships that you can define for your classes. You can create classes that are composed of other types or that manage lists of other type instances. You can design classes that simply use other objects. The potential for such relationships of composition or use is built into your classes (through the use of class type hints in method signatures, for example), but the actual object relationships take place at runtime, which can add flexibility to your design. You will see how to model these relationships in this chapter, and we'll explore them further throughout the book.

As part of the design process, you must decide when an operation should belong to a type and when it should belong to another class used by the type. Everywhere you turn, you are presented with choices, decisions that might lead to clarity and elegance or might mire you in compromise.

In this chapter, I will examine some issues that might influence a few of these choices.

Object-Oriented and Procedural Programming

How does object-oriented design differ from the more traditional procedural code? It is tempting to say that the primary distinction is that object-oriented code has objects in it. This is neither true nor useful. In PHP, you will often find procedural code using objects. You may also come across classes that contain tracts of procedural code. The presence of classes does not guarantee object-oriented design, even in a language like Java, which forces you to do most things inside a class.

One core difference between object-oriented and procedural code can be found in the way that responsibility is distributed. Procedural code takes the form of a sequential series of commands and method calls. The controlling code tends to take responsibility for handling differing conditions. This top-down control can result in the development of duplications and dependencies across a project. Object-oriented code tries to minimize these dependencies by moving responsibility for handling tasks away from client code and toward the objects in the system.

In this section I'll set up a simple problem and then analyze it in terms of both object-oriented and procedural code to illustrate these points. My project is to build a quick tool for reading from and writing to configuration files. In order to maintain focus on the structures of the code, I will omit implementation details in these examples.

I'll begin with a procedural approach to this problem. To start with, I will read and write text in the format

```
key:value
```

I need only two functions for this purpose:

```php
function readParams( $sourceFile ) {
    $prams = array();
    // read text parameters from $sourceFile
    return $prams;
}

function writeParams( $params, $sourceFile ) {
    // write text parameters to $sourceFile
}
```

The readParams() function requires the name of a source file. It attempts to open it, and reads each line, looking for key/value pairs. It builds up an associative array as it goes. Finally, it returns the array to the controlling code. writeParams() accepts an associative array and the path to a source file. It loops through the associative array, writing each key/value pair to the file. Here's some client code that works with the functions:

```php
$file = "./param.txt";
$array['key1'] = "val1";
$array['key2'] = "val2";
$array['key3'] = "val3";
writeParams( $array, $file );  // array written to file
$output = readParams( $file ); // array read from file
print_r( $output );
```

This code is relatively compact and should be easy to maintain. The writeParams() is called to create param.txt and to write to it with something like:

```
key1:val1
key2:val2

key3:val3
```

Then I'm told that the tool should support a simple XML format that looks like this:

```
<params>
    <param>
        <key>my key</key>
        <val>my val</val>
    </pram>
</params>
```

The parameter file should be read in XML mode if the parameter file ends in .xml. Although this is not difficult to accommodate, it threatens to make my code much harder to maintain. I really have two options at this stage. I can check the file extension in the controlling code, or I can test inside my read and write functions. Here I go for the latter approach:

```
function readParams( $source ) {
    $params = array();
    if ( preg_match( "/\.xml$/i", $source )) {
        // read XML parameters from $source
    } else {
        // read text parameters from $source
    }
    return $params;
}

function writeParams( $params, $source ) {
    if ( preg_match( "/\.xml$/i", $source )) {
        // write XML parameters to $source
    } else {
        // write text parameters to $source
    }
}
```

■**Note** Illustrative code always involves a difficult balancing act. It needs to be clear enough to make its point, which often means sacrificing error checking and fitness for its ostensible purpose. In other words, the example here is really intended to illustrate issues of design and duplication rather than the best way to parse and write file data. For this reason, I omit implementation where it is not relevant to the issue at hand.

As you can see, I have had to use the test for the XML extension in each of the functions. It is this repetition that might cause us problems down the line. If I were to be asked to include yet another parameter format, I would need to remember to keep the readParams() and writeParams() functions in line with one another.

Now I'll address the same problem with some simple classes. First, I create an abstract base class that will define the interface for the type:

```
abstract class ParamHandler {
    protected $source;
    protected $params = array();

    function __construct( $source ) {
        $this->source = $source;
    }

    function addParam( $key, $val ) {
        $this->params[$key] = $val;
    }

    function getAllParams() {
        return $this->params;
    }

    static function getInstance( $filename ) {
    if ( preg_match( "/\.xml$/i", $filename )) {
            return new XmlParamHandler( $filename );
        }
        return new TextParamHandler( $filename );
    }

    abstract function write();
    abstract function read();
}
```

I define the addParam() method to allow the user to add parameters to the protected $params property and getAllParams() to provide access to a copy of the array.

I also create a static getInstance() method that tests the file extension and returns a particular subclass according to the results. Crucially, I define two abstract methods, read() and write(), ensuring that any subclasses will support this interface.

■**Note** Placing a static method for generating child objects in the parent class is convenient. Such a design decision does have its own consequences, however. The ParamHandler type is now essentially limited to working with the concrete classes in this central conditional statement. What happens if you need to handle another format? Of course, if you are the maintainer of ParamHandler, you can always amend the getInstance() method. If you are a client coder, however, changing this library class may not be so easy (in fact, changing it won't be hard, but you face the prospect of having to reapply your patch every time you reinstall the package that provides it). I discuss issues of object creation in Chapter 9.

Now, I'll define the subclasses, once again omitting the details of implementation to keep the example clean:

```
class XmlParamHandler extends ParamHandler {

    function write() {
        // write XML
        // using $this->params
    }

    function read() {
        // read XML
        // and populate $this->prams
    }

}

class TextParamHandler extends ParamHandler {

    function write() {
        // write text
        // using $this->params
    }

    function read() {
        // read text
        // and populate $this->prams
    }

}
```

These classes simply provide implementations of the write() and read() methods. Each class will write and read according to the appropriate format.

Client code will write to both text and XML formats entirely transparently according to the file extension:

```
$test = ParamHandler::getInstance( "./params.xml" );
$test->addParam("key1", "val1" );
$test->addParam("key2", "val2" );
$test->addParam("key3", "val3" );
$test->write(); // writing in XML format
```

We can also read from either file format:

```
$test = ParamHandler::getInstance( "./params.txt" );
$test->read(); // reading in text format
```

So, what can we learn from these two approaches?

Responsibility

The controlling code in the procedural example takes responsibility for deciding about format, not once but twice. The conditional code is tidied away into functions, certainly, but this merely disguises the fact of a single flow making decisions as it goes. The call to readParams() must always take place in a different context from a call to writeParams(), so we are forced to repeat the file extension test in each function (or to perform variations on this test).

In the object-oriented version, this choice about file format is made in the static getInstance() method, which tests the file extension only once, serving up the correct subclass. The client code takes no responsibility for implementation. It uses the provided object with no knowledge of, or interest in, the particular subclass it belongs to. It knows only that it is working with a ParamHandler object, and that it will support write() and read(). While the procedural code busies itself about details, the object-oriented code works only with an interface, unconcerned about the details of implementation. Because responsibility for implementation lies with the objects and not with the client code, it would be easy to switch in support for new formats transparently.

Cohesion

Cohesion is the extent to which proximate procedures are related to one another. Ideally, you should create components that share a clear responsibility. If your code spreads related routines widely, you will find them harder to maintain as you have to hunt around to make changes.

Our ParamHandler classes collect related procedures into a common context. The methods for working with XML share a context in which they can share data and where changes to one method can easily be reflected in another if necessary (if you needed to change an XML element name, for example). The ParamHandler classes can therefore be said to have high cohesion.

The procedural example, on the other hand, separates related procedures. The code for working with XML is spread across functions.

Coupling

Tight coupling occurs when discrete parts of a system's code are tightly bound up with one another so that a change in one part necessitates changes in the others. Tight coupling is by no means unique to procedural code, though the sequential nature of such code makes it prone to the problem.

You can see this kind of coupling in the procedural example. The writeParams() and readParams() functions run the same test on a file extension to determine how they should work with data. Any change in logic you make to one will have to be implemented in the other. If you were to add a new format, for example, we would have to bring the functions into line with one another so that they both implement a new file extension test in the same way. This problem can only get worse as you add new parameter-related functions.

The object-oriented example decouples the individual subclasses from one another and from the client code. If you were required to add a new parameter format, you could simply create a new subclass, amending a single test in the static getInstance() method.

Orthogonality

The killer combination in components of tightly defined responsibilities together with independence from the wider system is sometimes referred to as orthogonality, in particular by Andrew Hunt and David Thomas in *The Pragmatic Programmer* (Addison-Wesley Professional, 1999).

Orthogonality, it is argued, promotes reuse in that components can be plugged into new systems without needing any special configuration. Such components will have clear inputs and outputs independent of any wider context. Orthogonal code makes change easier because the impact of altering an implementation will be localized to the component being altered. Finally, orthogonal code is safer. The effects of bugs should be limited in scope. An error in highly interdependent code can easily cause knock-on effects in the wider system.

There is nothing automatic about loose coupling and high cohesion in a class context. We could, after all, embed our entire procedural example into one misguided class. So how can you achieve this balance in your code? I usually start by considering the classes that should live in my system.

Choosing Your Classes

It can be surprisingly difficult to define the boundaries of your classes, especially as they will evolve with any system that you build.

It can seem straightforward when you are modeling the real world. Object-oriented systems often feature software representations of real things—Person, Invoice, and Shop classes abound. This would seem to suggest that defining a class is a matter of finding the *things* in your system and then giving them agency through methods. This is not a bad starting point, but it does have its dangers. If you see a class as a noun, a subject for any number of verbs, then you may find it bloating as ongoing development and requirement changes call for it to do more and more things.

Let's consider the ShopProduct example that we created in Chapter 3. Our system exists to offer products to a customer, so defining a ShopProduct class is an obvious choice, but is that the only decision we need to make? We provide methods such as getTitle() and getPrice() for accessing product data. When we are asked to provide a mechanism for outputting summary information for invoices and delivery notes, it seems to make sense to define a write() method. When the client asks us to provide the product summaries in different formats, we look again at our class. We duly create writeXML() and writeXHTML() methods in addition to the write() method. Or we add conditional code to write() to output different formats according to an option flag.

Either way, the problem here is that the ShopProduct class is now trying to do too much. It is struggling to manage strategies for display as well as for managing product data.

How *should* you think about defining classes? The best approach is to think of a class as having a primary responsibility and to make that responsibility as singular and focused as possible. Put the responsibility into words. It has been said that you should be able to describe a class's responsibility in 25 words or less, rarely using the words "and" or "or." If your sentence gets too long or mired in clauses, it is probably time to consider defining new classes along the lines of some of the responsibilities you have described.

So ShopProduct classes are responsible for managing product data. If we add methods for writing to different formats, we begin to add a new area of responsibility: product display. As you saw in Chapter 3, we actually defined two types based on these separate responsibilities. The ShopProduct type remained responsible for product data, and the ShopProductWriter type took on responsibility for displaying product information. Individual subclasses refined these responsibilities.

■**Note** Very few design rules are entirely inflexible. You will sometimes see code for saving object data in an otherwise unrelated class, for example. While this would seem to violate the rule that a class should have a singular responsibility, it can be the most convenient place for the functionality to live, because a method has to have full access to an instance's fields. Using local methods for persistence can also save us from creating a parallel hierarchy of persistence classes mirroring our savable classes, and thereby introducing unavoidable coupling. We deal with other strategies for object persistence in Chapter 12. Avoid religious adherence to design rules; they are not a substitute for analyzing the problem before you. Try to remain alive to the reasoning behind the rule, and emphasize that over the rule itself.

Polymorphism

Polymorphism, or class switching, is a common feature of object-oriented systems. You have encountered it several times already in this book.

Polymorphism is the maintenance of multiple implementations behind a common interface. This sounds complicated, but in fact, it should be very familiar to you by now. The need for polymorphism is often signaled by the presence of extensive conditional statements in your code.

When I first created the ShopProduct class in Chapter 3, I experimented with a single class which managed functionality for books and CDs in addition to generic products. In order to provide summary information, I relied on a conditional statement:

```
function getSummaryLine() {
    $base  = "$this->title ( $this->producerMainName, ";
    $base .= "$this->producerFirstName )";
    if ( $this->type == 'book' ) {
        $base .= ": page count - $this->numPages";
    } else if ( $this->type == 'cd' ) {
        $base .= ": playing time - $this->playLength";
    }
    return $base;
}
```

These statements suggested the shape for the two subclasses: CdProduct and BookProduct.

By the same token, the conditional statements in my procedural parameter example contained the seeds of the object-oriented structure I finally arrived at. I repeated the same condition in two parts of the script.

```
function readParams( $source ) {
    $params = array();
    if ( preg_match( "/\.xml$/i", $source )) {
        // read XML parameters from $source
    } else {
        // read text parameters from $source
    }
    return $params;
}

function writeParams( $params, $source ) {
    if ( preg_match( "/\.xml$/i", $source )) {
        // write XML parameters to $source
    } else {
        // write text parameters to $source
    }
}
```

Each clause suggested one of the subclasses I finally produced: XmlParamHandler and TextParamHandler, extending the abstract base class ParamHandler's write() and read() methods.

```
// could return XmlParamHandler or TextParamHandler
$test = ParamHandler::getInstance( $file );


$test->read();  // could be XmlParamHandler::read() or TextParamHandler::read()
$test->addParam("key1", "val1" );
$test->write(); // could be XmlParamHandler::write() or TextParamHandler::write()
```

It is important to note that polymorphism doesn't banish conditionals. Methods like `ParamHandler::getInstance()` will often determine which objects to return based on `switch` or `if` statements. These tend to centralize the conditional code into one place, though.

As you have seen, PHP enforces the interfaces defined by abstract classes. This is useful because we can be sure that a concrete child class will support exactly the same method signatures as those defined by an abstract parent. This includes all class type hints and access controls. Client code can, therefore, treat all children of a common superclass interchangeably (as long it only relies on only functionality defined in the parent). There is an important exception to this rule: there is no way of constraining the return type of a method.

▓**Note** At the time of this writing, there are plans to incorporate return type hinting in a future release of PHP. Whether this will happen, though, is by no means certain.

The fact that you cannot specify return types means that it is possible for methods in different subclasses to return different class types or primitives. This can undermine the interchangeability of types. You should try to be consistent with your return values. Some methods may be defined to take advantage of PHP's loose typing and return different types according to circumstances. Other methods enter into an implicit contract with client code, effectively promising that they will return a particular type. If this contract is laid down in an abstract superclass, it should be honored by its concrete children so that clients can be sure of consistent behavior. If you commit to return an object of a particular type, you can, of course, return an instance of a subtype. Although the interpreter does not enforce return types, you can make it a convention in your projects that certain methods will behave consistently. Use comments in the source code to specify a method's return type.

Encapsulation

Encapsulation simply means the hiding of data and functionality from a client. And once again, it is a key object-oriented concept.

On the simplest level, you encapsulate data by declaring properties `private` or `protected`. By hiding a property from client code, you enforce an interface and prevent the accidental corruption of an object's data.

Polymorphism illustrates another kind of encapsulation. By placing different implementations behind a common interface, you hide these underlying strategies from the client. This means that any changes that are made behind this interface are transparent to the wider system. You can add new classes or change the code in a class without causing errors. The interface is what matters, and not the mechanisms working beneath it. The more independent these mechanisms are kept, the less chance that changes or repairs will have a knock-on effect in your projects.

Encapsulation is, in some ways, the key to object-oriented programming. Your objective should be to make each part as independent as possible from its peers. Classes and methods should receive as much information as is necessary to perform their allotted tasks, which should be limited in scope and clearly identified.

The introduction of the `private`, `protected`, and `public` keywords have made encapsulation easier. Encapsulation is also a state of mind, though. PHP 4 provided no formal support for hiding data. Privacy had to be signaled using documentation and naming conventions. An underscore, for example, is a common way of signaling a private property:

```
var $_touchezpas;
```

Code had to be checked closely, of course, because privacy was not strictly enforced. Interestingly, though, errors were rare, because the structure and style of the code made it pretty clear which properties wanted to be left alone.

By the same token, even in PHP 5, we could break the rules and discover the exact subtype of an object that we are using in a class-switching context simply by using the instanceof operator.

```
function workWithProducts( ShopProduct $prod ) {

    if ( $prod instanceof cdproduct ) {

        // do cd thing

    } else if ( $prod instanceof bookproduct ) {

        // do book thing

    }

}
```

You may have a very good reason to do this, but in general, it carries a slightly uncertain odor. By querying the specific subtype in the example, I am setting up a dependency. While the specifics of the subtype were hidden by polymorphism, it would have been possible to have changed the ShopProduct inheritance hierarchy entirely with no ill effects. This code ends that. Now, if I need to rationalize the CdProduct and BookProduct classes, I may create unexpected side effects in the workWithProducts() method.

There are two lessons to take away from this example. First, encapsulation helps you to create orthogonal code. Second, the extent to which encapsulation is enforceable is beside the point. Encapsulation is a technique that should be observed equally by classes and their clients.

Forget How to Do It

If you are like me, the mention of a problem will set your mind racing, looking for mechanisms that might provide a solution. You might select functions that will address an issue, revisit clever regular expressions, track down PEAR packages. You probably have some pasteable code in an old project that does something somewhat similar. At the design stage, you can profit by setting all that aside for a while. Empty your head of procedures and mechanisms.

Think only about the key participants of your system: the types it will need and their interfaces. Of course, your knowledge of process will inform your thinking. A class that opens a file will need a path; database code will need to manage table names and passwords, and so on. Let the structures and relationships in your code lead you, though. You will find that the implementation falls into place easily behind a well-defined interface. You then have the flexibility to switch out, improve, or extend an implementation should you need to, without affecting the wider system.

In order to emphasize interface, think in terms of abstract base classes rather than concrete children. In my parameter-fetching code, for example, the interface is the most important aspect of the design. I want a type that reads and writes name/value pairs. It is this responsibility that is important about the type, not the actual persistence medium or the means of storing and retrieving data. I design the system around the abstract ParamHandler class, and only add in the concrete strategies for actually reading and writing parameters later on. In this way, I build both polymorphism and encapsulation into my system from the start. The structure lends itself to class switching.

Having said that, of course, I knew from the start that there would be text and XML implementations of `ParamHandler`, and there is no question that this influenced my interface. There is always a certain amount of mental juggling to do when designing interfaces.

The Gang of Four (*Design Patterns*) summed up this principle with the phrase "Program to an interface, not an implementation." It is a good one to add to your coder's handbook.

Four Signposts

Very few people get it absolutely right at the design stage. Most of us amend our code as requirements change or as we gain a deeper understanding of the nature of the problem we are addressing.

As you amend your code, it can easily drift beyond your control. A method is added here, and a new class there, and gradually your system begins to decay. As you have seen already, your code can point the way to its own improvement. These pointers in code are sometimes referred to as code smells—that is, features in code that *may* suggest particular fixes or at least call you to look again at your design. In this section, I distill some of the points already made into four signs that you should watch out for as you code.

Code Duplication

Duplication is one of the great evils in code. If you get a strange sense of déjà vu as you write a routine, chances are you have a problem.

Take a look at the instances of repetition in your system. Perhaps they belong together. Duplication generally means tight coupling. If you change something fundamental about one routine, will the similar routines need amendment? If this is the case, they probably belong in the same class.

The Class Who Knew Too Much

It can be a pain passing parameters around from method to method. Why not simply reduce the pain by using a global variable? With a global, everyone can get at the data.

Global variables have their place, but they do need to be viewed with some level of suspicion. That's quite a high level of suspicion, by the way. By using a global variable, or by giving a class any kind of knowledge about its wider domain, you anchor it into its context, making it less reusable and dependent on code beyond its control. Remember, you want to decouple your classes and routines and not create interdependence. Try to limit a class's knowledge of its context. I will look at some strategies for doing this later in the book.

The Jack of All Trades

Is your class trying to do too many things at once? If so, see if you can list the responsibilities of the class. You may find that one of them will form the basis of a good class itself.

Leaving an overzealous class unchanged can cause particular problems if you create subclasses. Which responsibility are you extending with the subclass? What would you do if you needed a subclass for more than one responsibility? You are likely to end up with too many subclasses or an overreliance on conditional code.

Conditional Statements

You will use if and switch statements with perfectly good reason throughout your projects. Sometimes, though, such structures can be a cry for polymorphism.

If you find that you are testing for certain conditions frequently within a class, especially if you find these tests mirrored across more than one method, this could be a sign that your one class should be two or more. See whether the structure of the conditional code suggests responsibilities that could be expressed in classes. The new classes should implement a shared abstract base class. The chances are that you will then have to work out how to pass the right class to client code. I will cover some patterns for creating objects in Chapter 9.

The UML

So far in this book, I have let the code speak for itself, and I have used short examples to illustrate concepts such as inheritance and polymorphism.

This is useful because PHP is a common currency here: it's a language we have in common, if you have read this far. As our examples grow in size and complexity, though, using code alone to illustrate the broad sweep of design becomes somewhat absurd. It is hard to see an overview in a few lines of code.

UML stands for Unified Modeling Language. The initials are correctly used with the definite article. This isn't just *a* unified modeling language, it is *the* Unified Modeling Language.

Perhaps this magisterial tone derives from the circumstances of the language's forging. According to Martin Fowler (*UML Distilled*, Addison-Wesley Professional, 1999), the UML emerged as a standard only after long years of intellectual and bureaucratic sparring among the great and good of the object-oriented design community.

The result of this struggle is a powerful graphical syntax for describing object-oriented systems. We will only scratch the surface in this section, but you will soon find that a little UML (sorry, a little of *the* UML) goes a long way.

Class diagrams in particular can describe structures and patterns so that their meaning shines through. This luminous clarity is often harder to find in code fragments and bullet points.

Class Diagrams

Although class diagrams are only one aspect of the UML, they are perhaps the most ubiquitous. Because they are particularly useful for describing object-oriented relationships, I will primarily use these in this book.

Representing Classes

As you might expect, classes are the main constituents of class diagrams. A class is represented by a named box, as in Figure 6–1.

Figure 6–1. *A class*

The class is divided into three sections, with the name displayed in the first. These dividing lines are optional when we present no more information than the class name. In designing a class diagram, we may find that the level of detail in Figure 6–1 is enough for some classes. We are not obligated to represent every field and method, or even every class in a class diagram.

Abstract classes are represented either by italicizing the class name, as in Figure 6–2, or by adding {abstract} to the class name, as in Figure 6–3. The first method is the more common of the two, but the second is more useful when you are making notes.

▨**Note** The {abstract} syntax is an example of a constraint. Constraints are used in class diagrams to describe the way in which specific elements should be used. There is no special structure for the text between the braces; it should simply provide a short clarification of any conditions that may apply to the element.

Figure 6–2. An abstract class

Figure 6–3. An abstract class defined using a constraint

Interfaces are defined in the same way as classes, except that they must include a stereotype (that is, an extension to the UML), as in Figure 6–4.

Figure 6–4. An interface

Attributes

Broadly speaking, attributes describe a class's properties. Attributes are listed in the section directly beneath the class name, as in Figure 6–5.

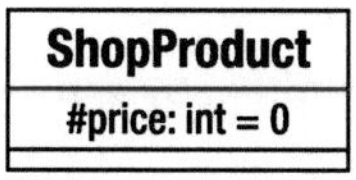

Figure 6–5. An attribute

Let's take a close look at the attribute in the example. The initial symbol represents the level of visibility, or access control, for the attribute. Table 6–1 shows the three symbols available.

Table 6–1. *Visibility Symbols*

Symbol	Visibility	Explanation
+	Public	Available to all code
-	Private	Available to the current class only
#	Protected	Available to the current class and its subclasses only

The visibility symbol is followed by the name of the attribute. In this case, I am describing the ShopProduct::$price property. A colon is used to separate the attribute name from its type (and optionally its default value).

Once again, you need only include as much detail as is necessary for clarity.

Operations

Operations describe methods, or more properly, they describe the calls that can be made on an instance of a class. Figure 6–6 shows two operations in the ShopProduct class.

ShopProduct
#price: int = 0
+setDiscount(amount:int)
+getTitle(): String

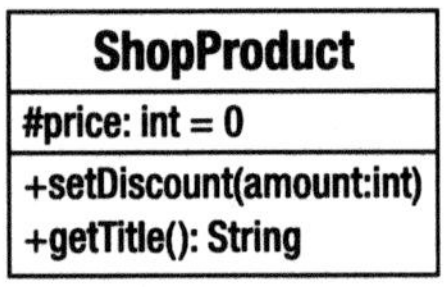

Figure 6–6. *Operations*

As you can see, operations use a similar syntax to that used by attributes. The visibility symbol precedes the method name. A list of parameters is enclosed in parentheses. The method's return type, if any, is delineated by a colon. Parameters are separated by commas, and follow the attribute syntax, with the attribute name separated from its type by a colon.

As you might expect, this syntax is relatively flexible. You can omit the visibility flag and the return type. Parameters are often represented by their type alone, as the argument name is not usually significant.

Describing Inheritance and Implementation

The UML describes the inheritance relationship as generalization. This relationship is signified by a line leading from the subclass to its parent. The line is tipped with an empty closed arrow.

Figure 6–7 shows the relationship between the ShopProduct class and its child classes.

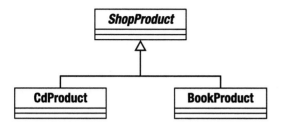

Figure 6–7. Describing inheritance

The UML describes the relationship between an interface and the classes that implement it as realization. So if the ShopProduct class were to implement the Chargeable interface, we could add it to our class diagram as in Figure 6–8.

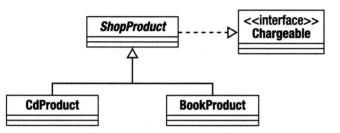

Figure 6–8. Describing interface implementation

Associations

Inheritance is only one of a number of relationships in an object-oriented system. An association occurs when a class property is declared to hold a reference to an instance (or instances) of another class.

In Figure 6–9, we model two classes and create an association between them.

Figure 6–9. A class association

At this stage, we are vague about the nature of this relationship. We have only specified that a Teacher object will have a reference to one or more Pupil objects or vice versa. This relationship may or may not be reciprocal.

You can use arrows to describe the direction of the association. If the Teacher class has an instance of the Pupil class but not the other way round, then you should make your association an arrow leading from the Teacher to the Pupil class. This association, which is called unidirectional, is shown in Figure 6–10.

Figure 6–10. *A unidirectional association*

If each class has a reference to the other, we can use a double-headed arrow to describe a bidirectional relationship, as in Figure 6–11.

Figure 6–11. *A bidirectional association*

You can also specify the number of instances of a class that are referenced by another in an association. You do this by placing a number or range beside each class. You can also use an asterisk (*) to stand for any number. In Figure 6–12, there can be one Teacher object and zero or more Pupil objects.

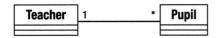

Figure 6–12. *Defining multiplicity for an association*

In Figure 6–13, there can be one Teacher object and between five and ten Pupil objects in the association.

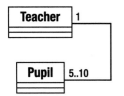

Figure 6–13. *Defining multiplicity for an association*

Aggregation and Composition

Aggregation and composition are similar to association. All describe a situation in which a class holds a permanent reference to one or more instances of another. With aggregation and composition, though, the referenced instances form an intrinsic part of the referring object.

In the case of aggregation, the contained objects are a core part of the container, but they can also be contained by other objects at the same time. The aggregation relationship is illustrated by a line that begins with an unfilled diamond.

In Figure 6–14, I define two classes: SchoolClass and Pupil. The SchoolClass class aggregates Pupil.

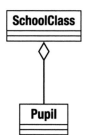

Figure 6–14. *Aggrgation*

Pupils make up a class, but the same `Pupil` object can be referred to by different `SchoolClass` instances at the same time. If I were to dissolve a school class, I would not necessarily delete the pupil, who may attend other classes.

Composition represents an even stronger relationship than this. In composition, the contained object can be referenced by its container only. It should be deleted when the container is deleted. Composition relationships are depicted in the same way as aggregation relationships, except that the diamond should be filled. We illustrate a composition relationship in Figure 6–15.

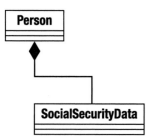

Figure 6–15. *Composition*

A `Person` class maintains a reference to a `SocialSecurityData` object. The contained instance can belong only to the containing `Person` object.

Describing Use

The use relationship is described as a dependency in the UML. It is the most transient of the relationships discussed in this section, because it does not describe a permanent link between classes.

A used class may be passed as an argument or acquired as a result of a method call.

The `Report` class in Figure 6–16 uses a `ShopProductWriter` object. The use relationship is shown by the broken line and open arrow that connects the two. It does not, however, maintain this reference as a property in the same way that a `ShopProductWriter` object maintains an array of `ShopProduct` objects.

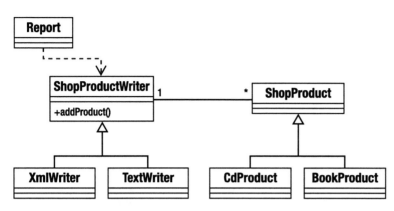

Figure 6–16. *A dependency relationship*

Using Notes

Class diagrams can capture the structure of a system, but they provide no sense of process. Figure 6–16 tells us about the classes in our system. From Figure 6–16 you know that a Report object uses a ShopProductWriter, but you don't know the mechanics of this. In Figure 6–17, I use a note to clarify things somewhat.

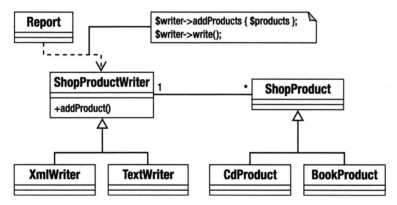

Figure 6–17. *Using a note to clarify a dependency*

As you can see, a note consists of a box with a folded corner. It will often contain scraps of pseudo-code.

This clarifies Figure 6–16; you can now see that the Report object uses a ShopProductWriter to output product data. This is hardly a revelation, but use relationships are not always so obvious. In some cases, even a note might not provide enough information. Luckily, you can model the interactions of objects in your system as well as the structure of your classes.

Sequence Diagrams

A sequence diagram is object based rather than class based. It is used to model a process in a system step by step.

Let's build up a simple diagram, modeling the means by which a Report object writes product data. A sequence diagram presents the participants of a system from left to right, as in Figure 6–18.

Figure 6–18. *Objects in a sequence diagram*

I have labeled my objects with class names alone. If I had more than one instance of the same class working independently in my diagram, I would include an object name using the format label:class (product1:ShopProduct, for example).

You show the lifetime of the process you are modeling from top to bottom, as in Figure 6–19.

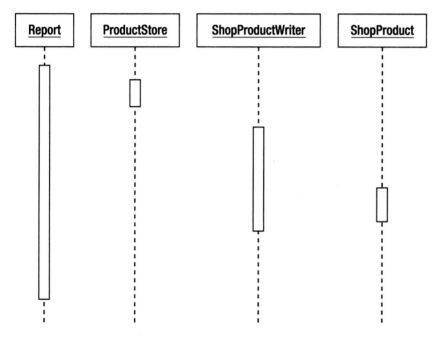

Figure 6–19. *Object lifelines in a sequence diagram*

The vertical broken lines represent the lifetime of the objects in the system. The larger boxes that follow the lifelines represent the focus of a process. If you read Figure 6–19 from top to bottom, you can see how the process moves among objects in the system. This is hard to read without showing the messages that are passed between the objects. I add these in Figure 6–20.

The arrows represent the messages sent from one object to another. Return values are often left implicit (though they can be represented by a broken line, passing from the invoked object to the message originator). Each message is labeled using the relevant method call. You can be quite flexible with your labeling, though there is some syntax. Square brackets represent a condition. So

```
[okToPrint]
write()
```

means that the write() invocation should only be made if the correct condition is met. An asterisk is used to indicate a repetition, optionally with further clarification in square brackets:

```
*[for each ShopProduct]
write()
```

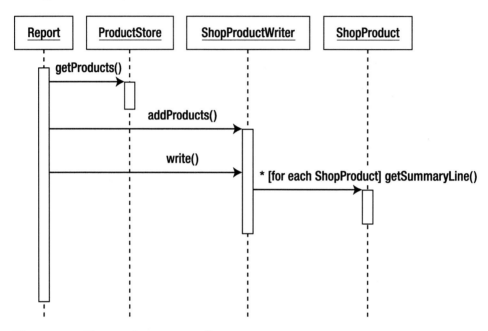

Figure 6–20. *The complete sequence diagram*

You can interpret Figure 6–20 from top to bottom. First, a Report object acquires a list of ShopProduct objects from a ProductStore object. It passes these to a ShopProductWriter object, which stores references to them (though we can only infer this from the diagram). The ShopProductWriter object calls ShopProduct::getSummaryLine() for every ShopProduct object it references, adding the result to its output.

As you can see, sequence diagrams can model processes, freezing slices of dynamic interaction and presenting them with surprising clarity.

▓**Note** Look at Figures 6–16 and 6–20. Notice how the class diagram illustrates polymorphism, showing the classes derived from `ShopProductWriter` and `ShopProduct`. Now notice how this detail becomes transparent when we model the communication among objects. Where possible, we want objects to work with the most general types available so that we can hide the details of implementation.

Summary

In this chapter, I went beyond the nuts and bolts of object-oriented programming to look at some key design issues. I examined features such as encapsulation, loose coupling, and cohesion that are essential aspects of a flexible and reusable object-oriented system. I went on to look at the UML, laying groundwork that will be essential in working with patterns later in the book.

PART 3

Patterns

■ ■ ■

CHAPTER 7

What Are Design Patterns? Why Use Them?

Most problems we encounter as programmers have been handled time and again by others in our community. Design patterns can provide us with the means to mine that wisdom. Once a pattern becomes a common currency, it enriches our language, making it easy to share design ideas and their consequences. Design patterns simply distill common problems, define tested solutions, and describe likely outcomes. Many books and articles focus on the details of computer languages, the available functions, classes and methods. Pattern catalogs concentrate instead on how you can move on from these basics (the "what") to an understanding of the problems and potential solutions in your projects (the "why" and "how").

In this chapter, I introduce you to design patterns and look at some of the reasons for their popularity.

This chapter will cover

- *Pattern basics*: What are design patterns?

- *Pattern structure*: The key elements of a design pattern.

- *Pattern benefits*: Why are patterns worth your time?

What Are Design Patterns?

In the world of software, a pattern is a tangible manifestation of an organization's tribal memory.

—Grady Booch in Core J2EE Patterns

[A pattern is] a solution to a problem in a context.

—The Gang of Four, Design Patterns: Elements of Reusable Object-Oriented Software

As these quotations imply, a design pattern is a problem analyzed with good practice for its solution explained.

Problems tend to recur, and as web programmers, we must solve them time and time again. How are we going to handle an incoming request? How can we translate this data into instructions for our system? How should we acquire data? Present results? Over time, we answer these questions with a greater or lesser degree of elegance and evolve an informal set of techniques that we use and reuse in our projects. These techniques are patterns of design.

Design patterns inscribe and formalize these problems and solutions, making hard-won experience available to the wider programming community. Patterns are (or should be) essentially bottom-up and not top-down. They are rooted in practice and not theory. That is not to say that there isn't a strong theoretical element to design patterns (as we will see in the next chapter), but patterns are based on real-world techniques used by real programmers. Renowned pattern-hatcher Martin Fowler says that he discovers patterns, he does not invent them. For this reason, many patterns will engender a sense of déjà vu as you recognize techniques you have used yourself.

A catalog of patterns is not a cookbook. Recipes can be followed slavishly; code can be copied and slotted into a project with minor changes. You do not always need even to understand all the code used in a recipe. Design patterns inscribe *approaches* to particular problems. The details of implementation may vary enormously according to the wider context. This context might include the programming language you are using, the nature of your application, the size of your project, and the specifics of the problem.

Let's say, for example that your project requires that you create a templating system. Given the name of a template file, you must parse it and build a tree of objects to represent the tags you encounter.

You start off with a default parser that scans the text for trigger tokens. When it finds a match, it hands on responsibility for the hunt to another parser object, which is specialized for reading the internals of tags. This continues examining template data until it either fails, finishes, or finds another trigger. If it finds a trigger, it too must hand on to a specialist— perhaps an argument parser. Collectively, these components form what is known as a recursive descent parser.

So these are your participants: a MainParser, a TagParser, and an ArgumentParser. You create a ParserFactory class to create and return these objects.

Of course, nothing is easy, and you're informed late in the game that you must support more than one syntax in your templates. Now, you need to create a parallel set of parsers according to syntax: an OtherTagParser, OtherArgumentParser, and so on.

This is your problem: you need to generate a different set of objects according to circumstance, and you want this to be more or less transparent to other components in the system. It just so happens that the Gang of Four define the following problem in their book's summary page for the pattern Abstract Factory, "Provide an interface for creating families of related or dependent objects without specifying their concrete classes."

That fits nicely. It is the nature of our problem that determines and shapes our use of this pattern. There is nothing cut and paste about the solution either, as you can see in Chapter 9, in which I cover Abstract Factory.

The very act of naming a pattern is valuable; it provides the kind of common vocabulary that has arisen naturally over the years in the older crafts and professions. Such shorthand greatly aids collaborative design as alternative approaches and their various consequences are weighed and tested. When you discuss your alternative parser families, for example, you can simply tell colleagues that the system creates each set using the Abstract Factory pattern. They will nod sagely, either immediately enlightened or making a mental note to look it up later. The point is that this bundle of concepts and consequences has a handle, which makes for a handy shorthand, as I'll illustrate later in this chapter.

Finally, it is illegal, according to international law, to write about patterns without quoting Christopher Alexander, an architecture academic whose work heavily influenced the original object-oriented pattern advocates. He states in *A Pattern Language* (Oxford University Press, 1977):

Each pattern describes a problem which occurs over and over again in our environment, and then describes the core of the solution to that problem, in such a way that you can use this solution a million times over, without ever doing it the same way twice.

It is significant that this definition (which applies to architectural problems and solutions) begins with the problem and its wider setting and proceeds to a solution. There has been some criticism in recent years that design patterns have been overused, especially by inexperienced programmers. This is often a sign that solutions have been applied where the problem and context are not present. Patterns are more than a particular organization of classes and objects, cooperating in a particular way. Patterns are structured to define the conditions in which solutions should be applied and to discuss the effects of the solution.

In this book, we will focus on a particularly influential strand in the patterns field: the form described in *Design Patterns: Elements of Reusable Object-Oriented Software* by Erich Gamma, Richard Helm, Ralph Johnson, and John Vlissides (Addison-Wesley Professional, 1995). It concentrates on patterns in object-oriented software development and inscribes some of the classic patterns that are present in most modern object-oriented projects.

The Gang of Four book is important, because it inscribes key patterns, but also because it describes the design principles that inform and motivate these patterns. We will look at some of these principles in the next chapter.

■**Note** The patterns described by the Gang of Four and in this book are really instances of a pattern language, that is, a catalog of problems and solutions organized together so that they complement one another, forming an interrelated whole. There are pattern languages for other problem spaces such as visual design and project management (and architecture, of course). When I discuss design patterns here, I refer to problems and solutions in object-oriented software development.

A Design Pattern Overview

At heart, a design pattern consists of four parts: the name, problem, solution, and consequences.

Name

Names matter. They enrich the language of programmers; a few short words can stand in for quite complex problems and solutions. They must balance brevity and description. The Gang of Four claims, "Finding good names has been one of the hardest parts of developing our catalog."

Martin Fowler agrees, "Pattern names are crucial, because part of the purpose of patterns is to create a vocabulary that allows developers to communicate more effectively" (*Patterns of Enterprise Application Architecture*, Addison-Wesley Professional, 2002).

In *Patterns of Enterprise Application Architecture*, Martin Fowler refines a database access pattern I first encountered in *Core J2EE Patterns* by Deepak Alur, Dan Malks, and John Crupi (Prentice Hall, 2003). Fowler defines two patterns that describe specializations of the older pattern. The logic of his approach is clearly correct (one of the new patterns models domain objects, while the other models database tables, a distinction that was vague in the earlier work). It was hard to train myself to think in terms of the new patterns. I had been using the name of the original in design sessions and documents for so long that it had become part of my language.

The Problem

No matter how elegant the solution (and some are very elegant indeed), the problem and its context are the grounds of a pattern. Recognizing a problem is harder than applying any one of the solutions in a pattern catalog. This is one reason that some pattern solutions can be misapplied or overused.

Patterns describe a problem space with great care. The problem is described in brief and then contextualized, often with a typical example and one or more diagrams. It is broken down into its specifics, its various manifestations. Any warning signs that might help in identifying the problem are described.

The Solution

The solution is summarized initially in conjunction with the problem. It is also described in detail often using UML class and interaction diagrams. The pattern usually includes a code example.

Although code may be presented, the solution is never cut and paste. The pattern describes an approach to a problem. There may be hundreds of nuances in implementation. Think about instructions for sowing a food crop. If you simply follow a set of steps blindly, you are likely to go hungry come harvest time. More useful would be a pattern-based approach that covers the various conditions that may apply. The basic solution to the problem (making your crop grow) will always be the same (plant seeds, irrigate, harvest crop), but the actual steps you take will depend on all sorts of factors such as your soil type, your location, the orientation of your land, local pests, and so on.

Martin Fowler refers to solutions in patterns as "half-baked." That is, the coder must take away the concept and finish it for himself.

Consequences

Every design decision you make will have wider consequences. This should include the satisfactory resolution of the problem in question, of course. A solution, once deployed, may be ideally suited to work with other patterns. There may also be dangers to watch for.

The Gang of Four Format

As I write, I have five pattern catalogs on the desk in front of me. A quick look at the patterns in each confirms that not one uses the same structure as the others. Some are more formal than others; some are fine-grained, with many subsections; others are discursive.

There are a number of well-defined pattern structures, including the original form developed by Christopher Alexander (the Alexandrian form), the narrative approach favored by the Portland Pattern Repository (the Portland form). Because the Gang of Four book is so influential, and because we will cover many of the patterns they describe, let's examine a few of the sections they include in their patterns:

- *Intent*: A brief statement of the pattern's purpose. You should be able to see the point of the pattern at a glance.

- *Motivation*: The problem described, often in terms of a typical situation. The anecdotal approach can help make the pattern easy to grasp.

- *Applicability*: An examination of the different situations in which you might apply the pattern. While the motivation describes a typical problem, this section defines specific situations and weighs the merits of the solution in the context of each.

- *Structure/Interaction*: These sections may contain UML class and interaction diagrams describing the relationships among classes and objects in the solution.

- *Implementation*: This section looks at the details of the solution. It examines any issues that may come up when applying the technique and provides tips for deployment.

- *Sample Code*: I always skip ahead to this section. I find that a simple code example often provides a way into a pattern. The example is often chopped down to the basics in order to lay the solution bare. It could be in any object-oriented language. Of course, in this book, it will always be PHP.

- *Known Uses*: Real systems in which the pattern (problem, context, and solution) occur. Some people say that for a pattern to be genuine, it must be found in at least three publicly available contexts. This is sometimes called the "rule of three."

- *Related Patterns*: Some patterns imply others. In applying one solution, you can create the context in which another becomes useful. This section examines these synergies. It may also discuss patterns that have similarities in problem or solution and any antecedents: patterns defined elsewhere on which the current pattern builds.

Why Use Design Patterns?

So what benefits can patterns bring? Given that a pattern is a problem defined and solution described, the answer should be obvious. Patterns can help you to solve common problems. There is more to patterns, of course.

A Design Pattern Defines a Problem

How many times have you reached a stage in a project and found that there is no going forward? The chances are you must backtrack some way before starting out again.

By defining common problems, patterns can help you to improve your design. Sometimes, the first step to a solution is recognizing that you have a problem.

A Design Pattern Defines a Solution

Having defined and recognized the problem (and made certain that it is the right problem), a pattern gives you access to a solution, together with an analysis of the consequences of its use. Although a pattern does not absolve you of the responsibility to consider the implications of a design decision, you can at least be certain that you are using a tried-and-tested technique.

Design Patterns Are Language Independent

Patterns define objects and solutions in object-oriented terms. This means that many patterns apply equally in more than one language. When I first started using patterns, I read code examples in C++ and Smalltalk and deployed my solutions in Java. Others transfer with modifications to the pattern's applicability or consequences but remain valid. Either way, patterns can help you as you move between languages. Equally, an application that is built on good object-oriented design principles can be relatively easy to port between languages (although there are always issues that must be addressed).

Patterns Define a Vocabulary

By providing developers with names for techniques, patterns make communication richer. Imagine a design meeting. I have already described my Abstract Factory solution, and now I need to describe my strategy for managing the data the system compiles. I describe my plans to Bob:

ME: I'm thinking of using a Composite.

BOB: I don't think you've thought that through.

OK, Bob didn't agree with me. He never does. But he knew what I was talking about, and therefore why my idea sucked. Let's play that scene through again without a design vocabulary.

ME: I intend to use a tree of objects that share the same type. The type's interface will provide methods for adding child objects of its own type. In this way, we can build up complex combinations of implementing objects at runtime.

BOB: Huh?

Patterns, or the techniques they describe, tend to interoperate. The Composite pattern lends itself to collaboration with Visitor:

ME: And then we can use Visitors to summarize the data.

BOB: You're missing the point.

Ignore Bob. I won't describe the tortuous nonpattern version of this; I will cover Composite in Chapter 10 and Visitor in Chapter 11.

The point is that without a pattern language, we would still use these techniques. They *precede* their naming and organization. If patterns did not exist, they would evolve on their own anyway. Any tool that is used sufficiently will eventually acquire a name.

Patterns Are Tried and Tested

So if patterns document good practice, is naming the only truly original thing about pattern catalogs? In some senses, that would seem to be true. Patterns represent best practice in an object-oriented context. To some highly experienced programmers, this may seem an exercise in repackaging the obvious. To the rest of us, patterns provide access to problems and solutions we would otherwise have to discover the hard way.

Patterns make design accessible. As pattern catalogs emerge for more and more specializations, even the highly experienced can find benefits as they move into new aspects of their fields. A GUI programmer can gain fast access to common problems and solutions in enterprise programming, for example. A web programmer can quickly chart strategies for avoiding the pitfalls that lurk in PDA and smart phone projects.

Patterns Are Designed for Collaboration

By their nature, patterns should be generative and composable. This means that you should be able to apply one pattern and thereby create conditions suitable for the application of another. In other words, in using a pattern you may find other doors opened for you.

Pattern catalogs are usually designed with this kind of collaboration in mind, and the potential for pattern composition is always documented in the pattern itself.

Design Patterns Promote Good Design

Design patterns demonstrate and apply principles of object-oriented design. So a study of design patterns can yield more than a specific solution in a context. You can come away with a new perspective on the ways that objects and classes can be combined to achieve an objective.

PHP and Design Patterns

There is little in this chapter that is specific to PHP, which is characteristic of our topic to some extent. Many patterns apply to many object-capable languages with few or no implementation issues.

This is not always the case, of course. Some enterprise patterns work well in languages in which an application process continues to run between server requests. PHP does not work that way. A new script execution is kicked off for every request. This means that some patterns need to be treated with more care. Front Controller, for example, often requires some serious initialization time. This is fine when the initialization takes place once at application startup but more of an issue when it must take place for every request. That is not to say that we can't use the pattern; I have deployed it with very good results in the past. We must simply ensure that we take account of PHP-related issues when we discuss the pattern. PHP forms the context for all the patterns that this book examines.

I referred to object-capable languages earlier in this section. You can code in PHP without defining any classes at all (although with PEAR's continuing development you will probably manipulate objects to some extent). Although this book focuses almost entirely on object-oriented solutions to programming problems, it is not a broadside in an advocacy war. Patterns and PHP can be a powerful mix, and they form the core of this book; they can, however, coexist quite happily with more traditional approaches. PEAR is an excellent testament to this. PEAR packages use design patterns elegantly. They tend to be object-oriented in nature. This makes them more, not less, useful in procedural projects. Because PEAR packages are self-enclosed and hide their complexity behind clean interfaces, they are easy to stitch into any kind of project.

Summary

In this chapter, I introduced design patterns, showed you their structure (using the Gang of Four form), and suggested some reasons why you might want to use design patterns in your scripts.

It is important to remember that design patterns are not snap-on solutions that can be combined like components to build a project. They are suggested approaches to common problems. These solutions embody some key design principles. It is these that we will examine in the next chapter.

■ ■ ■

CHAPTER 8

Some Pattern Principles

Although design patterns simply describe solutions to problems, they tend to emphasize solutions that promote reusability and flexibility. To achieve this, they manifest some key object-oriented design principles. We will encounter some of them in this chapter and in more detail throughout the rest of the book.

This chapter will cover

- *Composition*: How to use object aggregation to achieve greater flexibility than you could with inheritance alone

- *Decoupling*: How to reduce dependency between elements in a system

- *The power of the interface*: Patterns and polymorphism

- *Pattern categories*: The types of pattern that this book will cover

The Pattern Revelation

I first started working with objects in the Java language. As you might expect, it took a while before some concepts clicked. When it did happen, though, it happened very fast, almost with the force of revelation. The elegance of inheritance and encapsulation bowled me over. I could sense that this was a different way of defining and building systems. I *got* polymorphism, working with a type and switching implementations at runtime.

All the books on my desk at the time focused on language features and the very many APIs available to the Java programmer. Beyond a brief definition of polymorphism, there was little attempt to examine design strategies.

Language features alone do not engender object-oriented design. Although my projects fulfilled their functional requirements, the kind of design that inheritance, encapsulation, and polymorphism had seemed to offer continued to elude me.

My inheritance hierarchies grew wider and deeper as I attempted to build new classes for every eventuality. The structure of my systems made it hard to convey messages from one tier to another without giving intermediate classes too much awareness of their surroundings, binding them into the application and making them unusable in new contexts.

It wasn't until I discovered *Design Patterns*, otherwise known as the Gang of Four book, that I realized I had missed an entire design dimension. By that time, I had already discovered some of the core patterns for myself, but others contributed to a new way of thinking.

I discovered that I had overprivileged inheritance in my designs, trying to build too much functionality into my classes. But where else can functionality go in an object-oriented system?

I found the answer in composition. Software components can be defined at runtime by combining objects in flexible relationships. The Gang of Four boiled this down into a principle: "favor composition over inheritance." The patterns described ways in which objects could be combined at runtime to achieve a level of flexibility impossible in an inheritance tree alone.

Composition and Inheritance

Inheritance is a powerful way of designing for changing circumstances or contexts. It can limit flexibility, however, especially when classes take on multiple responsibilities.

The Problem

As you know, child classes inherit the methods and properties of their parents (as long as they are protected or public elements). You can use this fact to design child classes that provide specialized functionality.

Figure 8–1 presents a simple example using the UML.

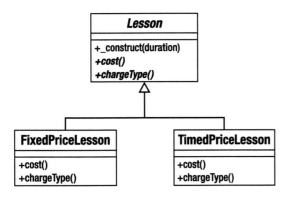

Figure 8–1. *A parent class and two child classes*

The abstract Lesson class in Figure 8–1 models a lesson in a college. It defines abstract cost() and chargeType() methods. The diagram shows two implementing classes, FixedPriceLesson and TimedPriceLesson, which provide distinct charging mechanisms for lessons.

Using this inheritance scheme, I can switch between lesson implementations. Client code will know only that it is dealing with a Lesson object, so the details of cost will be transparent.

What happens, though, if I introduce a new set of specializations? I need to handle lectures and seminars. Because these organize enrollment and lesson notes in different ways, they require separate classes. So now I have two forces that operate upon my design. I need to handle pricing strategies and separate lectures and seminars.

Figure 8–2 shows a brute-force solution.

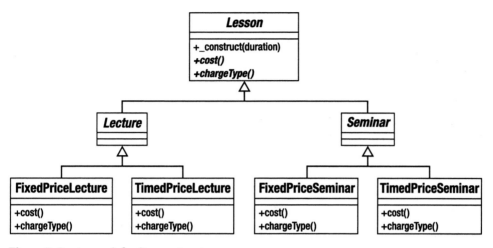

Figure 8–2. *A poor inheritance structure*

Figure 8–2 shows a hierarchy that is clearly faulty. I can no longer use the inheritance tree to manage my pricing mechanisms without duplicating great swathes of functionality. The pricing strategies are mirrored across the Lecture and Seminar class families.

At this stage, I might consider using conditional statements in the Lesson super class, removing those unfortunate duplications. Essentially, I remove the pricing logic from the inheritance tree altogether, moving it up into the super class. This is the reverse of the usual refactoring where you replace a conditional with polymorphism. Here is an amended Lesson class:

```
abstract class Lesson {
    protected $duration;
    const    FIXED = 1;
    const    TIMED = 2;
    private  $costtype;

    function __construct( $duration, $costtype=1 ) {
        $this->duration = $duration;
        $this->costtype = $costtype;
    }

    function cost() {
        switch ( $this->costtype ) {
            CASE self::TIMED :
                return (5 * $this->duration);
                break;
            CASE self::FIXED :
                return 30;
                break;
            default:
                $this->costtype = self::FIXED;
                return 30;
        }
    }
}
```

```
    function chargeType() {
        switch ( $this->costtype ) {
            CASE self::TIMED :
                return "hourly rate";
                break;
            CASE self::FIXED :
                return "fixed rate";
                break;
            default:
                $this->costtype = self::FIXED;
                return "fixed rate";
        }
    }

    // more lesson methods...
}

class Lecture extends Lesson {
    // Lecture-specific implementations ...
}

class Seminar extends Lesson {
    // Seminar-specific implementations ...
}
```

Here's how I might work with these classes:

```
$lecture = new Lecture( 5, Lesson::FIXED );

print "{$lecture->cost()} ({$lecture->chargeType()})\n";


$seminar= new Seminar( 3, Lesson::TIMED );

print "{$seminar->cost()} ({$seminar->chargeType()})\n";
```

And here's the output:

```
30 (fixed rate)

15 (hourly rate)
```

You can see the new class diagram in Figure 8–3.

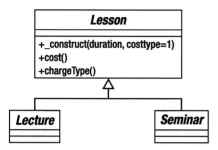

Figure 8–3. *Inheritance hierarchy improved by removing cost calculations from subclasses*

I have made the class structure much more manageable but at a cost. Using conditionals in this code is a retrograde step. Usually, you would try to replace a conditional statement with polymorphism. Here, I have done the opposite. As you can see, this has forced me to duplicate the conditional statement across the `chargeType()` and `cost()` methods.

I seem doomed to duplicate code.

Using Composition

I can use the Strategy pattern to compose my way out of trouble. Strategy is used to move a set of algorithms into a separate type. By moving cost calculations, I can simplify the `Lesson` type. You can see this in Figure 8–4.

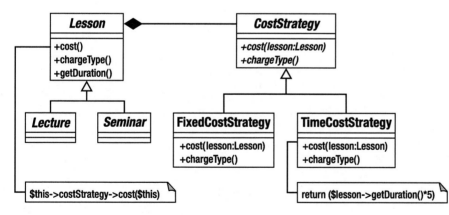

Figure 8–4. *Moving algorithms into a separate type*

I create an abstract class, `CostStrategy`, which defines the abstract methods `cost()` and `chargeType()`. The `cost()` method requires an instance of `Lesson`, which it will use to generate cost data. I provide two implementations for `CostStrategy`. `Lesson` objects work only with the `CostStrategy` type, not a specific implementation, so I can add new cost algorithms at any time by subclassing `CostStrategy`. This would require no changes at all to any `Lesson` classes.

Here's a simplified version of the new `Lesson` class illustrated in Figure 8–4:

```
abstract class Lesson {
    private   $duration;
    private   $costStrategy;

    function __construct( $duration, CostStrategy $strategy ) {
        $this->duration = $duration;
        $this->costStrategy = $strategy;
    }

    function cost() {
        return $this->costStrategy->cost( $this );
    }

    function chargeType() {
        return $this->costStrategy->chargeType( );
    }

    function getDuration() {
        return $this->duration;
    }

    // more lesson methods...
}

class Lecture extends Lesson {
    // Lecture-specific implementations ...
}

class Seminar extends Lesson {
    // Seminar-specific implementations ...
}
```

The Lesson class requires a CostStrategy object, which it stores as a property. The Lesson::cost()
method simply invokes CostStrategy::cost(). Equally, Lesson::chargeType() invokes
CostStrategy::chargeType(). This explicit invocation of another object's method in order to fulfill a
request is known as delegation. In my example, the CostStrategy object is the delegate of Lesson. The
Lesson class washes its hands of responsibility for cost calculations and passes on the task to a
CostStrategy implementation. Here, it is caught in the act of delegation:

```
function cost() {
    return $this->costStrategy->cost( $this );
}
```

Here is the CostStrategy class, together with its implementing children:

```
abstract class CostStrategy {
    abstract function cost( Lesson $lesson );
    abstract function chargeType();
}

class TimedCostStrategy extends CostStrategy {
    function cost( Lesson $lesson ) {
        return ( $lesson->getDuration() * 5 );
    }
    function chargeType() {
```

```
        return "hourly rate";
    }
}

class FixedCostStrategy extends CostStrategy {
    function cost( Lesson $lesson ) {
        return 30;
    }

    function chargeType() {
        return "fixed rate";
    }
}
```

I can change the way that any Lesson object calculates cost by passing it a different CostStrategy object at runtime. This approach then makes for highly flexible code. Rather than building functionality into my code structures statically, I can combine and recombine objects dynamically.

```
$lessons[] = new Seminar( 4, new TimedCostStrategy() );
$lessons[] = new Lecture( 4, new FixedCostStrategy() );

foreach ( $lessons as $lesson ) {
    print "lesson charge {$lesson->cost()}. ";
    print "Charge type: {$lesson->chargeType()}\n";
}

lesson charge 20. Charge type: hourly rate
```

```
lesson charge 30. Charge type: fixed rate
```

As you can see, one effect of this structure is that I have focused the responsibilities of my classes. CostStrategy objects are responsible solely for calculating cost, and Lesson objects manage lesson data.

So, composition can make your code more flexible, because objects can be combined to handle tasks dynamically in many more ways than you can anticipate in an inheritance hierarchy alone. There can be a penalty with regard to readability, though. Because composition tends to result in more types, with relationships that aren't fixed with the same predictability as they are in inheritance relationships, it can be slightly harder to digest the relationships in a system.

Decoupling

You saw in Chapter 6 that it makes sense to build independent components. A system with highly interdependent classes can be hard to maintain. A change in one location can require a cascade of related changes across the system.

The Problem

Reusability is one of the key objectives of object-oriented design, and tight coupling is its enemy. You can diagnose tight coupling when you see that a change to one component of a system necessitates many changes elsewhere. You shouldy aspire to create independent components so that you can make changes without a domino effect of unintended consequences. When you alter a component, the extent to which it is independent is related to the likelihood that your changes will cause other parts of your system to fail.

You saw an example of tight coupling in Figure 8–2. Because the costing logic was mirrored across the Lecture and Seminar types, a change to TimedPriceLecture would necessitate a parallel change to the same logic in TimedPriceSeminar. By updating one class and not the other, I would break my system—without any warning from the PHP engine. My first solution, using a conditional statement, produced a similar dependency between the cost() and chargeType() methods.

By applying the Strategy pattern, I distilled my costing algorithms into the CostStrategy type, locating them behind a common interface and implementing each only once.

Coupling of another sort can occur when many classes in a system are embedded explicitly into a platform or environment. Let's say that you are building a system that works with a MySQL database, for example. You might use functions such as mysql_connect() and mysql_query() to speak to the database server.

Should you be required to deploy the system on a server that does not support MySQL, you *could* convert your entire project to use SQLite. You would be forced to make changes throughout your code, though, and face the prospect of maintaining two parallel versions of your application.

The problem here is not the system's dependency on an external platform. Such a dependency is inevitable. You need to work with code that speaks to a database. The problem comes when such code is scattered throughout a project. Talking to databases is not the primary responsibility of most classes in a system, so the best strategy is to extract such code and group it together behind a common interface. In this way, you promote the independence of your classes. At the same time, by concentrating your gateway code in one place, you make it much easier to switch to a new platform without disturbing your wider system. This process, the hiding of implementation behind a clean interface, is known as encapsulation.

PEAR solves this problem with the PEAR::MDB2 package (which has superceded PEAR::DB). This provides a single point of access for multiple databases. More recently the bundled PDO extension has brought this model into the PHP language itself.

The MDB2 class provides a static method called connect() that accepts a Data Source Name (DSN) string. According to the makeup of this string, it returns a particular implementation of a class called MDB2_Driver_Common. So for the string "mysql://", the connect() method returns a MDB2_Driver_mysql object, while for a string that starts with "sqlite://", it would return an MDB2_Driver_sqlite object. You can see the class structure in Figure 8–5.

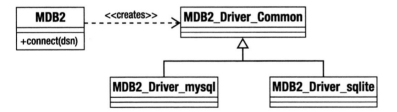

Figure 8–5. *The PEAR::MDB2 package decouples client code from database objects.*

The PEAR::MDB2 package, then, lets you decouple your application code from the specifics of your database platform . As long as you use uncontroversial SQL, you should be able to run a single system with MySQL, SQLite, MSSQL, and others without changing a line of code (apart from the DSN, of course, which is the single point at which the database context must be configured). In fact, the PEAR::MDB2 package can also help manage different SQL dialects to some extent—one reason you might still choose to use it, despite the speed and convenience of PDO.

Loosening Your Coupling

To handle database code flexibly, you should decouple the application logic from the specifics of the database platform it uses. You will see lots of opportunities for this kind of component separation of components in your own projects.

Imagine for example that the Lesson system must incorporate a registration component to add new lessons to the system. As part of the registration procedure, an administrator should be notified when a lesson is added. The system's users can't agree whether this notification should be sent by mail, or by text message. In fact, they're so argumentative, that you suspect they might want to switch to a new mode of communication in the future. What's more, they want to be notified of all sorts of things. So that a change to the notification mode in one place, will mean a similar alteration in many other places.

If you've hardcoded calls to a Mailer class, or a Texter class, then your system is tightly coupled to a particular notification mode. Just as it would be tightly coupled to a database platform by the use of a specialized database API.

Here is some code that hides the implementation details of a notifier from the system that uses it.

```
class RegistrationMgr {

    function register( Lesson $lesson ) {

        // do something with this Lesson


        // now tell someone

        $notifier = Notifier::getNotifier();

        $notifier->inform( "new lesson: cost ({$lesson->cost()})" );

    }

}


abstract class Notifier {


    static function getNotifier() {

        // acquire concrete class according to

        // configuration or other logic


        if ( rand(1,2) == 1 ) {

            return new MailNotifier();

        } else {
```

```
                return new TextNotifier();

        }

    }


    abstract function inform( $message );

}


class MailNotifier extends Notifier {

    function inform( $message ) {

        print "MAIL notification: {$message}\n";

    }

}


class TextNotifier extends Notifier {

    function inform( $message ) {

        print "TEXT notification: {$message}\n";

    }

}
```

I create RegistrationMgr, a sample client for my Notifier classes. The Notifier class is abstract, but it does implement a static method: getNotifier() which fetches a concrete Notifier object (TextNotifier or MailNotifier). In a real project, the choice of Notifier would be determined by a flexible mechanism, such as a configuration file. Here, I cheat and make the choice randomly. MailNotifier and TextNotifier do nothing more than print out the message they are passed along with an identifier to show which one has been called.

Notice how the knowledge of which concrete Notifier should be used has been focused in the Notifier::getNotifier() method. I could send notifier messages from a hundred different parts of my system, and a change in Notifier would only have to be made in that one method.

Here is some code that calls the RegistrationMgr,

```
$lessons1 = new Seminar( 4, new TimedCostStrategy() );

$lessons2 = new Lecture( 4, new FixedCostStrategy() );

$mgr = new RegistrationMgr();
```

```
$mgr->register( $lessons1 );

$mgr->register( $lessons2 );
```

and the output from a typical run

```
TEXT notification: new lesson: cost (20)
MAIL notification: new lesson: cost (30)
```

Figure 8–6 shows these classes.

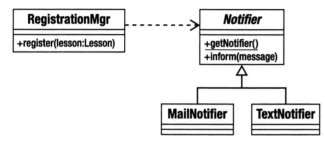

Figure 8–6. *The Notifier class separates client code from Notifier implementations.*

Notice how similar the structure in Figure 8–6 is to that formed by the MDB2 components shown in Figure 8–5

Code to an Interface, Not to an Implementation

This principle is one of the all-pervading themes of this book. You saw in Chapter 6 (and in the last section) that you can hide different implementations behind the common interface defined in a superclass. Client code can then require an object of the superclass's type rather than that of an implementing class, unconcerned by the specific implementation it is actually getting.

Parallel conditional statements, like the ones I built into Lesson::cost() and Lesson::chargeType(), are a common signal that polymorphism is needed. They make code hard to maintain, because a change in one conditional expression necessitates a change in its twins. Conditional statements are occasionally said to implement a "simulated inheritance."

By placing the cost algorithms in separate classes that implement CostStrategy, I remove duplication. I also make it much easier should I need to add new cost strategies in the future.

From the perspective of client code, it is often a good idea to require abstract or general types in your methods' parameters. By requiring more specific types, you could limit the flexibility of your code at runtime.

Having said that, of course, the level of generality you choose in your argument hints is a matter of judgment. Make your choice too general, and your method may become less safe. If you require the specific functionality of a subtype, then accepting a differently equipped sibling into a method could be risky.

Still, make your choice of argument hint too restricted, and you lose the benefits of polymorphism. Take a look at this altered extract from the Lesson class:

```
function __construct( $duration,
    FixedPriceStrategy $strategy ) {
    $this->duration = $duration;
    $this->costStrategy = $strategy;
}
```

There are two issues arising from the design decision in this example. First, the Lesson object is now tied to a specific cost strategy, which closes down my ability to compose dynamic components. Second, the explicit reference to the FixedPriceStrategy class forces me to maintain that particular implementation.

By requiring a common interface, I can combine a Lesson object with any CostStrategy implementation:

```
function __construct( $duration, CostStrategy $strategy ) {
    $this->duration = $duration;
    $this->costStrategy = $strategy;
}
```

I have, in other words, decoupled my Lesson class from the specifics of cost calculation. All that matters is the interface and the guarantee that the provided object will honor it.

Of course, coding to an interface can often simply defer the question of how to instantiate your objects. When I say that a Lesson object can be combined with any CostStrategy interface at runtime, I beg the question, "But where does the CostStrategy object come from?"

When you create an abstract super class, there is always the issue as to how its children should be instantiated. Which child do you choose and according to which condition? This subject forms a category of its own in the Gang of Four pattern catalog, and I will examine it further in the next chapter.

The Concept That Varies

It's easy to interpret a design decision once it has been made, but how do you decide where to start?

The Gang of Four recommend that you "encapsulate the concept that varies." In terms of my lesson example, the varying concept is the cost algorithm. Not only is the cost calculation one of two possible strategies in the example, but it is obviously a candidate for expansion: special offers, overseas student rates, introductory discounts, all sorts of possibilities present themselves.

I quickly established that subclassing for this variation was inappropriate, and I resorted to a conditional statement. By bringing my variation into the same class, I underlined its suitability for encapsulation.

The Gang of Four recommend that you actively seek varying elements in your classes and assess their suitability for encapsulation in a new type. Each alternative in a suspect conditional may be extracted to form a class extending a common abstract parent. This new type can then be used by the class or classes from which it was extracted. This has the effect of

- Focusing responsibility

- Promoting flexibility through composition

- Making inheritance hierarchies more compact and focused

- Reducing duplication

So how do you spot variation? One sign is the misuse of inheritance. This might include inheritance deployed according to multiple forces at one time (lecture/seminar, fixed/timed cost). It might also include subclassing on an algorithm where the algorithm is incidental to the core responsibility of the type. The other sign of variation suitable for encapsulation is, of course, a conditional expression.

Patternitis

One problem for which there is no pattern is the unnecessary or inappropriate use of patterns. This has earned patterns a bad name in some quarters. Because pattern solutions are neat, it is tempting to apply them wherever you see a fit, whether they truly fulfill a need or not.

The eXtreme Programming (XP) methodology offers a couple of principles that might apply here. The first is "You aren't going to need it" (often abbreviated to YAGNI). This is generally applied to application features, but it also makes sense for patterns.

When I build large environments in PHP, I tend to split my application into layers, separating application logic from presentation and persistence layers. I use all sorts of core and enterprise patterns in conjunction with one another.

When I am asked to build a feedback form for a small business web site, however, I may simply use procedural code in a single page script. I do not need enormous amounts of flexibility, I won't be building on the initial release. I don't need to use patterns that address problems in larger systems. Instead, I apply the second XP principle: "Do the simplest thing that works."

When you work with a pattern catalog, the structure and process of the solution are what stick in the mind, consolidated by the code example. Before applying a pattern, though, pay close attention to the problem, or "when to use it," section, and read up on the pattern's consequences. In some contexts, the cure may be worse than the disease.

The Patterns

This book is not a pattern catalog. Nevertheless, in the coming chapters, I will introduce a few of the key patterns in use at the moment, providing PHP implementations and discussing them in the broad context of PHP programming.

The patterns described will be drawn from key catalogs including *Design Patterns*, *Patterns of Enterprise Application Architecture* by Martin Fowler (Addison-Wesley, 2003) and *Core J2EE Patterns* by Alur et al. (Prentice Hall PTR, 2001). I use the Gang of Four's categorization as a starting point, dividing patterns as follows.

Patterns for Generating Objects

These patterns are concerned with the instantiation of objects. This is an important category given the principle "code to an interface." If you are working with abstract parent classes in your design, then you must develop strategies for instantiating objects from concrete subclasses. It is these objects that will be passed around your system.

Patterns for Organizing Objects and Classes

These patterns help you to organize the compositional relationships of your objects. More simply, these patterns show how you combine objects and classes.

Task-Oriented Patterns

These patterns describe the mechanisms by which classes and objects cooperate to achieve objectives.

Enterprise Patterns

I look at some patterns that describe typical Internet programming problems and solutions. Drawn largely from *Patterns of Enterprise Application Architecture* and *Core J2EE Patterns*, the patterns deal with presentation, and application logic.

Database Patterns

An examination of patterns that help with storing and retrieving data and with mapping objects to and from databases.

Summary

In this chapter, I examined some of the principles that underpin many design patterns. I looked at the use of composition to enable object combination and recombination at runtime, resulting in more flexible structures than would be available using inheritance alone. I introduced you to decoupling, the practice of extracting software components from their context to make them more generally applicable. I reviewed the importance of interface as a means of decoupling clients from the details of implementation.

In the coming chapters, I will examine some design patterns in detail.

CHAPTER 9

■ ■ ■

Generating Objects

Creating objects is a messy business. So many object-oriented designs deal with nice, clean abstract classes, taking advantage of the impressive flexibility afforded by polymorphism (the switching of concrete implementations at runtime). To achieve this flexibility though, I must devise strategies for object generation. This is the topic I will look at here.

This chapter will cover

- *The Singleton pattern*: A special class that generates one and only one object instance

- *The Factory Method pattern*: Building an inheritance hierarchy of creator classes

- *The Abstract Factory pattern*: Grouping the creation of functionally related products

- *The Prototype pattern*: Using clone to generate objects

Problems and Solutions in Generating Objects

Object creation can be a weak point in object-oriented design. In the previous chapter, you saw the principle "Code to an interface, not to an implementation." To this end, you are encouraged to work with abstract supertypes in your classes. This makes code more flexible, allowing you to use objects instantiated from different concrete subclasses at runtime. This has the side effect that object instantiation is deferred.

Here's a class that accepts a name string and instantiates a particular object:

```
abstract class Employee {
    protected $name;
    function __construct( $name ) {
        $this->name = $name;
    }
    abstract function fire();
}

class Minion extends Employee {
    function fire() {
        print "{$this->name}: I'll clear my desk\n";
    }
}
```

```
class NastyBoss {
    private $employees = array();

    function addEmployee( $employeeName ) {
        $this->employees[] = new Minion( $employeeName );
    }

    function projectFails() {
        if ( count( $this->employees ) > 0 ) {
            $emp = array_pop( $this->employees );
            $emp->fire();
        }
    }
}

$boss = new NastyBoss();
$boss->addEmployee( "harry" );
$boss->addEmployee( "bob" );
$boss->addEmployee( "mary" );
$boss->projectFails();

// output:
// mary: I'll clear my desk
```

As you can see, I define an abstract base class: Employee, with a downtrodden implementation: Minion. Given a name string, the NastyBoss::addEmployee() method instantiates a new Minion object. Whenever a NastyBoss object runs into trouble (via the NastyBoss::projectFails() method), it looks for a Minion to fire.

By instantiating a Minion object directly in the NastyBoss class, we limit flexibility. If a NastyBoss object could work with *any* instance of the Employee type, we could make our code amenable to variation at runtime as we add more Employee specializations. You should find the polymorphism in Figure 9-1 familiar.

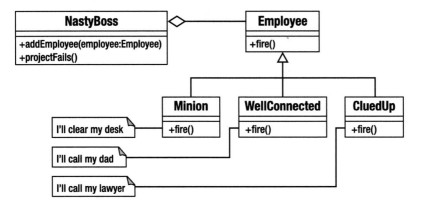

Figure 9-1. Working with an abstract type enables polymorphism.

If the NastyBoss class does not instantiate a Minion object, where does it come from? Authors often duck out of this problem by constraining an argument type in a method declaration and then conveniently omitting to show the instantiation in anything other than a test context.

```
class NastyBoss {
    private $employees = array();

    function addEmployee( Employee $employee ) {
        $this->employees[] = $employee;
    }

    function projectFails() {
        if ( count( $this->employees ) ) {
            $emp = array_pop( $this->employees );
            $emp->fire();
        }
    }
}

// new Employee class...
class CluedUp extends Employee {
    function fire() {
        print "{$this->name}: I'll call my lawyer\n";
    }
}

$boss = new NastyBoss();
$boss->addEmployee( new Minion( "harry" ) );
$boss->addEmployee( new CluedUp( "bob" ) );
$boss->addEmployee( new Minion( "mary" ) );
$boss->projectFails();
$boss->projectFails();
$boss->projectFails();
// output:
// mary: I'll clear my desk
// bob: I'll call my lawyer
// harry: I'll clear my desk
```

Although this version of the NastyBoss class works with the Employee type, and therefore benefits from polymorphism, I still haven't defined a strategy for object creation. Instantiating objects is a dirty business, but it has to be done. This chapter is about classes and objects that work with concrete classes so that the rest of your classes do not have to.

If there is a principle to be found here, it is "delegate object instantiation." I did this implicitly in the previous example by demanding that an Employee object is passed to the NastyBoss::addEmployee() method. I could, however, equally delegate to a separate class or method that takes responsibility for generating Employee objects. Here I add a static method to the Employee class that implements a strategy for object creation:

```
abstract class Employee {
    protected $name;
    private static $types = array( 'minion', 'cluedup', 'wellconnected' );

    static function recruit( $name ) {
        $num = rand( 1, count( self::$types ) )-1;
```

```
        $class = self::$types[$num];
        return new $class( $name );
    }

    function __construct( $name ) {
        $this->name = $name;
    }
    abstract function fire();
}

// new Employee class...

class WellConnected extends Employee {
    function fire() {
        print "{$this->name}: I'll call my dad\n";
    }
}
```

As you can see, this takes a name string and uses it to instantiate a particular Employee subtype at random. I can now delegate the details of instantiation to the Employee class's recruit() method:

```
$boss = new NastyBoss();
$boss->addEmployee( Employee::recruit( "harry" ) );
$boss->addEmployee( Employee::recruit( "bob" ) );
$boss->addEmployee( Employee::recruit( "mary" ) );
```

You saw a simple example of such a class in Chapter 4. I placed a static method in the ShopProduct class called getInstance(). getInstance() is responsible for generating the correct ShopProduct subclass based on a database query. The ShopProduct class, therefore, has a dual role. It defines the ShopProduct type, but it also acts as a factory for concrete ShopProduct objects.

▨**Note** I use the term "factory" frequently in this chapter. A factory is a class or method with responsibility for generating objects.

```
// class ShopProduct

    public static function getInstance( $id, PDO $dbh ) {
        $query = "select * from products where id = ?";
        $stmt = $dbh->prepare( $query );

        if ( ! $stmt->execute( array( $id ) ) ) {
            $error=$dbh->errorInfo();
            die( "failed: ".$error[1] );
        }

        $row = $stmt->fetch( );
        if ( empty( $row ) ) { return null; }

        if ( $row['type'] == "book" ) {
```

```
        // instantiate a BookProduct objec
    } else if ( $row['type'] == "cd" ) {
        $product = new CdProduct();
        // instantiate a CdProduct object
    } else {
        // instantiate a ShopProduct object
    }
    $product->setId( $row['id'] );
    $product->setDiscount( $row['discount'] );
    return $product;
}
```

The getInstance() method uses a large if/else statement to determine which subclass to instantiate. Conditionals like this are quite common in factory code. Although you should attempt to excise large conditional statements from your projects, doing so often has the effect of pushing the conditional back to the moment at which an object is generated. This is not generally a serious problem, because you remove parallel conditionals from your code in pushing the decision making back to this point.

In this chapter, then, I will examine some of the key Gang of Four patterns for generating objects.

The Singleton Pattern

The global variable is one of the great bugbears of the object-oriented programmer. The reasons should be familiar to you by now. Global variables tie classes into their context, undermining encapsulation (see Chapter 6, "Objects and Design," and Chapter 8, "Some Pattern Principles," for more on this). A class that relies on global variables becomes impossible to pull out of one application and use in another, without first ensuring that the new application itself defines the same global variables.

Although this is undesirable, the unprotected nature of global variables can be a greater problem. Once you start relying on global variables, it is perhaps just a matter of time before one of your libraries declares a global that clashes with another declared elsewhere. You have seen already that, if you are not using namespaces, PHP is vulnerable to class name clashes, but this is much worse. PHP will not warn you when globals collide. The first you will know about it is when your script begins to behave oddly. Worse still, you may not notice any issues at all in your development environment. By using globals, though, you potentially leave your users exposed to new and interesting conflicts when they attempt to deploy your library alongside others.

Globals remain a temptation, however. This is because there are times when the sin inherent in global access seems a price worth paying in order to give all your classes access to an object.

As I hinted, namespaces provide some protection from this. You can at least scope variables to a package, which means that third-party libraries are less likely to clash with your own system. Even so, the risk of collision exists within the namespace itself.

The Problem

Well-designed systems generally pass object instances around via method calls. Each class retains its independence from the wider context, collaborating with other parts of the system via clear lines of communication. Sometimes, though, you find that this forces you to use some classes as conduits for objects that do not concern them, introducing dependencies in the name of good design.

Imagine a Preferences class that holds application-level information. We might use a Preferences object to store data such as DSN strings (Data Source Names hold table and user information about a database), URL roots, file paths, and so on. This is the sort of information that will vary from installation to installation. The object may also be used as a notice board, a central location for messages that could be set or retrieved by otherwise unrelated objects in a system.

Passing a Preferences object around from object to object may not always be a good idea. Many classes that do not otherwise use the object could be forced to accept it simply so that they could pass it on to the objects that they work with. This is just another kind of coupling.

You also need to be sure that all objects in your system are working with the *same* Preferences object. You do not want objects setting values on one object, while others read from an entirely different one.

Let's distill the forces in this problem:

- A Preferences object should be available to any object in your system.

- A Preferences object should not be stored in a global variable, which can be overwritten.

- There should be no more than one Preferences object in play in the system. This means that *object Y* can set a property in the Preferences object, and *object Z* can retrieve the same property, without either one talking to the other directly (assuming both have access to the Preferences object).

Implementation

To address this problem, I can start by asserting control over object instantiation. Here, I create a class that cannot be instantiated from outside of itself. That may sound difficult, but it's simply a matter of defining a private constructor:

```
class Preferences {
    private $props = array();

    private function __construct() { }

    public function setProperty( $key, $val ) {
        $this->props[$key] = $val;
    }

    public function getProperty( $key ) {
        return $this->props[$key];
    }
}
```

Of course, at this point, the Preferences class is entirely unusable. I have taken access restriction to an absurd level. Because the constructor is declared private, no client code can instantiate an object from it. The setProperty() and getProperty() methods are therefore redundant.

I can use a static method and a static property to mediate object instantiation:

```
class Preferences {
    private $props = array();
    private static $instance;

    private function __construct() { }

    public static function getInstance() {
        if ( empty( self::$instance ) ) {
            self::$instance = new Preferences();
        }
```

```
        return self::$instance;
    }

    public function setProperty( $key, $val ) {
        $this->props[$key] = $val;
    }

    public function getProperty( $key ) {
        return $this->props[$key];
    }
}
```

The $instance property is private and static, so it cannot be accessed from outside the class. The getInstance() method has access though. Because getInstance() is public and static, it can be called via the class from anywhere in a script.

```
$pref = Preferences::getInstance();
$pref->setProperty( "name", "matt" );

unset( $pref ); // remove the reference

$pref2 = Preferences::getInstance();
print $pref2->getProperty( "name" ) ."\n"; // demonstrate value is not lost
```

The output is the single value we added to the Preferences object initially, available through a separate access:

```
matt
```

A static method cannot access object properties because it is, by definition, invoked in a class and not an object context. It can, however, access a static property. When getInstance() is called, I check the Preferences::$instance property. If it is empty, then I create an instance of the Preferences class and store it in the property. Then I return the instance to the calling code. Because the static getInstance() method is part of the Preferences class, I have no problem instantiating a Preferences object even though the constructor is private.

Figure 9-2 shows the Singleton pattern.

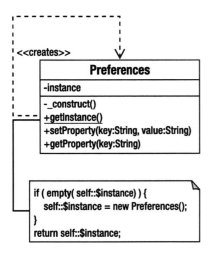

Figure 9-2. *An example of the Singleton pattern*

Consequences

So, how does the Singleton approach compare to using a global variable? First the bad news. Both Singletons and global variables are prone to misuse. Because Singletons can be accessed from anywhere in a system, they can serve to create dependencies that can be hard to debug. Change a Singleton, and classes that use it may be affected. Dependencies are not a problem in themselves. After all, we create a dependency every time we declare that a method requires an argument of a particular type. The problem is that the global nature of the Singleton lets a programmer bypass the lines of communication defined by class interfaces. When a Singleton is used, the dependency is hidden away inside a method and not declared in its signature. This can make it harder to trace the relationships within a system. Singleton classes should therefore be deployed sparingly and with care.

Nevertheless, I think that moderate use of the Singleton pattern can improve the design of a system, saving you from horrible contortions as you pass objects unnecessarily around your system.

Singletons represent an improvement over global variables in an object-oriented context. You cannot overwrite a Singleton with the wrong kind of data. This kind of protection is especially important in versions of PHP that do not support namespaces. Any name clash will be caught at compile time, ending script execution.

Factory Method Pattern

Object-oriented design emphasizes the abstract class over the implementation. That is, we work with generalizations rather than specializations. The Factory Method pattern addresses the problem of how to create object instances when your code focuses on abstract types. The answer? Let specialist classes handle instantiation.

The Problem

Imagine a personal organizer project. Among others, you manage Appointment objects. Your business group has forged a relationship with another company, and you must communicate appointment data to them using a format called BloggsCal. The business group warns you that you may face yet more formats as time wears on, though.

Staying at the level of interface alone, you can identify two participants right away. You need a data encoder that converts your Appointment objects into a proprietary format. Let's call that class ApptEncoder. You need a manager class that will retrieve an encoder and maybe work with it to communicate with a third party. You might call that CommsManager. Using the terminology of the pattern, the CommsManager is the creator, and the ApptEncoder is the product. You can see this structure in Figure 9-3.

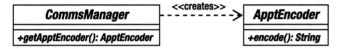

Figure 9-3. Abstract creator and product classes

How do you get your hands on a real concrete ApptEncoder, though?

You could demand that an ApptEncoder is passed to the CommsManager, but that simply defers your problem, and you want the buck to stop about here. Here I instantiate a BloggsApptEncoder object directly within the CommsManager class:

```
abstract class ApptEncoder {
    abstract function encode();
}

class BloggsApptEncoder extends ApptEncoder {
    function encode() {
        return "Appointment data encoded in BloggsCal format\n";
    }
}

class MegaApptEncoder extends ApptEncoder {
    function encode() {
        return "Appointment data encoded in MegaCal format\n";
    }
}
class CommsManager {
    function getApptEncoder() {
        return new BloggsApptEncoder();
    }
}
```

The CommsManager class is responsible for generating BloggsApptEncoder objects. When the sands of corporate allegiance inevitably shift and we are asked to convert our system to work with a new format called MegaCal, we can simply add a conditional into the CommsManager::getApptEncoder() method. This is the strategy we have used in the past, after all. Let's build a new implementation of CommsManager that handles both BloggsCal and MegaCal formats:

```
class CommsManager {
    const BLOGGS = 1;
```

```
        const MEGA = 2;
        private $mode = 1;

        function __construct( $mode ) {
            $this->mode = $mode;
        }

        function getApptEncoder() {
            switch ( $this->mode ) {
                case ( self::MEGA ):
                    return new MegaApptEncoder();
                default:
                    return new BloggsApptEncoder();
            }
        }
    }

$comms = new CommsManager( CommsManager::MEGA );
$apptEncoder = $comms->getApptEncoder();
print $apptEncoder->encode();
```

I use constant flags to define two modes in which the script might be run: MEGA and BLOGGS. I use a switch statement in the getApptEncoder() method to test the $mode property and instantiate the appropriate implementation of ApptEncoder.

There is little wrong with this approach. Conditionals are sometimes considered examples of bad "code smells," but object creation often requires a conditional at some point. You should be less sanguine if you see duplicate conditionals creeping into our code. The CommsManager class provides functionality for communicating calendar data. Imagine that the protocols we work with require you to provide header and footer data to delineate each appointment. I can extend the previous example to support a getHeaderText() method:

```
class CommsManager {
    const BLOGGS = 1;
    const MEGA = 2;
    private $mode ;

    function __construct( $mode ) {
        $this->mode = $mode;
    }

    function getHeaderText() {
        switch ( $this->mode ) {
            case ( self::MEGA ):
                return "MegaCal header\n";
            default:
                return "BloggsCal header\n";
        }
    }
    function getApptEncoder() {
        switch ( $this->mode ) {
            case ( self::MEGA ):
                return new MegaApptEncoder();
            default:
                return new BloggsApptEncoder();
```

```
        }
      }
}
```

As you can see, the need to support header output has forced me to duplicate the protocol conditional test. This will become unwieldy as I add new protocols, especially if I also add a getFooterText() method.

So, to summarize the problem:

- I do not know until runtime the kind of object I need to produce (BloggsApptEncoder or MegaApptEncoder).

- I need to be able to add new product types with relative ease. (SyncML support is just a new business deal away!)

- Each product type is associated with a context that requires other customized operations (getHeaderText(), getFooterText()).

Additionally, I am using conditional statements, and you have seen already that these are naturally replaceable by polymorphism. The Factory Method pattern enables you to use inheritance and polymorphism to encapsulate the creation of concrete products. In other words, you create a CommsManager subclass for each protocol, each one implementing the getApptEncoder() method.

Implementation

The Factory Method pattern splits creator classes from the products they are designed to generate. The creator is a factory class that defines a method for generating a product object. If no default implementation is provided, it is left to creator child classes to perform the instantiation. Typically, each creator subclass instantiates a parallel product child class.

I can redesignate CommsManager as an abstract class. That way I keep a flexible superclass and put all my protocol-specific code in the concrete subclasses. You can see this alteration in Figure 9-4.

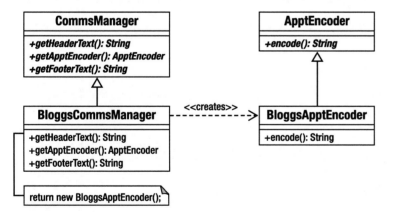

Figure 9-4. *Concrete creator and product classes*

Here's some simplified code:

```
abstract class ApptEncoder {
```

155

```
        abstract function encode();
}

class BloggsApptEncoder extends ApptEncoder {
    function encode() {
        return "Appointment data encode in BloggsCal format\n";
    }
}

abstract class CommsManager {
    abstract function getHeaderText();
    abstract function getApptEncoder();
    abstract function getFooterText();
}

class BloggsCommsManager extends CommsManager {
    function getHeaderText() {
        return "BloggsCal header\n";
    }

    function getApptEncoder() {
        return new BloggsApptEncoder();
    }

    function getFooterText() {
        return "BloggsCal footer\n";
    }
}
```

The BloggsCommsManager::getApptEncoder() method returns a BloggsApptEncoder object. Client code calling getApptEncoder() can expect an object of type ApptEncoder and will not necessarily know about the concrete product it has been given. In some languages, method return types are enforced, so client code calling a method like getApptEncoder() can be absolutely certain that it will receive an ApptEncoder object. In PHP, this is a matter of convention at present. It is important to document return types, or otherwise signal them through naming conventions.

▓**Note** At the time of this writing, hinted return types are a feature slated for a future release of PHP.

So when I am required to implement MegaCal, supporting it is simply a matter of writing a new implementation for my abstract classes. Figure 9-5 shows the MegaCal classes.

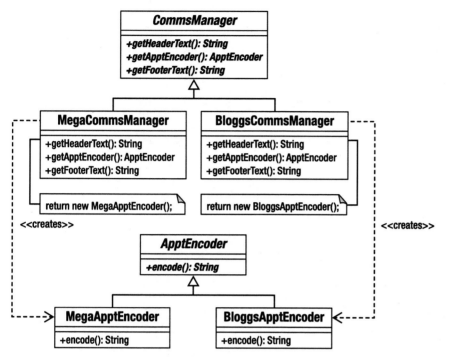

Figure 9-5. *Extending the design to support a new protocol*

Consequences

Notice that the creator classes mirror the product hierarchy. This is a common consequence of the Factory Method pattern and disliked by some as a special kind of code duplication. Another issue is the possibility that the pattern could encourage unnecessary subclassing. If your only reason for subclassing a creator is to deploy the Factory Method pattern, you may need to think again (that's why I introduced the header and footer constraints to our example here).

I have focused only on appointments in my example. If I extend it somewhat to include to-do items and contacts, I face a new problem. I need a structure that will handle sets of related implementations at one time. The Factory Method pattern is often used with the Abstract Factory pattern, as you will see in the next section.

Abstract Factory Pattern

In large applications, you may need factories that produce related sets of classes. The Abstract Factory pattern addresses this problem.

The Problem

Let's look again at the organizer example. I manage encoding in two formats, BloggsCal and MegaCal. I can grow this structure horizontally by adding more encoding formats, but how can I grow vertically, adding encoders for different types of PIM object? In fact, I have been working toward this pattern already.

In Figure 9-6, you can see the parallel families with which I will want to work. These are appointments (Appt), things to do (Ttd), and contacts (Contact).

The BloggsCal classes are unrelated to one another by inheritance (although they could implement a common interface), but they are functionally parallel. If the system is currently working with BloggsTtdEncoder, it should also be working with BloggsContactEncoder.

To see how I enforce this, you can begin with the interface as I did with the Factory Method pattern (see Figure 9-7).

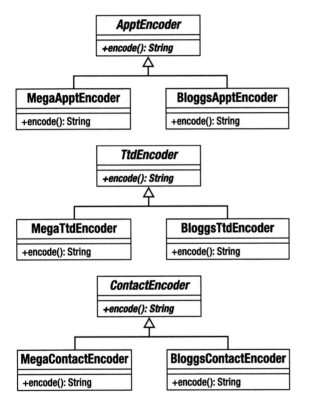

Figure 9-6. *Three product families*

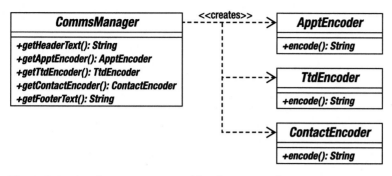

Figure 9-7. *An abstract creator and its abstract products*

Implementation

The abstract CommsManager class defines the interface for generating each of the three products
(ApptEncoder, TtdEncoder, and ContactEncoder). You need to implement a concrete creator in order to
actually generate the concrete products for a particular family. I illustrate that for the BloggsCal format
in Figure 9-8.

Here is a code version of CommsManager and BloggsCommsManager:

```
abstract class CommsManager {
    abstract function getHeaderText();
    abstract function getApptEncoder();
    abstract function getTtdEncoder();
    abstract function getContactEncoder();
    abstract function getFooterText();
}

class BloggsCommsManager extends CommsManager {
    function getHeaderText() {
        return "BloggsCal header\n";
    }

    function getApptEncoder() {
        return new BloggsApptEncoder();
    }

    function getTtdEncoder() {
        return new BloggsTtdEncoder();
    }

    function getContactEncoder() {
        return new BloggsContactEncoder();
    }
```

```
    function getFooterText() {
        return "BloggsCal footer\n";
    }
}
```

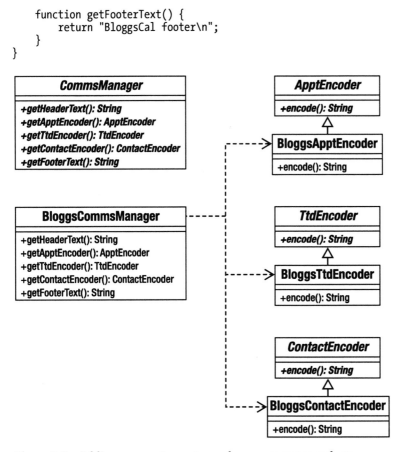

Figure 9-8. *Adding a concrete creator and some concrete products*

Notice that I use the Factory Method pattern in this example. getContact() is abstract in CommsManager and implemented in BloggsCommsManager. Design patterns tend to work together in this way, one pattern creating the context that lends itself to another. In Figure 9-9, I add support for the MegaCal format.

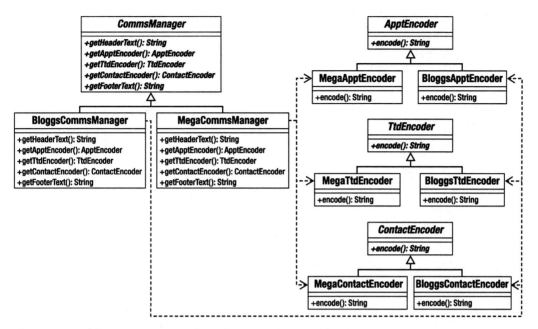

Figure 9-9. *Adding concrete creators and some concrete products*

Consequences

So what does this pattern buy you?

- First, you decouple your system from the details of implementation. I can add or remove any number of encoding formats in my example without causing a knock on effect.

- You enforce the grouping of functionally related elements of your system. So by using BloggsCommsManager, I am guaranteed that I will work only with BloggsCal-related classes.

- Adding new products can be a pain. Not only do I have to create concrete implementations of the new product but also we have to amend the abstract creator and every one of its concrete implementers in order to support it.

Many implementations of the Abstract Factory pattern use the Factory Method pattern. This may be because most examples are written in Java or C++. PHP, however, does not enforce a return type for a method, which affords us some flexibility that we might leverage.

Rather than create separate methods for each Factory Method, you can create a single make() method that uses a flag argument to determine which object to return:

```
abstract class CommsManager {
    const APPT    = 1;
    const TTD     = 2;
    const CONTACT = 3;
    abstract function getHeaderText();
    abstract function make( $flag_int );
    abstract function getFooterText();
}

class BloggsCommsManager extends CommsManager {
    function getHeaderText() {
        return "BloggsCal header\n";
    }
    function make( $flag_int ) {
        switch ( $flag_int ) {
            case self::APPT:
                return new BloggsApptEncoder();
            case self::CONTACT:
                return new BloggsContactEncoder();
            case self::TTD:
                return new BloggsTtdEncoder();
        }
    }

    function getFooterText() {
        return "BloggsCal footer\n";
    }
}
```

As you can see, I have made the class interface more compact. I've done this at a considerable cost, though. In using a factory method, you define a clear interface and force all concrete factory objects to honor it. In using a single make() method, I must remember to support all product objects in all the concrete creators. I also introduce parallel conditionals, as each concrete creator must implement the same flag tests. A client class cannot be certain that concrete creators generate all the products because the internals of make() are a matter of choice in each case.

On the other hand, you can build more flexible creators. The base creator class can provide a make() method that guarantees a default implementation of each product family. Concrete children could then modify this behavior selectively. It would be up to implementing creator classes to call the default make() method after providing their own implementation.

You will see another variation on the Abstract Factory pattern in the next section.

Prototype

The emergence of parallel inheritance hierarchies can be a problem with the Factory Method pattern. This is a kind of coupling that makes some programmers uncomfortable. Every time you add a product family, you are forced to create an associated concrete creator (the BloggsCal encoders are matched by BloggsCommsManager, for example). In a system that grows fast to encompass many products, maintaining this kind of relationship can quickly become tiresome.

One way of avoiding this dependency is to use PHP's clone keyword to duplicate existing concrete products. The concrete product classes themselves then become the basis of their own generation. This is the Prototype pattern. It enables you to replace inheritance with composition. This in turn promotes runtime flexibility and reduces the number of classes you must create.

The Problem

Imagine a Civilization-style web game in which units operate on a grid of tiles. Each tile can represent sea, plains, or forests. The terrain type constrains the movement and combat abilities of units occupying the tile. You might have a TerrainFactory object that serves up Sea, Forest, and Plains objects. You decide that you will allow the user to choose among radically different environments, so the Sea object is an abstract superclass implemented by MarsSea and EarthSea. Forest and Plains objects are similarly implemented. The forces here lend themselves to the Abstract Factory pattern. You have distinct product hierarchies (Sea, Plains, Forests), with strong family relationships cutting across inheritance (Earth, Mars). Figure 9-10 presents a class diagram that shows how you might deploy the Abstract Factory and Factory Method patterns to work with these products.

As you can see, I rely on inheritance to group the terrain family for the products that a factory will generate. This is a workable solution, but it requires a large inheritance hierarchy, and it is relatively inflexible. When you do not want parallel inheritance hierarchies, and when you need to maximize runtime flexibility, the Prototype pattern can be used in a powerful variation on the Abstract Factory pattern.

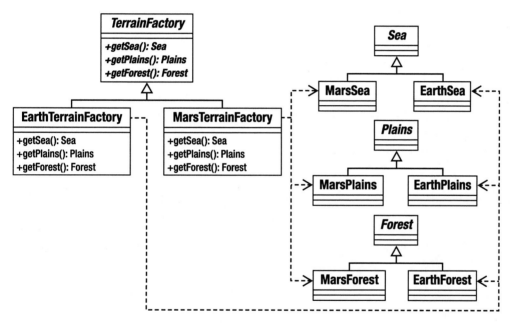

Figure 9-10. *Handling terrains with the Abstract Factory method*

Implementation

When you work with the Abstract Factory/Factory Method patterns, you must decide, at some point, which concrete creator we wish to work with, probably by checking some kind of preference flag. Since you must do this anyway, why not simply create a factory class that stores concrete products, and populate this during initialization? You can cut down on a couple of classes this way and, as you shall see, take advantage of other benefits. Here's some simple code that uses the Prototype pattern in a factory:

```
class Sea {}
class EarthSea extends Sea {}
class MarsSea extends Sea {}

class Plains {}
class EarthPlains extends Plains {}
class MarsPlains extends Plains {}

class Forest {}
class EarthForest extends Forest {}
class MarsForest extends Forest {}

class TerrainFactory {
    private $sea;
    private $forest;
    private $plains;

    function __construct( Sea $sea, Plains $plains, Forest $forest ) {
        $this->sea = $sea;
        $this->plains = $plains;
        $this->forest = $forest;
    }

    function getSea( ) {
        return clone $this->sea;
    }

    function getPlains( ) {
        return clone $this->plains;
    }

    function getForest( ) {
        return clone $this->forest;
    }
}

$factory = new TerrainFactory( new EarthSea(),
    new EarthPlains(),
    new EarthForest() );
print_r( $factory->getSea() );
print_r( $factory->getPlains() );
print_r( $factory->getForest() );
```

As you can see, I load up a concrete TerrainFactory with instances of product objects. When a client calls getSea(), I return a clone of the Sea object that I cached during initialization. Not only have I saved a couple of classes but I have bought additional flexibility. Want to play a game on a new planet with Earth-like seas and forests, but Mars-like plains? No need to write a new creator class—you can simply change the mix of classes you add to TerrainFactory:

```
$factory = new TerrainFactory( new EarthSea(),
    new MarsPlains(),
    new EarthForest() );
```

So the Prototype pattern allows you to take advantage of the flexibility afforded by composition. We get more than that, though. Because you are storing and cloning objects at runtime, you reproduce object state when you generate new products. Imagine that Sea objects have a $navigability property. The property influences the amount of movement energy a sea tile saps from a vessel and can be set to adjust the difficulty level of a game:

```
class Sea {
    private $navigability = 0;
    function __construct( $navigability ) {
        $this->navigability = $navigability;
    }
}
```

Now, when I initialize the TerrainFactory object, I can add a Sea object with a navigability modifier. This will then hold true for all Sea objects served by TerrainFactory:

```
$factory = new TerrainFactory( new EarthSea( -1 ),
    new EarthPlains(),
    new EarthForest() );
```

This flexibility is also apparent when the object you wish to generate is composed of other objects. Perhaps all Sea objects can contain Resource objects (FishResource, OilResource, etc.). According to a preference flag, we might give all Sea objects a FishResource by default. Remember that if your products reference other objects, you should implement a __clone() method in order to ensure that you make a deep copy.

Note I covered object cloning in Chapter 4. The clone keyword generates a shallow copy of any object to which it is applied. This means that the product object will have the same properties as the source. If any of the source's properties are objects, then these will not be copied into the product. Instead, the product will reference the *same* object properties. It is up to you to change this default and to customize object copying in any other way, by implementing a __clone() method. This is called automatically when the clone keyword is used.

```
class Contained { }

class Container {
    public $contained;
    function __construct() {
        $this->contained = new Contained();
    }

    function __clone() {
        // Ensure that cloned object holds a
        // clone of self::$contained and not
        // a reference to it
        $this->contained = clone $this->contained;
    }
}
```

But That's Cheating!

I promised that this chapter would deal with the logic of object creation, doing away with the sneaky buck-passing of many object-oriented examples. Yet some patterns here have slyly dodged the decision-making part of object creation, if not the creation itself.

The Singleton pattern is not guilty. The logic for object creation is built in and unambiguous. The Abstract Factory pattern groups the creation of product families into distinct concrete creators. How do we decide which concrete creator to use though? The Prototype pattern presents us with a similar problem. Both these patterns handle the creation of objects, but they defer the decision as to which object, or group of objects, should be created.

The particular concrete creator that a system chooses is often decided according to the value of a configuration switch of some kind. This could be located in a database, a configuration file, or a server file (such as Apache's directory-level configuration file, usually called .htaccess), or it could even be hard-coded as a PHP variable or property. Because PHP applications must be reconfigured for every request, you need script initialization to be as painless as possible. For this reason, I often opt to hard-code configuration flags in PHP code. This can be done by hand or by writing a script that autogenerates a class file. Here's a crude class that includes a flag for calendar protocol types:

```
class Settings {
    static $COMMSTYPE = 'Bloggs';
}
```

Now that I have a flag (however inelegant), I can create a class that uses it to decide which CommsManager to serve on request. It is quite common to see a Singleton used in conjunction with the Abstract Factory pattern, so let's do that:

```
require_once( 'Settings.php' );

class AppConfig {
    private static $instance;
    private $commsManager;

    private function __construct() {
        // will run once only
        $this->init();
    }

    private function init() {
        switch ( Settings::$COMMSTYPE ) {
            case 'Mega':
                $this->commsManager = new MegaCommsManager();
                break;
            default:
                $this->commsManager = new BloggsCommsManager();
        }
    }

    public static function getInstance() {
        if ( empty( self::$instance ) ) {
            self::$instance = new self();
        }
        return self::$instance;
    }
```

```
    public function getCommsManager() {
        return $this->commsManager;
    }
}
```

The `AppConfig` class is a standard Singleton. For that reason, I can get an `AppConfig` instance anywhere in our system, and I will always get the same one. The `init()` method is invoked by the class's constructor and is therefore only run once in a process. It tests the `Settings::$COMMSTYPE` property, instantiating a concrete `CommsManager` object according to its value. Now my script can get a `CommsManager` object and work with it without ever knowing about its concrete implementations or the concrete classes it generates:

```
$commsMgr = AppConfig::getInstance()->getCommsManager();
$commsMgr->getApptEncoder()->encode();
```

Summary

This chapter covered some of the tricks you can use to generate objects. I examined the Singleton pattern, which provides global access to a single instance. I looked at the Factory Method pattern, which applies the principle of polymorphism to object generation. I combined Factory Method with the Abstract Factory pattern to generate creator classes that instantiate sets of related objects. Finally, I looked at the Prototype pattern and saw how object cloning can allow composition to be used in object generation.

■ ■ ■

CHAPTER 10

Patterns for Flexible Object Programming

With strategies for generating objects covered, we're free now to look at some strategies for structuring classes and objects. I will focus in particular on the principle that composition provides greater flexibility than inheritance. The patterns I examine in this chapter are once again drawn from the Gang of Four catalog.

This chapter will cover

- *The Composite pattern*: Composing structures in which groups of objects can be used as if they were individual objects

- *The Decorator pattern*: A flexible mechanism for combining objects at runtime to extend functionality

- *The Facade pattern*: Creating a simple interface to complex or variable systems

Structuring Classes to Allow Flexible Objects

Way back in Chapter 4, I said that beginners often confuse objects and classes. This was only half true. In fact, most of the rest of us occasionally scratch our heads over UML class diagrams, attempting to reconcile the static inheritance structures they show with the dynamic object relationships their objects will enter into off the page.

Remember the pattern principle "Favor composition over inheritance"? This principle distills this tension between the organization of classes and of objects. In order to build flexibility into our projects, we structure our classes so that their objects can be composed into useful structures at runtime.

This is a common theme running through the first two patterns of this chapter. Inheritance is an important feature in both, but part of its importance lies in providing the mechanism by which composition can be used to represent structures and extend functionality.

The Composite Pattern

The Composite pattern is perhaps the most extreme example of inheritance deployed in the service of composition. It is a simple and yet breathtakingly elegant design. It is also fantastically useful. Be warned, though, it is so neat, you might be tempted to overuse this strategy.

The Composite pattern is a simple way of aggregating and then managing groups of similar objects so that an individual object is indistinguishable to a client from a collection of objects. The pattern is, in fact, very simple, but it is also often confusing. One reason for this is the similarity in structure of the classes in the pattern to the organization of its objects. Inheritance hierarchies are trees, beginning with the super class at the root, and branching out into specialized subclasses. The inheritance tree of *classes* laid down by the Composite pattern is designed to allow the easy generation and traversal of a tree of *objects*.

If you are not already familiar with this pattern, you have every right to feel confused at this point. Let's try an analogy to illustrate the way that single entities can be treated in the same way as collections of things. Given broadly irreducible ingredients such as cereals and meat (or soya if you prefer), we can make a food product—a sausage, for example. We then act on the result as a single entity. Just as we eat, cook, buy, or sell meat, we can eat, cook, buy, or sell the sausage that the meat in part composes. We might take the sausage and combine it with the other composite ingredients to make a pie, thereby rolling a composite into a larger composite. We behave in the same way to the collection as we do to the parts. The Composite pattern helps us to model this relationship between collections and components in our code.

The Problem

Managing groups of objects can be quite a complex task, especially if the objects in question might also contain objects of their own. This kind of problem is very common in coding. Think of invoices, with line items that summarize additional products or services, or things-to-do lists with items that themselves contain multiple subtasks. In content management, we can't move for trees of sections, pages, articles, media components. Managing these structures from the outside can quickly become daunting.

Let's return to a previous scenario. I am designing a system based on a game called Civilization. A player can move units around hundreds of tiles that make up a map. Individual counters can be grouped together to move, fight, and defend themselves as a unit. Here I define a couple of unit types:

```
abstract class Unit {
    abstract function bombardStrength();
}

class Archer extends Unit {
    function bombardStrength() {
        return 4;
    }
}

class LaserCannonUnit extends Unit {
    function bombardStrength() {
        return 44;
    }
}
```

The Unit class defines an abstract bombardStrength() method, which sets the attack strength of a unit bombarding an adjacent tile. I implement this in both the Archer and LaserCannonUnit classes. These classes would also contain information about movement and defensive capabilities, but I'll keep things simple. I could define a separate class to group units together like this:

```
class Army {
    private $units = array();

    function addUnit( Unit $unit ) {
        array_push( $this->units, $unit );
    }
```

```
function bombardStrength() {
    $ret = 0;
    foreach( $this->units as $unit ) {
        $ret += $unit->bombardStrength();
    }
    return $ret;
}
}
```

The Army class has an addUnit() method that accepts a Unit object. Unit objects are stored in an array property called $units. I calculate the combined strength of my army in the bombardStrength() method. This simply iterates through the aggregated Unit objects, calling the bombardStrength() method of each one.

This model is perfectly acceptable as long as the problem remains as simple as this. What happens, though, if I were to add some new requirements? Let's say that an army should be able to combine with other armies. Each army should retain its own identity so that it can disentangle itself from the whole at a later date. The ArchDuke's brave forces may have common cause today with General Soames' push toward the exposed flank of the enemy, but a domestic rebellion may send his army scurrying home at any time. For this reason, I can't just decant the units from each army into a new force.

I could amend the Army class to accept Army objects as well as Unit objects:

```
function addArmy( Army $army ) {
    array_push( $this->armies, $army );
}
```

Then I'd need to amend the bombardStrength() method to iterate through all armies as well as units:

```
function bombardStrength() {
    $ret = 0;
    foreach( $this->units as $unit ) {
        $ret += $unit->bombardStrength();
    }

    foreach( $this->armies as $army ) {
        $ret += $army->bombardStrength();
    }

    return $ret;
}
```

This additional complexity is not too problematic at the moment. Remember, though, I would need to do something similar in methods like defensiveStrength(), movementRange(), and so on. My game is going to be richly featured. Already the business group is calling for troop carriers that can hold up to ten units to improve their movement range on certain terrains. Clearly, a troop carrier is similar to an army in that it groups units. It also has its own characteristics. I could further amend the Army class to handle TroopCarrier objects, but I know that there will be a need for still more unit groupings. It is clear that I need a more flexible model.

Let's look again at the model I have been building. All the classes I created shared the need for a bombardStrength() method. In effect, a client does not need to distinguish between an army, a unit, or a troop carrier. They are functionally identical. They need to move, attack, and defend. Those objects that contain others need to provide methods for adding and removing. These similarities lead us to an inevitable conclusion. Because container objects share an interface with the objects that they contain, they are naturally suited to share a type family.

Implementation

The Composite pattern defines a single inheritance hierarchy that lays down two distinct sets of responsibilities. We have already seen both of these in our example. Classes in the pattern must support a common set of operations as their primary responsibility. For us, that means the bombardStrength() method. Classes must also support methods for adding and removing child objects.

Figure 10–1 shows a class diagram that illustrates the Composite pattern as applied to our problem.

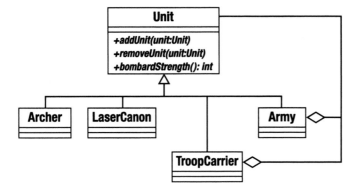

Figure 10–1. *The Composite pattern*

As you can see, all the units in this model extend the Unit class. A client can be sure, then, that any Unit object will support the bombardStrength() method. So an Army can be treated in exactly the same way as an Archer.

The Army and TroopCarrier classes are *composites*: designed to hold Unit objects. The Archer and LaserCannon classes are *leaves*, designed to support unit operations but not to hold other Unit objects. There is actually an issue as to whether leaves should honor the same interface as composites as they do in Figure 1. The diagram shows TroopCarrier and Army aggregating other units, even though the leaf classes are also bound to implement addUnit(), I will return to this question shortly. Here is the abstract Unit class:

```
abstract class Unit {
    abstract function addUnit( Unit $unit );
    abstract function removeUnit( Unit $unit );
    abstract function bombardStrength();
}
```

As you can see, I lay down the basic functionality for all Unit objects here. Now, let's see how a composite object might implement these abstract methods:

```
class Army extends Unit {
    private $units = array();

        function addUnit( Unit $unit ) {
        if ( in_array( $unit, $this->units, true ) ) {
            return;
        }
        $this->units[] = $unit;
    }
```

```php
    function removeUnit( Unit $unit ) {

        $this->units = array_udiff( $this->units, array( $unit ),

                        function( $a, $b ) { return ($a === $b)?0:1; } );

    }


    function bombardStrength() {
        $ret = 0;
        foreach( $this->units as $unit ) {
            $ret += $unit->bombardStrength();
        }
        return $ret;
    }
}
```

The addUnit() method checks that I have not yet added the same Unit object before storing it in the private $units array property. removeUnit() uses a similar check to remove a given Unit object from the property.

▪**Note** I use an anonymous callback function in the removeUnit() method. This checks the array elements in the $units property for equivalence. Anonymous functions were introduced in PHP 5.3. If you're running an older version of PHP, you can use the create_function() method to get a similar effect:

```php
        $this->units = array_udiff( $this->units, array( $unit ),
                        create_function( '$a,$b', 'return ($a === $b)?0:1;' ) );
```

Army objects, then, can store Units of any kind, including other Army objects, or leaves such as Archer or LaserCannonUnit. Because all units are guaranteed to support bombardStrength(), our Army::bombardStrength() method simply iterates through all the child Unit objects stored in the $units property, calling the same method on each.

One problematic aspect of the Composite pattern is the implementation of add and remove functionality. The classic pattern places add() and remove() methods in the abstract super class. This ensures that all classes in the pattern share a common interface. As you can see here, though, it also means that leaf classes must provide an implementation:

```php
class UnitException extends Exception {}

class Archer extends Unit {
    function addUnit( Unit $unit ) {
        throw new UnitException( get_class($this)." is a leaf" );
    }

    function removeUnit( Unit $unit ) {
        throw new UnitException( get_class($this)." is a leaf" );
    }
```

```
    function bombardStrength() {
        return 4;
    }
}
```

I do not want to make it possible to add a Unit object to an Archer object, so I throw exceptions if addUnit() or removeUnit() are called. I will need to do this for all leaf objects, so I could perhaps improve my design by replacing the abstract addUnit()/removeUnit() methods in Unit with default implementations like the one in the preceding example.

```
abstract class Unit {
    abstract function bombardStrength();

    function addUnit( Unit $unit ) {
        throw new UnitException( get_class($this)." is a leaf" );
    }

    function removeUnit( Unit $unit ) {
        throw new UnitException( get_class($this)." is a leaf" );
    }
}

class Archer extends Unit {
    function bombardStrength() {
        return 4;
    }
}
```

This removes duplication in leaf classes but has the drawback that a Composite is not forced at compile time to provide an implementation of addUnit() and removeUnit(), which could cause problems down the line.

I will look in more detail at some of the problems presented by the Composite pattern in the next section. Let's end this section by examining of some of its benefits.

- *Flexibility*: Because everything in the Composite pattern shares a common supertype, it is very easy to add new composite or leaf objects to the design without changing a program's wider context.

- *Simplicity*: A client using a Composite structure has a straightforward interface. There is no need for a client to distinguish between an object that is composed of others and a leaf object (except when adding new components). A call to Army::bombardStrength() may cause a cascade of delegated calls behind the scenes, but to the client, the process and result are exactly equivalent to those associated with calling Archer::bombardStrength().

- *Implicit reach*: Objects in the Composite pattern are organized in a tree. Each composite holds references to its children. An operation on a particular part of the tree, therefore, can have a wide effect. We might remove a single Army object from its Army parent and add it to another. This simple act is wrought on one object, but it has the effect of changing the status of the Army object's referenced Unit objects and of their own children.

- *Explicit reach*: Tree structures are easy to traverse. They can be iterated through in order to gain information or to perform transformations. We will look at a particularly powerful technique for this in the next chapter when we deal with the Visitor pattern.

Often you really see the benefit of a pattern only from the client's perspective, so here are a couple of armies:

```
// create an army
$main_army = new Army();

// add some units
$main_army->addUnit( new Archer() );
$main_army->addUnit( new LaserCannonUnit() );

// create a new army
$sub_army = new Army();

// add some units
$sub_army->addUnit( new Archer() );
$sub_army->addUnit( new Archer() );
$sub_army->addUnit( new Archer() );

// add the second army to the first
$main_army->addUnit( $sub_army );

// all the calculations handled behind the scenes
print "attacking with strength: {$main_army->bombardStrength()}\n";
```

I create a new Army object and add some primitive Unit objects. I repeat the process for a second Army object that I then add to the first. When I call Unit::bombardStrength() on the first Army object, all the complexity of the structure that I have built up is entirely hidden.

Consequences

If you're anything like me, you would have heard alarm bells ringing when you saw the code extract for the Archer class. Why do we put up with these redundant addUnit() and removeUnit() methods in leaf classes that do not need to support them? An answer of sorts lies in the transparency of the Unit type.

If a client is passed a Unit object, it knows that the addUnit() method will be present. The Composite pattern principle that primitive (leaf) classes have the same interface as composites is upheld. This does not actually help you much, because you still do not know how safe you might be calling addUnit() on any Unit object you might come across.

If I move these add/remove methods down so that they are available only to composite classes, then passing a Unit object to a method leaves me with the problem that I do not know by default whether or not it supports addUnit(). Nevertheless, leaving booby-trapped methods lying around in leaf classes makes me uncomfortable. It adds no value and confuses a system's design, because the interface effectively lies about its own functionality.

You can split composite classes off into their own CompositeUnit subtype quite easily. First of all, I excise the add/remove behavior from Unit:

```
abstract class Unit {
    function getComposite() {
        return null;
    }

    abstract function bombardStrength();
}
```

Notice the new getComposite() method. I will return to this in a little while. Now, I need a new abstract class to hold addUnit() and removeUnit(). I can even provide default implementations:

```
abstract class CompositeUnit extends Unit {
    private $units = array();

    function getComposite() {
        return $this;
    }

    protected function units() {
        return $this->units;
    }

    function removeUnit( Unit $unit ) {
                $this->units = array_udiff( $this->units, array( $unit ),

                        function( $a, $b ) { return ($a === $b)?0:1; } );

    }

    function addUnit( Unit $unit ) {
        if ( in_array( $unit, $this->units, true ) ) {
            return;
        }
        $this->units[] = $unit;
    }
}
```

The CompositeUnit class is declared abstract, even though it does not itself declare an abstract method. It does, however, extend Unit, and does not implement the abstract bombardStrength() method. Army (and any other composite classes) can now extend CompositeUnit. The classes in my example are now organized as in Figure 10–2.

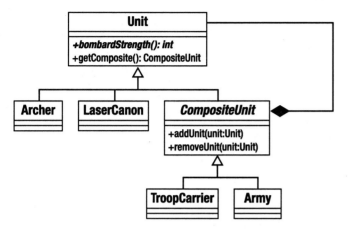

Figure 10–2. *Moving add/remove methods out of the base class*

The annoying, useless implementations of add/remove methods in the leaf classes are gone, but the client must still check to see whether it has a CompositeUnit before it can use addUnit().

This is where the getComposite() method comes into its own. By default, this method returns a null value. Only in a CompositeUnit class does it return CompositeUnit. So if a call to this method returns an object, we should be able to call addUnit() on it. Here's a client that uses this technique:

```
class UnitScript {
    static function joinExisting( Unit $newUnit,
                                  Unit $occupyingUnit ) {
        $comp;

        if ( ! is_null( $comp = $occupyingUnit->getComposite() ) ) {
            $comp->addUnit( $newUnit );
        } else {
            $comp = new Army();
            $comp->addUnit( $occupyingUnit );
            $comp->addUnit( $newUnit );
        }
        return $comp;
    }
}
```

The joinExisting() method accepts two Unit objects. The first is a newcomer to a tile, and the second is a prior occupier. If the second Unit is a CompositeUnit, then the first will attempt to join it. If not, then a new Army will be created to cover both units. I have no way of knowing at first whether the $occupyingUnit argument contains a CompositeUnit. A call to getComposite() settles the matter, though. If getComposite() returns an object, I can add the new Unit object to it directly. If not, I create the new Army object and add both.

I could simplify this model further by having the Unit::getComposite() method return an Army object prepopulated with the current Unit. Or I could return to the previous model (which did not distinguish structurally between composite and leaf objects) and have Unit::addUnit() do the same thing: create an Army object, and add both Unit objects to it. This is neat, but it presupposes that you know in advance the type of composite you would like to use to aggregate your units. Your business logic will determine the kinds of assumptions you can make when you design methods like getComposite() and addUnit().

These contortions are symptomatic of a drawback to the Composite pattern. Simplicity is achieved by ensuring that all classes are derived from a common base. The benefit of simplicity is sometimes bought at a cost to type safety. The more complex your model becomes, the more manual type checking you are likely to have to do. Let's say that I have a Cavalry object. If the rules of the game state that you cannot put a horse on a troop carrier, I have no automatic way of enforcing this with the Composite pattern:

```
class TroopCarrier {

    function addUnit( Unit $unit ) {
        if ( $unit instanceof Cavalry ) {
            throw new UnitException("Can't get a horse on the vehicle");
        }
        super::addUnit( $unit );
    }

    function bombardStrength() {
        return 0;
    }
}
```

I am forced to use the instanceof operator to test the type of the object passed to addUnit(). Too many special cases of this kind, and the drawbacks of the pattern begin to outweigh its benefits. Composite works best when most of the components are interchangeable.

Another issue to bear in mind is the cost of some Composite operations. The Army :: bombardStrength() method is typical in that it sets off a cascade of calls to the same method down the tree. For a large tree with lots of subarmies, a single call can cause an avalanche behind the scenes. bombardStrength() is not itself very expensive, but what would happen if some leaves performed a complex calculation to arrive at their return values? One way around this problem is to cache the result of a method call of this sort in the parent object, so that subsequent invocations are less expensive. You need to be careful, though, to ensure that the cached value does not grow stale. You should devise strategies to wipe any caches whenever any operations take place on the tree. This may require that you give child objects references to their parents.

Finally, a note about persistence. The Composite pattern is elegant, but it doesn't lend itself neatly to storage in a relational database. This is because, by default, you access the entire structure only through a cascade of references. So to construct a Composite structure from a database in the natural way you would have to make multiple expensive queries. You can get round this problem by assigning an ID to the whole tree, so that all components can be drawn from the database in one go. Having acquired all the objects, however, you would still have the task of recreating the parent/child references which themselves would have to be stored in the database. This is not difficult, but it is somewhat messy.

While Composites sit uneasily with relational databases, they lend themselves very well indeed to storage in XML. This is because XML elements are often themselves composed of trees of subelements.

Composite in Summary

So the Composite pattern is useful when you need to treat a collection of things in the same way as you would an individual, either because the collection is intrinsically like a component (armies and archers), or because the context gives the collection the same characteristics as the component (line items in an invoice). Composites are arranged in trees, so an operation on the whole can affect the parts, and data from the parts is transparently available via the whole. The Composite pattern makes such operations and queries transparent to the client. Trees are easy to traverse (as we shall see in the next chapter). It is easy to add new component types to Composite structures.

On the downside, Composites rely on the similarity of their parts. As soon as we introduce complex rules as to which composite object can hold which set of components, our code can become hard to manage. Composites do not lend themselves well to storage in relational databases but are well suited to XML persistence.

The Decorator Pattern

While the Composite pattern helps us to create a flexible representation of aggregated components, the Decorator pattern uses a similar structure to help us to modify the functionality of concrete components. Once again, the key to this pattern lies in the importance of composition at runtime. Inheritance is a neat way of building on characteristics laid down by a parent class. This neatness can lead you to hard-code variation into your inheritance hierarchies, often causing inflexibility.

The Problem

Building all your functionality into an inheritance structure can result in an explosion of classes in a system. Even worse, as you try to apply similar modifications to different branches of your inheritance tree, you are likely to see duplication emerge.

Let's return to our game. Here, I define a `Tile` class and a derived type:

```
abstract class Tile {
    abstract function getWealthFactor();
}

class Plains extends Tile {
    private $wealthfactor = 2;
    function getWealthFactor() {
        return $this->wealthfactor;
    }
}
```

I define a `Tile` class. This represents a square on which my units might be found. Each tile has certain characteristics. In this example, I have defined a getWealthFactor() method that affects the revenue a particular square might generate if owned by a player. As you can see, `Plains` objects have a wealth factor of 2. Obviously, tiles manage other data. They might also hold a reference to image information so that the board could be drawn. Once again, I'll keep things simple here.

I need to modify the behavior of the `Plains` object to handle the effects of natural resources and human abuse. I wish to model the occurrence of diamonds on the landscape, and the damage caused by pollution. One approach might be to inherit from the `Plains` object:

```
class DiamondPlains extends Plains {
    function getWealthFactor() {
        return parent::getWealthFactor() + 2;
    }
}

class PollutedPlains extends Plains {
    function getWealthFactor() {
        return parent::getWealthFactor() - 4;
    }
}
```

I can now acquire a polluted tile very easily:

```
$tile = new PollutedPlains();
print $tile->getWealthFactor();
```

You can see the class diagram for this example in Figure 10–3.

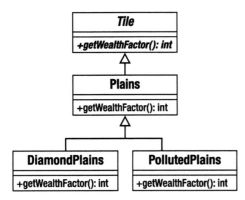

Figure 10–3. *Building variation into an inheritance tree*

This structure is obviously inflexible. I can get plains with diamonds. I can get polluted plains. But can I get them both? Clearly not, unless I am willing to perpetrate the horror that is PollutedDiamondPlains. This situation can only get worse when I introduce the Forest class, which can also have diamonds and pollution.

This is an extreme example, of course, but the point is made. Relying entirely on inheritance to define your functionality can lead to a multiplicity of classes and a tendency toward duplication.

Let's take a more commonplace example at this point. Serious web applications often have to perform a range of actions on a request before a task is initiated to form a response. You might need to authenticate the user, for example, and to log the request. Perhaps you should process the request to build a data structure from raw input. Finally, you must perform your core processing. You are presented with the same problem.

You can extend the functionality of a base ProcessRequest class with additional processing in a derived LogRequest class, in a StructureRequest class, and in an AuthenticateRequest class. You can see this class hierarchy in Figure 10–4.

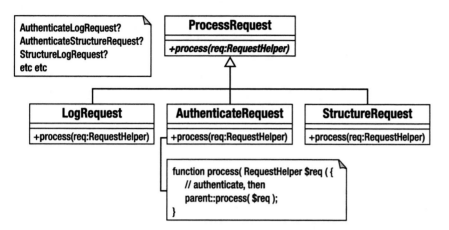

Figure 10-4. *More hard-coded variations*

What happens, though, when you need to perform logging and authentication but not data preparation? Do you create a LogAndAuthenticateProcessor class? Clearly, it is time to find a more flexible solution.

Implementation

Rather than use only inheritance to solve the problem of varying functionality, the Decorator pattern uses composition and delegation. In essence, Decorator classes hold an instance of another class of their own type. A Decorator will implement an operation so that it calls the same operation on the object to which it has a reference before (or after) performing its own actions. In this way it is possible to build a pipeline of decorator objects at runtime.

Let's rewrite our game example to illustrate this:

```
abstract class Tile {
    abstract function getWealthFactor();
}

class Plains extends Tile {
    private $wealthfactor = 2;
    function getWealthFactor() {
        return $this->wealthfactor;
    }
}

abstract class TileDecorator extends Tile {
    protected $tile;
    function __construct( Tile $tile ) {
        $this->tile = $tile;
    }
}
```

Here, I have declared Tile and Plains classes as before but introduced a new class: TileDecorator. This does not implement getWealthFactor(), so it must be declared abstract. I define a constructor that requires a Tile object, which it stores in a property called $tile. I make this property protected so that child classes can gain access to it. Now I'll redefine the Pollution and Diamond classes:

```
class DiamondDecorator extends TileDecorator {
    function getWealthFactor() {
        return $this->tile->getWealthFactor()+2;
    }
}

class PollutionDecorator extends TileDecorator {
    function getWealthFactor() {
        return $this->tile->getWealthFactor()-4;
    }
}
```

Each of these classes extends TileDecorator. This means that they have a reference to a Tile object. When getWealthFactor() is invoked, each of these classes invokes the same method on its Tile reference before making its own adjustment.

By using composition and delegation like this, you make it easy to combine objects at runtime. Because all the objects in the pattern extend Tile, the client does not need to know which combination it is working with. It can be sure that a getWealthFactor() method is available for any Tile object, whether it is decorating another behind the scenes or not.

```
$tile = new Plains();
print $tile->getWealthFactor(); // 2
```

Plains is a component. It simply returns 2

```
$tile = new DiamondDecorator( new Plains() );
print $tile->getWealthFactor(); // 4
```

DiamondDecorator has a reference to a Plains object. It invokes getWealthFactor() before adding its own weighting of 2:

```
$tile = new PollutionDecorator(
            new DiamondDecorator( new Plains() ));
print $tile->getWealthFactor(); // 0
```

PollutionDecorator has a reference to a DiamondDecorator object which has its own Tile reference. You can see the class diagram for this example in Figure 10–5.

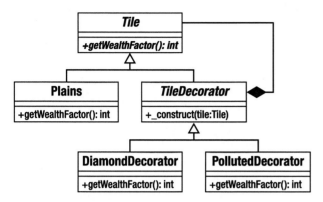

Figure 10–5. *The Decorator pattern*

This model is very extensible. You can add new decorators and components very easily. With lots of decorators you can build very flexible structures at runtime. The component class, Plains in this case, can be significantly modified in very many ways without the need to build the totality of the modifications into the class hierarchy. In plain English, this means you can have a polluted Plains object that has diamonds without having to create a PollutedDiamondPlains object.

The Decorator pattern builds up pipelines that are very useful for creating filters. The Java IO package makes great use of decorator classes. The client coder can combine decorator objects with core components to add filtering, buffering, compression, and so on to core methods like read(). My web request example can also be developed into a configurable pipeline. Here's a simple implementation that uses the Decorator pattern:

```
class RequestHelper{}

abstract class ProcessRequest {
    abstract function process( RequestHelper $req );
}

class MainProcess extends ProcessRequest {
    function process( RequestHelper $req ) {
        print __CLASS__.": doing something useful with request\n";
    }
}

abstract class DecorateProcess extends ProcessRequest {
    protected $processrequest;
    function __construct( ProcessRequest $pr ) {
        $this->processrequest = $pr;
    }
}
```

As before, we define an abstract super class (ProcessRequest), a concrete component (MainProcess), and an abstract decorator (DecorateProcess). MainProcess::process() does nothing but report that it has been called. DecorateProcess stores a ProcessRequest object on behalf of its children. Here are some simple concrete decorator classes:

```
class LogRequest extends DecorateProcess {
    function process( RequestHelper $req ) {
        print __CLASS__.": logging request\n";
        $this->processrequest->process( $req );
    }
}

class AuthenticateRequest extends DecorateProcess {
    function process( RequestHelper $req ) {
        print __CLASS__.": authenticating request\n";
        $this->processrequest->process( $req );
    }
}

class StructureRequest extends DecorateProcess {
    function process( RequestHelper $req ) {
        print __CLASS__.": structuring request data\n";
        $this->processrequest->process( $req );
    }
}
```

Each process() method outputs a message before calling the referenced ProcessRequest object's own process() method. You can now combine objects instantiated from these classes at runtime to build filters that perform different actions on a request, and in different orders. Here's some code to combine objects from all these concrete classes into a single filter:

```
$process = new AuthenticateRequest( new StructureRequest(
                                    new LogRequest (
                                    new MainProcess()
                                    )));
$process->process( new RequestHelper() );
```

This code will give the following output:

```
Authenticate
Request: authenticating request
StructureRequest: structuring request data
LogRequest: logging request
MainProcess: doing something useful with request
```

▨**Note** This example is, in fact, also an instance of an enterprise pattern called Intercepting Filter. Intercepting Filter is described in *Core J2EE Patterns*.

Consequences

Like the Composite pattern, Decorator can be confusing. It is important to remember that both composition and inheritance are coming into play at the same time. So LogRequest inherits its interface from ProcessRequest, but it is acting as a wrapper around another ProcessRequest object.

Because a decorator object forms a wrapper around a child object, it helps to keep the interface as sparse as possible. If you build a heavily featured base class, then decorators are forced to delegate to all public methods in their contained object. This can be done in the abstract decorator class but still introduces the kind of coupling that can lead to bugs.

Some programmers create decorators that do not share a common type with the objects they modify. As long as they fulfill the same interface as these objects, this strategy can work well. You get the benefit of being able to use the built-in interceptor methods to automate delegation (implementing __call() to catch calls to nonexistent methods and invoking the same method on the child object automatically). However, by doing this you also lose the safety afforded by class type checking. In our examples so far, client code can demand a Tile or a ProcessRequest object in its argument list and be certain of its interface, whether or not the object in question is heavily decorated.

The Facade Pattern

You may have had occasion to stitch third-party systems into your own projects in the past. Whether or not the code is object oriented, it will often be daunting, large, and complex. Your own code, too, may become a challenge to the client programmer who needs only to access a few features. The Facade pattern is a way of providing a simple, clear interface to complex systems.

The Problem

Systems tend to evolve large amounts of code that is really only useful within the system itself. Just as classes define clear public interfaces and hide their guts away from the rest of the world, so should well-designed systems. However, it is not always clear which parts of a system are designed to be used by client code and which are best hidden.

As you work with subsystems (like web forums or gallery applications), you may find yourself making calls deep into the logic of the code. If the subsystem code is subject to change over time, and your code interacts with it at many different points, you may find yourself with a serious maintenance problem as the subsystem evolves.

Similarly, when you build your own systems, it is a good idea to organize distinct parts into separate tiers. Typically, you may have a tier responsible for application logic, another for database interaction, another for presentation, and so on. You should aspire to keep these tiers as independent of one another as you can, so that a change in one area of your project will have minimal repercussions elsewhere. If code from one tier is tightly integrated into code from another, then this objective is hard to meet.

Here is some deliberately confusing procedural code that makes a song-and-dance routine of the simple process of getting log information from a file and turning it into object data:

```
function getProductFileLines( $file ) {
    return file( $file );
}

function getProductObjectFromId( $id, $productname ) {
    // some kind of database lookup
    return new Product( $id, $productname );
}
```

```php
function getNameFromLine( $line ) {
    if ( preg_match( "/.*-(.*)\s\d+/", $line, $array ) ) {
        return str_replace( '_',' ', $array[1] );
    }
    return '';
}

function getIDFromLine( $line ) {
    if ( preg_match( "/^(\d{1,3})-/", $line, $array ) ) {
        return $array[1];
    }
    return -1;
}

class Product {
    public $id;
    public $name;
    function __construct( $id, $name ) {
        $this->id = $id;
        $this->name = $name;
    }
}
```

Let's imagine that the internals of this code to be more complicated than they actually are, and that I am stuck with using it rather than rewriting it from scratch. In order to turn a file that contains lines like

```
234-ladies_jumper 55
532-gents_hat 44
```

into an array of objects, I must call all of these functions (note that for the sake of brevity I don't extract the final number, which represents a price):

```php
$lines = getProductFileLines( 'test.txt' );
$objects = array();
foreach ( $lines as $line ) {
    $id = getIDFromLine( $line );
    $name = getNameFromLine( $line );
    $objects[$id] = getProductObjectFromID( $id, $name  );
}
```

If I call these functions directly like this throughout my project, my code will become tightly wound into the subsystem it is using. This could cause problems if the subsystem changes or if I decide to switch it out entirely. I really need to introduce a gateway between the system and the rest of our code.

Implementation

Here is a simple class that provides an interface to the procedural code you encountered in the previous section:

```php
class ProductFacade {
    private $products = array();

    function __construct( $file ) {
        $this->file = $file;
        $this->compile();
```

```
    }

    private function compile() {
        $lines = getProductFileLines( $this->file );
        foreach ( $lines as $line ) {
            $id = getIDFromLine( $line );
            $name = getNameFromLine( $line );
            $this->products[$id] = getProductObjectFromID( $id, $name  );
        }
    }

    function getProducts() {
        return $this->products;
    }

    function getProduct( $id ) {
        return $this->products[$id];
    }
}
```

From the point of view of client code, now access to Product objects from a log file is much simplified:

```
$facade = new ProductFacade( 'test.txt' );
$facade->getProduct( 234 );
```

Consequences

A Facade is really a very simple concept. It is just a matter of creating a single point of entry for a tier or subsystem. This has a number of benefits. It helps to decouple distinct areas in a project from one another. It is useful and convenient for client coders to have access to simple methods that achieve clear ends. It reduces errors by focusing use of a subsystem in one place, so changes to the subsystem should cause failure in a predictable location. Errors are also minimized by Facade classes in complex subsystems where client code might otherwise use internal functions incorrectly.

Despite the simplicity of the Facade pattern, it is all too easy to forget to use it, especially if you are familiar with the subsystem you are working with. There is a balance to be struck, of course. On the one hand, the benefit of creating simple interfaces to complex systems should be clear. On the other hand, one could abstract systems with reckless abandon, and then abstract the abstractions. If you are making significant simplifications for the clear benefit of client code, and/or shielding it from systems that might change, then you are probably right to implement the Facade pattern.

Summary

In this chapter, I looked at a few of the ways that classes and objects can be organized in a system. In particular, I focused on the principle that composition can be used to engender flexibility where inheritance fails. In both the Composite and Decorator patterns, inheritance is used to promote composition and to define a common interface that provides guarantees for client code.

You also saw delegation used effectively in these patterns. Finally, I looked at the simple but powerful Facade pattern. Facade is one of those patterns that many people have been using for years without having a name to give it. Facade lets you provide a clean point of entry to a tier or subsystem. In PHP, the Facade pattern is also used to create object wrappers that encapsulate blocks of procedural code.

CHAPTER 11

■ ■ ■

Performing and Representing Tasks

In this chapter, we get active. I look at patterns that help you to get things done, whether interpreting a minilanguage or encapsulating an algorithm.

This chapter will cover

- *The Interpreter pattern*: Building a minilanguage interpreter that can be used to create scriptable applications

- *The Strategy pattern*: Identifying algorithms in a system and encapsulating them into their own types

- *The Observer pattern*: Creating hooks for alerting disparate objects about system events

- *The Visitor pattern*: Applying an operation to all the nodes in a tree of objects

- *The Command pattern*: Creating command objects that can be saved and passed around

The Interpreter Pattern

Languages are written in other languages (at least at first). PHP itself, for example, is written in C. By the same token, odd as it may sound, you can define and run your own languages using PHP. Of course, any language you might create will be slow and somewhat limited. Nonetheless, minilanguages can be very useful, as you will see in this chapter.

The Problem

When you create web (or command line) interfaces in PHP, you give the user access to functionality. The trade-off in interface design is between power and ease of use. As a rule, the more power you give your user, the more cluttered and confusing your interface becomes. Good interface design can help a lot here, of course, but if 90 percent of users are using the same 30 percent of your features, the costs of piling on the functionality may outweigh the benefits. You may wish to consider simplifying your system for most users. But what of the power users, that 10 percent who use your system's advanced features? Perhaps you can accommodate them in a different way. By offering such users a domain language (often called a DSL—Domain Specific Language), you might actually extend the power of your application.

Of course, you have a programming language at hand right away. It's called PHP. Here's how you could allow your users to script your system:

```
$form_input = $_REQUEST['form_input'];
// contains: "print file_get_contents('/etc/passwd');"
eval( $form_input );
```

This approach to making an application scriptable is clearly insane. Just in case the reasons are not blatantly obvious, they boil down to two issues: security and complexity. The security issue is well addressed in the example. By allowing users to execute PHP via your script, you are effectively giving them access to the server the script runs on. The complexity issue is just as big a drawback. No matter how clear your code is, the average user is unlikely to extend it easily and certainly not from the browser window.

A minilanguage, though, can address both these problems. You can design flexibility into the language, reduce the possibility that the user can do damage, and keep things focused.

Imagine an application for authoring quizzes. Producers design questions and establish rules for marking the answers submitted by contestants. It is a requirement that quizzes must be marked without human intervention, even though some answers can be typed into a text field by users.

Here's a question:

```
How many members in the Design Patterns gang?
```

You can accept "four" or "4" as correct answers. You might create a web interface that allows a producer to use regular expression for marking responses:

```
^4|four$
```

Most producers are not hired for their knowledge of regular expressions, however. To make everyone's life easier, you might implement a more user-friendly mechanism for marking responses:

```
$input equals "4" or $input equals "four"
```

You propose a language that supports variables, an operator called equals and Boolean logic (or and and). Programmers love naming things, so let's call it MarkLogic. It should be easy to extend, as you envisage lots of requests for richer features. Let's leave aside the issue of parsing input for now and concentrate on a mechanism for plugging these elements together at runtime to produce an answer. This, as you might expect, is where the Interpreter pattern comes in.

Implementation

A language is made up of expressions (that is, things that resolve to a value). As you can see in Table 11-1, even a tiny language like MarkLogic needs to keep track of a lot of elements.

Table 11–1. *Elements of the MarkLogic Grammar*

Description	EBNF Name	Class Name	Example
Variable	variable	VariableExpression	$input
String literal	<stringLiteral>	LiteralExpression	"four"
Boolean and	indexer	BooleanAndExpression	-$input equals '4' and $other equals '6'
Boolean or	orExpr	BooleanOrExpression	-$input equals '4' or $other equals '6'
Equality test	equalsExpr	EqualsExpression	$input equals '4'

Table 11–1 lists EBNF names. So what is EBNF all about? It's a notation that you can use to describe a language grammar. EBNF stands for Extended Backus-Naur Form. It consists of a series of lines (called productions), each one consisting of a name and a description that takes the form of references to other productions and to terminals (that is, elements that are not themselves made up of references to other productions). Here is one way of describing my grammar using EBNF:

```
expr     ::= operand (orExpr | andExpr )*
operand  ::= ( '(' expr ')' | <stringLiteral> | variable ) ( eqExpr )*
orExpr   ::= 'or' operand
andExpr  ::= 'and' operand
eqExpr   ::= 'equals' operand
variable ::= '$' <word>
```

Some symbols have special meanings (that should be familiar from regular expression notation): * means zero or more, for example, and | means or. You can group elements using brackets. So in the example, an expression (expr) consists of an operand followed by zero or more of either orExpr or andExpr. An operand can be a bracketed expression, a quoted string (I have omitted the production for this), or a variable followed by zero or more instances of eqExpr. Once you get the hang of referring from one production to another, EBNF becomes quite easy to read.

In Figure 11–1, I represent the elements of my grammar as classes.

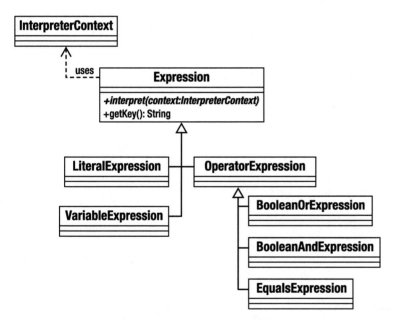

Figure 11–1. *The Interpreter classes that make up the MarkLogic language*

As you can see, BooleanAndExpression and its siblings inherit from OperatorExpression. This is because these classes all perform their operations upon other Expression objects. VariableExpression and LiteralExpression work directly with values.

All Expression objects implement an interpret() method that is defined in the abstract base class, Expression. The interpret() method expects an InterpreterContext object that is used as a shared data store. Each Expression object can store data in the InterpreterContext object. The InterpreterContext will then be passed along to other Expression objects. So that data can be retrieved easily from the InterpreterContext, the Expression base class implements a getKey() method that returns a unique handle. Let's see how this works in practice with an implementation of Expression:

```
abstract class Expression {
    private static $keycount=0;
    private $key;
    abstract function interpret( InterpreterContext $context );

    function getKey() {
        if ( ! asset( $this->key ) ) {
            self::$keycount++;
            $this->key=self::$keycount;
        }
        return $this->key;
    }
}

class LiteralExpression extends Expression {
    private $value;

    function __construct( $value ) {
        $this->value = $value;
    }

    function interpret( InterpreterContext $context ) {
        $context->replace( $this, $this->value );
    }
}

class InterpreterContext {
    private $expressionstore = array();

    function replace( Expression $exp, $value ) {
        $this->expressionstore[$exp->getKey()] = $value;
    }

    function lookup( Expression $exp ) {
        return $this->expressionstore[$exp->getKey()];
    }
}

$context = new InterpreterContext();
$literal = new LiteralExpression( 'four');
$literal->interpret( $context );
print $context->lookup( $literal ) . "\n";
```

Here's the output:

```
four
```

I'll begin with the InterpreterContext class. As you can see, it is really only a front end for an associative array, $expressionstore, which I use to hold data. The replace() method accepts an Expression object as key and a value of any type, and adds the pair to $expressionstore. It also provides a lookup() method for retrieving data.

The Expression class defines the abstract interpret() method and a concrete getKey() method that uses a static counter value to generate, store, and return an identifier.

This method is used by InterpreterContext::lookup() and InterpreterContext::replace() to index data.

The LiteralExpression class defines a constructor that accepts a value argument. The interpret() method requires a InterpreterContext object. I simply call replace(), using getKey() to define the key for retrieval and the $value property. This will become a familiar pattern as you examine the other expression classes. The interpret() method always inscribes its results upon the InterpreterContext object.

I include some client code as well, instantiating both an InterpreterContext object and a LiteralExpression object (with a value of "four"). I pass the InterpreterContext object to LiteralExpression::interpret(). The interpret() method stores the key/value pair in InterpreterContext, from where I retrieve the value by calling lookup().

Here's the remaining terminal class. VariableExpression is a little more complicated:

```
class VariableExpression extends Expression {
    private $name;
    private $val;

    function __construct( $name, $val=null ) {
        $this->name = $name;
        $this->val = $val;
    }

    function interpret( InterpreterContext $context ) {
        if ( ! is_null( $this->val ) ) {
            $context->replace( $this, $this->val );
            $this->val = null;
        }
    }

    function setValue( $value ) {
        $this->val = $value;
    }

    function getKey() {
        return $this->name;
    }
}
$context = new InterpreterContext();
$myvar = new VariableExpression( 'input', 'four');
$myvar->interpret( $context );
print $context->lookup( $myvar ). "\n";
// output: four

$newvar = new VariableExpression( 'input' );
$newvar->interpret( $context );
print $context->lookup( $newvar ). "\n";
// output: four
```

```
$myvar->setValue("five");
$myvar->interpret( $context );
print $context->lookup( $myvar ). "\n";
// output: five
print $context->lookup( $newvar ) . "\n";
// output: five
```

The VariableExpression class accepts both name and value arguments for storage in property variables. I provide the setValue() method so that client code can change the value at any time.

The interpret() method checks whether or not the $val property has a nonnull value. If the $val property has a value, it sets it on the InterpreterContext. I then set the $val property to null. This is in case interpret() is called again after another identically named instance of VariableExpression has changed the value in the InterpreterContext object. This is quite a limited variable, accepting only string values as it does. If you were going to extend your language, you should consider having it work with other Expression objects, so that it could contain the results of tests and operations. For now, though, VariableExpression will do the work I need of it. Notice that I have overridden the getKey() method so that variable values are linked to the variable name and not to an arbitrary static ID.

Operator expressions in the language all work with two other Expression objects in order to get their job done. It makes sense, therefore, to have them extend a common superclass. Here is the OperatorExpression class:

```
abstract class OperatorExpression extends Expression {
    protected $l_op;
    protected $r_op;

    function __construct( Expression $l_op, Expression $r_op ) {
        $this->l_op = $l_op;
        $this->r_op = $r_op;
    }

    function interpret( InterpreterContext $context ) {
        $this->l_op->interpret( $context );
        $this->r_op->interpret( $context );
        $result_l = $context->lookup( $this->l_op );
        $result_r = $context->lookup( $this->r_op  );
        $this->doInterpret( $context, $result_l, $result_r );
    }

    protected abstract function doInterpret( InterpreterContext $context,
                                             $result_l,
                                             $result_r );
}
```

OperatorExpression is an abstract class. It implements interpret(), but it also defines the abstract doInterpret() method.

The constructor demands two Expression objects, $l_op and $r_op, which it stores in properties.

The interpret() method begins by invoking interpret() on both its operand properties (if you have read the previous chapter, you might notice that I am creating an instance of the Composite pattern here). Once the operands have been run, interpret() still needs to acquire the values that this yields. It does this by calling InterpreterContext::lookup() for each property. It then calls doInterpret(), leaving it up to child classes to decide what to do with the results of these operations.

■**Note** doInterpret() is an instance of the Template Method pattern. In this pattern, a parent class both defines and calls an abstract method, leaving it up to child classes to provide an implementation. This can streamline the development of concrete classes, as shared functionality is handled by the superclass, leaving the children to concentrate on clean, narrow objectives.

Here's the EqualsExpression class, which tests two Expression objects for equality:

```
class EqualsExpression extends OperatorExpression {
    protected function doInterpret( InterpreterContext $context,
                                    $result_l, $result_r ) {
        $context->replace( $this, $result_l == $result_r );
    }
}
```

EqualsExpression only implements the doInterpret() method, which tests the equality of the operand results it has been passed by the interpret() method, placing the result in the InterpreterContext object.

To wrap up the Expression classes, here are BooleanOrExpression and BooleanAndExpression:

```
class BooleanOrExpression extends OperatorExpression {
    protected function doInterpret( InterpreterContext $context,
                                    $result_l, $result_r ) {
        $context->replace( $this, $result_l || $result_r );
    }
}
```

```
class BooleanAndExpression extends OperatorExpression {
    protected function doInterpret( InterpreterContext $context,
                                    $result_l, $result_r ) {
        $context->replace( $this, $result_l && $result_r );
    }
}
```

Instead of testing for equality, the BooleanOrExpression class applies a logical or operation and stores the result of that via the InterpreterContext::replace() method. BooleanAndExpression, of course, applies a logical and operation.

I now have enough code to execute the minilanguage fragment I quoted earlier. Here it is again:

```
$input equals "4" or $input equals "four"
```

Here's how I can build this statement up with my Expression classes:

```
$context = new InterpreterContext();
$input = new VariableExpression( 'input' );
$statement = new BooleanOrExpression(
    new EqualsExpression( $input, new LiteralExpression( 'four' ) ),
    new EqualsExpression( $input, new LiteralExpression( '4' ) )
);
```

I instantiate a variable called 'input' but hold off on providing a value for it. I then create a BooleanOrExpression object that will compare the results from two EqualsExpression objects. The first of these objects compares the VariableExpression object stored in $input with a LiteralExpression containing the string "four"; the second compares $input with a LiteralExpression object containing the string "4".

Now, with my statement prepared, I am ready to provide a value for the input variable, and run the code:

```
foreach ( array( "four", "4", "52" ) as $val ) {
    $input->setValue( $val );
    print "$val:\n";
    $statement->interpret( $context );
    if ( $context->lookup( $statement ) ) {
        print "top marks\n\n";
    } else {
        print "dunce hat on\n\n";
    }
}
```

In fact, I run the code three times, with three different values. The first time through, I set the temporary variable $val to "four", assigning it to the input VariableExpression object using its setValue() method. I then call interpret() on the topmost Expression object (the BooleanOrExpression object that contains references to all other expressions in the statement). Here are the internals of this invocation step by step:

- $statement calls interpret() on its $l_op property (the first EqualsExpression object).

- The first EqualsExpression object calls interpret() on *its* $l_op property (a reference to the input VariableExpression object which is currently set to "four").

- The input VariableExpression object writes its current value to the provided InterpreterContext object by calling InterpreterContext::replace().

- The first EqualsExpression object calls interpret() on its $r_op property (a LiteralExpression object charged with the value "four").

- The LiteralExpression object registers its key and its value with InterpreterContext.

- The first EqualsExpression object retrieves the values for $l_op ("four") and $r_op ("four") from the InterpreterContext object.

- The first EqualsExpression object compares these two values for equality and registers the result (true) together with its key with the InterpreterContext object.

- Back at the top of the tree the $statement object (BooleanOrExpression) calls interpret() on its $r_op property. This resolves to a value (false, in this case) in the same way as the $l_op property did.

- The $statement object retrieves values for each of its operands from the InterpreterContext object and compares them using ||. It is comparing true and false, so the result is true. This final result is stored in the InterpreterContext object.

And all that is only for the first iteration through the loop. Here is the final output:

```
four:
top marks
```

```
4:
top marks
```

```
52:
dunce hat on
```

You may need to read through this section a few times before the process clicks. The old issue of object versus class trees might confuse you here. Expression classes are arranged in an inheritance hierarchy just as Expression objects are composed into a tree at runtime. As you read back through the code, keep this distinction in mind.

Figure 11–2 shows the complete class diagram for the example.

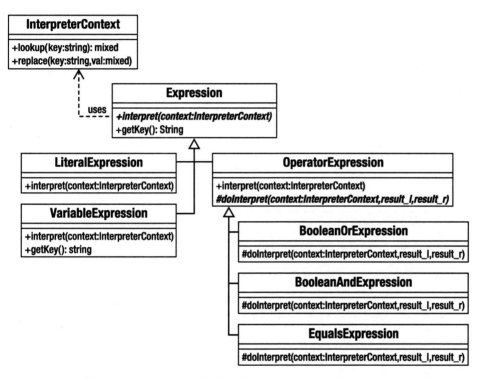

Figure 11–2. *The Interpreter pattern deployed*

Interpreter Issues

Once you have set up the core classes for an Interpreter pattern implementation, it becomes easy to extend. The price you pay is in the sheer number of classes you could end up creating. For this reason, Interpreter is best applied to relatively small languages. If you have a need for a full programming language, you would do better to look for a third-party tool to use.

Because Interpreter classes often perform very similar tasks, it is worth keeping an eye on the classes you create with a view to factoring out duplication.

Many people approaching the Interpreter pattern for the first time are disappointed, after some initial excitement, to discover that it does not address parsing. This means that you are not yet in a position to offer your users a nice, friendly language. Appendix B contains some rough code to illustrate one strategy for parsing a minilanguage.

The Strategy Pattern

Classes often try to do too much. It's understandable: you create a class that performs a few related actions. As you code, some of these actions need to be varied according to circumstances. At the same time, your class needs to be split into subclasses. Before you know it, your design is being pulled apart by competing forces.

The Problem

Since I have recently built a marking language, I'm sticking with the quiz example. Quizzes need questions, so you build a Question class, giving it a mark() method. All is well until you need to support different marking mechanisms.

Imagine you are asked to support the simple MarkLogic language, marking by straight match and marking by regular expression. Your first thought might be to subclass for these differences, as in Figure 11–3.

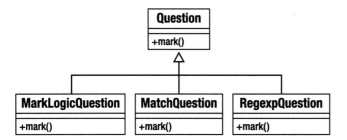

Figure 11–3. *Defining subclasses according to marking strategies*

This would serve you well as long as marking remains the only aspect of the class that varies. Imagine, though, that you are called on to support different kinds of questions: those that are text based and those that support rich media. This presents you with a problem when it comes to incorporating these forces in one inheritance tree as you can see in Figure 11–4.

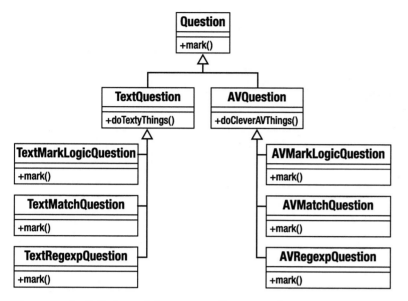

Figure 11–4. *Defining subclasses according to two forces*

Not only have the number of classes in the hierarchy ballooned, but you also necessarily introduce repetition. Your marking logic is reproduced across each branch of the inheritance hierarchy.

Whenever you find yourself repeating an algorithm across siblings in an inheritance tree (whether through subclassing or repeated conditional statements), consider abstracting these behaviors into their own type.

Implementation

As with all the best patterns, Strategy is simple and powerful. When classes must support multiple implementations of an interface (multiple marking mechanisms, for example), the best approach is often to extract these implementations and place them in their own type, rather than to extend the original class to handle them.

So, in the example, your approach to marking might be placed in a Marker type. Figure 11–5 shows the new structure.

Remember the Gang of Four principle "favor composition over inheritance"? This is an excellent example. By defining and encapsulating the marking algorithms, you reduce subclassing and increase flexibility. You can add new marking strategies at any time without the need to change the Question classes at all. All Question classes know is that they have an instance of a Marker at their disposal, and that it is guaranteed by its interface to support a mark() method. The details of implementation are entirely somebody else's problem.

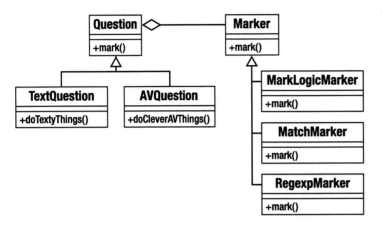

Figure 11–5. Extracting algorithms into their own type

Here are the Question classes rendered as code:

```
abstract class Question {
    protected $prompt;
    protected $marker;

    function __construct( $prompt, Marker $marker ) {
        $this->marker=$marker;
        $this->prompt = $prompt;
    }

    function mark( $response ) {
        return $this->marker->mark( $response );
    }
}

class TextQuestion extends Question {
    // do text question specific things
}

class AVQuestion extends Question {
    // do audiovisual question specific things
}
```

As you can see, I have left the exact nature of the difference between TextQuestion and AVQuestion to the imagination. The Question base class provides all the real functionality, storing a prompt property and a Marker object. When Question::mark() is called with a response from the end user, the method simply delegates the problem solving to its Marker object.

Now to define some simple Marker objects:

```
abstract class Marker {
    protected $test;

    function __construct( $test ) {
```

```
        $this->test = $test;
    }

    abstract function mark( $response );
}

class MarkLogicMarker extends Marker {
    private $engine;
    function __construct( $test ) {
        parent::__construct( $test );
        // $this->engine = new MarkParse( $test );
    }

    function mark( $response ) {
        // return $this->engine->evaluate( $response );
        // dummy return value
        return true;
    }
}

class MatchMarker extends Marker {
    function mark( $response ) {
        return ( $this->test == $response );
    }
}

class RegexpMarker extends Marker {
    function mark( $response ) {
        return ( preg_match( $this->test, $response ) );
    }
}
```

There should be little if anything that is particularly surprising about the Marker classes themselves. Note that the MarkParse object is designed to work with the simple parser developed in Appendix B. This isn't necessary for the sake of this example though, so I simply return a dummy value of true from MarkLogicMarker::mark(). The key here is in the structure that I have defined, rather than in the detail of the strategies themselves. I can swap RegexpMarker for MatchMarker, with no impact on the Question class.

Of course, you must still decide what method to use to choose between concrete Marker objects. I have seen two real-world approaches to this problem. In the first, producers use radio buttons to select the marking strategy they prefer. In the second, the structure of the marking condition is itself used: a match statement was left plain:

five

A MarkLogic statement was preceded by a colon:

:$input equals 'five'

and a regular expression used forward slashes:

/f.ve/

Here is some code to run the classes through their paces:

$markers = array(new RegexpMarker("/f.ve/"),

```
                    new MatchMarker( "five" ),
                    new MarkLogicMarker( '$input equals "five"' )
        );

foreach ( $markers as $marker ) {
    print get_class( $marker )."\n";
    $question = new TextQuestion( "how many beans make five", $marker );
    foreach ( array( "five", "four" ) as $response ) {
        print "\tresponse: $response: ";
        if ( $question->mark( $response ) ) {
            print "well done\n";
        } else {
            print "never mind\n";
        }
    }
}
}
```

I construct three strategy objects, using each in turn to help construct a TextQuestion object. The TextQuestion object is then tried against two sample responses.

The MarkLogicMarker class shown here is a placeholder at present, and its mark() method always returns true. The commented out code does work, however, with the parser example shown in Appendix B, or could be made to work with a third-party parser.

Here is the output:

```
RegexpMarker
        response: five: well done
        response: four: never mind
MatchMarker
        response: five: well done
        response: four: never mind
MarkLogicMarker
        response: five: well done
        response: four: well done
```

Remember that the MarkLogicMarker in the example is a dummy which always returns true, so it marked both responses correct.

In the example, I passed specific data (the $response variable) from the client to the strategy object via the mark() method. Sometimes, you may encounter circumstances in which you don't always know in advance how much information the strategy object will require when its operation is invoked. You can delegate the decision as to what data to acquire by passing the strategy an instance of the client itself. The strategy can then query the client in order to build the data it needs.

The Observer Pattern

Orthogonality is a virtue I have described before. One of objectives as programmers should be to build components that can be altered or moved with minimal impact on other components. If every change you make to one component necessitates a ripple of changes elsewhere in the codebase, the task of development can quickly become a spiral of bug creation and elimination.

Of course, orthogonality is often just a dream. Elements in a system must have embedded references to other elements. You can, however, deploy various strategies to minimize this. You have seen various examples of polymorphism in which the client understands a component's interface but the actual component may vary at runtime.

In some circumstances, you may wish to drive an even greater wedge between components than this. Consider a class responsible for handling a user's access to a system:

```
class Login {
    const LOGIN_USER_UNKNOWN = 1;
    const LOGIN_WRONG_PASS = 2;
    const LOGIN_ACCESS = 3;
    private $status = array();

    function handleLogin( $user, $pass, $ip ) {
        switch ( rand(1,3) ) {
            case 1:
                $this->setStatus( self::LOGIN_ACCESS, $user, $ip );
                $ret = true;
                break;
            case 2:
                $this->setStatus( self::LOGIN_WRONG_PASS, $user, $ip );
                $ret = false;
                break;
            case 3:
                $this->setStatus( self::LOGIN_USER_UNKNOWN, $user, $ip );
                $ret = false;
                break;
        }
        return $ret;
    }

    private function setStatus( $status, $user, $ip ) {
        $this->status = array( $status, $user, $ip );
    }

    function getStatus() {
        return $this->status;
    }

}
```

In a real-world example, of course, the handleLogin() method would validate the user against a storage mechanism. As it is, this class fakes the login process using the rand() function. There are three potential outcomes of a call to handleLogin(). The status flag may be set to LOGIN_ACCESS, LOGIN_WRONG_PASS, or LOGIN_USER_UNKNOWN.

Because the Login class is a gateway guarding the treasures of your business team, it may excite much interest during development and in the months beyond. Marketing might call you up and ask that you keep a log of IP addresses. You can add a call to your system's Logger class:

```
function handleLogin( $user, $pass, $ip ) {
    switch ( rand(1,3) ) {
        case 1:
            $this->setStatus( self::LOGIN_ACCESS, $user, $ip );
            $ret = true;
            break;
        case 2:
```

```
                    $this->setStatus( self::LOGIN_WRONG_PASS, $user, $ip );
                    $ret = false;
                    break;
                case 3:
                    $this->setStatus( self::LOGIN_USER_UNKNOWN, $user, $ip );
                    $ret = false;
                    break;
            }
            Logger::logIP( $user, $ip, $this->getStatus() );
            return $ret;
    }
```

Worried about security, the system administrators might ask for notification of failed logins. Once again, you can return to the login method and add a new call:

```
        if ( ! $ret ) {
            Notifier::mailWarning( $user, $ip,
                                  $this->getStatus()  );
        }
```

The business development team might announce a tie-in with a particular ISP and ask that a cookie be set when particular users log in, and so on, and on.

These are all easy enough requests to fulfill but at a cost to your design. The Login class soon becomes very tightly embedded into this particular system. You cannot pull it out and drop it into another product without going through the code line by line and removing everything that is specific to the old system. This isn't too hard, of course, but then you are off down the road of cut-and-paste coding. Now that you have two similar but distinct Login classes in your systems, you find that an improvement to one will necessitate the same changes in the other, until inevitably and gracelessly they fall out of alignment with one another.

So what can you do to save the Login class? The Observer pattern is a powerful fit here.

Implementation

At the core of the Observer pattern is the unhooking of client elements (the observers) from a central class (the subject). Observers need to be informed when events occur that the subject knows about. At the same time, you do not want the subject to have a hard-coded relationship with its observer classes.

To achieve this, you can allow observers to register themselves with the subject. You give the Login class three new methods, attach(), detach(), and notify(), and enforce this using an interface called Observable:

```
interface Observable {
    function attach( Observer $observer );
    function detach( Observer $observer );
    function notify();
}

// ... Login class
class Login implements Observable {

    private $observers;
    //...

    function __construct() {
```

```
        $this->observers = array();

    }


    function attach( Observer $observer ) {
        $this->observers[] = $observer;
    }

    function detach( Observer $observer ) {
        $newobservers = array();
        foreach ( $this->observers as $obs ) {
            if (  ($obs !== $observer) ) {
                $newobservers[]=$obs;
            }
        }
        $this->observers = $newobservers;
    }

    function notify() {
        foreach ( $this->observers as $obs ) {
            $obs->update( $this );
        }
    }
}
//...
```

So the Login class manages a list of observer objects. These can be added by a third party using the attach() method and removed via detach(). The notify() method is called to tell the observers that something of interest has happened. The method simply loops through the list of observers, calling update() on each one.

The Login class itself calls notify() from its handleLogin() method.

```
function handleLogin( $user, $pass, $ip ) {
        switch ( rand(1,3) ) {
            case 1:
                $this->setStatus( self::LOGIN_ACCESS, $user, $ip );
                $ret = true; break;
            case 2:
                $this->setStatus( self::LOGIN_WRONG_PASS, $user, $ip );
                $ret = false; break;
            case 3:
                $this->setStatus( self::LOGIN_USER_UNKNOWN, $user, $ip );
                $ret = false; break;
        }
        $this->notify();
        return $ret;
    }
```

Here's the interface for the Observer class:

```
interface Observer {
    function update( Observable $observable );
}
```

Any object that uses this interface can be added to the Login class via the attach() method. Here's create a concrete instance:

```
class SecurityMonitor extends Observer {
    function update( Observable $observable ) {
        $status = $observable->getStatus();
        if ( $status[0] == Login::LOGIN_WRONG_PASS ) {
            // send mail to sysadmin
            print __CLASS__.":\tsending mail to sysadmin\n";
        }
    }
}
$login = new Login();
$login->attach( new SecurityMonitor() );
```

Notice how the observer object uses the instance of Observable to get more information about the event. It is up to the subject class to provide methods that observers can query to learn about state. In this case, I have defined a method called getStatus() that observers can call to get a snapshot of the current state of play.

This addition also highlights a problem, though. By calling Login::getStatus(), the SecurityMonitor class assumes more knowledge than it safely can. It is making this call on an Observable object, but there's no guarantee that this will also be a Login object. I have a couple of options here. I could extend the Observable interface to include a getStatus() declaration and perhaps rename it to something like ObservableLogin to signal that it is specific to the Login type.

Alternatively, I can keep the Observable interface generic and make the Observer classes responsible for ensuring that their subjects are of the correct type. They could even handle the chore of attaching themselves to their subject. Since there will be more than one type of Observer, and since I'm planning to perform some housekeeping that is common to all of them, here's an abstract superclass to handle the donkey work:

```
abstract class LoginObserver implements Observer {
    private $login;
    function __construct( Login $login ) {
        $this->login = $login;
        $login->attach( $this );
    }

    function update( Observable $observable ) {
        if ( $observable === $this->login ) {
            $this->doUpdate( $observable );
        }
    }

    abstract function doUpdate( Login $login );
}
```

The LoginObserver class requires a Login object in its constructor. It stores a reference and calls Login::attach(). When update() is called, it checks that the provided Observable object is the correct reference. It then calls a Template Method: doUpdate(). I can now create a suite of LoginObserver objects all of whom can be secure they are working with a Login object and not just any old Observable:

```
class SecurityMonitor extends LoginObserver {
    function doUpdate( Login $login ) {
        $status = $login->getStatus();
        if ( $status[0] == Login::LOGIN_WRONG_PASS ) {
```

```
                // send mail to sysadmin
                print __CLASS__.":\tsending mail to sysadmin\n";
            }
        }
}

class GeneralLogger  extends LoginObserver {
    function doUpdate( Login $login ) {
        $status = $login->getStatus();
        // add login data to log
        print __CLASS__.":\tadd login data to log\n";
    }
}

class PartnershipTool extends LoginObserver {
    function doUpdate( Login $login ) {
        $status = $login->getStatus();
        // check IP address
        // set cookie if it matches a list
        print __CLASS__.":\tset cookie if IP matches a list\n";
    }
}
```

Creating and attaching LoginObserver classes is now achieved in one go at the time of instantiation:

```
$login = new Login();
new SecurityMonitor( $login );
new GeneralLogger( $login );
new PartnershipTool( $login );
```

So now I have created a flexible association between the subject classes and the observers. You can see the class diagram for the example in Figure 11–6.

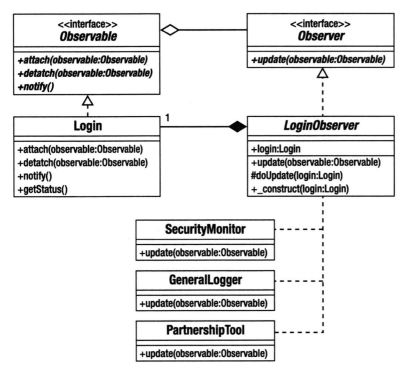

Figure 11–6. *The Observer pattern*

PHP provides built-in support for the Observer pattern through the bundled SPL (Standard PHP Library) extension. The SPL is a set of tools that help with common largely object-oriented problems. The Observer aspect of this OO Swiss Army knife consists of three elements: SplObserver, SplSubject, and SplObjectStorage. SplObserver and SplSubject are interfaces and exactly parallel the Observer and Observable interfaces shown in this section's example. SplObjectStorage is a utility class designed to provide improved storage and removal of objects. Here's an edited version of the Observer implementation:

```
class Login implements SplSubject {
    private $storage;
    //...

    function __construct() {
        $this->storage = new SplObjectStorage();
    }
    function attach( SplObserver $observer ) {
        $this->storage->attach( $observer );
    }

    function detach( SplObserver $observer ) {
        $this->storage->detach( $observer );
    }
```

```
        function notify() {
            foreach ( $this->storage as $obs ) {
                $obs->update( $this );
            }
        }
        //...
}

abstract class LoginObserver implements SplObserver {
        private $login;
        function __construct( Login $login ) {
            $this->login = $login;
            $login->attach( $this );
        }

        function update( SplSubject $subject ) {
            if ( $subject === $this->login ) {
                $this->doUpdate( $subject );
            }
        }

        abstract function doUpdate( Login $login );
}
```

There are no real differences as far as SplObserver (which was Observer) and SplSubject (which was Observable) are concerned, except, of course, I no longer need to declare the interfaces, and I must alter my type hinting according to the new names. SplObjectStorage provides you with a really useful service however. You may have noticed that in my initial example my implementation of Login::detach() applied array_udiff (together with an anonymous function) to the $observable array, in order to find and remove the argument object. The SplObjectStorage class does this work for you under the hood. It implements attach() and detach() methods and can be passed to foreach and iterated like an array.

Note You can read more about SPL in the PHP documentation at http://www.php.net/spl. In particular, you will find many iterator tools there. I cover PHP's built-in Iterator interface in Chapter 13, "Database Patterns."

Another approach to the problem of communicating between an Observable class and its Observer could be to pass specific state information via the update() method, rather than an instance of the subject class. For a quick-and-dirty solution, this is often the approach I would take initially. So in the example, update() would expect a status flag, the username, and IP address (probably in an array for portability), rather than an instance of Login. This saves you from having to write a state method in the Login class. On the other hand, where the subject class stores a lot of state, passing an instance of it to update() allows observers much more flexibility.

You could also lock down type completely, by making the Login class refuse to work with anything other than a specific type of observer class (LoginObserver perhaps). If you want to do that, then you may consider some kind of runtime check on objects passed to the attach() method; otherwise, you may need to reconsider the Observable interface altogether.

Once again, I have used composition at runtime to build a flexible and extensible model. The Login class can be extracted from the context and dropped into an entirely different project without qualification. There, it might work with a different set of observers.

The Visitor Pattern

As you have seen, many patterns aim to build structures at runtime, following the principle that composition is more flexible than inheritance. The ubiquitous Composite pattern is an excellent example of this. When you work with collections of objects, you may need to apply various operations to the structure that involve working with each individual component. Such operations can be built into the components themselves. After all, components are often best placed to invoke one another.

This approach is not without issues. You do not always know about all the operations you may need to perform on a structure. If you add support for new operations to your classes on a case-by-case basis, you can bloat your interface with responsibilities that don't really fit. As you might guess, the Visitor pattern addresses these issues.

The Problem

Think back to the Composite example from the previous chapter. For a game, I created an army of components such that the whole and its parts can be treated interchangeably. You saw that operations can be built into components. Typically, leaf objects perform an operation and composite objects call on their children to perform the operation.

```
class Army extends CompositeUnit {

    function bombardStrength() {
        $ret = 0;
        foreach( $this->units() as $unit ) {
            $ret += $unit->bombardStrength();
        }
        return $ret;
    }
}

class LaserCannonUnit extends Unit {
    function bombardStrength() {
        return 44;
    }
}
```

Where the operation is integral to the responsibility of the composite class, there is no problem. There are more peripheral tasks, however, that may not sit so happily on the interface.

Here's an operation that dumps textual information about leaf nodes. It could be added to the abstract Unit class.

```
// Unit
function textDump( $num=0 ) {
    $ret = "";
    $pad = 4*$num;
    $ret .= sprintf( "%{$pad}s", "" );
    $ret .= get_class($this).": ";
    $ret .= "bombard: ".$this->bombardStrength()."\n";
```

```
        return $ret;
    }
```

This method can then be overridden in the `CompositeUnit` class:

```
// CompositeUnit
function textDump( $num=0 ) {
    $ret = parent::textDump( $num );
    foreach ( $this->units as $unit ) {
        $ret .= $unit->textDump( $num + 1 );
    }
    return $ret;
}
```

I could go on to create methods for counting the number of units in the tree, for saving components to a database, and for calculating the food units consumed by an army.

Why would I want to include these methods in the composite's interface? There is only one really compelling answer. I include these disparate operations here because this is where an operation can gain easy access to related nodes in the composite structure.

Although it is true that ease of traversal is part of the Composite pattern, it does not follow that every operation that needs to traverse the tree should therefore claim a place in the Composite's interface.

So these are the forces at work. I want to take full advantage of the easy traversal afforded by my object structure, but I want to do this without bloating the interface.

Implementation

I'll begin with the interfaces. In the abstract `Unit` class, I define an `accept()` method:

```
function accept( ArmyVisitor $visitor ) {
    $method = "visit".get_class( $this );
    $visitor->$method( $this );
}

protected function setDepth( $depth ) {
    $this->depth=$depth;
}

function getDepth() {
    return $this->depth;
}
```

As you can see, the `accept()` method expects an `ArmyVisitor` object to be passed to it. PHP allows you dynamically to define the method on the `ArmyVisitor` you wish to call. This saves me from implementing `accept()` on every leaf node in my class hierarchy. While I was in the area, I also added two methods of convenience `getDepth()` and `setDepth()`. These can be used to store and retrieve the depth of a unit in a tree. `setDepth()` is invoked by the unit's parent when it adds it to the tree from `CompositeUnit::addUnit()`.

```
function addUnit( Unit $unit ) {
    foreach ( $this->units as $thisunit ) {
        if ( $unit === $thisunit ) {
            return;
        }
    }
```

```
        $unit->setDepth($this->depth+1);
        $this->units[] = $unit;
    }
```

The only other accept() method I need to define is in the abstract composite class:

```
function accept( ArmyVisitor $visitor ) {
    $method = "visit".get_class( $this );
    $visitor->$method( $this );
    foreach ( $this->units as $thisunit ) {
        $thisunit->accept( $visitor );
    }
}
```

This method does the same as Unit::accept(), with one addition. It constructs a method name based on the name of the current class and invokes that method on the provided ArmyVisitor object. So if the current class is Army, then it invokes ArmyVisitor::visitArmy(), and if the current class is TroopCarrier, it invokes ArmyVisitor::visitTroopCarrier(), and so on. Having done this, it then loops through any child objects calling accept(). In fact, because accept() overrides its parent operation, I could factor out the repetition here:

```
function accept( ArmyVisitor $visitor ) {
    parent::accept( $visitor );
    foreach ( $this->units as $thisunit ) {
        $thisunit->accept( $visitor );
    }
}
```

Eliminating repetition in this way can be very satisfying, though in this case I have saved only one line, arguably at some cost to clarity. In either case, the accept() method allows me to do two things:

- Invoke the correct visitor method for the current component.

- Pass the visitor object to all the current element children via the accept() method (assuming the current component is composite).

I have yet to define the interface for ArmyVisitor. The accept() methods should give you some clue. The visitor class should define accept() methods for each of the concrete classes in the class hierarchy. This allows me to provide different functionality for different objects. In my version of this class, I also define a default visit() method that is automatically called if implementing classes choose not to provide specific handling for particular Unit classes.

```
abstract class ArmyVisitor  {
    abstract function visit( Unit $node );

    function visitArcher( Archer $node ) {
        $this->visit( $node );
    }

    function visitCavalry( Cavalry $node ) {
        $this->visit( $node );
    }

    function visitLaserCannonUnit( LaserCannonUnit $node ) {
        $this->visit( $node );
    }
```

```
    function visitTroopCarrierUnit( TroopCarrierUnit $node ) {
        $this->visit( $node );
    }

    function visitArmy( Army $node ) {
        $this->visit( $node );
    }
}
```

So now it's just a matter of providing implementations of ArmyVisitor, and I am ready to go. Here is the simple text dump code reimplemented as an ArmyVisitor object:

```
class TextDumpArmyVisitor extends ArmyVisitor {
    private $text="";

    function visit( Unit $node ) {
        $ret = "";
        $pad = 4*$node->getDepth();
        $ret .= sprintf( "%{$pad}s", "" );
        $ret .= get_class($node).": ";
        $ret .= "bombard: ".$node->bombardStrength()."\n";
        $this->text .= $ret;
    }

    function getText() {
        return $this->text;
    }
}
```

Let's look at some client code and then walk through the whole process:

```
$main_army = new Army();
$main_army->addUnit( new Archer() );
$main_army->addUnit( new LaserCannonUnit() );
$main_army->addUnit( new Cavalry() );

$textdump = new TextDumpArmyVisitor();
$main_army->accept( $textdump  );
print $textdump->getText();
```

This code yields the following output:

```
Army: bombard: 50
    Archer: bombard: 4
    LaserCannonUnit: bombard: 44
    Cavalry: bombard: 2
```

I create an Army object. Because Army is composite, it has an addUnit() method that I use to add some more Unit objects. I then create the TextDumpArmyVisitor object. I pass this to the Army::accept(). The accept() method constructs a method call and invokes TextDumpArmyVisitor::visitArmy(). In this case, I have provided no special handling for Army objects, so the call is passed on to the generic visit() method. visit() has been passed a reference to the Army object. It invokes its methods (including the newly added, getDepth(), which tells anyone who needs to know how far down the object hierarchy the unit is) in order to generate summary data. The call to visitArmy() complete, the Army::accept()

operation now calls accept() on its children in turn, passing the visitor along. In this way, the ArmyVisitor class visits every object in the tree.

With the addition of just a couple of methods, I have created a mechanism by which new functionality can be plugged into my composite classes without compromising their interface and without lots of duplicated traversal code.

On certain squares in the game, armies are subject to tax. The tax collector visits the army and levies a fee for each unit it finds. Different units are taxable at different rates. Here's where I can take advantage of the specialized methods in the visitor class:

```php
class TaxCollectionVisitor extends ArmyVisitor {
    private $due=0;
    private $report="";

    function visit( Unit $node ) {
        $this->levy( $node, 1 );
    }

    function visitArcher( Archer $node ) {
        $this->levy( $node, 2 );
    }

    function visitCavalry( Cavalry $node ) {
        $this->levy( $node, 3 );
    }

    function visitTroopCarrierUnit( TroopCarrierUnit $node ) {
        $this->levy( $node, 5 );
    }

    private function levy( Unit $unit, $amount ) {
        $this->report .= "Tax levied for ".get_class( $unit );
        $this->report .= ": $amount\n";
        $this->due += $amount;
    }

    function getReport() {
        return $this->report;
    }

    function getTax() {
        return $this->due;
    }
}
```

In this simple example, I make no direct use of the Unit objects passed to the various visit methods. I do, however, use the specialized nature of these methods, levying different fees according to the specific type of the invoking Unit object.

Here's some client code:

```php
$main_army = new Army();
$main_army->addUnit( new Archer() );
$main_army->addUnit( new LaserCannonUnit() );
$main_army->addUnit( new Cavalry() );
```

```
$taxcollector = new TaxCollectionVisitor();
$main_army->accept( $taxcollector );
print "TOTAL: ";
print $taxcollector->getTax()."\n";
```

The TaxCollectionVisitor object is passed to the Army object's accept() method as before. Once again, Army passes a reference to itself to the visitArmy() method, before calling accept() on its children. The components are blissfully unaware of the operations performed by their visitor. They simply collaborate with its public interface, each one passing itself dutifully to the correct method for its type.

In addition to the methods defined in the ArmyVisitor class, TaxCollectionVisitor provides two summary methods, getReport() and getTax(). Invoking these provides the data you might expect:

```
Tax levied for Army: 1
Tax levied for Archer: 2
Tax levied for LaserCannonUnit: 1
Tax levied for Cavalry: 3
TOTAL: 7
```

Figure 11–7 shows the participants in this example.

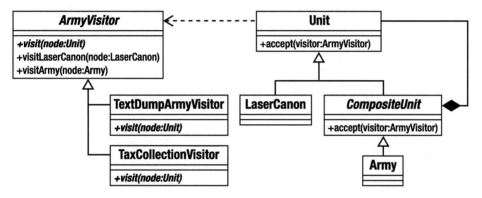

Figure 11–7. *The Visitor pattern*

Visitor Issues

The Visitor pattern, then, is another that combines simplicity and power. There are a few things to bear in mind when deploying this pattern, however.

First, although it is perfectly suited to the Composite pattern, Visitor can, in fact, be used with any collection of objects. So you might use it with a list of objects where each object stores a reference to its siblings, for example.

By externalizing operations, you may risk compromising encapsulation. That is, you may need to expose the guts of your visited objects in order to let visitors do anything useful with them. You saw, for example, that for the first Visitor example, I was forced to provide an additional method in the Unit interface in order to provide information for TextDumpArmyVisitor objects. You also saw this dilemma previously in the Observer pattern.

Because iteration is separated from the operations that visitor objects perform, you must relinquish a degree of control. For example, you cannot easily create a visit() method that does something both before and after child nodes are iterated. One way around this would be to move responsibility for iteration into the visitor objects. The trouble with this is that you may end up duplicating the traversal code from visitor to visitor.

By default, I prefer to keep traversal internal to the visited classes, but externalizing it provides you with one distinct advantage. You can vary the way that you work through the visited classes on a visitor-by-visitor basis.

The Command Pattern

In recent years, I have rarely completed a web project without deploying this pattern. Originally conceived in the context of graphical user interface design, command objects make for good enterprise application design, encouraging a separation between the controller (request and dispatch handling) and domain model (application logic) tiers. Put more simply, the Command pattern makes for systems that are well organized and easy to extend.

The Problem

All systems must make decisions about what to do in response to a user's request. In PHP, that decision-making process is often handled by a spread of point-of-contact pages. In selecting a page (feedback.php), the user clearly signals the functionality and interface she requires. Increasingly, PHP developers are opting for a single-point-of-contact approach (as I will discuss in the next chapter). In either case, however, the receiver of a request must delegate to a tier more concerned with application logic. This delegation is particularly important where the user can make requests to different pages. Without it, duplication inevitably creeps into the project.

So, imagine you have a project with a range of tasks that need performing. In particular, the system must allow some users to log in and others to submit feedback. You could create login.php and feedback.php pages that handle these tasks, instantiating specialist classes to get the job done. Unfortunately, user interface in a system rarely maps neatly to the tasks that the system is designed to complete. You may require login and feedback capabilities on every page, for example. If pages must handle many different tasks, then perhaps you should think of tasks as things that can be encapsulated. In doing this, you make it easy to add new tasks to your system, and you build a boundary between your system's tiers. This, of course, brings us to the Command pattern.

Implementation

The interface for a command object could not get much simpler. It requires a single method: execute().

In Figure 11–8, I have represented Command as an abstract class. At this level of simplicity, it could be defined instead as an interface. I tend to use abstracts for this purpose, because I often find that the base class can also provide useful common functionality for its derived objects.

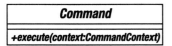

Figure 11–8. *The Command class*

There are up to three other participants in the Command pattern: the client, which instantiates the command object; the invoker, which deploys the object; and the receiver on which the command operates.

The receiver can be given to the command in its constructor by the client, or it can be acquired from a factory object of some kind. I like the latter approach, keeping the constructor method clear of arguments. All Command objects can then be instantiated in exactly the same way.

Here's a concrete Command class:

```
abstract class Command {
    abstract function execute( CommandContext $context );
}

class LoginCommand extends Command {
    function execute( CommandContext $context ) {
        $manager = Registry::getAccessManager();
        $user = $context->get( 'username' );
        $pass = $context->get( 'pass' );
        $user_obj = $manager->login( $user, $pass );
        if ( is_null( $user_obj ) ) {
            $context->setError( $manager->getError() );
            return false;
        }
        $context->addParam( "user", $user_obj );
        return true;
    }
}
```

The LoginCommand is designed to work with an AccessManager object. AccessManager is an imaginary class whose task is to handle the nuts and bolts of logging users into the system. Notice that the Command::execute() method demands a CommandContext object (known as RequestHelper in *Core J2EE Patterns*). This is a mechanism by which request data can be passed to Command objects, and by which responses can be channeled back to the view layer. Using an object in this way is useful, because I can pass different parameters to commands without breaking the interface. The CommandContext is essentially an object wrapper around an associative array variable, though it is frequently extended to perform additional helpful tasks. Here is a simple CommandContext implementation:

```
class CommandContext {
    private $params = array();
    private $error = "";

    function __construct() {
        $this->params = $_REQUEST;
    }

    function addParam( $key, $val ) {
        $this->params[$key]=$val;
    }

    function get( $key ) {
        return $this->params[$key];
    }

    function setError( $error ) {
        $this->error = $error;
    }

    function getError() {
```

```
        return $this->error;
    }
}
```

So, armed with a CommandContext object, the LoginCommand can access request data: the submitted username and password. I use Registry, a simple class with static methods for generating common objects, to return the AccessManager object with which LoginCommand needs to work. If AccessManager reports an error, the command lodges the error message with the CommandContext object for use by the presentation layer, and returns false. If all is well, LoginCommand simply returns true. Note that Command objects do not themselves perform much logic. They check input, handle error conditions, and cache data as well as calling on other objects to perform the operations they must report on. If you find that application logic creeps into your command classes, it is often a sign that you should consider refactoring. Such code invites duplication, as it is inevitably copied and pasted between commands. You should at least look at where the functionality belongs. It may be best moved down into your business objects, or possibly into a Facade layer. I am still missing the client, the class that generates command objects, and the invoker, the class that works with the generated command. The easiest way of selecting which command to instantiate in a web project is by using a parameter in the request itself. Here is a simplified client:

```
class CommandNotFoundException extends Exception {}

class CommandFactory {
    private static $dir = 'commands';

    static function getCommand( $action='Default' ) {
        if ( preg_match( '/\W/', $action ) ) {
            throw new Exception("illegal characters in action");
        }
        $class = UCFirst(strtolower($action))."Command";
        $file = self::$dir.DIRECTORY_SEPARATOR."{$class}.php";
        if ( ! file_exists( $file ) ) {
            throw new CommandNotFoundException( "could not find '$file'" );
        }
        require_once( $file );
        if ( ! class_exists( $class ) ) {
            throw new CommandNotFoundException( "no '$class' class located" );
        }
        $cmd = new $class();
        return $cmd;
    }
}
```

The CommandFactory class simply looks in a directory called commands for a particular class file. The file name is constructed using the CommandContext object's $action parameter, which in turn should have been passed to the system from the request. If the file is there, and the class exists, then it is returned to the caller. I could add even more error checking here, ensuring that the found class belongs to the Command family, and that the constructor is expecting no arguments, but this version will do fine for my purposes. The strength of this approach is that you can drop a new Command object into the commands directory at any time, and the system will immediately support it.

The invoker is now simplicity itself:

```
class Controller {
    private $context;
    function __construct() {
        $this->context = new CommandContext();
```

```
    }

    function getContext() {
        return $this->context;
    }

    function process() {
        $cmd = CommandFactory::getCommand( $this->context->get('action') );
        if ( ! $cmd->execute( $this->context ) ) {
            // handle failure
        } else {
            // success
            // dispatch view now..
        }
    }
}

$controller = new Controller();
// fake user request
$context = $controller->getContext();
$context->addParam('action', 'login' );
$context->addParam('username', 'bob' );
$context->addParam('pass', 'tiddles' );
$controller->process();
```

Before I call Controller::process(), I fake a web request by setting parameters on the CommandContext object instantiated in the controller's constructor. The process() method delegates object instantiation to the CommandFactory object. It then invokes execute() on the returned command. Notice how the controller has no idea about the command's internals. It is this independence from the details of command execution that makes it possible for you to add new Command classes with a relatively small impact on this framework.

Here's one more Command class:

```
class FeedbackCommand extends Command {

    function execute( CommandContext $context ) {
        $msgSystem = Registry::getMessageSystem();
        $email = $context->get( 'email' );
        $msg   = $context->get( 'msg' );
        $topic = $context->get( 'topic' );
        $result = $msgSystem->send( $email, $msg, $topic );
        if ( ! $result ) {
            $context->setError( $msgSystem->getError() );
            return false;
        }
        return true;
    }
}
```

▨**Note** I will return to the Command pattern in Chapter 12 with a fuller implementation of a Command factory class. The framework for running commands presented here is a simplified version of another pattern that you will encounter: the Front Controller.

As long as this class is contained within a file called FeedbackCommand.php, and is saved in the correct commands folder, it will be run in response to a "feedback" action string, without the need for any changes in the controller or CommandFactory classes.

Figure 11–9 shows the participants of the Command pattern.

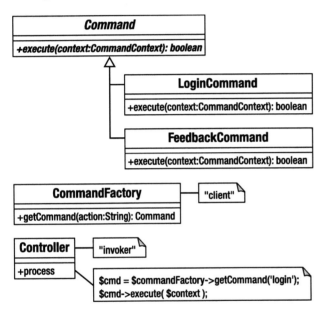

Figure 11–9. Command pattern participants

Summary

In this chapter, I wrapped up my examination the Gang of Four patterns. I designed a minilanguage and built its engine with the Interpreter pattern. You encountered in the Strategy pattern another way of using composition to increase flexibility and reduce the need for repetitive subclassing. The Observer pattern solved the problem of notifying disparate and varying components about system events. You revisited the Composite example, and with the Visitor pattern learned how to pay a call on, and apply many operations to, every component in a tree. Finally, you saw how the Command pattern can help you to build an extensible tiered system.

In the next chapter, I will step beyond the Gang of Four to examine some patterns specifically oriented toward enterprise programming.

CHAPTER 12

■ ■ ■

Enterprise Patterns

PHP is first and foremost a language designed for the Web. And since its support for objects was significantly extended in PHP 5, you can now take advantage of patterns hatched in the context of other object-oriented languages, particularly Java.

I develop a single example in this chapter, using it to illustrate the patterns I cover. Remember, though, that by choosing to use one pattern, you are not committed to using all the patterns that work well with it. Nor should you feel that the implementations presented here are the only way you might go about deploying these patterns. Use the examples here to help you understand the thrust of the patterns described, and feel free to extract what you need for your projects.

Because of the amount of material to cover, this is one this book's longest and most involved chapters, and it may be a challenge to traverse in one sitting. It is divided into an introduction and two main parts. These dividing lines might make good break points.

I also describe the individual patterns in the "Architecture Overview" section. Although these are interdependent to some extent, you should be able to jump straight to any particular pattern and work through it independently, moving on to related patterns at your leisure.

This chapter will cover

- *Architecture overview*: An introduction to the layers that typically comprise an enterprise application

- *Registry pattern*: Managing application data

- *Presentation layer*: Tools for managing and responding to requests and for presenting data to the user

- *Business logic layer*: Getting to the real purpose of your system: addressing business problems

Architecture Overview

With a lot of ground to cover, let's kick off with an overview of the patterns to come, followed by an introduction to building layered, or tiered, applications.

221

The Patterns

These are the patterns I explore in this chapter. You may read from start to finish or dip in to those patterns that fit your needs or pique your interest. Note that the Command pattern is not described individually here (I wrote about it in Chapter 11), but it is encountered once again in both the Front Controller and Application Controller patterns.

- *Registry*: This pattern is useful for making data available to all classes in a process. Through careful use of serialization, it can also be used to store information across a session or even across instances of an application.

- *Front Controller*: Use this for larger systems in which you know that you will need as much flexibility as possible in managing many different views and commands.

- *Application Controller*: Create a class to manage view logic and command selection.

- *Template View*: Create pages that manage display and user interface only, incorporating dynamic information into display markup with as little raw code as possible.

- *Page Controller*: Lighter weight but less flexible than Front Controller, Page Controller addresses the same need. Use this pattern to manage requests and handle view logic if you want fast results and your system is unlikely to grow substantially in complexity.

- *Transaction Script*: When you want to get things done fast, with minimal up-front planning, fall back on procedural library code for your application logic. This pattern does not scale well.

- *Domain Model*: At the opposite pole from Transaction Script, use this pattern to build object-based models of your business participants and processes.

Applications and Layers

Many (most, in fact) of the patterns in this chapter are designed to promote the independent operation of several distinct tiers in an application. Just as classes represent specializations of responsibilities, so do the tiers of an enterprise system, albeit on a coarser scale. Figure 12–1 shows a typical breakdown of the layers in a system.

The structure shown in Figure 12–1 is not written in stone: some of these tiers may be combined, and different strategies used for communication between them, depending on the complexity of your system. Nonetheless, Figure 12–1 illustrates a model that emphasizes flexibility and reuse, and many enterprise applications follow it to a large extent.

- The *view layer* contains the interface that a system's users actually see and interact with. It is responsible for presenting the results of a user's request and providing the mechanism by which the next request can be made to the system.

- The *command and control layer* processes the request from the user. Based on this analysis, it delegates to the business logic layer any processing required in order to fulfill the request. It then chooses which view is best suited to present the results to the user. In practice, this and the view layer are often combined into a single *presentation layer*. Even so, the role of display should be strictly separated from those of request handling and business logic invocation.

- The *business logic layer* is responsible for seeing to the business of a request. It performs any required calculations and marshals the resulting data.

- The *data layer* insulates the rest of the system from the mechanics of saving and acquiring persistent information. In some systems, the command and control layer uses the data layer to acquire the business objects with which it needs to work. In other systems, the data layer is hidden as far as possible.

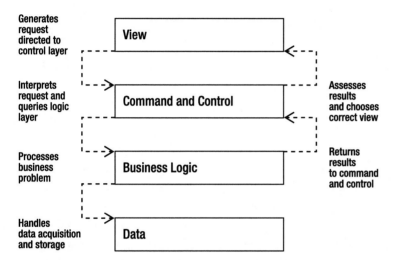

Figure 12-1. *The layers or tiers in a typical enterprise system*

So what is the point of dividing a system in this way? As with so much else in this book, the answer lies with decoupling. By keeping business logic independent of the view layer, you make it possible to add new interfaces to your system with little or no rewriting.

Imagine a system for managing event listings (this will be a very familiar example by the end of the chapter). The end user will naturally require a slick HTML interface. Administrators maintaining the system may require a command line interface for building into automated systems. At the same time, you may be developing versions of the system to work with cell phones and other handheld devices. You may even begin to consider SOAP or a RESTful API.

If you originally combined the underlying logic of your system with the HTML view layer (which is still a common strategy despite the many strictures against it), these requirements would trigger an instant rewrite. If, on the other hand, you had created a tiered system, you would be able to bolt on new presentation strategies without the need to reconsider your business logic and data layers.

By the same token, persistence strategies are subject to change. Once again, you should be able to switch between storage models with minimal impact on the other tiers in a system.

Testing is another good reason for creating systems with separate tiers. Web applications are notoriously hard to test. Any kind of automated test tends to get caught up in the need to parse the HTML interface at one end and to work with live databases at the other. This means that tests must work with fully deployed systems and risk undermining the very system that they were written to protect. In any tier, the classes that face other tiers are often written so that they extend an abstract superclass or implement an interface. This supertype can then support polymorphism. In a test context, an entire tier can be replaced by a set of dummy objects (often called "stubs" or "mock objects"). In this way, you can test business logic using a fake data layer, for example. You can read more about testing in Chapter 18.

Layers are useful even if you think that testing is for wimps, and your system will only ever have a single interface. By creating tiers with distinct responsibilities, you build a system whose constituent parts are easier to extend and debug. You limit duplication by keeping code with the same kinds of responsibility in one place (rather than lacing a system with database calls, for example, or with display strategies). Adding to a system is relatively easy, because your changes tend to be nicely vertical as opposed to messily horizontal.

A new feature, in a tiered system, might require a new interface component, additional request handling, some more business logic, and an amendment to your storage mechanism. That's vertical change. In a nontiered system, you might add your feature and then remember that five separate pages reference your amended database table, or was it six? There may be dozens of places where your new interface may potentially be invoked, so you need to work through your system adding code for that. This is horizontal amendment.

In reality, of course, you never entirely escape from horizontal dependencies of this sort, especially when it comes to navigation elements in the interface. A tiered system can help to minimize the need for horizontal amendment, however.

Note While many of these patterns have been around for a while (patterns reflect well-tried practices, after all), the names and boundaries are drawn either from Martin Fowler's key work on enterprise patterns, *Patterns of Enterprise Application Architecture*, or from the influential *Core J2EE Patterns* by Alur et al. For the sake of consistency, I have tended to use Fowler's naming conventions where the two sources diverge. This is because Fowler's work is less focused on a single technology and, therefore, has the wider application. Alur et al. tend to concentrate on Enterprise Java Beans in their work, which means that many patterns are optimized for distributed architectures. This is clearly a niche concern in the PHP world.

If you find this chapter useful, I would recommend both books as a next step. Even if you don't know Java, as an object-oriented PHP programmer, you should find the examples reasonably easy to decipher.

All the examples in this chapter revolve around a fictional listings system with the whimsical-sounding name "Woo," which stands for something like "What's On Outside."

Participants of the system include venues (theaters, clubs, and cinemas), spaces (screen 1, the stage upstairs) and events (*The Long Good Friday, The Importance of Being Earnest*).

The operations I will cover include creating a venue, adding a space to a venue, and listing all venues in the system.

Remember that the aim of this chapter is to illustrate key enterprise design patterns and not to build a working system. Reflecting the interdependent nature of design patterns, most of these examples overlap to a large extent with code examples, making good use of ground covered elsewhere in the chapter. As this code is mainly designed to demonstrate enterprise patterns, much of it does not fulfill all the criteria demanded by a production system. In particular, I omit error checking where it might stand in the way of clarity. You should approach the examples as a means of illustrating the patterns they implement, rather than as building blocks in a framework or application.

Cheating Before We Start

Most of the patterns in this book find a natural place in the layers of an enterprise architecture. But some patterns are so basic that they stand outside of this structure. The Registry pattern is a good example of this. In fact, Registry is a powerful way of breaking out of the constraints laid down by layering. It is the exception that allows for the smooth running of the rule.

Registry

The Registry pattern is all about providing systemwide access to objects. It is an article of faith that globals are bad. Like other sins, though, global data is fatally attractive. This is so much the case that object-oriented architects have felt it necessary to reinvent globals under a new name. You encountered the Singleton pattern in Chapter 9. It is true that singleton objects do not suffer from all the ills that beset global variables. In particular, you cannot overwrite a singleton by accident. Singletons, then, are low-fat globals. You should remain suspicious of singleton objects, though, because they invite you to anchor your classes into a system, thereby introducing coupling.

Even so, singletons are so useful at times that many programmers (including me) can't bring themselves to give them up.

The Problem

As you have seen, many enterprise systems are divided into layers, with each layer communicating with its neighbors only through tightly defined conduits. This separation of tiers makes an application flexible. You can replace or otherwise develop each tier with the minimum impact on the rest of the system. What happens, though, when you acquire information in a tier that you later need in another noncontiguous layer?

Let's say that I acquire configuration data in an `ApplicationHelper` class:

```
// woo\controller\ApplicationHelper
function getOptions() {
    if ( ! file_exists( "data/woo_options.xml" ) ) {
        throw new woo_base_AppException(
            "Could not find options file" );
    }
    $options = simplexml_load_file( "data/woo_options.xml" );
    $dsn = (string)$options->dsn;
    // what do we do with this now?
    // ...
}
```

Acquiring the information is easy enough, but how would I get it to the data layer where it is later used? And what about all the other configuration information I must disseminate throughout my system?

One answer would be to pass this information around the system from object to object: from a controller object responsible for handling requests, through to objects in the business logic layer, and on to an object responsible for talking to the database.

This is entirely feasible. In fact, you could pass the ApplicationHelper object itself around, or alternatively, a more specialized Context object. Either way, contextual information is transmitted through the layers of your system to the object or objects that need it.

The trade-off is that in order to do this, you must alter the interface of all the objects that relay the context object whether they need to use it or not. Clearly, this undermines loose coupling to some extent.

The Registry pattern provides an alternative that is not without its own consequences.

A *registry* is simply a class that provides access to data (usually, but not exclusively, objects) via static methods (or via instance methods on a singleton). Every object in a system, therefore, has access to these objects.

The term "Registry" is drawn from Fowler's *Patterns of Enterprise Application Architecture*, but like all patterns, implementations pop up everywhere. David Hunt and David Thomas (*The Pragmatic Programmer*) liken a registry class to a police incident notice board. Detectives on one shift leave evidence and sketches on the board, which are then picked up by new detectives on another shift. I have also seen the Registry pattern called Whiteboard and Blackboard.

Implementation

Figure 12–2 shows a Registry object whose job it is to store and serve Request objects.

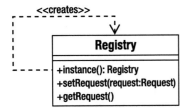

Figure 12–2. A simple registry

Here is this class in code form:

```
class Registry {
    private static $instance;
    private $request;

    private function __construct() { }

    static function instance() {
        if ( ! isset( self::$instance ) ) { self::$instance = new self(); }
        return self::$instance;
```

```
    }

    function getRequest() {
        return $this->request;
    }

    function setRequest( Request $request ) {
        $this->request = $request;
    }
}
// empty class for testing
class Request {}
```

You can then add a Request object in one part of a system:

```
$reg = Registry::instance();
$reg->setRequest( new Request() );
```

and access it from another part of the system:

```
$reg = Registry::instance();
print_r( $reg->getRequest() );
```

As you can see, the Registry is simply a singleton (see Chapter 9 if you need a reminder about singleton classes). The code creates and returns a sole instance of the Registry class via the instance() method. This can then be used to set and retrieve a Request object. Despite the fact that PHP does not enforce return types, the value returned by getRequest() is *guaranteed* to be a Request object because of the type hint in setRequest().

I have been known to throw caution to the winds and use a key-based system, like this:

```
class Registry {
    private static $instance;
    private $values = array();

    private function __construct() { }

    static function instance() {
        if ( ! isset( self::$instance ) ) { self::$instance = new self(); }
        return self::$instance;
    }

    function get( $key ) {
        if ( isset( $this->values[$key] ) ) {
            return $this->values[$key];
        }
        return null;
    }

    function set( $key, $value ) {
        $this->values[$key] = $value;
    }
}
```

The benefit here is that you don't need to create methods for every object you wish to store and serve. The downside, though, is that you reintroduce global variables by the back door. The use of arbitrary strings as keys for the objects you store means that there is nothing stopping one part of your system overwriting a key/value pair when adding an object. I have found it useful to use this map-like structure during development and shift over to explicitly named methods when I'm clear about the data I am going to need to store and retrieve.

You can also use registry objects as factories for common objects in your system. Instead of storing a provided object, the registry class creates an instance and then caches the reference. It may do some setup behind the scenes as well, maybe retrieving data from a configuration file or combining a number of objects.

```
//class Registry...
function treeBuilder() {
    if ( ! isset( $this->treeBuilder ) ) {
        $this->treeBuilder = new TreeBuilder( $this->conf()->get('treedir') );
    }
    return $this->treeBuilder;
}

function conf() {
    if ( ! isset( $this->conf ) ) {
        $this->conf = new Conf();
    }
    return $this->conf;
}
```

TreeBuilder and Conf are just dummy classes, included to demonstrate a point. A client class that needs a TreeBuilder object can simply call Registry::treeBuilder(), without bothering itself with the complexities of initialization. Such complexities may include application-level data such as the dummy Conf object, and most classes in a system should be insulated from them.

Registry objects can be useful for testing, too. The static instance() method can be used to serve up a child of the Registry class primed with dummy objects. Here's how I might amend instance() to achieve this:

```
static function testMode( $mode=true ) {
    self::$instance=null;
    self::$testmode=$mode;
}

static function instance() {
    if ( self::$testmode ) {
        return new MockRegistry();
    }
    if ( ! isset( self::$instance ) ) { self::$instance = new self(); }
    return self::$instance;
}
```

When you need to put your system through its paces, you can use test mode to switch in a fake registry. This can serve up stubs (objects that fake a real environment for testing purposes) or mocks (similar objects that also analyze calls made to them and assess them for correctness).

```
Registry::testMode();
$mockreg = Registry::instance();
```

You can read more about mock and stub objects in Chapter 18, "Testing with PHPUnit."

Registry, Scope, and PHP

The term *scope* is often used to describe the visibility of an object or value in the context of code structures. The lifetime of a variable can also be measured over time. There are three levels of scope you might consider in this sense. The standard is the period covered by an HTTP request.

PHP also provides built-in support for session variables. These are serialized and saved to the file system or the database at the end of a request, and then restored at the start of the next. A session ID stored in a cookie or passed around in query strings is used to keep track of the session owner. Because of this, you can think of some variables having session scope. You can take advantage of this by storing some objects between requests, saving a trip to the database. Clearly, you need to be careful that you don't end up with multiple versions of the same object, so you may need to consider a locking strategy when you check an object that also exists in a database into a session.

In other languages, notably Java and Perl (running on the ModPerl Apache module), there is the concept of application scope. Variables that occupy this space are available across all instances of the application. This is fairly alien to PHP, but in larger applications, it is very useful to have access to an applicationwide space for accessing configuration variables. You can build a registry class that emulates application scope, though you must be aware of some pretty considerable caveats.

Figure 12–3 shows a possible structure for Registry classes that work on the three levels I have described.

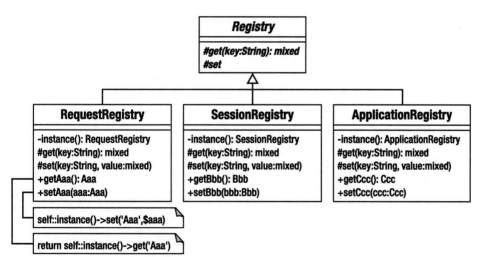

Figure 12–3. *Implementing registry classes for different scopes*

The base class defines two protected methods, get() and set(). They are not available to client code, because I want to enforce type for get and set operations. The base class may define other public methods such as isEmpty(), isPopulated(), and clear(), but I'll leave those as an exercise for you to do.

■Note In a real-world system, you might want to extend this structure to include another layer of inheritance. You might keep the concrete get() and set() methods in their respective implementations, but specialize the public getAaa() and setAaa() methods into domain-specific classes. The new specializations would become the singletons. That way you could reuse the core save and retrieve operations across multiple applications.

Here is the abstract class as code:

```
namespace woo\base;

abstract class Registry {
    abstract protected function get( $key );
    abstract protected function set( $key, $val );
}
```

■Note Notice that I'm using namespaces in these examples. Because I will be building a complete, if basic, system in this chapter, it makes sense to use a package hierarchy, and to take advantage of the brevity and clarity that namespaces can bring to a project.

The request level class is pretty straightforward. In another variation from my previous example, I keep the Registry sole instance hidden and provide static methods to set and get objects. Apart from that, it's simply a matter of maintaining an associative array.

```
namespace woo\base;
// ...
class RequestRegistry extends Registry {
    private $values = array();
    private static $instance;

    private function __construct() {}
    static function instance() {
        if ( ! isset(self::$instance) ) { self::$instance = new self(); }
        return self::$instance;
    }

    protected function get( $key ) {
```

```
        if ( isset( $this->values[$key] ) ) {
            return $this->values[$key];
        }
        return null;
    }

    protected function set( $key, $val ) {
        $this->values[$key] = $val;
    }

    static function getRequest() {
        return self::instance()->get('request');
    }

    static function setRequest( \woo\controller\Request $request ) {
        return self::instance()->set('request', $request );
    }
}
```

The session-level implementation simply uses PHP's built-in session support:

```
namespace woo\base;
// ...
class SessionRegistry extends Registry {
    private static $instance;
    private function __construct() {
        session_start();
    }

    static function instance() {
        if ( ! isset(self::$instance) ) { self::$instance = new self(); }
        return self::$instance;
    }

    protected function get( $key ) {
        if ( isset( $_SESSION[__CLASS__][$key] ) ) {
            return $_SESSION[__CLASS__][$key];
        }
        return null;
    }

    protected function set( $key, $val ) {
        $_SESSION[__CLASS__][$key] = $val;
    }

    function setComplex( Complex $complex ) {
        self::instance()->set('complex', $complex);
    }

    function getComplex( ) {
        return self::instance()->get('complex');
    }
}
```

As you can see, this class uses the $_SESSION superglobal to set and retrieve values. I kick off the session in the constructor with the session_start() method. As always with sessions, you must ensure that you have not yet sent any text to the user before using this class.

As you might expect, the application-level implementation is more of an issue. As with all code examples in this chapter, this is an illustration rather than production-quality code:

```
namespace woo\base;
// ...
class ApplicationRegistry extends Registry {
    private static $instance;
    private $freezedir = "data";
    private $values = array();
    private $mtimes = array();

    private function __construct() { }

    static function instance() {
        if ( ! isset(self::$instance) ) { self::$instance = new self(); }
        return self::$instance;
    }

    protected function get( $key ) {
        $path = $this->freezedir . DIRECTORY_SEPARATOR . $key;
        if ( file_exists( $path ) ) {
            clearstatcache();
            $mtime=filemtime( $path );
            if ( ! isset($this->mtimes[$key] ) ) { $this->mtimes[$key]=0; }
            if ( $mtime > $this->mtimes[$key] ) {
                $data = file_get_contents( $path );
                $this->mtimes[$key]=$mtime;
                return ($this->values[$key]=unserialize( $data ));
            }
        }
        if ( isset( $this->values[$key] ) ) {
            return $this->values[$key];
        }
        return null;
    }
    protected function set( $key, $val ) {
        $this->values[$key] = $val;
        $path = $this->freezedir . DIRECTORY_SEPARATOR . $key;
        file_put_contents( $path, serialize( $val ) );
        $this->mtimes[$key]=time();
    }

    static function getDSN() {
        return self::instance()->get('dsn');
    }
}
```

```
        static function setDSN( $dsn ) {
            return self::instance()->set('dsn', $dsn);
        }
    }
```

This class uses serialization to save and restore individual properties. The get() function checks for the existence of the relevant value file. If the file exists and has been modified since the last read, the method unserializes and returns its contents. Because it's not particularly efficient to open a file for each variable you are managing, you might want to take a different approach here—placing all properties into a single save file. The set() method changes the property referenced by $key both locally and in the save file. It updates the $mtimes property. This is the array of modification times that is used to test save files. Later, if get() is called, the file can be tested against the corresponding entry in $mtimes to see if it has been modified since this object's last write.

If the shm (System V shared memory) extension is enabled in your PHP install, you might use its functions to implement an application registry. Here's a simplified example:

```
namespace woo\base;
// ...

class MemApplicationRegistry extends Registry {
    private static $instance;
    private $values=array();
    private $id;
    const DSN=1;

    private function __construct() {
        $this->id = @shm_attach(55, 10000, 0600);
        if ( ! $this->id ) {
            throw new Exception("could not access shared memory");
        }
    }

    static function instance() {
        if ( ! isset(self::$instance) ) { self::$instance = new self(); }
        return self::$instance;
    }

    protected function get( $key ) {
        return shm_get_var( $this->id, $key );
    }

    protected function set( $key, $val ) {
        return shm_put_var( $this->id, $key, $val );
    }

    static function getDSN() {
        return self::instance()->get(self::DSN);
    }

    static function setDSN( $dsn ) {
        return self::instance()->set(self::DSN, $dsn);
```

```
    }

}
```

If you intend to use a variation on this code example, make sure you check out the next section: there are some serious issues that you should consider.

Consequences

Because both `SessionRegistry` and `ApplicationRegistry` serialize data to the file system, it is important to restate the obvious point that objects retrieved in different requests are identical copies and not references to the same object. This should not matter with `SessionRegistry`, because the same user is accessing the object in each instance. With `ApplicationRegistry`, this could be a serious problem. If you are saving data promiscuously, you could arrive at a situation where two processes conflict. Take a look at these steps:

```
Process 1 retrieves an object
Process 2 retrieves an object
Process 1 alters object
Process 2 alters object
Process 1 saves object
Process 2 saves object
```

The changes made by Process 1 are overwritten by the save of Process 2. If you really want to create a shared space for data, you will need to work on `ApplicationRegistry` to implement a locking scheme to prevent collisions like this. Alternatively, you can treat `ApplicationRegistry` as a largely read-only resource. This is the way that I use the class in examples later in this chapter. It sets data initially, and thereafter, interactions with it are read-only. The code only calculates new values and writes them if the storage file cannot be found. You can, therefore, force a reload of configuration data only by deleting the storage file. You may wish to enhance the class so read-only behavior is enforced.

Another point to remember is that not every object is suitable for serialization. In particular, if you are storing a resource of any type (a database connection handle, for example), it will not serialize. You will have to devise strategies for disposing of the handle on serialization and reacquiring it on unserialization.

■**Note** One way of managing serialization is to implement the magic methods __sleep() and __wakeup(). __sleep() is called automatically when an object is serialized. You can use it to perform any cleaning up before the object is saved. It should return an array of strings representing the fields you would like to have saved. The __wakeup() method is invoked when an object is unserialized. You can use this to resume any file or database handles the object may have been using at the time of storage.

Although serialization is a pretty efficient business in PHP, you should be careful of what you save. A simple-seeming object may contain a reference to an enormous collection of objects pulled from a database.

Registry objects make their data globally available. This means that any class that acts as a client for a registry will exhibit a dependency that is not declared in its interface. This can become a serious problem if you begin to rely on Registry objects for lots of the data in your system. Registry objects are best used sparingly, for a well-defined set of data items.

The Presentation Layer

When a request hits your system, you must interpret the requirement it carries, then you must invoke any business logic needed, and finally return a response. For simple scripts, this whole process often takes place entirely inside the view itself, with only the heavyweight logic and persistence code split off into libraries.

■**Note** A *view* is an individual element in the view layer. It can be a PHP page (or a collection of composed view elements) whose primary responsibility is to display data and provide the mechanism by which new requests can be generated by the user. It could also be a template in a templating system such as Smarty.

As systems grow in size, this default strategy becomes less tenable with request processing, business logic invocation, and view dispatch logic necessarily duplicated from view to view.

In this section, I look at strategies for managing these three key responsibilities of the presentation layer. Because the boundaries between the view layer and the command and control layer are often fairly blurred, it makes sense to treat them together under the common term "presentation layer."

Front Controller

This pattern is diametrically opposed to the traditional PHP application with its multiple points of entry. The Front Controller pattern presents a central point of access for all incoming requests, ultimately delegating to a view the task of presenting results back to the user. This is a key pattern in the Java enterprise community. It is covered in great detail in *Core J2EE Patterns*, which remains one of the most influential enterprise patterns resources. The pattern is not universally loved in the PHP community, partly because of the overhead that initialization sometimes incurs.

Most systems I write tend to gravitate toward the Front Controller. That is, I may not deploy the entire pattern to start with, but I will be aware of the steps necessary to evolve my project into a Front Controller implementation should I need the flexibility it affords.

The Problem

Where requests are handled at multiple points throughout a system, it is hard to keep duplication from the code. You may need to authenticate a user, translate terms into different languages, or simply access common data. When a request requires common actions from view to view, you may find yourself copying and pasting operations. This can make alteration difficult, as a simple amendment may need to be deployed across several points in your system. For this reason, it becomes easy for some parts of your code to fall out of alignment with others. Of course, a first step might be to centralize common operations into library code, but you are still left with the calls to the library functions or methods distributed throughout your system.

Difficulty in managing the progression from view to view is another problem that can arise in a system where control is distributed among its views. In a complex system, a submission in one view may lead to any number of result pages, according to the input and the success of any operations performed at the logic layer. Forwarding from view to view can get messy, especially if the same view might be used in different flows.

Implementation

At heart, the Front Controller pattern defines a central point of entry for every request. It processes the request and uses it to select an operation to perform. Operations are often defined in specialized command objects organized according to the Command pattern.

Figure 12–4 shows an overview of a Front Controller implementation.

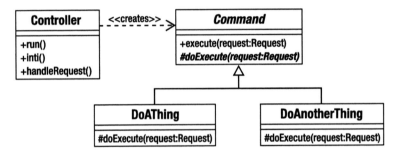

Figure 12–4. *A Controller class and a command hierarchy*

In fact, you are likely to deploy a few helper classes to smooth the process, but let's begin with the core participants. Here is a simple Controller class:

```
namespace woo\controller;

//...
class Controller {
    private $applicationHelper;
    private function __construct() {}

    static function run() {
        $instance = new Controller();
        $instance->init();
        $instance->handleRequest();
    }
```

```
    function init() {
        $applicationHelper
            = ApplicationHelper::instance();
        $applicationHelper->init();
    }

    function handleRequest() {
        $request = new \woo\controller\Request();
        $cmd_r = new \woo\command\CommandResolver();
        $cmd = $cmd_r->getCommand( $request );
        $cmd->execute( $request );
    }
}
```

Simplified as this is, and bereft of error handling, there isn't much more to the Controller class. A controller sits at the tip of a system delegating to other classes. It is these other classes that do most of the work.

run() is merely a convenience method that calls init() and handleRequest(). It is static, and the constructor is private, so the only option for client code is to kick off execution of the system. I usually do this in a file called index.php that contains only a couple of lines of code:

```
require( "woo/controller/Controller.php" );
\woo\controller\Controller::run();
```

The distinction between the init() and handleRequest() methods is really one of category in PHP. In some languages, init() would be run only at application startup, and handleRequest() or equivalent would be run for each user request. This class observes the same distinction between setup and request handling, even though init() is called for each request.

The init() method obtains an instance of a class called ApplicationHelper. This class manages configuration data for the application as a whole. init() calls a method in ApplicationHelper, also called init(), which, as you will see, initializes data used by the application.

The handleRequest() method uses a CommandResolver to acquire a Command object, which it runs by calling Command::execute().

ApplicationHelper

The ApplicationHelper class is not essential to Front Controller. Most implementations must acquire basic configuration data, though, so I should develop a strategy for this. Here is a simple ApplicationHelper:

```
namespace woo\controller;
//...
class ApplicationHelper {
    private static $instance;
    private $config = "/tmp/data/woo_options.xml";

    private function __construct() {}

    static function instance() {
        if ( ! self::$instance ) {
            self::$instance = new self();
        }
```

```
        return self::$instance;
    }


    function init() {
        $dsn = \woo\base\ApplicationRegistry::getDSN( );
        if ( ! is_null( $dsn ) ) {
            return;
        }
        $this->getOptions();
    }

    private function getOptions() {
        $this->ensure( file_exists( $this->config  ),
                                "Could not find options file" );

        $options = SimpleXml_load_file( $this->config );
        print get_class( $options );
        $dsn = (string)$options->dsn;
        $this->ensure( $dsn, "No DSN found" );
        \woo\base\ApplicationRegistry::setDSN( $dsn );
        // set other values
    }

    private function ensure( $expr, $message ) {
        if ( ! $expr ) {
            throw new \woo\base\AppException( $message );
        }
    }
}
```

This class simply reads a configuration file and makes values available to clients. As you can see, it is another singleton, which is a useful way of making it available to any class in the system. You could alternatively make it a standard class and ensure that it is passed around to any interested objects. I have already discussed the trade-offs involved there both earlier in this chapter and in Chapter 9.

The fact that I am using an ApplicationRegistry here suggests a refactoring. It may be worth making ApplicationHelper itself the registry rather than have two singletons in a system with overlapping responsibilities. This would involve the refactoring suggested in the previous section (splitting core ApplicationRegistry functionality from storage and retrieval of domain-specific objects). I will leave that for you to do!

So the init() method is responsible for loading configuration data. In fact, it checks the ApplicationRegistry to see if the data is already cached. If the Registry object is already populated, init() does nothing at all. This is useful for systems that do lots of very expensive initialization. Complicated setup may be acceptable in a language that separates application initialization from individual requests. In PHP, you need to minimize initialization.

Caching is very useful for ensuring that complex and time-consuming initialization processes take place in an initial request only (probably one run by you), with all subsequent requests benefiting from the results.

If this *is* the first run (or if the cache files have been deleted—a crude but effective way of forcing configuration data to be re-read), then the getOptions() method is invoked.

In real life, this would probably do a lot more work than the example shows. This version satisfies itself with acquiring a DSN. getOptions() first checks that the configuration file exists (the path is stored in a property called $config). It then attempts to load XML data from the file and sets the DSN.

▩**Note** In these examples, both ApplicationRegistry and ApplicationHelper use hard-coded paths to work with files. In a real-world deployment, these file paths would probably be configurable and acquired through a registry or configuration object. The actual paths could be set at installation time by a build tool such as PEAR or Phing (see Chapters 15 and 19 for more on these tools).

Notice that the class uses a trick to throw exceptions. Rather than pepper the code with conditionals and throw statements like this:

```
if ( ! file_exists( $this->config ) ) {
    throw new \woo\base\AppException(
            "Could not find options file" );
}
```

the class centralizes the test expression and the throw statement in a method called ensure(). You can confirm that a condition is true (and throw an exception otherwise) in a single (albeit split) line:

```
$this->ensure( file_exists( $this->config ),
                        "Could not find options file" );
```

The cache approach taken here allows for the best of both worlds. The system can maintain an easy-to-use XML configuration file, but caching means that its values can be accessed at near native speed. Of course, if your end users are programmers too, or if you don't intend to change configuration very often, you could include PHP data structures directly in the helper class (or in a separate file that it then includes). While risky, this approach is certainly the fastest.

CommandResolver

A controller needs a way of deciding how to interpret an HTTP request so that it can invoke the right code to fulfill that request. You could easily include this logic within the Controller class itself, but I prefer to use a specialist class for the purpose. That makes it easy to refactor for polymorphism if necessary.

A front controller often invokes application logic by running a Command object (I introduced the Command pattern in Chapter 11). The Command that is chosen is usually selected according to a parameter in the request or according to the structure of the URL itself (you might, for example, use Apache configuration to make concrete-seeming URLs yield a key for use in selecting a Command). In these examples, I will use a simple parameter: cmd.

There is more than one way of using the given parameter to select a command. You can test the parameter against a configuration file or data structure (a *logical* strategy). Or you can test it directly against class files on the file system (a *physical* strategy).

A logical strategy is more flexible, but also more labor intensive, in terms of both setup and maintenance. You can see an example of this approach in the "Application Controller" section.

You saw an example of a command factory that used a physical strategy in the last chapter. Here is a slight variation that uses reflection for added safety:

```
namespace woo\command;
//...

class CommandResolver {
    private static $base_cmd;
    private static $default_cmd;

    function __construct() {
        if ( ! self::$base_cmd ) {
            self::$base_cmd = new \ReflectionClass( "\woo\command\Command" );
            self::$default_cmd = new DefaultCommand();
        }
    }

    function getCommand( \woo\controller\Request $request ) {
        $cmd = $request->getProperty( 'cmd' );
        $sep = DIRECTORY_SEPARATOR;
        if ( ! $cmd ) {
            return self::$default_cmd;
        }
        $cmd=str_replace( array('.', $sep), "", $cmd );
        $filepath = "woo{$sep}command{$sep}{$cmd}.php";
        $classname = "woo\\command\\{$cmd}";
        if ( file_exists( $filepath ) ) {
            @require_once( "$filepath" );
            if ( class_exists( $classname) ) {
                $cmd_class = new ReflectionClass($classname);
                if ( $cmd_class->isSubClassOf( self::$base_cmd ) ) {
                    return $cmd_class->newInstance();
                } else {
                    $request->addFeedback( "command '$cmd' is not a Command" );
                }
            }
        }

        $request->addFeedback( "command '$cmd' not found" );
        return clone self::$default_cmd;
    }
}
```

This simple class looks for a request parameter called cmd. Assuming that this is found, and that it maps to a real class file in the command directory, *and* that the class file contains the right kind of class, the method creates and returns an instance of the relevant class.

If any of these conditions are not met, the getCommand() method degrades gracefully by serving up a default Command object.

You may wonder why this code takes it on trust that the Command class it locates does not require parameters:

```
if ( $cmd_class->isSubClassOf( self::$base_cmd ) ) {
    return $cmd_class->newInstance();
}
```

The answer to this lies in the signature of the Command class itself.

```
Namespace woo\command;
//...

abstract class Command {

    final function __construct() { }

    function execute( \woo\controller\Request $request ) {
        $this->doExecute( $request );
    }

    abstract function doExecute( \woo\controller\Request $request );
}
```

By declaring the constructor method final, I make it impossible for a child class to override it. No Command class, therefore, will ever require arguments to its constructor.

Remember that you should never use input from the user without checking it first. I have included a test to ensure that there is no path element to the provided "cmd" string, so that only files in the correct directory can be invoked (and not something like ../../../tmp/DodgyCommand.php). You can make code even safer by only accepting command strings that match values in a configuration file.

When creating command classes, you should be careful to keep them as devoid of application logic as you possibly can. As soon as they begin to do application-type stuff, you'll find that they turn into a kind of tangled transaction script, and duplication will soon creep in. Commands are a kind of relay station: they should interpret a request, call into the domain to juggle some objects, and then lodge data for the presentation layer. As soon as they begin to do anything more complicated than this, it's probably time to refactor. The good news is that refactoring is relatively easy. It's not hard to spot when a command is trying to do too much, and the solution is usually clear. Move that functionality down to a facade or domain class.

Request

Requests are magically handled for us by PHP and neatly packaged up in superglobal arrays. You might have noticed that I still use a class to represent a request. A Request object is passed to CommandResolver, and later on to Command.

Why do I not let these classes simply query the $_REQUEST, $_POST, or $_GET arrays for themselves? I could do that, of course, but by centralizing request operations in one place, I open up new options. You could, for example, apply filters to the incoming request. Or, as the next example shows, you could gather request parameters from somewhere other than an HTTP request, allowing the application to be run from the command line or from a test script. Of course, if your application uses sessions, you may have to provide an alternative storage mechanism for use in a command line context. The Registry pattern would work well for you there, allowing you to generate different Registry classes according to the context of the application.

The Request object is also a useful repository for data that needs to be communicated to the view layer. In that respect, Request can also provide response capabilities.

Here is a simple Request class:

```
namespace woo\controller;
//...

class Request {
    private $properties;
    private $feedback = array();

    function __construct() {
        $this->init();
        \woo\base\RequestRegistry::setRequest($this );
    }

    function init() {
        if ( isset( $_SERVER['REQUEST_METHOD'] ) ) {
            $this->properties = $_REQUEST;
            return;
        }

        foreach( $_SERVER['argv'] as $arg ) {
            if ( strpos( $arg, '=' ) ) {
                list( $key, $val )=explode( "=", $arg );
                $this->setProperty( $key, $val );
            }
        }
    }

    function getProperty( $key ) {
        if ( isset( $this->properties[$key] ) ) {
            return $this->properties[$key];
        }
    }

    function setProperty( $key, $val ) {
        $this->properties[$key] = $val;
    }

    function addFeedback( $msg ) {
        array_push( $this->feedback, $msg );
    }

    function getFeedback( ) {
        return $this->feedback;
    }

    function getFeedbackString( $separator="\n" ) {
        return implode( $separator, $this->feedback );
    }
}
```

As you can see, most of this class is taken up with mechanisms for setting and acquiring properties. The init() method is responsible for populating the private $properties array. Notice that it works with command line arguments as well as the HTTP requests. This is extremely useful when it comes to testing and debugging.

Once you have a Request object, you should be able to access an HTTP parameter via the getProperty() method, which accepts a key string and returns the corresponding value (as stored in the $properties array). You can also add data via setProperty().

The class also manages a $feedback array. This is a simple conduit through which controller classes can pass messages to the user.

A Command

You have already seen the Command base class, and Chapter 11 covered the Command pattern in detail, so there's no need to go too deep into Commands. Let's round things off, though, with a simple concrete Command object:

```
namespace woo\command;
//...

class DefaultCommand extends Command {
    function doExecute( \woo\controller\Request $request ) {
        $request->addFeedback( "Welcome to WOO" );
        include( "woo/view/main.php");
    }
}
```

This is the Command object that is served up by CommandResolver if no explicit request for a particular Command is received.

As you may have noticed, the abstract base class implements execute() itself, calling down to the doExecute() implementation of its child class. This allows us to add setup and cleanup code to all commands simply by altering the base class.

The execute() method is passed a Request object that gives access to user input, as well as to the setFeedback() method. DefaultCommand makes use of this to set a welcome message.

Finally, the command dispatches control to a view, simply by calling include(). Embedding the map from command to view in the Command classes is the simplest dispatch mechanism, but for small systems, it can be perfectly adequate. A more flexible strategy can be seen in the "Application Controller" section.

The file main.php contains some HTML and a call into the Request object to check for any feedback (I'll cover views in more detail shortly). I now have all the components in place to run the system. Here's what I see:

```
<html>
<head>
<title>Woo! it's Woo!</title>
</head>
<body>

<table>
<tr>
<td>
Welcome to WOO</td>
</tr>
</table>
```

```
</body>
</html>
```

As you can see, the feedback message set in by the default command has found its way into the output. Let's review the full process that leads to this outcome.

Overview

It is possible that the detail of the classes covered in this section might disguise the simplicity of the Front Controller pattern. Figure 12–5 shows a sequence diagram that illustrates the life cycle of a request.

As you can see, the front controller delegates initialization to the ApplicationHelper object (which uses caching to short-circuit any expensive setup). The Controller then acquires a Command object from the CommandResolver object. Finally, it invokes Command::execute() to kick off the application logic.

In this implementation of the pattern, the Command itself is responsible for delegating to the view layer. You can see a refinement of this in the next section.

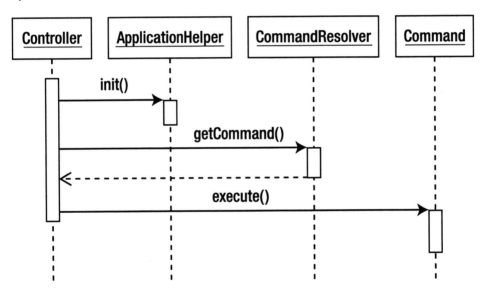

Figure 12–5. *The front controller in operation*

Consequences

Front Controller is not for the fainthearted. It does require a lot of up-front development before you begin to see benefits. This is a serious drawback if your project requires fast turnaround or if it is small enough that the Front Controller framework would weigh in heavier than the rest of the system.

Having said that, once you have successfully deployed a Front Controller in one project, you will find that you can reuse it for others with lightning speed. You can abstract much of its functionality into library code, effectively building yourself a reusable framework.

The requirement that all configuration information is loaded up for every request is another drawback. All approaches will suffer from this to some extent, but Front Controller often requires additional information, such as logical maps of commands and views.

This overhead can be eased considerably by caching such data. The most efficient way of doing this is to add the data to your system as native PHP. This is fine if you are the sole maintainer of a system, but if you have nontechnical users, you may need to provide a configuration file. You can still automate the native PHP approach, though, by creating a system that reads a configuration file and then builds PHP data structures, which it writes to a cache file. Once the native PHP cache has been created, the system will use it in preference to the configuration file until a change is made and the cache must be rebuilt. Less efficient but much easier is the approach I took in the ApplicationRegistry class—simply serialize the data.

On the plus side, Front Controller centralizes the presentation logic of your system. This means that you can exert control over the way that requests are processed and views selected in one place (well, in one set of classes, anyway). This reduces duplication and decreases the likelihood of bugs.

Front Controller is also very extensible. Once you have a core up and running, you can add new Command classes and views very easily.

In this example, commands handled their own view dispatch. If you use the Front Controller pattern with an object that helps with view (and possibly command) selection, then the pattern allows for excellent control over navigation, which is harder to maintain elegantly when presentation control is distributed throughout a system. I cover such an object in the next section.

Application Controller

Allowing commands to invoke their own views is acceptable for smaller systems, but it is not ideal. It is preferable to decouple your commands from your view layer as much as possible.

An application controller takes responsibility for mapping requests to commands, and commands to views. This decoupling means that it becomes easier to switch in alternative sets of views without changing the codebase. It also allows the system owner to change the flow of the application, again without the need for touching any internals. By allowing for a logical system of Command resolution, the pattern also makes it easier for the same Command to be used in different contexts within a system.

The Problem

Remember the nature of the example problem. An administrator needs to be able to add a venue to the system and to associate a space with it. The system might, therefore, support the AddVenue and AddSpace commands. According to the examples so far, these commands would be selected using a direct map from a request parameter (cmd=AddVenue) to a class (AddVenue).

Broadly speaking, a successful call to the AddVenue command should lead to an initial call to the AddSpace command. This relationship might be hard-coded into the classes themselves, with AddVenue invoking AddSpace on success. AddSpace might then include a view that contains the form for adding the space to the venue.

Both commands may be associated with at least two different views, a core view for presenting the input form and an error or "thank you" screen. According to the logic already discussed, the Command classes themselves would include those views (using conditional tests to decide which view to present in which circumstances).

This level of hard-coding is fine, as long as the commands will always be used in the same way. It begins to break down, though, if I want a special view for AddVenue in some circumstances, and if I want to alter the logic by which one command leads to another (perhaps one flow might include an additional screen between a successful venue addition and the start of a space addition). If each of your commands is only used once, in one relationship to other commands, and with one view, then you should hard-code your commands' relationship with each other and their views. Otherwise, you should read on.

An application controller class can take over this logic, freeing up Command classes to concentrate on their job, which is to process input, invoke application logic, and handle any results.

Implementation

As always, the key to this pattern is the interface. An application controller is a class (or a set of classes) that the front controller can use to acquire commands based on a user request and to find the right view to present after the command has been run. You can see the bare bones of this relationship in Figure 12–6.

As with all patterns in this chapter, the aim is to make things as simple as possible for the client code—hence the spartan front controller class. Behind the interface, though, I must deploy an implementation. The approach laid out here is just one way of doing it. As you work through this section, remember that the essence of the pattern lies in the way that the participants, the application controller, the commands, and the views, interact, and not with the specifics of this implementation.

Let's begin with the code that uses the application controller.

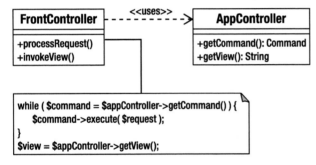

Figure 12–6. *The Application Controller pattern*

The Front Controller

Here is how the FrontController might work with the AppController class (simplified and stripped of error handling):

```
function handleRequest() {
    $request = new Request();
    $app_c = \woo\base\ApplicationRegistry::appController();

    while( $cmd = $app_c->getCommand( $request ) ) {
        $cmd->execute( $request );
```

```
    }
    $this->invokeView( $app_c->getView( $request ) );
}

function invokeView( $target ) {
    include( "woo/view/$target.php" );
    exit;
}
```

As you can see, the principal difference from the previous Front Controller example is that here Command objects are retrieved and executed in a loop. The code also uses AppController to get the name of the view that it should include. Notice that this code uses a registry object to acquire the AppController.

So how do I move from a cmd parameter to a chain of commands and ultimately a view?

Implementation Overview

A Command class might demand a different view according to different stages of operation. The default view for the AddVenue command might be a data input form. If the user adds the wrong kind of data, the form may be presented again, or an error page may be shown. If all goes well, and the venue is created in the system, then I may wish to forward to another in a chain of Command objects: AddSpace, perhaps.

The Command objects tell the system of their current state by setting a status flag. Here are the flags that this minimal implementation recognizes (set as a property in the Command superclass):

```
private static $STATUS_STRINGS = array (
    'CMD_DEFAULT'=>0,
    'CMD_OK' => 1,
    'CMD_ERROR' => 2,
    'CMD_INSUFFICIENT_DATA' => 3
);
```

The application controller finds and instantiates the correct Command class using the Request object. Once it has been run, the Command will be associated with a status. This combination of Command and status can be compared against a data structure to determine which command should be run next, or—if no more commands should be run—which view to serve up.

The Configuration File

The system's owner can determine the way that commands and views work together by setting a set of configuration directives. Here is an extract:

```
<control>
    <view>main</view>
    <view status="CMD_OK">main</view>
    <view status="CMD_ERROR">error</view>

    <command name="ListVenues">
        <view>listvenues</view>
    </command>

    <command name="QuickAddVenue">
```

```
        <classroot name="AddVenue" />
        <view>quickadd</view>
    </command>

    <command name="AddVenue">
        <view>addvenue</view>
        <status value="CMD_OK">
          <forward>AddSpace</forward>
        </status>
    </command>

    <command name="AddSpace">
        <view>addspace</view>
        <status value="CMD_OK">
            <forward>ListVenues</forward>
        </status>
    </command>
    ...
</control>
```

This simplified XML fragment shows one strategy for abstracting the flow of commands and their relationship to views from the Command classes themselves. The directives are all contained within a control element. The logic here is search based. The outermost elements defined are the most generic. They can be overridden by their equivalents within command elements.

So the first element, view, defines the default view for all commands if no other directive contradicts this order. The other view elements on the same level declare status attributes (which correspond to flags set in the Command class). Each status represents a flag that might be set by a Command object to signal its progress with a task. Because these elements are more specific than the first view element, they have priority. If a command sets the CMD_OK flag, then the corresponding view "menu" is the one that will be included, unless an even more specific element overrides this.

Having set these defaults, the document presents the command elements. By default, these elements map directly to Command classes (and their class files on the file system) as in the previous CommandResolver example. So if the cmd parameter is set to AddVenue, then the corresponding element in the configuration document is selected. The string "AddVenue" is used to construct a path to the AddVenue.php class file.

Aliases are supported, however. So if cmd is set to QuickAddVenue, then the following element is used:

```
<command name="QuickAddVenue">
    <classroot name="AddVenue" />
    <view>quickadd</view>
</command>
```

Here, the command element named QuickAddVenue does not map to a class file. That mapping is defined by the classroot element. This makes it possible to reference the AddVenue class in the context of many different flows, and many different views.

Command elements work from outer elements to inner elements, with the inner, more specific, elements having priority. By setting a view element within a command, I ensure that the command is tied to that view.

```
<command name="AddVenue">
```

```
    <view>addvenue</view>
    <status value="CMD_OK">
      <forward>AddSpace</forward>
    </status>
</command>
```

So here, the addvenue view is associated with the AddVenue command (as set in the Request object's cmd parameter). This means that the addvenue.php view will always be included when the AddVenue command is invoked. Always, that is, unless the status condition is matched. If the AddVenue class sets a flag of CMD_OK, the default view for the Command is overridden.

The status element could simply contain another view that would be included in place of the default. Here, though, the forward element comes into play. By forwarding to another command, the configuration file delegates all responsibility for handling views to the new element.

Parsing the Configuration File

This is a reasonably flexible model for controlling display and command flow logic. The document, though, is not something that you would want to parse for every single request. You have already seen a solution to this problem. The ApplicationHelper class provides a mechanism for caching configuration data.

Here is an extract:

```
private function getOptions() {
    $this->ensure( file_exists( $this->config ),
                        "Could not find options file" );
    $options = @SimpleXml_load_file( $this->config );

    // ...set DSN...

    $map = new ControllerMap();

    foreach ( $options->control->view as $default_view ) {
        $stat_str = trim($default_view['status']);
        $status = \woo\command\Command::statuses( $stat_str );
        $map->addView( 'default', $status, (string)$default_view );
    }
    // ... more parse code omitted ...
    \woo\base\ApplicationRegistry::setControllerMap( $map );
}
```

Parsing XML, even with the excellent SimpleXML package, is a wordy business and not particularly challenging, so I leave most of the details out here. The key thing to note is that the getOptions() method is only invoked if configuration has not been cached into the ApplicationRegistry object.

Storing the Configuration Data

The cached object in question is a ControllerMap. ControllerMap is essentially a wrapper around three arrays. I could use raw arrays, of course, but ControllerMap gives us the security of knowing that each array will follow a particular format. Here is the ControllerMap class:

```
namespace woo\controller;
```

```
//...

class ControllerMap {
    private $viewMap = array();
    private $forwardMap = array();
    private $classrootMap = array();

    function addClassroot( $command, $classroot ) {
        $this->classrootMap[$command]=$classroot;
    }

    function getClassroot( $command ) {
        if ( isset( $this->classrootMap[$command] ) ) {
            return $this->classrootMap[$command];
        }
        return $command;
    }

    function addView( $command='default', $status=0, $view ) {
        $this->viewMap[$command][$status]=$view;
    }

    function getView( $command, $status ) {
        if ( isset( $this->viewMap[$command][$status] ) ) {
            return $this->viewMap[$command][$status];
        }
        return null;
    }

    function addForward( $command, $status=0, $newCommand ) {
        $this->forwardMap[$command][$status]=$newCommand;
    }

    function getForward( $command, $status ) {
        if ( isset( $this->forwardMap[$command][$status] ) ) {
            return $this->forwardMap[$command][$status];
        }
        return null;
    }
}
```

The $classroot property is simply an associative array that maps command handles (that is, the names of the command elements in configuration) to the roots of Command class names (that is, AddVenue, as opposed to woo_command_AddVenue). This is used to determine whether the cmd parameter is an alias to a particular class file. During the parsing of the configuration file, the addClassroot() method is called to populate this array.

The $forwardMap and $viewMap arrays are both two-dimensional, supporting combinations of commands and statuses.

Recall this fragment:

```
<command name="AddVenue">
    <view>addvenue</view>
    <status value="CMD_OK">
      <forward>AddSpace</forward>
    </status>
</command>
```

Here is the call the parse code will make to add the correct element to the $viewMap property:

```
$map->addView( 'AddVenue', 0, 'addvenue' );
```

and here is the call for populating the $forwardMap property:

```
$map->addForward( 'AddVenue', 1, 'AddSpace' );
```

The application controller class uses these combinations in a particular search order. Let's say the AddVenue command has returned CMD_OK (which maps to 1, while 0 is CMD_DEFAULT). The application controller will search the $forwardMap array from the most specific combination of Command and status flag to the most general. The first match found will be the command string that is returned:

```
$viewMap['AddVenue'][1];  //  AddVenue CMD_OK [MATCHED]
$viewMap['AddVenue'][0];  //  AddVenue CMD_DEFAULT
$viewMap['default'][1];   //  DefaultCommand CMD_OK
$viewMap['default'][0];   //  DefaultCommand CMD_DEFAULT
```

The same hierarchy of array elements is searched in order to retrieve a view.

Here is an application controller:

```
namespace woo\controller;
//..

class AppController {
    private static $base_cmd;
    private static $default_cmd;
    private $controllerMap;
    private $invoked = array();

    function __construct( ControllerMap $map ) {
        $this->controllerMap = $map;
        if ( ! self::$base_cmd ) {
            self::$base_cmd = new \ReflectionClass( "\\woo\\command\\Command" );
            self::$default_cmd = new \woo\command\DefaultCommand();
        }
    }

    function getView( Request $req ) {
        $view = $this->getResource( $req, "View" );
        return $view;
    }

    function getForward( Request $req ) {
        $forward = $this->getResource( $req, "Forward" );
        if ( $forward ) {
```

```
            $req->setProperty( 'cmd', $forward );
        }
        return $forward;
    }

    private function getResource( Request $req,
                                  $res ) {
        // get the previous command and its execution status
        $cmd_str = $req->getProperty( 'cmd' );
        $previous = $req->getLastCommand();
        $status = $previous->getStatus();
        if (! $status ) { $status = 0; }
        $acquire = "get$res";
        // find resource for previous command and its status
        $resource = $this->controllerMap->$acquire( $cmd_str, $status );
        // alternatively find resource for command and status 0
        if ( ! $resource ) {
            $resource = $this->controllerMap->$acquire( $cmd_str, 0 );
        }

        // or command 'default' and command status
        if ( ! $resource ) {
            $resource = $this->controllerMap->$acquire( 'default', $status );
        }

        // all else has failed get resource for 'default', status 0
        if ( ! $resource ) {
            $resource = $this->controllerMap->$acquire( 'default', 0 );
        }

        return $resource;
    }

    function getCommand( Request $req ) {
        $previous = $req->getLastCommand();
        if ( ! $previous ) {
            // this is the first command this request
            $cmd = $req->getProperty('cmd');
            if ( ! $cmd ) {
                // no cmd property - using default
                $req->setProperty('cmd', 'default' );
                return  self::$default_cmd;
            }
        } else {
            // a command has been run already in this request
            $cmd = $this->getForward( $req );
            if ( ! $cmd ) { return null; }
        }
```

```
        // we now have a command name in $cmd
        // turn it into a Command object
        $cmd_obj = $this->resolveCommand( $cmd );
        if ( ! $cmd_obj ) {
            throw new \woo\base\AppException( "couldn't resolve '$cmd'" );
        }

        $cmd_class = get_class( $cmd_obj );
        if ( isset( $this->invoked[$cmd_class] ) ) {
            throw new \woo\base\AppException( "circular forwarding" );
        }

        $this->invoked[$cmd_class]=1;
        // return the Command object
        return $cmd_obj;
    }

    function resolveCommand( $cmd ) {
        $classroot = $this->controllerMap->getClassroot( $cmd );
        $filepath = "woo/command/$classroot.php";
        $classname = "\\woo\\command\\{$classroot}";
        if ( file_exists( $filepath ) ) {
            require_once( "$filepath" );
            if ( class_exists( $classname) ) {
                $cmd_class = new ReflectionClass($classname);
                if ( $cmd_class->isSubClassOf( self::$base_cmd ) ) {
                    return $cmd_class->newInstance();
                }
            }
        }
        return null;
    }
}
```

The getResource() method implements the search for both forwarding and view selection. It is called by getView() and getForward(), respectively. Notice how it searches from the most specific combination of command string and status flag to the most generic.

getCommand() is responsible for returning as many commands as have been configured into a forwarding chain. It works like this: when the initial request is received, there should be a cmd property available, and no record of a previous Command having been run in this request. The Request object stores this information. If the cmd request property has not been set, then the method uses default, and returns the default Command class. The $cmd string variable is passed to resolveCommand(), which uses it to acquire a Command object.

When getCommand() is called for the second time in the request, the Request object will be holding a reference to the Command previously run. getCommand() then checks to see if any forwarding is set for the combination of that Command and its status flag (by calling getForward()). If getForward() finds a match, it returns a string that can be resolved to a Command and returned to the Controller.

Another thing to note in getCommand() is the essential check I impose to prevent circular forwarding. I maintain an array indexed by Command class names. If an element is already present when I come to add it, I know that this command has been retrieved previously. This puts us at risk of falling into an infinite loop, which is something I *really* don't want, so I throw an exception if this happens.

The strategies an application controller might use to acquire views and commands can vary considerably; the key is that these are hidden away from the wider system. Figure 12–7 shows the high-level process by which a front controller class uses an application controller to acquire first a Command object and then a view.

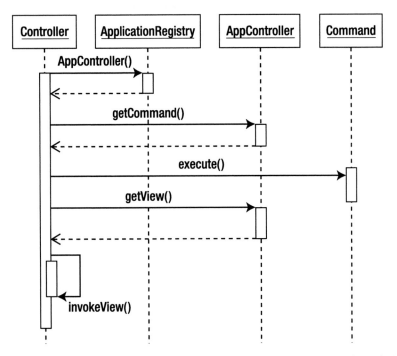

Figure 12–7. *Using an application controller to acquire commands and views*

The Command Class

You may have noticed that the AppController class relies on previous commands having been stored in the Request object. This is done by the Command base class:

```
namespace woo\command;
//....

abstract class Command {

    private static $STATUS_STRINGS = array (
        'CMD_DEFAULT'=>0,
        'CMD_OK' => 1,
        'CMD_ERROR' => 2,
        'CMD_INSUFFICIENT_DATA' => 3
```

```
);
private $status = 0;

final function __construct() { }

function execute( \woo\controller\Request  $request ) {
    $this->status = $this->doExecute( $request );
    $request->setCommand( $this );
}

function getStatus() {
    return $this->status;
}

static function statuses( $str='CMD_DEFAULT' ) {
    if ( empty( $str ) ) { $str = 'CMD_DEFAULT'; }
    // convert string into a status number
    return self::$STATUS_STRINGS[$str];
}
abstract function doExecute( \woo\controller\Request $request );

}
```

The Command class defines an array of status strings (severely cut for the sake of this example). It provides the statuses() method for converting a string ("CMD_OK") to its equivalent number, and getStatus() for revealing the current Command object's status flag. If you want to be strict, statuses() could throw an exception on failure. As it is, the method returns null by default if the right element is not defined. The execute() method uses the return value of the abstract doExecute() to set the status flag, and to cache itself in the Request object.

A Concrete Command

Here is how a simple AddVenue command might look:

```
namespace woo\command;
//...

class AddVenue extends Command {

    function doExecute( \woo\controller\Request $request ) {
        $name = $request->getProperty("venue_name");
        if ( ! $name ) {
            $request->addFeedback( "no name provided" );
            return self::statuses('CMD_INSUFFICIENT_DATA');
        } else {
            $venue_obj = new \woo\domain\Venue( null, $name );
            $request->setObject( 'venue', $venue_obj );
            $request->addFeedback( "'$name' added ({$venue_obj->getId()})" );
            return self::statuses('CMD_OK');
        }

    }
}
```

Some of this code will make more sense in the next chapter. For now here's a stub Venue object that would work with this command:

```
namespace woo\domain;

class Venue {
    private $id;
    private $name;

    function __construct( $id, $name ) {
        $this->name = $name;
        $this->id = $id;
    }

    function getName() {
        return $this->name;
    }
    function getId() {
        return $this->id;
    }
}
```

Returning to the command, the key thing to note is that the doExecute() method returns a status flag that the abstract base class stores in a property. The decision as to how to respond to the fact that this object has been invoked and has set this status is entirely driven by the configuration file. So according to the example XML, if CMD_OK is returned, the forwarding mechanism will cause the AddSpace class to be instantiated. This chain of events is triggered in this way only if the request contains cmd=AddVenue. If the request contains cmd=QuickAddVenue, then no forwarding will take place, and the quickaddvenue view will be displayed.

Note that this example does not include any code for saving a Venue object to the database. I'll get to that in the next chapter.

Consequences

A fully featured instance of the Application Controller pattern can be a pain to set up because of the sheer amount of work that must go into acquiring and applying metadata that describes the relationships between command and request, command and command, and command and view.

For this reason, I tend to implement something like this when my application tells me it is needed. I usually hear this whisper when I find myself adding conditionals to my commands that invoke different views or invoke other commands according to circumstances. It is at about this time that I feel that command flow and display logic are beginning to spiral out of my control.

Of course, an application controller can use all sorts of mechanisms to build its associations among commands and views, not just the approach I have taken here. Even if you're starting off with a fixed relationship among a request string, a command name, and a view in all cases, you could still benefit from building an application controller to encapsulate this. It will give you considerable flexibility when you must refactor in order to accommodate more complexity.

Page Controller

Much as I like the Front Controller pattern, it is not always the right approach to take. The investment in up-front design tends to reward the larger system and penalize simple need-results-now projects. The Page Controller pattern will probably be familiar to you already as it is a common strategy. Nevertheless, it is worth exploring some of the issues.

The Problem

Once again, the problem is your need to manage the relationship among request, domain logic, and presentation. This is pretty much a constant for enterprise projects. What differs, though, are the constraints placed on you.

If you have a relatively simple project, and one where big up-front design could threaten your deadline without adding huge amounts of value, Page Controller can be a good option for managing requests and views.

Let's say that you want to present a page that displays a list of all venues in the Woo system. Even with the database retrieval code finished, without Front Controller already in place, I have a daunting task to get just this simple result.

The view is a list of venues; the request is for a list of venues. Errors permitting, the request does not lead to a new view, as you might expect in a complex task. The simplest thing that works here is to associate the view and the controller—often in the same page.

Implementation

Although the practical reality of Page Controller projects can become fiendish, the pattern is simple. Control is related to a view, or to a set of views. In the simplest case, this means that the control sits in the view itself, although it can be abstracted, especially when a view is closely linked with others (that is when you might need to forward to different pages in different circumstances).

Here is the simplest flavor of Page Controller:

```php
<?php
require_once("woo/domain/Venue.php");
try {
    $venues = \woo\domain\Venue::findAll();
} catch ( Exception $e ) {
    include( 'error.php' );
    exit(0);
}

// default page follows
?>
<html>
<head>
<title>Venues</title>
</head>
<body>

<h1>Venues</h1>

<?php foreach( $venues as $venue ) { ?>
```

```
    <?php print $venue->getName(); ?><br />
<?php } ?>

</body>
</html>
```

This document has two elements to it. The view element handles display, while the controller element manages the request and invokes application logic. Even though view and controller inhabit the same page, they are rigidly separated.

There is very little to this example (aside from the database work going on behind the scenes, of which you'll find more in the section "The Data Layer"). The PHP block at the top of the page attempts to get a list of Venue objects, which it stores in the $venues global variable.

If an error occurs, the page delegates to a page called error.php by using include(), followed by exit() to kill any further processing on the current page. I prefer this mechanism to an HTTP forward, which is much more expensive and loses any environment you may have set up in memory. If no include takes place, then the HTML at the bottom of the page (the view) is shown.

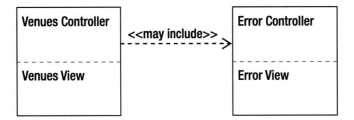

Figure 12–8. *Page Controllers embedded in views*

This will do as a quick test, but a system of any size or complexity will probably need more support than that.

The Page Controller code was previously implicitly separated from the view. Here, I make the break starting with a rudimentary Page Controller base class:

```
namespace woo\controller;
//...

abstract class PageController {
    private $request;
    function __construct() {
        $request = \woo\base\RequestRegistry::getRequest();
        if ( is_null( $request ) ) { $request = new Request(); }
        $this->request = $request;
    }

    abstract function process();

    function forward( $resource ) {
        include( $resource );
        exit( 0 );
```

```
    }

    function getRequest() {
        return $this->request;
    }
}
```

This class uses some of the tools that you have already looked at, in particular the Request and RequestRegistry classes. The PageController class's main roles are to provide access to a Request object and to manage the including of views. This list of purposes would quickly grow in a real project as more child classes discover a need for common functionality.

A child class could live inside the view, and thereby display it by default as before, or it could stand separate from the view. The latter approach is cleaner, I think, so that's the path I take. Here is a PageController that attempts to add a new venue to the system:

```
namespace woo\controller;
//...

class AddVenueController extends PageController {
    function process() {
        try {
            $request = $this->getRequest();
            $name = $request->getProperty( 'venue_name' );
            if ( is_null( $request->getProperty('submitted') ) ) {
                $request->addFeedback("choose a name for the venue");
                $this->forward( 'add_venue.php' );
            } else if ( is_null( $name ) ) {
                $request->addFeedback("name is a required field");
                $this->forward( 'add_venue.php' );
            }

            // just creating the object is enough to add it
            // to the database
            $venue = new \woo\domain\Venue( null, $name );
            $this->forward( "ListVenues.php" );
        } catch ( Exception $e ) {
            $this->forward( 'error.php' );
        }
    }
}

$controller = new AddVenueController();
$controller->process();
```

The AddVenueController class only implements the process() method. process() is responsible for checking the user's submission. If the user has not submitted a form, or has completed the form incorrectly, the default view (add_venue.php) is included, providing feedback and presenting the form. If I successfully add a new user, then the method invokes forward() to send the user to the ListVenues page controller.

Note the format I used for the view. I tend to differentiate view files from class files by using all lowercase file names in the former and camel case (running words together and using capital letters to show the boundaries) in the latter.

Here is the view associated with the AddVenueController class:

```php
<?php
require_once( "woo/base/RequestRegistry.php" );
$request = \woo\base\RequestRegistry::getRequest();
?>
<html>
<head>
<title>Add Venue</title>
</head>
<body>
<h1>Add Venue</h1>

<table>
<tr>
<td>
<?php
print $request->getFeedbackString("</td></tr><tr><td>");
?>
</td>
</tr>
</table>

<form action="AddVenue.php" method="get">
    <input type="hidden" name="submitted" value="yes"/>
    <input type="text" name="venue_name" />
</form>
</body>

</html>
```

As you can see, the view does nothing but display data and provide the mechanism for generating a new request. The request is made to the PageController, not back to the view. Remember, it is the PageController class that is responsible for processing requests.

You can see an overview of this more complicated version of the Page Controller pattern in Figure 12–9.

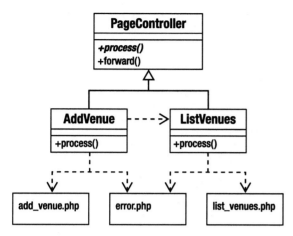

Figure 12–9. *A Page Controller class hierarchy and its include relationships*

Consequences

This approach has the great merit that it immediately makes sense to anyone with any Web experience. I make a request for venues.php, and that is precisely what I get. Even an error is within the bounds of expectation, with "server error" and "page not found" pages an everyday reality.

Things get a little more complicated if you separate the view from the page controller class, but the near one-to-one relationship between the participants is clear enough.

One potential area of confusion lies with the inclusion of views. A page controller includes its view once it has completed processing. In some circumstances, though, it might use the same inclusion code to include another page controller. So, for example, when AddVenue successfully adds a venue, it no longer needs to display the addition form. Instead it delegates to another page controller called ListVenues. You need to be clear about when you are delegating to a view and when you are delegating to another page controller. It is the responsibility of the page controller to ensure that its views have the data they need to do their jobs.

Although a page controller class might delegate to Command objects, the benefit of doing so is not as marked as it is with Front Controller. Front controller classes need to work out what the purpose of a request is; page controller classes already know this. The light request checking and logic layer calls that you would put in a Command sit just as easily in a page controller class, and you benefit from the fact that you do not need a mechanism to select your Command objects.

Duplication can be a problem, but the use of a common superclass can factor away a lot of that. You can also save on setup time, because you can avoid loading data you won't be needing in the current context. Of course, you could do that with Front Controller too, but the process of discovering what is needed, and what is not, would be much more complicated.

The real drawback to the pattern lies in situations where the paths through your views are complex—especially when the same view is used in different ways at different times (add and edit screens are a good example of this). You can find that you get tangled up in conditionals and state checking, and it becomes hard to get an overview of your system.

It is not impossible to start with Page Controller and move toward the Front Controller pattern, however. This is especially true if you are using a PageController superclass.

As a rule of thumb, if I estimate a system should take me less than a week or so to complete, and that it isn't going to need more phases in the future, I would choose Page Controller and benefit from fast turnaround. If I were building a large project that needs to grow over time and has complex view logic, I would go for a Front Controller every time.

Template View and View Helper

Template View is pretty much what you get by default in PHP, in that I can commingle presentation markup (HTML) and system code (native PHP). As I have said before, this is both a blessing and a curse, because the ease with which these can be brought together represents a temptation to combine application and display logic in the same place with potentially disastrous consequences.

In PHP then, programming the view is largely a matter of restraint. If it isn't strictly a matter of display, treat any code with the greatest suspicion.

To this end, the View Helper pattern (Alur et al.) provides for a helper class that may be specific to a view or shared between multiple views to help with any tasks that require more than the smallest amount of code.

The Problem

These days it is becoming rarer to find SQL queries and other business logic embedded directly in display pages, but it still happens. I have covered this particular evil in great detail in previous chapters, so I'll keep this brief.

Web pages that contain too much code can be hard for web producers to work with, as presentation components become tangled up in loops and conditionals.

Business logic in the presentation forces you to stick with that interface. You can't switch in a new view easily without porting across a lot of application code too.

With many operations recurring from view to view, systems that embed application code in their templates tend to fall prey to duplication as the same code structures are pasted from page to page. Where this happens, bugs and maintenance nightmares surely follow.

To prevent this from happening, you should handle application processing elsewhere and allow views to manage presentation only. This is often achieved by making views the passive recipients of data. Where a view does need to interrogate the system, it is a good idea to provide a View Helper object to do any involved work on the view's behalf.

Implementation

Once you have created a wider framework, the view layer is not a massive programming challenge. Of course, it remains a huge design and information architecture issue, but that's another book!

Template View was so named by Fowler. It is a staple pattern used by most enterprise programmers. In some languages, an implementation might involve cooking up a templating system that translates tags to values set by the system. You have that option in PHP too. You could use a templating engine like the excellent Smarty. My preferred option, though, is to use PHP's existing functionality, but to use it with care.

In order for a view to have something to work with, it must be able to acquire data. I like to define a View Helper that views can use. From this, they can get access to the Request object and, through it, to any other objects that they need to do their job.

Here is a simple View Helper class:

```
namespace woo\view;
class VH {
    static function getRequest() {
        return \woo\base\RequestRegistry::getRequest();
    }
}
```

All this class does at present is provide access to a Request object. You can extend it to provide additional functionality as your application evolves. If you find yourself doing something in a view that takes up more than a couple of lines, chances are it belongs in the View Helper. In a larger application, you may provide multiple View Helper objects in an inheritance hierarchy in order to provide different tools for different parts of your system.

Here is a simple view that uses both the View Helper and the Request object:

```
<?php
require_once("woo/view/ViewHelper.php");
$request = \woo\view\VH::getRequest();  // Controller caches this
$venue = $request->getObject('venue'); // Command caches this
?>

<html>
<head>
<title>Add a Space for venue <?php echo $venue->getName() ?></title>
</head>
<body>
<h1>Add a Space for Venue '<?php print $venue->getName() ?>'</h1>
<table>
<tr>
<td>
<?php print $request->getFeedbackString("</td></tr><tr><td>"); ?>
</td>
</tr>
</table>

<form method="post">
    <input type="text"
     value="<?php echo $request->getProperty( 'space_name' ) ?>" name="space_name"/>
    <input type="hidden" name="venue_id" value="<?php echo $venue->getId() ?>" />
    <input type="submit" value="submit" />
</form>

</body>
</html>
```

The view (add_space.php) gets a Request object from the View Helper (VH) and uses its methods to supply the dynamic data for the page. In particular, the getFeedback() method returns any messages set by commands, and getObject() acquires any objects cached for the view layer. getProperty() is used to access any parameters set in the HTTP request. If you run this view on its own, the Venue and Request objects will not have been made available. Check back to the Controller class to see where the Request object is set, and to the AddVenue command class to see the Venue object being stored on the Request.

You could simplify things still further here by making the View Helper a proxy that delegates for the Request object's most useful methods, saving the view layer the bother of even acquiring a reference to Request.

Clearly, this example doesn't banish code from the view, but it does severely limit the amount and kind of coding that needs to be done. The page contains simple print statements and a few method calls. A designer should be able to work around code of this kind with little or no effort.

Slightly more problematic are if statements and loops. These are difficult to delegate to a View Helper, because they are usually bound up with formatted output. I tend to keep both simple conditionals and loops (which are very common in building tables that display rows of data) inside the Template View, but to keep them as simple as possible, I delegate things like test clauses where possible.

Consequences

There is something slightly disturbing about the way that data is passed to the view layer, in that a view doesn't really have a fixed interface that guarantees its environment. I tend to think of every view as entering into a contract with the system at large. The view effectively says to the application, "If I am invoked, then I have a right to access object This, object That, and object TheOther." It is up to the application to ensure that this is the case.

Surprisingly, I have always found that this works perfectly well for me, though you could make views stricter by adding assertions to view-specific helper classes. If you go as far as this, you could go for complete safety and provide accessor methods in the helper classes that do away with the need for the evil Request::getObject() method, which is clearly just a wrapper around an associative array.

While I like type safety where I can get it, I find the thought of building a parallel system of views and View Helper classes exhausting in the extreme. I tend to register objects dynamically for the view layer, through a Request object, a SessionRegistry, or a RequestRegistry.

While templates are often essentially passive, populated with data resulting from the last request, there may be times when the view needs to make an ancillary request. The View Helper is a good place to provide this functionality, keeping any knowledge of the mechanism by which data is required hidden from the view itself. Even the View Helper should do as little work as possible, delegating to a command or contacting the domain layer via a facade.

▨**Note** You saw the Facade pattern in Chapter 10. Alur et al. look at one use of Facades in enterprise programming in the Session Facade pattern (which is designed to limit fine-grained network transactions). Fowler also describes a pattern called Service Layer, which provides a simple point of access to the complexities within a layer.

The Business Logic Layer

If the control layer orchestrates communication with the outside world and marshals a system's response to it, the logic layer gets on with the *business* of an application. This layer should be as free as possible of the noise and trauma generated as query strings are analyzed, HTML tables are constructed, and feedback messages composed. Business logic is about doing the stuff that needs doing—the true purpose of the application. Everything else exists just to support these tasks.

In a classic object-oriented application, the business logic layer is often composed of classes that model the problems that the system aims to address. As you shall see, this is a flexible design decision. It also requires significant up-front planning.

Let's begin, then, with the quickest way of getting a system up and running.

Transaction Script

The Transaction Script pattern (*Patterns of Enterprise Application Architecture*) describes the way that many systems evolve of their own accord. It is simple, intuitive, and effective, although it becomes less so as systems grow. A transaction script handles a request inline, rather than delegating to specialized objects. It is the quintessential quick fix. It is also a hard pattern to categorize, because it combines elements from other layers in this chapter. I have chosen to present it as part of the business logic layer, because the pattern's motivation is to achieve the business aims of the system.

The Problem

Every request must be handled in some way. As you have seen, many systems provide a layer that assesses and filters incoming data. Ideally, though, this layer should then call on classes that are designed to fulfill the request. These classes could be broken down to represent forces and responsibilities in a system, perhaps with a facade interface. This approach requires a certain amount of careful design, however. For some projects (typically small in scope and urgent in nature) such a development overhead can be unacceptable. In this case, you may need to build your business logic into a set of procedural operations. Each operation will be crafted to handle a particular request.

The problem, then, is the need to provide a fast and effective mechanism for fulfilling a system's objectives without a potentially costly investment in complex design.

The great benefit of this pattern is the speed with which you can get results. Each script takes input and manipulates the database to ensure an outcome. Beyond organizing related methods within the same class and keeping the Transaction Script classes in their own tier (that is, as independent as possible of the command and control and view layers), there is little up-front design required.

While business logic layer classes tend to be clearly separated from the presentation layer, they are often more embedded in the data layer. This is because retrieving and storing data is key to the tasks that such classes often perform. You will see mechanisms for decoupling logic objects from the database later in the chapter. Transaction Script classes, though, usually know all about the database (though they can use gateway classes to handle the details of their actual queries).

Implementation

Let's return to my events listing example. In this case, the system supports three relational database tables: venue, space, and event. A venue may have a number of spaces (a theater can have more than one stage, for example; a dance club may have different rooms, and so on). Each space plays host to many events. Here is the schema:

```
CREATE TABLE 'venue' (
  'id' int(11) NOT NULL auto_increment,
  'name' text,
  PRIMARY KEY ('id')
```

```
)
CREATE TABLE 'space' (
  'id' int(11) NOT NULL auto_increment,
  'venue' int(11) default NULL,
  'name' text,
  PRIMARY KEY ('id')
)
CREATE TABLE 'event' (
  'id' int(11) NOT NULL auto_increment,
  'space' int(11) default NULL,
  'start' mediumtext,
  'duration' int(11) default NULL,
  'name' text,
  PRIMARY KEY ('id')
)
```

Clearly, the system will need mechanisms for adding both venues and events. Each of these represents a single transaction. I could give each method its own class (and organize my classes according to the Command pattern that you encountered in Chapter 11). In this case, though, I am going to place the methods in a single class, albeit as part of an inheritance hierarchy. You can see the structure in Figure 12–10.

So why does this example include an abstract superclass? In a script of any size, I would be likely to add more concrete classes to this hierarchy. Since most of these will work with the database, a common superclass is an excellent place to put core functionality for making database requests.

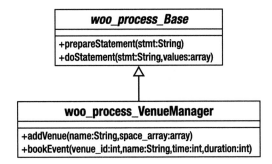

Figure 12–10. *A Transaction Script class with its superclass*

In fact, this is a pattern in its own right (Fowler has named it Layer Supertype), albeit one that most programmers use without thinking. Where classes in a layer share characteristics, it makes sense to group them into a single type, locating utility operations in the base class. You will see this a lot in the rest of this chapter.

In this case, the base class acquires a PDO object, which it stores in a static property. It also provides methods for caching database statements and making queries.

```
namespace woo\process;
//...
```

```
abstract class Base {
    static $DB;
    static $stmts = array();

    function __construct() {
        $dsn = \woo\base\ApplicationRegistry::getDSN( );
        if ( is_null( $dsn ) ) {
            throw new \woo\base\AppException( "No DSN" );
        }

        self::$DB = new \PDO( $dsn );
        self::$DB->setAttribute(\PDO::ATTR_ERRMODE, \PDO::ERRMODE_EXCEPTION);
    }

    function prepareStatement( $stmt_s ) {
        if ( isset( self::$stmts[$stmt_s] ) ) {
            return self::$stmts[$stmt_s];
        }
        $stmt_handle = self::$DB->prepare($stmt_s);
        self::$stmts[$stmt_s]=$stmt_handle;
        return $stmt_handle;
    }

    protected function doStatement( $stmt_s, $values_a ) {
        $sth = $this->prepareStatement( $stmt_s );
        $sth->closeCursor();
        $db_result = $sth->execute( $values_a );
        return $sth;
    }
}
```
I use the ApplicationRegistry class to acquire a DSN string, which I pass to the PDO constructor.

The prepareStatement() method simply calls the PDO class's prepare() method, which returns a statement handle. This is eventually passed to the execute() method. To run a query, though, in this method, I cache the resource in a static array called $stmts. I use the SQL statement itself as the array element's index.

prepareStatement() can be called directly by child classes, but it is more likely to be invoked via doStatement(). This accepts an SQL statement and a mixed array of values (strings and integers). This array should contain the values that are to be passed to the database in executing the statement. The method then uses the SQL statement in a call to prepareStatement(), acquiring a statement resource that it uses with the PDOStatment::execute() method. If an error occurs, I throw an exception. As you will see, all this work is hidden from the transaction scripts. All they need to do is formulate the SQL and get on with business logic.

Here is the start of the VenueManager class, which sets up my SQL statements:

```
namespace woo\process;
//...

class VenueManager extends Base {
    static $add_venue =   "INSERT INTO venue
                            ( name )
```

```
                               values( ? )";
       static $add_space   = "INSERT INTO space
                               ( name, venue )
                               values( ?, ? )";
       static $check_slot = "SELECT id, name
                             FROM event
                             WHERE space = ?
                             AND (start+duration) > ?
                             AND start < ?";
       static $add_event =  "INSERT INTO event
                             ( name, space, start, duration )
                             values( ?, ?, ?, ? )";
       //...
```

Not much new here. These are the SQL statements that the transaction scripts will use. They are constructed in a format accepted by the PDO class's prepare() method. The question marks are placeholders for the values that will be passed to execute().

Now to define the first method designed to fulfill a specific business need:

```
function addVenue( $name, $space_array ) {
    $ret = array();
    $ret['venue'] = array( $name );
    $this->doStatement( self::$add_venue, $ret['venue']);
    $v_id = self::$DB->lastInsertId();
    $ret['spaces'] = array();
    foreach ( $space_array as $space_name ) {
        $values = array( $space_name, $v_id );
        $this->doStatement( self::$add_space, $values);
        $s_id = self::$DB->lastInsertId();
        array_unshift( $values, $s_id );
        $ret['spaces'][] = $values;
    }
    return $ret;
}
```

As you can see, addVenue() requires a venue name and an array of space names. It uses these to populate the venue and space tables. It also creates a data structure that contains this information, along with the newly generated ID values for each row.

This method is spared lots of tedious database work by the superclass. I pass the venue name provided by the caller to doStatement(). If there's an error with this, remember, an exception is thrown. I don't catch any exceptions here, so anything thrown by doStatement() or (by extension) prepareStatement() will also be thrown by this method. This is the result I want, although I should to make it clear that this method throws exceptions in my documentation.

Having created the venue row, I loop through $space_array, adding a row in the space table for each element. Notice that I include the venue ID as a foreign key in each of the space rows I create, associating the row with the venue.

The second transaction script is similarly straightforward:

```
function bookEvent( $space_id, $name, $time, $duration ) {
    $values = array( $space_id, $time, ($time+$duration) );
    $stmt = $this->doStatement( self::$check_slot, $values, false ) ;
```

```
        if ( $result = $stmt->fetch() ) {
            throw new \woo\base\AppException( "double booked! try again" );
        }
        $this->doStatement( self::$add_event,
            array( $name, $space_id, $time, $duration ) );
    }
```

The purpose of this script is to add an event to the events table, associated with a space. Notice that I use the SQL statement contained in $check_slot to make sure that the proposed event does not clash with another in the same space.

Consequences

The Transaction Script pattern is an effective way of getting good results fast. It is also one of those patterns many programmers have used for years without imagining it might need a name. With a few good helper methods like those I added to the base class, you can concentrate on application logic without getting too bogged down in database fiddle-faddling.

I have seen Transaction Script appear in a less welcome context. I thought I was writing a much more complex and object-heavy application than would usually suit this pattern. As the pressure of deadlines began to tell, I found that I was placing more and more logic in what was intended to be a thin facade onto a Domain Model (see the next section). Although the result was less elegant than I had wanted, I have to admit that the application did not appear to suffer for its implicit redesign.

In most cases, you would choose a Transaction Script approach with a small project when you are certain it isn't going to grow into a large one. The approach does not scale well, because duplication often begins to creep in as the scripts inevitably cross one another. You can go some way to factoring this out, of course, but you probably will not be able to excise it completely.

In my example, I decide to embed database code in the transaction script classes themselves. As you saw, though, the code wants to separate the database work from the application logic. I can make that break absolute by pulling it out of the class altogether and creating a gateway class whose role it is to handle database interactions on the system's behalf.

Domain Model

The Domain Model is the pristine logical engine that many of the other patterns in this chapter strive to create, nurture, and protect. It is an abstracted representation of the forces at work in your project. It's a kind of plane of forms, where your business problems play out their nature unencumbered by nasty material issues like databases and web pages.

If that seems a little flowery, let's bring it down to reality. A Domain Model is a representation of the real-world participants of your system. It is in the Domain Model that the object-as-thing rule of thumb is truer than elsewhere. Everywhere else, objects tend to embody responsibilities. In the Domain Model, they often describe a set of attributes, with added agency. They are *things* that do *stuff.*

The Problem

If you have been using Transaction Script, you may find that duplication becomes a problem as different scripts need to perform the same tasks. That can be factored out to a certain extent, but over time, it's easy to fall into cut-and-paste coding.

You can use a Domain Model to extract and embody the participants and process of your system. Rather than using a script to add space data to the database, and then associate event data with it, you can create Space and Event classes. Booking an event in a space can then become as simple as a call to Space::bookEvent(). A task like checking for a time clash becomes Event::intersects(), and so on.

Clearly, with an example as simple as Woo, a Transaction Script is more than adequate. But as domain logic gets more complex, the alternative of a Domain Model becomes increasingly attractive. Complex logic can be handled more easily, and you need less conditional code when you model the application domain.

Implementation

Domain Models can be relatively simple to design. Most of the complexity associated with the subject lies in the patterns that are designed to keep the model pure—that is, to separate it from the other tiers in the application.

Separating the participants of a Domain Model from the presentation layer is largely a matter of ensuring that they keep to themselves. Separating the participants from the data layer is much more problematic. Although the ideal is to consider a Domain Model only in terms of the problems it represents and resolves, the reality of the database is hard to escape.

It is common for Domain Model classes to map fairly directly to tables in a relational database, and this certainly makes life easier. Figure 12–11, for example, shows a class diagram that sketches some of the participants of the Woo system.

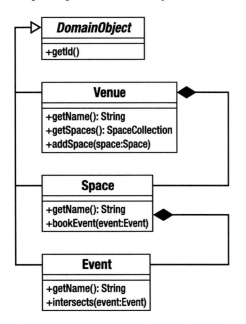

Figure 12–11. *An extract from a Domain Model*

The objects in Figure 12–11 mirror the tables that were set up for the Transaction Script example. This direct association makes a system easier to manage, but it is not always possible, especially if you are working with a database schema that precedes your application. Such an association can itself be the source of problems. If you're not careful, you can end up modeling the database, rather than the problems and forces you are attempting to address.

Just because a Domain Model often mirrors the structure of a database does not mean that its classes should have any knowledge of it. By separating the model from the database, you make the entire tier easier to test and less likely to be affected by changes of schema, or even changes of storage mechanism. It also focuses the responsibility of each class on its core tasks.

Here is a simplified Venue object, together with its parent class:

```
namespace woo\domain;



abstract class DomainObject {
    private $id;

    function __construct( $id=null ) {
        $this->id = $id;
    }

    function getId( ) {
        return $this->id;
    }

    static function getCollection( $type ) {
        return array(); // dummy
    }

    function collection() {
        return self::getCollection( get_class( $this ) );
    }
}


class Venue extends DomainObject {
    private $name;
    private $spaces;

    function __construct( $id=null, $name=null ) {
        $this->name = $name;
        $this->spaces = self::getCollection("\\woo\\domain\\Space");
        parent::__construct( $id );
    }

    function setSpaces( SpaceCollection $spaces ) {
        $this->spaces = $spaces;
    }

    function getSpaces() {
        return $this->spaces;
    }

    function addSpace( Space $space ) {
```

```
        $this->spaces->add( $space );
        $space->setVenue( $this );
    }

    function setName( $name_s ) {
        $this->name = $name_s;
        $this->markDirty();
    }

    function getName( ) {
        return $this->name;
    }
}
```

There a few points that distinguish this class from one intended to run without persistence. Instead of an array, I am using an object of type SpaceCollection to store any Space objects the Venue might contain. (Though I could argue that a type-safe array is a bonus whether you are working with a database or not!) Because this class works with a special collection object rather than an array of Space objects, the constructor needs to instantiate an empty collection on startup. It does this by calling a static method on the layer supertype.

▓**Note** In this chapter and the next I will discuss amendments to both the Venue and Space objects. These are simple domain objects and share a common functional core. If you're coding along, you should be able to apply concepts I discuss to either class. A Space class may not maintain a collection of Space objects for example, but it might manage Event objects in exactly the same way.

```
$this->spaces = self::getCollection("\\woo\\domain\\Space");
```

I will return to this system's collection objects in the next chapter, for now, though, the superclass simply returns an empty array.

I expect an $id parameter in the constructor that I pass to the superclass for storage. It should come as no surprise to learn that the $id parameter represents the unique ID of a row in the database. Notice also that I call a method on the superclass called markDirty() (this will be covered when you encounter the Unit of Work pattern).

Consequences

The design of a Domain Model needs to be as simple or complicated as the business processes you need to emulate. The beauty of this is that you can focus on the forces in your problem as you design the model and handle issues like persistence and presentation in other layers—in theory, that is.

In practice, I think that most developers design their domain models with at least one eye on the database. No one wants to design structures that will force you (or, worse, your colleagues) into somersaults of convoluted code when it comes to getting your objects in and out of the database.

This separation between Domain Model and the data layer comes at a considerable cost in terms of design and planning. It is possible to place database code directly in the model (although you would probably want to design a gateway to handle the actual SQL). For relatively simple models, especially if each class broadly maps to a table, this approach can be a real win, saving you the considerable design overhead of devising an external system for reconciling your objects with the database.

Summary

I have covered an enormous amount of ground here (although I have also left out a lot). You should not feel daunted by the sheer volume of code in this chapter. Patterns are meant to be used in the right circumstances, and combined when useful. Use those described in this chapter that you feel meet the needs of your project, and do not feel that you must build an entire framework before embarking on a project. On the other hand, there *is* enough material here to form the basis of a framework, or just as likely, to provide some insight into the architecture of some of the prebuilt frameworks you might choose to deploy.

And there's more! I left you teetering on the edge of persistence, with just a few tantalizing hints about collections and mappers to tease you. In the next chapter, I will look at some patterns for working with databases and for insulating your objects from the details of data storage.

CHAPTER 13

■ ■ ■

Database Patterns

Most web applications of any complexity handle persistence to a greater or lesser extent. Shops must recall their products and their customer records. Games must remember their players and the state of play. Social networking sites must keep track of your 238 friends and your unaccountable liking for boy-bands of the '80s and '90s. Whatever the application, the chances are it's keeping score behind the scenes. In this chapter, I look at some patterns that can help.

This chapter will cover

- *The Data Layer interface*: Patterns that define the points of contact between the storage layer and the rest of the system

- *Object watching*: Keeping track of objects, avoiding duplicates, automating save and insert operations

- *Flexible queries*: Allowing your client coders to construct queries without thinking about the underlying database

- *Creating lists of found objects*: Building iterable collections

- *Managing your database components*: The welcome return of the Abstract Factory pattern

The Data Layer

In discussions with clients, it's usually the presentation layer that dominates. Fonts, colors, and ease of use are the primary topics of conversation. Amongst developers it is often the database that looms large. It's not the database itself that concerns us; we can trust that to do its job unless we're very unlucky. No, it's the mechanisms we use to translate the rows and columns of a database table into data structures that cause the problems. In this chapter, I look at code that can help with this process.

Not everything presented here sits in the Data layer itself. Rather I have grouped some of the patterns that help to solve persistence problems. All of these patterns are described by one or more of Clifton Nock, Martin Fowler, and Alur et al.

Data Mapper

If you thought I glossed over the issue of saving and retrieving Venue objects from the database in the "Domain Model" section of Chapter 12, here is where you might find at least some answers. The Data Mapper pattern is described by both Alur et al in *Core J2EE Patterns* (as Data Access Object) and Martin Fowler in *Patterns of Enterprise Application Architecture* (in fact, Data Access Object is not an exact match, as it generates data transfer objects, but since such objects are designed to become the real thing if you add water, the patterns are close enough).

As you might imagine, a data mapper is a class that is responsible for handling the transition from database to object.

The Problem

Objects are not organized like tables in a relational database. As you know, database tables are grids made up of rows and columns. One row may relate to another in a different (or even the same) table by means of a foreign key. Objects, on the other hand, tend to relate to one another more organically. One object may contain another, and different data structures will organize the same objects in different ways, combining and recombining objects in new relationships at runtime. Relational databases are optimized to manage large amounts of tabular data, whereas classes and objects encapsulate smaller focussed chunks of information.

This disconnect between classes and relational databases is often described as the object-relational impedance mismatch (or simply impedance mismatch).

So how do you make that transition? One answer is to give a class (or a set of classes) responsibility for just that problem, effectively hiding the database from the domain model and managing the inevitable rough edges of the translation.

Implementation

Although with careful programming, it may be possible to create a single Mapper class to service multiple objects, it is common to see an individual Mapper for a major class in the Domain Model.

Figure 13–1 shows three concrete Mapper classes and an abstract superclass.

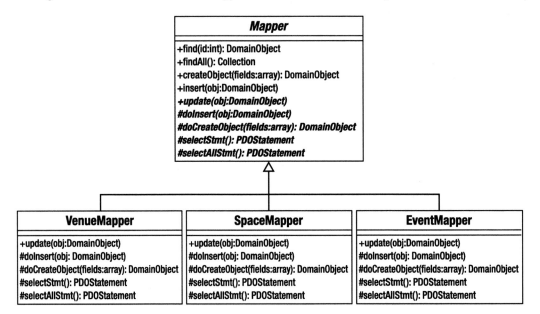

Figure 13–1. Mapper classes

In fact, since the Space objects are effectively subordinate to Venue objects, it may be possible to factor the SpaceMapper class into VenueMapper. For the sake of these exercises, I'm going to keep them separate.

As you can see, the classes present common operations for saving and loading data. The base class stores common functionality, delegating responsibility for handling object-specific operations to its children. Typically, these operations include actual object generation and constructing queries for database operations.

The base class often performs housekeeping before or after an operation, which is why Template Method is used for explicit delegation (calls from concrete methods like insert() to abstract ones like doInsert(), etc.). Implementation determines which of the base class methods are made concrete in this way, as you will see later in the chapter.

Here is a simplified version of a Mapper base class:

```
namespace woo\mapper;
//...

abstract class Mapper {
    protected static $PDO;
    function __construct() {

        if ( ! isset(self::$PDO) ) {
            $dsn = \woo\base\ApplicationRegistry::getDSN( );
            if ( is_null( $dsn ) ) {
                throw new \woo\base\AppException( "No DSN" );
            }
            self::$PDO = new \PDO( $dsn );
            self::$PDO->setAttribute(\PDO::ATTR_ERRMODE, \PDO::ERRMODE_EXCEPTION);
        }
    }

    function find( $id ) {
        $this->selectStmt()->execute( array( $id ) );
        $array = $this->selectStmt()->fetch( );
        $this->selectStmt()->closeCursor( );
        if ( ! is_array( $array ) ) { return null; }
        if ( ! isset( $array['id'] ) ) { return null; }
        $object = $this->createObject( $array );
        return $object;
    }

    function createObject( $array ) {
        $obj = $this->doCreateObject( $array );
        return $obj;
    }

    function insert( \woo\domain\DomainObject $obj ) {
        $this->doInsert( $obj );
    }

    abstract function update( \woo\domain\DomainObject $object );
    protected abstract function doCreateObject( array $array );
    protected abstract function doInsert( \woo\domain\DomainObject $object );
    protected abstract function selectStmt();
}
```

277

The constructor method uses an `ApplicationRegistry` to get a DSN for use with the PDO extension. A standalone singleton or a request-scoped registry really come into their own for classes like this. There isn't always a sensible path from the control layer to a `Mapper` along which data can be passed. Another way of managing mapper creation would be to hand it off to the `Registry` class itself. Rather than instantiate it, the mapper would expect to be *provided* with a PDO object as a constructor argument.

```
namespace woo\mapper;
//...
abstract class Mapper {
    protected $PDO;
    function __construct( \PDO $pdo ) {
        $this->pdo = $pdo;
    }
}
```

Client code would acquire a new `VenueMapper` from `Registry` using `\woo\base\Request Registry::getVenueMapper( )`. This would instantiate a mapper, generating the PDO object too. For subsequent requests, the method would return the cached mapper. The trade-off here is that you make `Registry` much more knowledgeable about your system, but your mappers remain ignorant of global configuration data.

The `insert()` method does nothing but delegate to `doInsert()`. This would be something that I would factor out in favor of an abstract `insert()` method were it not for the fact that I know that the implementation will be useful here in due course.

`find()` is responsible for invoking a prepared statement (provided by an implementing child class) and acquiring row data. It finishes up by calling `createObject()`. The details of converting an array to an object will vary from case to case, of course, so the details are handled by the abstract `doCreateObject()` method. Once again, `createObject()` seems to do nothing but delegate to the child implementation, and once again, I'll soon add the housekeeping that makes this use of the Template Method pattern worth the trouble.

Child classes will also implement custom methods for finding data according to specific criteria (I will want to locate `Space` objects that belong to `Venue` objects, for example).

You can take a look at the process from the child's perspective here:

```
namespace woo\mapper;
//...

class VenueMapper extends Mapper {
    function __construct() {
        parent::__construct();
        $this->selectStmt = self::$PDO->prepare(
                            "SELECT * FROM venue WHERE id=?");
        $this->updateStmt = self::$PDO->prepare(
                            "update venue set name=?, id=? where id=?");
        $this->insertStmt = self::$PDO->prepare(
                            "insert into venue ( name )
                             values( ? )");
    }

    function getCollection( array $raw ) {
        return new SpaceCollection( $raw, $this );
    }
    protected function doCreateObject( array $array ) {
        $obj = new \woo\domain\Venue( $array['id'] );
        $obj->setname( $array['name'] );
```

```
        return $obj;
    }

    protected function doInsert( \woo\domain\DomainObject $object ) {
        print "inserting\n";
        debug_print_backtrace();
        $values = array( $object->getName() );
        $this->insertStmt->execute( $values );
        $id = self::$PDO->lastInsertId();
        $object->setId( $id );
    }

    function update( \woo\domain\DomainObject $object ) {
        print "updating\n";
        $values = array( $object->getName(), $object->getId(), $object->getId() );
        $this->updateStmt->execute( $values );
    }

    function selectStmt() {
        return $this->selectStmt;
    }
}
```

Once again, this class is stripped of some of the goodies that are still to come. Nonetheless, it does its job. The constructor prepares some SQL statements for use later on. These could be made static and shared across VenueMapper instances, or as described earlier, a single Mapper object could be stored in a Registry, thereby saving the cost of repeated instantiation. These are refactorings I will leave to you!

The Mapper class implements find(), which invokes selectStmt() to acquire the prepared SELECT statement. Assuming all goes well, Mapper invokes VenueMapper::doCreateObject(). It's here that I use the associative array to generate a Venue object.

From the point of view of the client, this process is simplicity itself:

```
$mapper = new \woo\mapper\VenueMapper();
$venue = $mapper->find( 12 );
print_r( $venue );
```

The print_r() method is a quick way of confirming that find() was successful. In my system (where there is a row in the venue table with ID 12), the output from this fragment is as follows:

```
woo\domain\Venue Object
(
    [name:woo\domain\Venue:private] => The Eyeball Inn
    [spaces:woo\domain\Venue:private] =>
    [id:woo\domain\DomainObject:private] => 12
)
```

The doInsert() and update() methods reverse the process established by find(). Each accepts a DomainObject, extracts row data from it, and calls PDOStatement::execute() with the resulting information. Notice that the doInsert() method sets an ID on the provided object. Remember that objects are passed by reference in PHP, so the client code will see this change via its own reference.

Another thing to note is that doInsert() and update() are not really type safe. They will accept any DomainObject subclass without complaint. You should perform an instanceof test and throw an Exception if the wrong object is passed. This will guard against the inevitable bugs.

Once again, here is a client perspective on inserting and updating:

```
$venue = new \woo\domain\Venue();
$venue->setName( "The Likey Lounge-yy" );
// add the object to the database
$mapper->insert( $venue );
// find the object again - just prove it works!
$venue = $mapper->find( $venue->getId() );
print_r( $venue );
// alter our object
$venue->setName( "The Bibble Beer Likey Lounge-yy" );
// call update to enter the amended data
$mapper->update( $venue );
// once again, go back to the database to prove it worked
$venue = $mapper->find( $venue->getId() );
print_r( $venue );
```

Handling Multiple Rows

The find() method is pretty straightforward, because it only needs to return a single object. What do you do, though, if you need to pull lots of data from the database? Your first thought may be to return an array of objects. This will work, but there is a major problem with the approach.

If you return an array, each object in the collection will need to be instantiated first, which, if you have a result set of 1,000 objects, may be needlessly expensive. An alternative would be to simply return an array and let the calling code sort out object instantiation. This is possible, but it violates the very purpose of the Mapper classes.

There is one way you can have your cake and eat it. You can use the built-in Iterator interface.

The Iterator interface requires implementing classes to define methods for querying a list. If you do this, your class can be used in foreach loops just like an array. There are some people who say that iterator implementations are unnecessary in a language like PHP with such good support for arrays. Tish and piffle! I will show you at least three good reasons for using PHP's built-in Iterator interface in this chapter.

Table 13–1 shows the methods that the Iterator interface requires.

Table 13–1. Methods Defined by the Iterator Interface

Name	Description
rewind()	Send pointer to start of list.
current()	Return element at current pointer position.
key()	Return current key (i.e., pointer value).
next()	Return element at current pointer and advance pointer.
valid()	Confirm that there is an element at the current pointer position.

In order to implement an Iterator, you need to implement its methods and keep track of your place within a dataset. How you acquire that data, order it, or otherwise filter it is hidden from the client.

Here is an Iterator implementation that wraps an array but also accepts a Mapper object in its constructor for reasons that will become apparent:

```
namespace woo\mapper;
//...

abstract class Collection implements \Iterator {
    protected $mapper;
    protected $total = 0;
    protected $raw = array();

    private $result;
    private $pointer = 0;
    private $objects = array();

    function __construct( array $raw=null, Mapper $mapper=null ) {
        if ( ! is_null( $raw ) && ! is_null( $mapper ) ) {
            $this->raw = $raw;
            $this->total = count( $raw );
        }
        $this->mapper = $mapper;
    }

    function add( \woo\domain\DomainObject $object ) {
        $class = $this->targetClass();
        if ( ! ($object instanceof $class ) ) {
            throw new Exception("This is a {$class} collection");
        }
        $this->notifyAccess();
        $this->objects[$this->total] = $object;
        $this->total++;
    }

    abstract function targetClass();

    protected function notifyAccess() {
        // deliberately left blank!
    }
    private function getRow( $num ) {
        $this->notifyAccess();
        if ( $num >= $this->total || $num < 0 ) {
            return null;
        }
        if ( isset( $this->objects[$num]) ) {
            return $this->objects[$num];
        }

        if ( isset( $this->raw[$num] ) ) {
            $this->objects[$num]=$this->mapper->createObject( $this->raw[$num] );
            return $this->objects[$num];
        }
    }

    public function rewind() {
```

```
        $this->pointer = 0;
    }

    public function current() {
        return $this->getRow( $this->pointer );
    }

    public function key() {
        return $this->pointer;
    }

    public function next() {
        $row = $this->getRow( $this->pointer );
        if ( $row ) { $this->pointer++; }
        return $row;
    }

    public function valid() {
        return ( ! is_null( $this->current() ) );
    }
}
```

The constructor expects to be called with no arguments or with two (the raw data that may eventually be transformed into objects and a mapper reference).

Assuming that the client has set the $raw argument (it will be a Mapper object that does this), this is stored in a property together with the size of the provided dataset. If raw data is provided an instance of the Mapper is also required, since it's this that will convert each row into an object.

If no arguments were passed to the constructor, the class starts out empty, though note that there is the add() method for adding to the collection.

The class maintains two arrays: $objects and $raw. If a client requests a particular element, the getRow() method looks first in $objects to see if it has one already instantiated. If so, that gets returned. Otherwise, the method looks in $raw for the row data. $raw data is only present if a Mapper object is also present, so the data for the relevant row can be passed to the Mapper::createObject() method you encountered earlier. This returns a DomainObject object, which is cached in the $objects array with the relevant index. The newly created DomainObject object is returned to the user.

The rest of the class is simple manipulation of the $pointer property and calls to getRow(). Apart, that is, from the notifyAccess() method, which will become important when you encounter the Lazy Load pattern.

You may have noticed that the Collection class is abstract. You need to provide specific implementations for each domain class:

```
namespace woo\mapper;
//...


class VenueCollection
        extends Collection
        implements \woo\domain\VenueCollection {

    function targetClass( ) {
        return "\woo\domain\Venue";
    }
}
```

The VenueCollection class simply extends Collection and implements a targetClass() method. This, in conjunction with the type checking in the super class's add() method, ensures that only Venue objects can be added to the collection. You could provide additional checking in the constructor as well if you wanted to be even safer.

Clearly, this class should only work with a VenueMapper. In practical terms, though, this is a reasonably type-safe collection, especially as far as the Domain Model is concerned.

There are parallel classes for Event and Space objects, of course.

Note that VenueCollection implements an interface: woo\domain\VenueCollection. This is part of the Separated Interface trick I will describe shortly. In effect, it allows the domain package to define its requirements for a Collection independently of the mapper package. Domain objects hint for woo\domain\VenueCollection objects and not woo\mapper\VenueCollection objects, so that, at a later date, the mapper implementation might be removed. It could then be replaced with an entirely different implementing class without many changes within the domain package.

Here is the \woo\domain\VenueCollection interface, together with its siblings.

```
namespace woo\domain;


interface VenueCollection extends \Iterator {
    function add( DomainObject $venue );
}

interface SpaceCollection extends \Iterator {
    function add( DomainObject $space );
}

interface EventCollection extends \Iterator {
    function add( DomainObject $event );
}
```

Figure 13–2 shows some Collection classes.

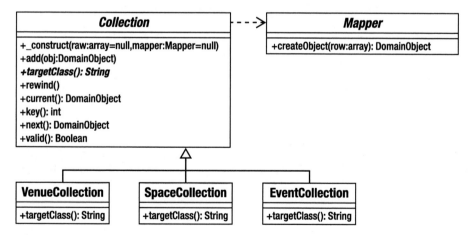

Figure 13–2. Managing multiple rows with collections

Because the Domain Model needs to instantiate Collection objects, and because I may need to switch the implementation at some point (especially for testing purposes), I provide a factory class in the Domain layer for generating Collection objects on a type-by-type basis. Here's how I get an empty VenueCollection object:

```
$collection = \woo\domain\HelperFactory::getCollection("woo\\domain\\Venue");
$collection->add( new \woo\domain\Venue( null, "Loud and Thumping" ) );
$collection->add( new \woo\domain\Venue( null, "Eeezy" ) );
$collection->add( new \woo\domain\Venue( null, "Duck and Badger" ) );

foreach( $collection as $venue ) {
    print $venue->getName()."\n";
}
```

With the implementation I have built here, there isn't much else you can do with this collection, but adding elementAt(), deleteAt(), count(), and similar methods is a trivial exercise. (And fun, too! Enjoy!)

The DomainObject superclass is a good place for convenience methods that acquire collections.

```
// namespace woo\domain;
// ...

// DomainObject

    static function getCollection( $type ) {
        return HelperFactory::getCollection( $type );
    }

    function collection() {
        return self::getCollection( get_class( $this ) );
    }
```

The class supports two mechanisms for acquiring a Collection object: static and instance. In both cases, the methods simply call HelperFactory::getCollection() with a class name. You saw the static getCollection() method used in the Domain Model example Chapter 12. Figure 13–3 shows the HelperFactory. Notice that it can be used to acquire both collections and mappers.

A variation on the structure displayed in Figure 13–3 would have you create interfaces within the domain package for Mapper and Collection which, of course would need to be implemented by their mapper counterparts. In this way, domain objects can be completely insulated from the mapper package (except within the HelperFactory itself, of course). This basic pattern, which Fowler calls Separated Interface, would be useful if you knew that some users might need to switch out the entire mapper package and replace it with an equivalent. If I were to implement Separated Interface, getFinder() would commit to return an instance of a Finder interface, and my Mapper objects would implement this. However, in most instances, you can leave this refinement as a possible future refactor. In these examples, getFinder() returns Mapper objects pure and simple.

In light of all this, the Venue class can be extended to manage the persistence of Space objects. The class provides methods for adding individual Space objects to its SpaceCollection or for switching in an entirely new SpaceCollection.

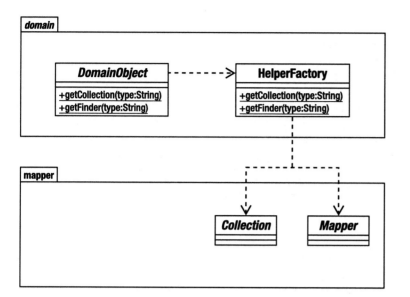

Figure 13–3. *Using a factory object as an intermediary to acquire persistence tools*

```
// Venue
// namespace woo\domain;
// ...

    function setSpaces( SpaceCollection $spaces ) {
        $this->spaces = $spaces;
    }

    function getSpaces() {
        if ( ! isset( $this->spaces ) ) {
            $this->spaces = self::getCollection("woo\\domain\\Space");
        }
        return $this->spaces;
    }

    function addSpace( wSpace $space ) {
        $this->getSpaces()->add( $space );
        $space->setVenue( $this );
    }
```

The setSpaces() operation is really designed to be used by the VenueMapper class in constructing the
Venue. It takes it on trust that all Space objects in the collection refer to the current Venue. It would be
easy enough to add checking to the method. This version keeps things simple though. Notice that I only
instantiate the $spaces property when getSpaces() is called. Later on, I'll demonstrate how you can
extend this lazy instantiation to limit database requests.

The VenueMapper needs to set up a SpaceCollection for each Venue object it creates.

```
// VenueMapper
```

```
// namespace woo\mapper;
// ...

    protected function doCreateObject( array $array ) {
        $obj = new w\woo\domain\Venue( $array['id'] );
        $obj->setname( $array['name'] );
        $space_mapper = new SpaceMapper();
        $space_collection = $space_mapper->findByVenue( $array['id'] );
        $obj->setSpaces( $space_collection );
        return $obj;
    }
```

The VenueMapper::doCreateObject() method gets a SpaceMapper and acquires a SpaceCollection from it. As you can see, the SpaceMapper class implements a findByVenue() method. This brings us to the queries that generate multiple objects. For the sake of brevity, I omitted the Mapper::findAll() method from the original listing for woo\mapper\Mapper. Here it is restored:

```
//Mapper
// namespace woo\mapper;
// ...

  function findAll( ) {
        $this->selectAllStmt()->execute( array() );
        return $this->getCollection(
            $this->selectAllStmt()->fetchAll( PDO::FETCH_ASSOC ) );
    }
```

This method calls a child method: selectAllStmt(). Like selectStmt(), this should contain a prepared statement object primed to acquire all rows in the table. Here's the PDOStatement object as created in the SpaceMapper class:

```
// SpaceMapper::__construct()
        $this->selectAllStmt = self::$PDO->prepare(
                            "SELECT * FROM space");
//...
        $this->findByVenueStmt = self::$PDO->prepare(
                            "SELECT * FROM space where venue=?");
```

I included another statement here, $findByVenueStmt, which is used to locate Space objects specific to an individual Venue.

The findAll() method calls another new method, getCollection(), passing it its found data. Here is SpaceMapper::getCollection():

```
    function getCollection( array $raw ) {
        return new SpaceCollection( $raw, $this );
    }
```

A full version of the Mapper class should declare getCollection() and selectAllStmt() as abstract methods, so all mappers are capable of returning a collection containing their persistent domain objects. In order to get the Space objects that belong to a Venue, however, I need a more limited collection. You have already seen the prepared statement for acquiring the data; now, here is the SpaceMapper::findByVenue() method, which generates the collection:

```
    function findByVenue( $vid ) {
        $this->findByVenueStmt->execute( array( $vid ) );
        return new SpaceCollection(
```

```
                                    $this->findByVenueStmt->fetchAll(), $this );
    }
```

The findByVenue() method is identical to findAll() except for the SQL statement used. Back in the VenueMapper, the resulting collection is set on the Venue object via Venue::setSpaces().

So Venue objects now arrive fresh from the database, complete with all their Space objects in a neat type-safe list. None of the objects in that list are instantiated before being requested.

Figure 13–4 shows the process by which a client class might acquire a SpaceCollection and how the SpaceCollection class interacts with SpaceMapper::createObject() to convert its raw data into an object for returning to the client.

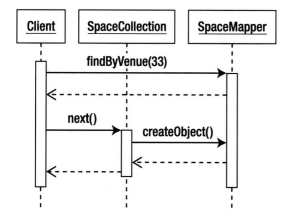

Figure 13–4. *Acquiring a SpaceCollection and using it to get a Space object*

Consequences

The drawback with the approach I took to adding Space objects to Venue ones is that I had to take two trips to the database. In most instances, I think that is a price worth paying. Also note that the work in Venue::doCreateObject() to acquire a correctly populated SpaceCollection could be moved to Venue::getSpaces() so that the secondary database connection would only occur on demand. Here's how such a method might look:

```
// Venue
// namespace woo\domain;
// ...

    function getSpaces() {
        if ( ! isset( $this->spaces ) ) {
            $finder = self::getFinder( 'woo\\domain\\Space' );
            $this->spaces = $finder->findByVenue( $this->getId() );
        }
        return $this->spaces;
    }
```

If efficiency becomes an issue, however, it should be easy enough to factor out SpaceMapper altogether and retrieve all the data you need in one go using an SQL join.

Of course, your code may become less portable as a result of that, but efficiency optimization always comes at a price!

Ultimately, the granularity of your Mapper classes will vary. If an object type is stored solely by another, then you may consider only having a Mapper for the container.

The great strength of this pattern is the strong decoupling it effects between the Domain layer and database. The Mapper objects take the strain behind the scenes and can adapt to all sorts of relational twistedness.

Perhaps the biggest drawback with the pattern is the sheer amount of slog involved in creating concrete Mapper classes. However, there is a large amount of boilerplate code that can be automatically generated. A neat way of generating the common methods for Mapper classes is through reflection. You can query a domain object, discover its setter and getter methods (perhaps in tandem with an argument naming convention), and generate basic Mapper classes ready for amendment. This is how all the Mapper classes featured in this chapter were initially produced.

One issue to be aware of with mappers is the danger of loading too many objects at one time. The Iterator implementation helps us here, though. Because a Collection object only holds row data at first, the secondary request (for a Space object) is only made when a particular Venue is accessed and converted from array to object. This form of lazy loading can be enhanced even further, as you shall see.

You should be careful of ripple loading. Be aware as you create your mapper that the use of another one to acquire a property for your object may be the tip of a very large iceberg. This secondary mapper may itself use yet more in constructing its own object. If you are not careful, you could find that what looks on the surface like a simple find operation sets off tens of other similar operations.

You should also be aware of any guidelines your database application lays down for building efficient queries and be prepared to optimize (on a database-by-database basis if necessary). SQL statements that apply well to multiple database applications are nice; fast applications are much nicer. Although introducing conditionals (or strategy classes) to manage different versions of the same queries is a chore, and potentially ugly in the former case, don't forget that all this mucky optimization is neatly hidden away from client code.

Identity Map

Do you remember the nightmare of pass-by-value errors in PHP 4? The sheer confusion that ensued when two variables that you thought pointed to a single object turned out to refer to different but cunningly similar ones? Well, the nightmare has returned.

The Problem

Here's some test code created to try out the Data Mapper example:

```
$venue = new \woo\domain\Venue();
$venue->setName( "The Likey Lounge" );
$mapper->insert( $venue );
$venue = $mapper->find( $venue->getId() );
print_r( $venue );
$venue->setName( "The Bibble Beer Likey Lounge" );
$mapper->update( $venue );
$venue = $mapper->find( $venue->getId() );
print_r( $venue );
```

The purpose of this code was to demonstrate that an object that you add to the database could also be extracted via a Mapper and would be identical. Identical, that is, in every way except for being the *same* object. I cheated this problem by assigning the new Venue object over the old. Unfortunately, you won't always have that kind of control over the situation. The same object may be referenced at several different times within a <u>single</u> request. If you alter one version of it and save that to the database, can you be sure that another version of the object (perhaps stored already in a Collection object) won't be written over your changes?

Not only are duplicate objects risky in a system, they also represent a considerable overhead. Some popular objects could be loaded three or four times in a process, with all but one of these trips to the database entirely redundant.

Fortunately, fixing this problem is relatively straightforward.

Implementation

An identity map is simply an object whose task it is to keep track of all the objects in a system, and thereby help to ensure that nothing that should be one object becomes two.

In fact, the Identity Map itself does not prevent this from happening in any active way. Its role is to manage information about objects. Here is a simple Identity Map:

```
namespace woo\domain;
//...

class ObjectWatcher {
    private $all = array();
    private static $instance;

    private function __construct() { }

    static function instance() {
        if ( ! self::$instance ) {
            self::$instance = new ObjectWatcher();
        }
        return self::$instance;
    }

    function globalKey( DomainObject $obj ) {
        $key = get_class( $obj ).".".$obj->getId();
        return $key;
    }

    static function add( DomainObject $obj ) {
        $inst = self::instance();
        $inst->all[$inst->globalKey( $obj )] = $obj;
    }

    static function exists( $classname, $id ) {
        $inst = self::instance();
        $key = "$classname.$id";
        if ( isset( $inst->all[$key] ) ) {
            return $inst->all[$key];
        }
        return null;
    }
}
```

Figure 13–5 shows how an Identity Map object might integrate with other classes you have seen.

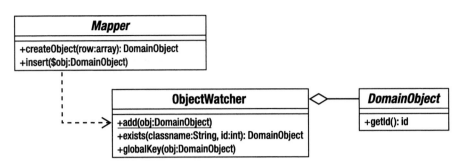

Figure 13–5. Identity Map

The main trick with an Identity Map is, pretty obviously, identifying objects. This means that you need to tag each object in some way. There are a number of different strategies you can take here. The database table key that all objects in the system already use is no good because the ID is not guaranteed to be unique across all tables.

You could also use the database to maintain a global key table. Every time you created an object, you would iterate the key table's running total and associate the global key with the object in its own row. The overhead of this is relatively slight, and it would be easy to do.

As you can see, I have gone for an altogether simpler approach. I concatenate the name of the object's class with its table ID. There can be no two objects of type woo\domain\Event with an ID of 4, so my key of woo\domain\Event.4 is safe enough for my purposes.

The globalKey() method handles the details of this. The class provides an add() method for adding new objects. Each object is labeled with its unique key in an array property, $all.

The exists() method accepts a class name and an $id rather than an object. I don't want to have to instantiate an object to see whether or not it already exists! The method builds a key from this data and checks to see if it indexes an element in the $all property. If an object is found, a reference is duly returned.

There is only one class where I work with the ObjectWatcher class in its role as an Identity Map. The Mapper class provides functionality for generating objects, so it makes sense to add the checking there.

```
// Mapper
namespace woo\mapper;
// ...

  private function getFromMap( $id ) {
        return \woo\domain\ObjectWatcher::exists
                ( $this->targetClass(), $id );
    }

    private function addToMap( \woo\domain\DomainObject $obj ) {
        return \woo\domain\ObjectWatcher::add( $obj );
    }

    function find( $id ) {
        $old = $this->getFromMap( $id );
        if ( $old ) { return $old; }
        // work with db
        return $object;
    }
```

```
function createObject( $array ) {
    $old = $this->getFromMap( $array['id']);
    if ( $old ) { return $old; }
    // construct object
    $this->addToMap( $obj );
    return $obj;
}

function insert( \woo\domain\DomainObject $obj ) {
    // handle insert. $obj will be updated with new id
    $this->addToMap( $obj );
}
```

The class provides two convenience methods: addToMap() and getFromMap(). These save the bother of remembering the full syntax of the static call to ObjectWatcher. More importantly, they call down to the child implementation (VenueMapper, etc.) to get the name of the class currently awaiting instantiation.

This is achieved by calling targetClass(), an abstract method that is implemented by all concrete Mapper classes. It should return the name of the class that the Mapper is designed to generate. Here is the SpaceMapper class's implementation of targetClass():

```
protected function targetClass() {
    return "woo\\domain\\Space";
}
```

Both find() and createObject() first check for an existing object by passing the table ID to getFromMap(). If an object is found, it is returned to the client and method execution ends. If, however, there is no version of this object in existence yet, object instantiation goes ahead. In createObject(), the new object is passed to addToMap() to prevent any clashes in the future.

So why am I going through part of this process twice, with calls to getFromMap() in both find() and createObject()? The answer lies with Collections. When these generate objects, they do so by calling createObject(). I need to make sure that the row encapsulated by a Collection object is not stale and ensure that the latest version of the object is returned to the user.

Consequences

As long as you use the Identity Map in all contexts in which objects are generated from or added to the database, the possibility of duplicate objects in your process is practically zero.

Of course, this only works *within* your process. Different processes will inevitably access versions of the same object at the same time. It is important to think through the possibilities for data corruption engendered by concurrent access. If there is a serious issue, you may need to consider a locking strategy. You might also consider storing objects in shared memory or using an external object caching system like Memcached. You can learn about Memcached at http://danga.com/memcached/ and about PHP support for it at http://www.php.net/memcache.

Unit of Work

When do you save your objects? Until I discovered the Unit of Work pattern (written up by David Rice in Martin Fowler's *Patterns of Enterprise Application Architecture*), I sent out save orders from the Presentation layer upon completion of a command. This turned out to be an expensive design decision.

The Unit of Work pattern helps you to save only those objects that need saving.

The Problem

One day, I echoed my SQL statements to the browser window to track down a problem and had a shock. I found that I was saving the same data over and over again in the same request. I had a neat system of composite commands, which meant that one command might trigger several others, and each one was cleaning up after itself.

Not only was I saving the same object twice, I was saving objects that didn't need saving.

This problem then is similar in some ways to that addressed by Identity Map. That problem involved unnecessary object loading; this problem lies at the other end of the process. Just as these issues are complementary, so are the solutions.

Implementation

To determine what database operations are required, you need to keep track of various events that befall your objects. Probably the best place to do that is in the objects themselves.

You also need to maintain a list of objects scheduled for each database operation (insert, update, delete). I am only going to cover insert and update operations here. Where might be a good place to store a list of objects? It just so happens that I already have an ObjectWatcher object, so I can develop that further:

```
// ObjectWatcher
// ...
    private $all = array();
    private $dirty = array();
    private $new = array();
    private $delete = array(); // unused in this example
    private static $instance;
// ...
    static function addDelete( DomainObject $obj ) {

        $self = self::instance();

        $self->delete[$self->globalKey( $obj )] = $obj;

    }

    static function addDirty( DomainObject $obj ) {
        $inst = self::instance();
        if ( ! in_array( $obj, $inst->new, true ) ) {
            $inst->dirty[$inst->globalKey( $obj )] = $obj;
        }
    }

    static function addNew( DomainObject $obj ) {
        $inst = self::instance();
        // we don't yet have an id
        $inst->new[] = $obj;
    }

    static function addClean( DomainObject $obj ) {
        $self = self::instance();
        unset( $self->delete[$self->globalKey( $obj )] );
        unset( $self->dirty[$self->globalKey( $obj )] );
```

```
        $self->new = array_filter( $self->new,
            function( $a ) use ( $obj ) { return !( $a === $obj ); }
            );
    }

    function performOperations() {
        foreach ( $this->dirty as $key=>$obj ) {
            $obj->finder()->update( $obj );
        }
        foreach ( $this->new as $key=>$obj ) {
            $obj->finder()->insert( $obj );
        }
        $this->dirty = array();
        $this->new = array();
    }
```

The ObjectWatcher class remains an Identity Map and continues to serve its function of tracking all objects in a system via the $all property. This example simply adds more functionality to the class.

You can see the Unit of Work aspects of the ObjectWatcher class in Figure 13–6.

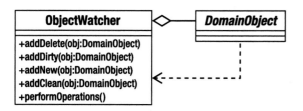

Figure 13–6. Unit of Work

Objects are described as "dirty" when they have been changed since extraction from the database. A dirty object is stored in the $dirty array property (via the addDirty() method) until the time comes to update the database. Client code may decide that a dirty object should not undergo update for its own reasons. It can ensure this by marking the dirty object as clean (via the addClean() method). As you might expect, a newly created object should be added to the $new array (via the addNew() method). Objects in this array are scheduled for insertion into the database. I am not implementing delete functionality in these examples, but the principle should be clear enough.

The addDirty() and addNew() methods each add an object to their respective array properties. addClean(), however, *removes* the given object from the $dirty array, marking it as no longer pending update.

When the time finally comes to process all objects stored in these arrays, the performOperations() method should be invoked (probably from the controller class, or its helper). This method loops through the $dirty and $new arrays either updating or adding the objects.

The ObjectWatcher class now provides a mechanism for updating and inserting objects. The code is still missing a means of adding objects to the ObjectWatcher object.

Since it is these objects that are operated upon, they are probably best placed to perform this notification. Here are some utility methods I can add to the DomainObject class. Notice also the constructor method.

```
// DomainObject
namespace woo\domain;
//...
```

```
abstract class DomainObject {
    private $id = -1;

    function __construct( $id=null ) {
        if ( is_null( $id ) ) {
            $this->markNew();
        } else {
            $this->id = $id;
        }
    }

    function markNew() {
        ObjectWatcher::addNew( $this );
    }

    function markDeleted() {
        ObjectWatcher::addDelete( $this );
    }

    function markDirty() {
        ObjectWatcher::addDirty( $this );
    }

    function markClean() {
        ObjectWatcher::addClean( $this );
    }

    function setId( $id ) {
        $this->id = $id;
    }

    function getId( ) {
        return $this->id;
    }

    function finder() {
        return self::getFinder( get_class( $this ) );
    }

    static function getFinder( $type ) {
        return HelperFactory::getFinder( $type );
    }
    //...
```

Before looking at the Unit of Work code, it is worth noting that the Domain class here has finder() and getFinder() methods. These work in exactly the same way as collection() and getCollection(), querying a simple factory class, HelperFactory, in order to acquire Mapper objects when needed. This relationship was illustrated in Figure 13–3.

As you can see, the constructor method marks the current object as new (by calling markNew()) if no $id property has been passed to it. This qualifies as magic of a sort and should be treated with some caution. As it stands, this code slates a new object for insertion into the database without any intervention from the object creator. Imagine a coder new to your team writing a throwaway script to test some domain behavior. No sign of persistence code there, so all should be safe enough, shouldn't it? Now imagine these test objects, perhaps with interesting throwaway names, making their way into persistent storage. Magic is nice, but clarity is nicer. It may be better to require client code to pass some kind of flag into the constructor in order to queue the new object for insertion.

I also need to add some code to the Mapper class:

```
// Mapper
    function createObject( $array ) {
        $old = $this->getFromMap( $array['id']);
        if ( $old ) { return $old; }
        $obj = $this->doCreateObject( $array );
        $this->addToMap( $obj );
        $obj->markClean();
        return $obj;
    }
```

Because setting up an object involves marking it new via the constructor's call to ObjectWatcher::addNew(), I must call markClean(), or every single object extracted from the database will be saved at the end of the request, which is not what I want.

The only thing remaining to do is to add markDirty() invocations to methods in the Domain Model classes. Remember, a dirty object is one that has been changed since it was retrieved from the database. This is the one aspect of this pattern that has a slightly fishy odor. Clearly, it's important to ensure that all methods that mess up the state of an object are marked dirty, but the manual nature of this task means that the possibility of human error is all too real.

Here are some methods in the Space object that call markDirty():

```
namespace woo\domain;

//...

class Space extends DomainObject {

//...

    function setName( $name_s ) {
        $this->name = $name_s;
        $this->markDirty();
    }

    function setVenue( Venue $venue ) {
        $this->venue = $venue;
        $this->markDirty();
    }
```

Here is some code for adding a new Venue and Space to the database, taken from a Command class:

```
        $venue = new \woo\domain\Venue( null, "The Green Trees" );
        $venue->addSpace(
            new \woo\domain\Space( null, 'The Space Upstairs' ) );
        $venue->addSpace(
            new \woo\domain\Space( null, 'The Bar Stage' ) );

        // this could be called from the controller or a helper class
        \woo\domain\ObjectWatcher::instance()->performOperations();
```

I have added some debug code to the ObjectWatcher, so you can see what happens at the end of the request:

```
inserting The Green Trees
inserting The Space Upstairs
inserting The Bar Stage
```

Because a high-level controller object usually calls the performOperations() method, all you need to do in most cases is create or modify an object, and the Unit of Work class (ObjectWatcher) will do its job just once at the end of the request.

Consequences

This pattern is very useful, but there are a few issues to be aware of. You need to be sure that all modify operations actually do mark the object in question as dirty. Failing to do this can result in hard-to-spot bugs.

You may like to look at other ways of testing for modified objects. Reflection sounds like a good option there, but you should look into the performance implications of such testing— the pattern is meant to improve efficiency, not undermine it.

Lazy Load

Lazy Load is one of those core patterns most Web programmers learn for themselves very quickly, simply because it's such an essential mechanism for avoiding massive database hits, which is something we all want to do.

The Problem

In the example that has dominated this chapter, I have set up a relationship between Venue, Space, and Event objects. When a Venue object is created, it is automatically given a SpaceCollection object. If I were to list every Space object in a Venue, this would automatically kick off a database request to acquire all the Events associated with each Space. These are stored in an EventCollection object. If I don't wish to view any events, I have nonetheless made several journeys to the database for no reason. With many venues, each with two or three spaces, and with each space managing tens, perhaps hundreds, of events, this is a costly process.

Clearly, we need to throttle back this automatic inclusion of collections in some instances. Here is the code in SpaceMapper that acquires Event data:

```
protected function doCreateObject( array $array ) {
    $obj = new \woo\domain\Space( $array['id'] );
    $obj->setname( $array['name'] );
    $ven_mapper = new VenueMapper();
    $venue = $ven_mapper->find( $array['venue'] );
    $obj->setVenue( $venue );
    $event_mapper = new EventMapper();
    $event_collection = $event_mapper->findBySpaceId( $array['id'] );
    $obj->setEvents( $event_collection );
    return $obj;
}
```

The doCreateObject() method first acquires the Venue object with which the space is associated. This is not costly, because it is almost certainly already stored in the ObjectWatcher object. Then the method calls the EventMapper::findBySpaceId() method. This is where the system could run into problems.

Implementation

As you may know, a Lazy Load means to defer acquisition of a property until it is actually requested by a client.

As you have seen, the easiest way of doing this is to make the deferral explicit in the containing object. Here's how I might do this in the Space object:

```
// Space
function getEvents() {
    if ( is_null($this->events) ) {
        $this->events = self::getFinder('woo\\domain\\Event')
            ->findBySpaceId( $this->getId() );
    }
    return $this->events;
}
```

This method checks to see whether or not the $events property is set. If it isn't set, then the method acquires a finder (that is, a Mapper) and uses its own $id property to get the EventCollection with which it is associated. Clearly, for this method to save us a potentially unnecessary database query, I would also need to amend the SpaceMapper code so that it does not automatically preload an EventCollection object as it does in the preceding example!

This approach will work just fine, although it is a little messy. Wouldn't it be nice to tidy the mess away?

This brings us back to the Iterator implementation that goes to make the Collection object. I amalready hiding one secret behind that interface (the fact that raw data may not yet have been used to instantiate a domain object at the time a client accesses it). Perhaps I can hide still more.

The idea here is to create an EventCollection object that defers its database access until a request is made of it. This means that a client object (such as Space, for example) need never know that it is holding an empty Collection in the first instance. As far as a client is concerned, it is holding a perfectly normal EventCollection.

Here is the DeferredEventCollection object:

```
namespace woo\mapper;
//...

class DeferredEventCollection extends EventCollection {
    private $stmt;
    private $valueArray;
    private $run=false;

    function __construct( Mapper $mapper, \PDOStatement $stmt_handle,
                          array $valueArray ) {
        parent::__construct( null, $mapper );
        $this->stmt = $stmt_handle;
        $this->valueArray = $valueArray;
    }

    function notifyAccess() {
        if ( ! $this->run ) {
            $this->stmt->execute( $this->valueArray );
            $this->raw = $this->stmt->fetchAll();
            $this->total = count( $this->raw );
        }
        $this->run=true;
```

```
        }
}
```

As you can see, this class extends a standard EventCollection. Its constructor requires EventMapper and PDOStatement objects and an array of terms that should match the prepared statement. In the first instance, the class does nothing but store its properties and wait. No query has been made of the database.

You may remember that the Collection base class defines the empty method called notifyAccess() that I mentioned in the "Data Mapper" section. This is called from any method whose invocation is the result of a call from the outside world.

DeferredEventCollection overrides this method. Now if someone attempts to access the Collection, the class knows it is time to end the pretense and acquire some real data. It does this by calling the PDOStatement::execute() method. Together with PDOStatement::fetch(), this yields an array of fields suitable for passing along to Mapper::createObject().

Here is the method in EventMapper that instantiates a DeferredEventCollection:

```
// EventMapper
namespace woo\mapper;
// ...
function findBySpaceId( $s_id ) {
        return new DeferredEventCollection(
                    $this,
                    $this->selectBySpaceStmt, array( $s_id ) );
    }
```

Consequences

Lazy loading is a good habit to get into, whether or not you explicitly add deferred loading logic to your domain classes.

Over and above type safety, the particular benefit of using a collection rather than an array for your properties is the opportunity this gives you to retrofit lazy loading should you need it.

Domain Object Factory

The Data Mapper pattern is neat, but it does have some drawbacks. In particular a Mapper class takes a lot on board. It composes SQL statements; it converts arrays to objects and, of course, converts objects back to arrays, ready to add data to the database. This versatility makes a Mapper class convenient and powerful. It can reduce flexibility to some extent, however. This is especially true when a mapper must handle many different kinds of query or where other classes need to share a Mapper's functionality. For the remainder of this chapter, I will decompose Data Mapper, breaking it down into a set of more focused patterns. These finer-grained patterns combine to duplicate the overall responsibilities managed in Data Mapper, and some or all can be used in conjunction with that pattern. They are well defined by Clifton Nock in *Data Access Patterns* (Addison Wesley 2003), and I have used his names where overlaps occur.

Let's start with a core function: the generation of domain objects.

The Problem

You have already encountered a situation in which the Mapper class displays a natural fault line. The createObject() method is used internally by Mapper, of course, but Collection objects also need it to create domain objects on demand. This requires us to pass along a Mapper reference when creating a

Collection object. While there's nothing wrong with allowing callbacks (as you have seen in the Visitor and Observer patterns,), it's neater to move responsibility for domain object creation into its own type. This can then be shared by Mapper and Collection classes alike.

The Domain Object Factory is described in *Data Access Patterns*.

Implementation

Imagine a set of Mapper classes, broadly organized so that each faces its own domain object. The Domain Object Factory pattern simply requires that you extract the createObject() method from each Mapper and place it in its own class in a parallel hierarchy. Figure 13–7 shows these new classes:

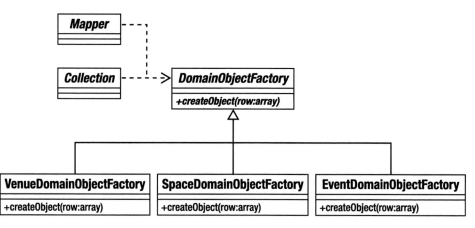

Figure 13–7. Domain Object Factory classes

Domain Object Factory classes have a single core responsibility, and as such, they tend to be simple:

```
namespace woo\mapper;
// ...

abstract class DomainObjectFactory {
    abstract function createObject( array $array );
}
```

Here's a concrete implementation:

```
namespace woo\mapper;
// ...
class VenueObjectFactory extends DomainObjectFactory {
    function createObject( array $array ) {
        $obj = new \woo\domain\Venue( $array['id'] );
        $obj->setname( $array['name'] );
        return $obj;
    }
}
```

Of course, you might also want to cache objects to prevent duplication and prevent unnecessary trips to the database as I did within the Mapper class. You could move the addToMap() and getFromMap()

methods here, or you could build an observer relationship between the ObjectWatcher and your createObject() methods. I'll leave the details up to you. Just remember, it's up to you to prevent clones of your domain objects running amok in your system!

Consequences

The Domain Object Factory decouples database row data from object field data. You can perform any number of adjustments within the createObject() method. This process is transparent to the client, whose responsibility it is to provide the raw data.

By snapping this functionality away from the Mapper class, it becomes available to other components. Here's an altered Collection implementation, for example:

```
namespace woo\mapper;
// ...

abstract class Collection {
    protected $dofact;
    protected $total = 0;
    protected $raw = array();

    // ...

    function __construct( array $raw=null, ➥
\woo\mapper\DomainObjectFactory $dofact=null ) {
        if ( ! is_null( $raw ) && ! is_null( $dofact ) ) {
            $this->raw = $raw;
            $this->total = count( $raw );
        }
        $this->dofact = $dofact;
    }
// ...
```

The DomainObjectFactory can be used to generate objects on demand:

```
if ( isset( $this->raw[$num] ) ) {
    $this->objects[$num]=$this->dofact->createObject( $this->raw[$num] );
    return $this->objects[$num];
}
```

Because Domain Object Factories are decoupled from the database, they can be used for testing more effectively. I might, for example, create a mock DomainObjectFactory to test the Collection code. It's much easier to do this than it would be to emulate an entire Mapper object (you can read more about mock and stub objects in Chapter 18).

One general effect of breaking down a monolithic component into composable parts is an unavoidable proliferation of classes. The potential for confusion should not be underestimated. Even when every component and its relationship with its peers is logical and clearly defined, I often find it challenging to chart packages containing tens of similarly named components.

This is going to get worse before it gets better. Already, I can see another fault line appearing in Data Mapper. The Mapper::getCollection() method was convenient, but once again, other classes might want to acquire a Collection object for a domain type, without having to go to a database facing class. So I have two related abstract components: Collection and DomainObjectFactory. According to the domain object I am working with, I will require a different set of concrete implementations: VenueCollection and VenueDomainObjectFactory, for example, or SpaceCollection and SpaceDomainObjectFactory. This problem leads us directly to the Abstract Factory pattern of course.

Figure 13–8 shows the PersistenceFactory class. I'll be using this to organize the various components that make up the next few patterns.

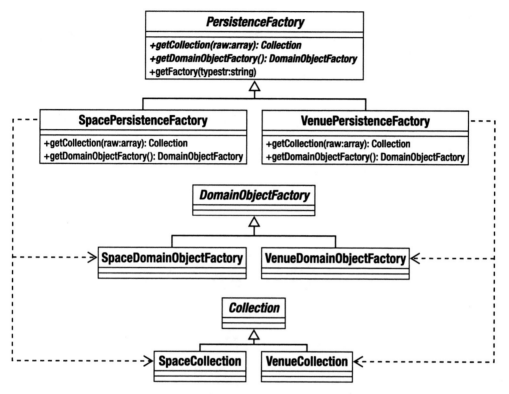

Figure 13–8. *Using the Abstract Factory pattern to organize related components*

The Identity Object

The mapper implementation I have presented here suffers from a certain inflexibility when it comes to locating domain objects. Finding an individual object is no problem. Finding all relevant domain objects is just as easy. Anything in between, though, requires you to add a special method to craft the query (EventMapper::findBySpaceId() is a case in point).

An identity object (also called a Data Transfer Object by Alur et al.) encapsulates query criteria, thereby decoupling the system from database syntax.

The Problem

It's hard to know ahead of time what you or other client coders are going to need to search for in a database. The more complex a domain object, the greater the number of filters you might need in your query. You can address this problem to some extent by adding more methods to your Mapper classes on a case-by-case basis. This is not very flexible, of course, and can involve duplication as you are required to craft many similar but differing queries both within a single Mapper class and across the mappers in your system.

An identity object encapsulates the conditional aspect of a database query in such a way that different combinations can be combined at runtime. Given a domain object called Person, for example, a client might be able to call methods on an identity object in order to specify a male, aged above 30 and below 40, who is under 6 feet tall. The class should be designed so conditions can combined flexibly (perhaps you're not interested in your target's height, or maybe you want to remove the lower age limit). An identity object limits a client coder's options to some extent. If you haven't written code to accommodate an income field, then this cannot be factored into a query without adjustment. The ability to apply different combinations of conditions does provide a step forward in flexibility, however. Let's see how this might work:

Implementation

An identity object will typically consist of a set of methods you can call to build query criteria. Having set the object's state, you can pass it on to a method responsible for constructing the SQL statement.

Figure 13–9 shows a typical set of IdentityObject classes.

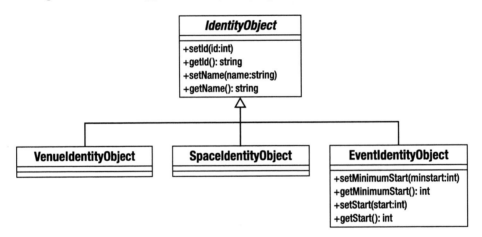

Figure 13–9. *Managing query criteria with identity objects*

You can use a base class to manage common operations and to ensure that your criteria objects share a type. Here's an implementation which is simpler even than the classes shown in Figure 13–9:

```
namespace woo\mapper;
//...

class IdentityObject {
    private $name = null;
    function setName( $name ) {
        $this->name=$name;
    }

    function getName() {
        return $this->name;
    }
```

```
}

class EventIdentityObject
    extends IdentityObject {
    private $start = null;
    private $minstart = null;

    function setMinimumStart( $minstart ) {
        $this->minstart = $minstart;
    }

    function getMinimumStart() {
        return $this->minstart;
    }

    function setStart( $start ) {
        $this->start = $start;
    }

    function getStart() {
        return $this->start;
    }
}
```

Nothing's too taxing here. The classes simply store the data provided and give it up on request. Here's some code that might use SpaceIdentityObject to build a WHERE clause:

```
$idobj = new EventIdentityObject();
$idobj->setMinimumStart( time() );
$idobj->setName( "A Fine Show" );
$comps = array();
$name = $idobj->getName();
if ( ! is_null( $name ) ) {
    $comps[] = "name = '{$name}'";
}
$minstart = $idobj->getMinimumStart();
if ( ! is_null( $minstart ) ) {
    $comps[] = "start > {$minstart}";
}

$start = $idobj->getStart();
if ( ! is_null( $start ) ) {
    $comps[] = "start = '{$start}'";
}

$clause = " WHERE " . implode( " and ", $comps );
```

This model will work well enough, but it does not suit my lazy soul. For a large domain object, the sheer number of getters and setters you would have to build is daunting. Then, following this model, you'd have to write code to output each condition in the WHERE clause. I couldn't even be bothered to handle all cases in my example code (no setMaximumStart() method for me), so imagine my joy at building identity objects in the real world.

Luckily, there are various strategies you can deploy to automate both the gathering of data and the generation of SQL. In the past, for example, I have populated associative arrays of field names in the base class. These were themselves indexed by comparison types: greater than, equal, less than or equal to. The child classes provide convenience methods for adding this data to the underlying structure. The SQL builder can then loop through the structure to build its query dynamically. I'm sure implementing such a system is just a matter of coloring in, so I'm going to look at a variation on it here.

I will use a fluent interface. That is a class whose setter methods return object instances, allowing your users to chain objects together in fluid, language-like way. This will satisfy my laziness, but still, I hope, give the client coder a flexible way of defining criteria.

I start by creating woo\mapper\Field, a class designed to hold comparison data for each field that will end up in the WHERE clause:

```
namespace woo\mapper;

class Field {
    protected $name=null;
    protected $operator=null;
    protected $comps=array();
    protected $incomplete=false;

    // sets up the field name (age, for example)
    function __construct( $name ) {
        $this->name = $name;
    }

    // add the operator and the value for the test
    // (> 40, for example) and add to the $comps property
    function addTest( $operator, $value ) {
        $this->comps[] = array( 'name' => $this->name,
            'operator' => $operator, 'value' => $value );
    }

    // comps is an array so that we can test one field in more than one way
    function getComps() { return $this->comps; }

    // if $comps does not contain elements, then we have
    // comparison data and this field is not ready to be used in
    // a query
    function isIncomplete() { return empty( $this->comps); }
}
```

This simple class accepts and stores a field name. Through the addTest() method the class builds an array of operator and value elements. This allows us to maintain more than one comparison test for a single field. Now, here's the new IdentityObject class:

```
namespace woo\mapper;

class IdentityObject {
    protected $currentfield=null;
    protected $fields = array();
    private $and=null;
    private $enforce=array();

    // an identity object can start off empty, or with a field
    function __construct( $field=null, array $enforce=null ) {
        if ( ! is_null( $enforce ) ) {
            $this->enforce = $enforce;
        }
```

```php
        if ( ! is_null( $field ) ) {
            $this->field( $field );
        }
}

// field names to which this is constrained
function getObjectFields() {
    return $this->enforce;
}

// kick off a new field.
// will throw an error if a current field is not complete
// (ie age rather than age > 40)
// this method returns a reference to the current object
// allowing for fluent syntax
function field( $fieldname ) {
    if ( ! $this->isVoid() && $this->currentfield->isIncomplete() ) {
        throw new \Exception("Incomplete field");
    }
    $this->enforceField( $fieldname );
    if ( isset( $this->fields[$fieldname] ) ) {
        $this->currentfield=$this->fields[$fieldname];
    } else {
        $this->currentfield = new Field( $fieldname );
        $this->fields[$fieldname]=$this->currentfield;
    }
    return $this;
}

// does the identity object have any fields yet
function isVoid() {
    return empty( $this->fields );
}

// is the given fieldname legal?
function enforceField( $fieldname ) {
    if ( ! in_array( $fieldname, $this->enforce ) &&
         ! empty( $this->enforce ) ) {
        $forcelist = implode( ', ', $this->enforce );
        throw new \Exception("{$fieldname} not a legal field ($forcelist)");
    }
}

// add an equality operator to the current field
// ie 'age' becomes age=40
// returns a reference to the current object (via operator())
function eq( $value ) {
    return $this->operator( "=", $value );
}

// less than
function lt( $value ) {
    return $this->operator( "<", $value );
}
```

```
    // greater than
    function gt( $value ) {
        return $this->operator( ">", $value );
    }


    // does the work for the operator methods
    // gets the current field and adds the operator and test value
    // to it
    private function operator( $symbol, $value ) {
        if ( $this->isVoid() ) {
            throw new \Exception("no object field defined");
        }
        $this->currentfield->addTest( $symbol, $value );
        return $this;
    }

    // return all comparisons built up so far in an associative array
    function getComps() {
        $ret = array();
        foreach ( $this->fields as $key => $field ) {
            $ret = array_merge( $ret, $field->getComps() );
        }
        return $ret;
    }
}
```

The easiest way to work out what's going on here is to start with some client code and work backward.

```
$idobj->field("name")->eq("The Good Show")
      ->field("start")->gt( time() )
                      ->lt( time()+(24*60*60) );
```

I begin by creating the IdentityObject. Calling add() causes a Field object to be created and assigned as the $currentfield property. Notice that add() returns a reference to the identity object. This allows us to hang more method calls off the back of the call to add(). The comparison methods eq(), gt(), and so forth each call operator(). This checks that there is a current Field object to work with, and if so, it passes along the operator symbol and the provided value. Once again, eq() returns an object reference, so that I can add new tests or call add() again to begin work with a new field.

Notice the way that the client code is almost sentence-like: field "name" equals "The Good Show" and field "start" is greater than the current time, but less than a day away.

Of course, by losing those hard-coded methods, I also lose some safety. This is what the $enforce array is designed for. Subclasses can invoke the base class with a set of constraints:

```
namespace woo\mapper;

class EventIdentityObject extends IdentityObject {
    function __construct( $field=null ) {
        parent::__construct( $field,
            array('name', 'id','start','duration',  'space' ) );
    }
}
```

The `EventIdentityObject` class now enforces a set of fields. Here's what happens if I try to work with a random field name:

```
PHP Fatal error:  Uncaught exception 'Exception' with message 'banana not a ➥
legal field (name, id, start, duration, space)'...
```

Consequences

Identity objects allow client coders to define search criteria without reference to a database query. They also save you from having to build special query methods for the various kinds of find operation your user might need.

Part of the point of an identity object is to shield users from the details of the database. It's important, therefore, that if you build an automated solution like the fluent interface in the preceding example, the labels you use should refer explicitly to your domain objects and not to the underlying column names. Where these differ, you should construct a mechanism for aliasing between them.

Where you use specialized entity objects, one for each domain object, it is useful to use an abstract factory (like `PersistenceFactory` described in the previous section) to serve them up along with other domain object related objects.

Now that I can represent search criteria, I can use this to build the query itself.

The Selection Factory and Update Factory Patterns

I have already pried a few responsibilities from the `Mapper` classes. With these patterns in place a `Mapper` does not need to create objects or collections. With query criteria handled by Identity Objects, it must no longer manage multiple variations on the `find()` method. The next stage is to remove responsibility for query creation.

The Problem

Any system that speaks to a database must generate queries, but the system itself is organized around domain objects and business rules rather than the database. Many of the patterns in this chapter can be said to bridge the gap between the tabular database and the more organic, treelike structures of the domain. There is, however, a moment of translation—the point at which domain data is transformed into a form that a database can understand. It is at this point that the true decoupling takes place.

Implementation

Of course, you have seen some of this functionality before in the Data Mapper pattern. In this specialization, though, I can benefit from the additional functionality afforded by the identity object pattern. This will tend to make query generation more dynamic, simply because the potential number of variations is so high.

Figure 13–10 shows my simple selection and update factories.

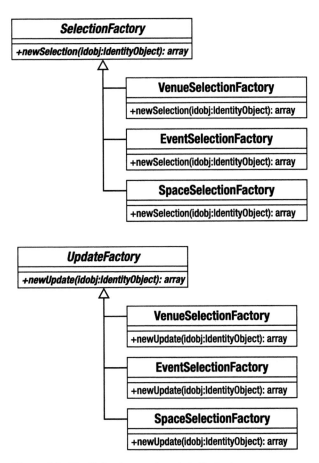

Figure 13–10. *Selection and update factories*

Selection and update factories are, once again, typically organized so that they parallel the domain objects in a system (possibly mediated via identity objects). Because of this, they are also candidates for my PersistenceFactory: the Abstract Factory I maintain as a one-stop shop for domain object persistence tools. Here is an implementation of a base class for update factories:

```
namespace woo\mapper;

abstract class UpdateFactory {

    abstract function newUpdate( \woo\domain\DomainObject $obj );

    protected function buildStatement( $table, array $fields, array $conditions=null ) {
        $terms = array();
        if ( ! is_null( $conditions ) ) {
            $query  = "UPDATE {$table} SET ";
```

```
        $query .= implode ( " = ?,", array_keys( $fields ) )." = ?";
        $terms = array_values( $fields );
        $cond = array();
        $query .= " WHERE ";
        foreach ( $conditions as $key=>$val ) {
            $cond[]="$key = ?";
            $terms[]=$val;
        }
        $query .= implode( " AND ", $cond );
    } else {
        $query  = "INSERT INTO {$table} (";
        $query .= implode( ",", array_keys($fields) );
        $query .= ") VALUES (";
        foreach ( $fields as $name => $value ) {
            $terms[]=$value;
            $qs[]='?';
        }
        $query .= implode( ",", $qs );
        $query .= ")";
    }
    return array( $query, $terms );
    }
}
```

In interface terms, the only thing that this class does is define the newUpdate() method. This will
return an array containing a query string, and a list of terms to apply to it. The buildStatement() method
does the generic work involved in building the update query, with the work specific to individual domain
objects handled by child classes. buildStatement() accepts a table name, an associative array of fields
and their values, and a similar associative array of conditions. The method combines these to create the
query. Here's a concrete UpdateFactory class:

```
namespace woo\mapper;
//...

class VenueUpdateFactory extends UpdateFactory {

    function newUpdate( \woo\domain\DomainObject $obj ) {
        // not type checking removed
        $id = $obj->getId();
        $cond = null;
        $values['name'] = $obj->getName();
        if ( $id > -1 ) {
            $cond['id'] = $id;
        }
        return $this->buildStatement( "venue", $values, $cond );
    }
}
```

In this implementation, I work directly with a DomainObject. In systems where one might operate on
many objects at once in an update, I could use an identity object to define the set on which I would like
to act. This would form the basis of the $cond array, which here only holds id data.

newUpdate() distills the data required to generate a query. This is the process by which object data is
transformed to database information.

Notice that the newUpdate() method will accept any DomainObject. This is so that all UpdateFactory classes can share an interface. It would be a good idea to add some further type checking to ensure the wrong object is not passed in.

You can see a similar structure for SelectionFactory classes. Here is the base class:

```
namespace woo\mapper;

//...

abstract class SelectionFactory {
    abstract function newSelection( IdentityObject $obj );

    function buildWhere( IdentityObject $obj ) {
        if ( $obj->isVoid() ) {
            return array( "", array() );
        }
        $compstrings = array();
        $values = array();
        foreach ( $obj->getComps() as $comp ) {
            $compstrings[] = "{$comp['name']} {$comp['operator']} ?";
            $values[] = $comp['value'];
        }
        $where = "WHERE " . implode( " AND ", $compstrings );
        return array( $where, $values );
    }
}
```

Once again, this class defines the public interface in the form of an abstract class. newSelection() expects an IdentityObject. Also requiring an IdentityObject but local to the type is the utility method buildWhere(). This uses the IdentityObject::getComps() method to acquire the information necessary to build a WHERE clause, and to construct a list of values, both of which it returns in a two element array.

Here is a concrete SelectionFactory class:

```
namespace woo\mapper;

//...

class VenueSelectionFactory extends SelectionFactory {

    function newSelection( IdentityObject $obj ) {
        $fields = implode( ',', $obj->getObjectFields() );
        $core = "SELECT $fields FROM venue";
        list( $where, $values ) = $this->buildWhere( $obj );
        return array( $core." ".$where, $values );
    }
}
```

This builds the core of the SQL statement and then calls buildWhere() to add the conditional clause. In fact, the only thing that differs from one concrete SelectionFactory to another in my test code is the name of the table. If I don't find that I require unique specializations soon, I will refactor these subclasses out of existence and use a single concrete SelectionFactory. This would query the table name from the PersistenceFactory.

Consequences

The use of a generic identity object implementation makes it easier to use a single parameterized
SelectionFactory class. If you opt for hard-coded identity objects—that is, identity objects which consist
of a list of getter and setter methods—you are more likely to have to build an individual
SelectionFactory per domain object.

One of the great benefits of query factories combined with identity objects is the range of queries
you can generate. This can also cause caching headaches. These methods generate queries on the fly,
and it's difficult to know when you're duplicating effort. It may be worth building a means of comparing
identity objects so that you can return a cached string without all that work. A similar kind of database
statement pooling might be considered at a higher level too.

Another issue with the combination of patterns I have presented in the latter part of this chapter is
the fact that they're flexible, but they're not *that* flexible. By this, I mean they are designed to be
extremely adaptable within limits. There is not much room for exceptional cases here, though. Mapper
classes, while more cumbersome to create and maintain, are very accommodating of any kind of
performance kludge or data juggling you might need to perform behind their clean APIs. These more
elegant patterns suffer from the problem that, with their focused responsibilities and emphasis on
composition, it can be hard to cut across the cleverness and do something dumb but powerful.

Luckily, I have not lost my higher level interface—there's still a controller level where I can head
cleverness off at the pass if necessary.

What's Left of Data Mapper Now?

So, I have stripped object, query, and collection generation from Data Mapper, to say nothing of the
management of conditionals. What could possibly be left of it? Well, something that is very much like a
mapper is needed in vestigial form. I still need an object that sits above the others I have created and
coordinates their activities. It can help with caching duties and handle database connectivity (although
the database-facing work could be delegated still further). Clifton Nock calls these data layer controllers
domain object assemblers.

Here is an example:

```
namespace woo\mapper;

//...

class DomainObjectAssembler {
    protected static $PDO;

    function __construct( PersistenceFactory $factory ) {
        $this->factory = $factory;
        if ( ! isset(self::$PDO) ) {
            $dsn = \woo\base\ApplicationRegistry::getDSN( );
            if ( is_null( $dsn ) ) {
                throw new \woo\base\AppException( "No DSN" );
            }
            self::$PDO = new \PDO( $dsn );
            self::$PDO->setAttribute(\PDO::ATTR_ERRMODE, \PDO::ERRMODE_EXCEPTION);
        }
    }

    function getStatement( $str ) {
        if ( ! isset( $this->statements[$str] ) ) {
            $this->statements[$str] = self::$PDO->prepare( $str );
```

```
        }
        return $this->statements[$str];
    }

    function findOne( IdentityObject $idobj ) {
        $collection = $this->find( $idobj );
        return $collection->next();
    }

    function find( IdentityObject $idobj ) {
        $selfact = $this->factory->getSelectionFactory(  );
        list ( $selection, $values ) = $selfact->newSelection( $idobj );
        $stmt = $this->getStatement( $selection );
        $stmt->execute( $values );
        $raw = $stmt->fetchAll();
        return $this->factory->getCollection( $raw );
    }

    function insert( \woo\domain\DomainObject $obj ) {
        $upfact = $this->factory->getUpdateFactory(  );
        list( $update, $values ) = $upfact->newUpdate( $obj );
        $stmt = $this->getStatement( $update );
        $stmt->execute( $values );
        if ( $obj->getId() < 0 ) {
            $obj->setId( self::$PDO->lastInsertId()  );
        }
        $obj->markClean();
    }
}
```

As you can see, this is not an abstract class. Instead of itself breaking down into specializations, it uses the PersistenceFactory to ensure that it gets the correct components for the current domain object.

Figure 13–11 shows the high-level participants I built up as I factored out Mapper.

Aside from making the database connection and performing queries, the class manages SelectionFactory and UpdateFactory objects. In the case of selections, it also works either with a Collection class or directly with a DomainObjectFactory to generate return values.

From a client's point of view, acquiring a DomainObjectFactory is easy. It's simply a matter of getting the correct concrete PersistenceFactory object:

```
$factory = \woo\mapper\PersistenceFactory::getFactory("woo\\domain\\Venue" );
$finder = new \woo\mapper\DomainObjectAssembler( $factory );
```

Although, of course, it would be even easier to add a getFinder() method to the PersistenceFactory itself and transform the previous example into a one-liner like this:

```
$finder = \woo\mapper\PersistenceFactory::getFinder( 'woo\\domain\\Venue' );
```

I'll leave that to you, however.

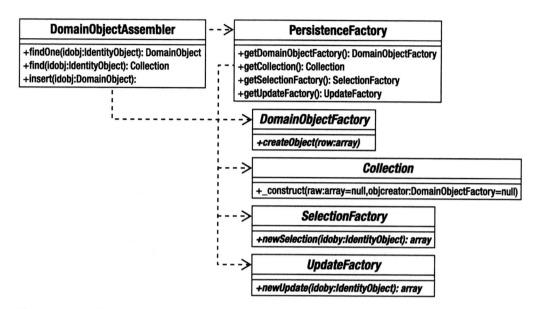

Figure 13–11. *Some of the persistence classes developed in this chapter*

A client coder might then go on to acquire a collection of Venue objects:

```
$idobj = $factory->getIdentityObject()->field('name')
        ->eq('The Eyeball Inn');
$collection = $finder->find( $idobj );


foreach( $collection as $venue ) {
    print $venue->getName()."\n";
}
```

Summary

As always, the patterns you choose to use will depend on the nature of your problem. I naturally gravitate toward a Data Mapper working with an identity object. I like neat automated solutions, but I also need to know I can break out of the system and go manual when I need to, while maintaining a clean interface and a decoupled database layer. I may need to optimize an SQL query, for example, or use a join to acquire data across multiple tables. Even if you're using a complex pattern-based third-party framework, you may find that the fancy object-relational mapping on offer does not do quite what you want. One test of a good framework, and of a good home-grown system, is the ease with which you can plug your own hack into place without degrading the overall integrity of the system as a whole. I love elegant, beautifully composed solutions, but I'm also a pragmatist!

Once again, I have covered a lot in this chapter. We examined the following patterns:

- *Data Mapper*: Create specialist classes for mapping Domain Model objects to and from relational databases.

- *Identity Map*: Keep track of all the objects in your system to prevent duplicate instantiations and unnecessary trips to the database.

- *Unit of Work*: Automate the process by which objects are saved to the database, ensuring that only objects that have been changed are updated and only those that have been newly created are inserted.

- *Lazy Load*: Defer object creation, and even database queries, until they are actually needed.

- *Domain Object Factory*: Encapsulate object creation functionality.

- *Identity Object*: Allow clients to construct query criteria without reference to the underlying database.

- *Query (Selection and Update) Factory*: Encapsulate the logic for constructing SQL queries.

- *Domain Object Assembler*: Construct a controller that manages the high-level process of data storage and retrieval.

In the next chapter, we take a welcome break from code, and I'll introduce some of the wider practices that can contribute to a successful project.

PART 4

■ ■ ■

Practice

CHAPTER 14

■ ■ ■

Good (and Bad) Practice

So far in this book, I have focused on coding, concentrating particularly on the role of design in building flexible and reusable tools and applications. Development doesn't end with code, however. It is possible to come away from books and courses with a solid understanding of a language, yet still encounter problems when it comes to running and deploying a project.

In this chapter, I will move beyond code to introduce some of the tools and techniques that form the underpinnings of a successful development process. This chapter will cover

- *Third-party packages*: Where to get them, when to use them

- *Build*: Creating and deploying packages

- *Version control*: Bringing harmony to the development process

- *Documentation*: Writing code that is easy to understand, use, and extend

- *Unit testing*: A tool for automated bug detection and prevention

- *Continuous integration*: Using this practice and set of tools to automate project builds and tests and be alerted of problems as they occur

Beyond Code

When I first graduated from working on my own and took a place in a development team, I was astonished at how much stuff other developers seemed to have to know. Good-natured arguments simmered endlessly over issues of vital-seeming importance: Which is the best text editor? Should the team standardize on an integrated development environment? Should we impose a coding standard? How should we test our code? Should we document as we develop? Sometimes these issues seemed more important than the code itself, and my colleagues seemed to have acquired their encyclopedic knowledge of the domain through some strange process of osmosis.

The books I had read on PHP, Perl, and Java certainly didn't stray from the code itself to any great extent. As I have already discussed, most books on programming platforms rarely divert from their tight focus on functions and syntax to take in code design. If design is off topic, you can be sure that wider issues such as version control and testing are rarely discussed. This is not a criticism—if a book professes to cover the main features of a language, it should be no surprise that this is all it does.

In learning about code, however, I found that I had neglected many of the mechanics of a project's day-to-day life. I discovered that some of these details were critical to the success or failure of projects I helped develop. In this chapter, and in more detail in coming chapters, I will look beyond code to explore some of the tools and techniques on which the success of your projects may depend.

Borrowing a Wheel

When faced with a challenging but discrete requirement in a project (the need to parse a particular format, perhaps, or use a novel protocol in talking to a remote server), there is a lot to be said for building a component that addresses the need. It can also be one of the best ways to learn your craft. In creating a package, you gain insight into a problem and file away new techniques that might have wider application. You invest at once in your project and in your own skills. By keeping functionality internal to your system, you can save your users from having to download third-party packages. Occasionally, too, you may sidestep thorny licensing issues. There's nothing like the sense of satisfaction you can get when you test a component you designed yourself and find that, wonder of wonders, it works—it does exactly what you wrote on the tin.

There is a dark side to all this, of course. Many packages represent an investment of thousands of man-hours: a resource that you may not have on hand. You may be able to address this by developing only the functionality needed specifically by your project, while a third-party tool might fulfill a myriad of other needs as well. The question remains though: if a freely available tool exists, why are you squandering your talents in reproducing it? Do you have the time and resources to develop, test, and debug your package? Might not this time be better deployed elsewhere?

I am one of the worst offenders when it comes to wheel reinvention. Picking apart problems and inventing solutions to them is a fundamental part of what we do as coders. Getting down to some serious architecture is a more rewarding prospect than writing some glue to stitch together three or four existing components. When this temptation comes over me, I remind myself of projects past. Although the choice to build from scratch has never killed a project in my experience, I have seen it devour schedules and murder profit margins. There I sit with a manic gleam in my eye, hatching plots and spinning class diagrams, failing to notice as I obsess over the details of my component that the big picture is now a distant memory.

Now, when I map out a project, I try to develop a feel for what belongs inside the codebase and what should be treated as a third-party requirement. For example, your application may generate (or read) an RSS feed; you may need to validate e-mail addresses and automate mailouts, authenticate users, or read from a standard-format configuration file. All of these needs can be fulfilled by external packages.

Once you have defined your needs, your first stop should be the PEAR web site at http://pear.php.net. PEAR (PHP Extension and Application Repository) is an officially maintained and quality-controlled repository of packages. It is also a mechanism for installing packages seamlessly and managing package interdependencies. I will cover PEAR in more detail in the next chapter, in which I look at the way that you can use PEAR functionality to prepare your own packages. To give you some idea of what's available in the PEAR repository, here are just a very few of the things you can do with PEAR packages:

- Cache output with Cache_Lite.

- Test the efficiency of your code with Benchmark.

- Abstract the details of database access with MDB2.

- Manipulate Apache .htaccess files with File_HtAccess.

- Extract or encode news feeds with XML_RSS.

- Send mail with attachments with Mail_Mime.

- Parse configuration file formats with Config.

- Password protected environments with Auth.

The PEAR web site provides a list of packages categorized by topic. You may find packages that broadly address your needs there, or you may need to cast your net wider (using the major search engines). Either way, you should always take time to assess existing packages before setting out to potentially reinvent that wheel.

The fact that you have a need, and that a package exists to address it, should not be the start and end of your deliberations. Although it is preferable to use a package where it will save you otherwise unnecessary development, in some cases, it can add an overhead without real gain. Your client's need for your application to send mail, for example, does not mean that you should automatically use PEAR's

Mail package. PHP provides a perfectly good `mail()` function, so initially this would probably be your first stop. As soon as you realize that you have a requirement to validate all e-mail addresses according to the RFC822 standard and that the design team wants to send image attachments with the e-mails, you may begin to weigh the options differently. As it happens, there are PEAR packages for both these features.

Many programmers, myself included, often place too much emphasis on the creation of original code, sometimes to the detriment of their projects. This emphasis on authorship may be one reason that there often seems to be more creation than actual use of reusable code.

Effective programmers see original code as just one of the tools available to aid them in engineering a project's successful outcome. Such programmers look at the resources they have at hand and deploy them effectively. If a package exists to take some strain, then that is a win. To steal and paraphrase an aphorism from the Perl world: good coders are lazy.

Playing Nice

The truth of Sartre's famous dictum that "Hell is other people" is proved on a daily basis in some software projects. This might describe the relationship between clients and developers, symptomized by the many ways that lack of communication leads to creeping features and skewed priorities. But the cap fits too for happily communicative and cooperative team members when it comes to sharing code.

As soon as a project has more than one developer, version control becomes an issue. A single coder may work on code in place, saving a copy of her working directory at key points in development. Introduce another programmer to the mix, and this strategy breaks down in minutes. If the new developer works in the same development directory, then there is a real chance that one programmer will overwrite the work of his colleague when saving, unless both are very careful to always work on different files.

Alternatively, our two developers can each take a version of the codebase to work on separately. That works fine until the moment comes to reconcile the two versions. Unless the developers have worked on entirely different sets of files, the task of merging two or more development strands rapidly becomes an enormous headache.

This is where Subversion and similar tools come in. Using Subversion, you can check out your own version of a codebase and work on it until you are happy with the result. You can then update your version with any changes that your colleagues have been making. Subversion will automatically merge these changes into your files, notifying you of any conflicts it cannot handle. Once you have tested this new hybrid, you can save it to the central Subversion repository, making it available to other developers.

Subversion provides you with other benefits. It keeps a complete record of all stages of a project, so you can roll back to, or grab a snapshot of, any point in the project's lifetime. You can also create branches, so that you can maintain a public release at the same time as a bleeding-edge development version.

Once you have used version control on a project, you will not want to attempt another without it. Working simultaneously with multiple branches of a project can be a conceptual challenge, especially at first, but the benefits soon become clear. Version control is just too useful to live without. I cover Subversion in Chapter 17.

Giving Your Code Wings

Have you ever seen your code grounded because it is just too hard to install? This is especially true for projects that are developed in place. Such projects settle into their context, with passwords and directories, databases and helper application invocations programmed right into the code. Deploying a project of this kind can be a major undertaking, with teams of programmers picking through source code to amend settings so that they fit the new environment.

This problem can be eased to some degree by providing a centralized configuration file or class so that settings can be changed in one place, but even then installation can be a chore. The difficulty or ease of installation will have a major impact upon the popularity of any application you distribute. It will also impede or encourage multiple and frequent deployment during development.

As with any repetitive and time-consuming task, installation should be automated. An installer can determine default values for install locations, check and change permissions, create databases, and initialize variables, among other tasks. In fact, an installer can do just about anything you need to get an application from a source directory in a distribution to full deployment.

This doesn't absolve the user from the responsibility for adding information about his environment to the code, of course, but it can make the process as easy as answering a few questions or providing a couple of command line switches.

For developers, installers have the further virtue of memory. Once an installer has been run from a distribution directory, it can cache many of its settings, making subsequent installations even easier. So the second time you install from a distribution directory, you may not need to provide configuration information like database names and install directories. These are remembered from the first installation. This is important for developers who frequently update their local development space using version control. Version control makes it easy to acquire the latest version of a project. There is little point, however, to removing impedance from the acquisition of code if you have a bottleneck restricting its deployment.

There are various build tools available to the developer. PEAR, for example, is, in part, an installation solution. Most of the time, you will use the PEAR installer to deploy code from the official PEAR repository. It is possible, however, to create your own PEAR packages that can be downloaded and installed by users with ease. The PEAR installer is best suited to self-enclosed, functionally focused packages. It is relatively rigid about the roles and install locations of the files a package should contain, and it tends to concentrate upon the process of placing file A in location B. I cover this aspect of PEAR in detail in Chapter 15.

If you need greater flexibility than this, as you might for application installation, you may prefer an installer that is more flexible and extensible. In Chapter 19, I will look at an application called Phing. This open source project is a port of the popular Ant build tool that is written in and for Java. Phing is written in and for PHP, but it's architecturally similar to Ant and uses the same XML format for its build files.

Where PEAR does a few things very well and offers the simplest possible configuration, Phing is more daunting at first, but with the tradeoff of immense flexibility. Not only can you use Phing to automate anything from file copying to XSLT transformation, you can easily write and incorporate your own tasks should you need to extend the tool. Phing is written using PHP's object-oriented features, and its design emphasizes modularity and ease of extension.

Documentation

My code is so sparse and elegant that it doesn't need documenting. Its purpose is luminously clear at the slightest of glances. I know your code is the same. The others, though, have a problem.

All irony aside, it is true that good code documents itself to some extent. By defining a clear interface and well-defined responsibility for each class and method, and naming each descriptively, you communicate your code's intent. However, you can improve the transparency of your work still further by avoiding unnecessary obfuscation: clarity beats cleverness unless cleverness brings with it immense, and required, gains in efficiency.

The naming of properties, variables, and arguments, too, can play a tremendous role in making your code easy for others to read. Choose descriptive names, where possible. I often add information about the type of a variable to the name—especially for argument variables.

```
public function setName( $name_str, $age_int ) {
    //...
}
```

No matter how clear your code is, though, it can never be quite clear enough on its own. You have seen that object-oriented design often involves combining many classes together in relationships of inheritance, aggregation, or both. When you look at a single class in such a structure, it is often very hard to extrapolate the bigger picture without some kind of explicit pointer.

At the same time, every programmer knows what a pain it is to write documentation. You tend to neglect it during development because the code is in flux, and really your project is about getting the code right. Then when you have reached a point of stability, you suddenly see the enormity of the task of documenting your work. Who would have thought that you would create so many classes and methods? Now your deadline is looming, so it's time to cut your losses and concentrate on quality assurance.

This is an understandable but shortsighted attitude, as you will discover when you return to your code for a second phase in a year's time. Here's a programmer quoted on the popular repository for Internet Relay Chat (IRC) witticism `http://www.bash.org`:

> <@Logan>: I spent a minute looking at my own code by accident.

> <@Logan>: I was thinking "What the hell is this guy doing?"

Without documentation, you are destined to play out that story: wasting your time second-guessing decisions you probably made for very good reasons (if you only knew what they were). This is bad enough, but the situation becomes worse, and more expensive, when you hand off your work to a colleague. Undocumented code will cost you expensive workdays, as your new hire is forced to pepper your code with debug messages, and work her way through fat printouts of promiscuously interrelated classes.

Clearly the answer is to document and to do it as you code, but can the process be streamlined? As you might imagine, the answer is "yes," and once again, the solution is borrowed from a Java tool. phpDocumentor (`http://www.phpdoc.org/`) is a reimplementation of JavaDoc, the documentation application that ships with the Java SDK. From a coder's perspective, the principle is simple. Add specially formatted comments above all classes, most methods, and some properties, and phpDocumentor will incorporate them into a hyperlinked web of documents. Even if you omit these comments, the application will read the code, summarizing and linking up the classes it finds. This is a benefit in itself, allowing you to click from class to class and to observe inheritance relationships at a glance.

I examine phpDocumentor in Chapter 16.

Testing

When you create a class, you are probably pretty sure that it works. You will, after all, have put it through its paces during development. You'll also have run your system with the component in place, checking that it integrates well, and your new functionality is available and performing as expected.

Can you be sure that your class will carry on working as expected though? That might seem like a silly question. After all, you've checked your code once; why should it stop working arbitrarily? Well, of course it won't; nothing happens arbitrarily, and if you never add another line of code to your system, you can probably breathe easy. If, on the other hand, your project is active, then it's inevitable that your component's context will change, and highly likely that the component itself will be altered in any number of ways.

Let's look at these issues in turn. First, how can changing a component's context introduce errors? Even in a system where components are nicely decoupled from one another, they remain interdependent. Objects used by your class return values, perform actions, and accept data. If any of these behaviors change, the effects on the operation of your class might cause the kind of error that's easy to catch—the kind where your system falls over with a convenient error message that includes a file name and line number. Much more insidious, though, is the kind of change that does not cause an engine-level error, but nonetheless confuses your component. If your class makes an assumption based on another class's data, a change in that data might cause it to make a wrong decision. Your class is now in error and without a change to a line of code.

And it's likely that you will go on altering the class you've just completed. Often, these changes will be minor and obvious. So minor in fact, that you won't feel the need to run through the careful checks you performed during development. You'll have probably forgotten them all, anyhow, unless you kept them in some way (perhaps commented out at the bottom of your class file as I sometimes do). Small changes, though, have a way of causing large unintended consequences—consequences that might have been caught had you thought to put a test harness in place.

A test harness is a set of automated tests that can be applied to your system as a whole or to its individual classes. Well deployed, a test harness helps you to prevent bugs from occurring and from *recurring*. A single change may cause a cascade of errors, and the test harness can help you to locate and eliminate these. This means you can make changes with some confidence that you are not breaking anything. It is quite satisfying to make an improvement to your system and then see a list of failed tests. These are all errors that might have been propagated within your system but that now it will not suffer.

Continuous Integration

Have you ever made a schedule that made everything okay? You start with an assignment: code maybe, or a school project. It's big and scary, and failure lurks. But you get out a sheet of paper and you slice it up into manageable tasks. You determine the books to read and the components to write. Maybe you highlight the tasks in different colors. Individually, none of the tasks is actually that scary, it turns out. And gradually, as you plan, you conquer the deadline. As long as you do a little bit every day, you'll be fine. You can relax.

Sometimes, though, that schedule takes on a talismanic power. You hold it up like a shield, to protect yourself from doubt, and from the creeping fear that perhaps this time you'll crash and burn. And it's only after several weeks that you realize the schedule is not magic on its own. You actually have to do the work, too. By then, of course, lulled by the schedule's reassuring power, you have let things slide. There's nothing for it but to make a new schedule. This time it will be less reassuring.

Test and build are like that, too. You have to run your tests. You have to build your projects, and build them in fresh environments regularly, otherwise the magic won't work.

And if writing tests is a pain, running them can be a chore. Especially as they gain in complexity and failures interrupt your plans. Of course, if you were running them more often, you'd probably have fewer failures, and those you did have would stand a good chance of relating to new code that's fresh in your mind.

It's easy to get comfortable in a sandbox. After all, you've got all your toys there. Little scriptlets that make your life easy, development tools, and useful libraries. The trouble is, your project may be getting too comfortable in your sandbox, too. It may begin to rely on uncommitted code, or dependencies that you have left out of your build files. That means it's broken anywhere else but where you work.

The only answer is to build, build, and build again. And do it in a reasonably virgin environment each time.

Of course, it's all very well to advise this. It's quite another matter to do it. Coders as a breed tend to like to code. They want to keep the meetings and the housekeeping to a minimum. That's where Continuous Integration (CI) comes in. CI is both a practice and a set of tools to make the practice as easy as it possibly can be. Ideally, builds and tests should be entirely automatic, or at least launchable from a single command or click. Any problems will be tracked, and you will be notified before an issue becomes too serious. I will talk more about CI in Chapter 20.

Summary

A developer's aim is always to deliver a working system. Writing good code is an essential part of this aim's fulfillment, but it is not the whole story.

In this chapter, I introduced PEAR (which is also the subject of the next chapter). I discussed two great aids to collaboration: documentation and version control. You saw that version control requires automated build, and I introduced Phing, a PHP implementation of Ant, a Java build tool. I discussed software testing, and introduced CI, a set of tools to automate build and testing.

■ ■ ■

CHAPTER 15

An Introduction to PEAR and Pyrus

Programmers aspire to produce reusable code. This is one of the great goals in object-oriented coding. We like to abstract useful functionality from the messiness of specific context, turning it into a tool that can be used again and again. To come at this from another angle, if programmers love the reusable, they hate duplication. By creating libraries that can be reapplied, programmers avoid the need to implement similar solutions across multiple projects.

Even if we avoid duplication in our own code, though, there is a wider issue. For every tool you create, how many other programmers have implemented the same solution? This is wasted effort on an epic scale: wouldn't it be much more sensible for programmers to collaborate and to focus their energies on making a single tool better, rather than producing hundreds of variations on a theme? This is where PEAR (PHP Extension and Application Repository) comes in.

PEAR is a repository of quality-controlled PHP packages that extend the functionality of PHP. It is also a client-server mechanism for distributing and installing packages and for managing interpackage dependencies.

This chapter will cover

- *PEAR basics*: What is this strange fruit?

- *Installing PEAR packages*: All it takes is one command.

- Working with Pyrus, PEAR's younger sibling

- *Adding PEAR packages to your projects*: An example and some notes on error handling.

- `package.xml`: The anatomy of a build file.

- *Creating your own channel*: Providing transparent dependency management and package downloads for users.

What Is PEAR?

At its core, PEAR is a collection of packages, organized into broad categories, such as networking, mail, and XML. The PEAR repository is managed centrally, so that when you use an official PEAR package, you can be sure of its quality.

You can browse the available packages at `http://pear.php.net`. Before you create a tool for a project, you should get into the habit of checking the PEAR site to see if someone has got there first.

Support for PEAR comes bundled with PHP (at least up until the time of this writing), which means that some of the core packages may be available on your system straightaway (unless PHP was compiled to exclude it using the `-without-pear` configure flag). Packages are installed in a configurable location (on Linux or Unix systems this will often be /usr/local/lib/php). You can check this using the pear command line application:

```
$ pear config-get php_dir
/usr/local/lib/php
```

The core packages (known as the PEAR Foundation Classes) provide a backbone for the wider repository—including core functions such as error handling and the processing of command line arguments.

Note If you use a Unix distribution to install PHP, you may begin with a minimal installation. For example, to get PHP and PEAR on Fedora 12 you would need issue these commands:

```
sudo yum install php
sudo yum install php-pear
```

See your distribution's documentation if you wish to use its package management tools to manage PHP. You have already seen the pear application in action. This is a tool for interacting with all aspects of PEAR, and as such, it is an important part of PEAR in itself. The pear application supports a number of subcommands. We used config-get, which shows the value of a particular configuration setting. You can see all settings and their values with the config-show subcommand:

$ pear config-show

```
$ pear config-show
Configuration (channel pear.php.net):
=====================================
Auto-discover new Channels      auto_discover     <not set>
Default Channel                 default_channel   pear.php.net
HTTP Proxy Server Address       http_proxy        <not set>
PEAR server [DEPRECATED]        master_server     pear.php.net
Default Channel Mirror          preferred_mirror  pear.php.net
Remote Configuration File       remote_config     <not set>
PEAR executables directory      bin_dir           /usr/bin
...
```

Phar Out with Pyrus

Before I go any further, I should introduce a newcomer to the PEAR world. Pyrus is the next generation of the PEAR application. The name comes from the genus of trees and shrubs that includes the pear tree. Incidentally, Pirus is the Latin for "pear tree." You can get Pyrus at http://pear2.php.net. The application you will download is a phar package (PHP Archive). If you are familiar with Java, you will recognize a PHP analog to the jar file. A phar is essentially a bundle of code compressed into a zip file. It's a neat way of passing round library code. After download you can simply run Pyrus like this:

php pyrus.phar

```
Pyrus version 2.0.0a1 SHA-1: 27EB8EB427EA50C05691185B41BBA0F0666058D0
Pyrus: No user configuration file detected
It appears you have not used Pyrus before, welcome! Initialize install?
...
```

As you can see, Pyrus will offer you configuration options on first run. You'll need to tell it where to save a configuration file, and where you want it to save packages. You should decide whether you want to use PEAR or Pyrus for your development. While they will both install PEAR packages, their installation locations are not entirely compatible.

At the time of this writing, Pyrus requires PHP 5.3.1, so it's pretty new. That means you may experience usage issues at times (the current version seems incapable of uninstalling packages, for example). You may be stuck with PHP 5.2 for a while yet. If that's the case, you'll need to stick with PEAR. Third-party tools that work with PEAR may not yet be ready for Pyrus. On the other hand, Pyrus is the future. Migrating now may work out cheaper in the long run.

Because there are good reasons to go either way, I'll try to steer a path between both PEAR and Pyrus in this chapter.

So, to bring you up to date, Pyrus does not support a config-get command. It does, however support config-show.

$ php pyrus.phar config-show

```
Pyrus version 2.0.0a1 SHA-1: 27EB8EB427EA50C05691185B41BBA0F0666058D0
Using PEAR installation found at /usr/share/pear2
System paths:
  php_dir => /usr/share/pear2/php
  ext_dir => /usr/lib/php/modules
...
```

Note Although Pyrus will run out of the box with a standard PHP build, once again, the PHP installed by some Linux distributions may not provide everything you need. Pyrus requires the extensions phar, simplexml, libxml2, spl, and pcre. In order to make Pyrus runnable, Fedora 12 required an additional install:

```
yum install php-xml
```

Your favorite distribution may have its own installation issues. Remember also that you need at least PHP 5.3.1 to be in this game.

Although both PEAR and Pyrus support many subcommands, you will probably get the most use out of one in particular. install is used for installing PEAR packages.

Installing a Package

Once you have selected your package, you can download and install it with a single command. Here is the process for installing Log, a package that provides enhanced support for error logging:

```
$ pear install pear/Log
```

■**Note** In most instances, you will need root privileges to install, update, and remove packages with PEAR, because this involves writing to areas of the computer outside of your home space. If you do not have write permissions for these areas, however, all is not lost. In the section "Creating Your Own PEAR Packages," I describe how to change the default installation locations. This will allow you to install packages within your own writeable space.

It really is as simple as that. The PEAR installer is bundled with PHP and locates, downloads, and installs the Log package on your behalf. Here's the command's output:

```
Did not download optional dependencies: pear/DB, pear/MDB2,
      use --alldeps to download automatically
pear/Log can optionally use package "pear/DB" (version >= 1.3)
pear/Log can optionally use package "pear/MDB2" (version >= 2.0.0RC1)
downloading Log-1.12.0.tgz ...
Starting to download Log-1.12.0.tgz (38,479 bytes)
.........done: 44,555 bytes
install ok: channel://pear.php.net/Log-1.9.11
```

The Log package has some optional dependencies, which you can safely ignore unless you require functionality associated with the missing packages. Notice the last line. PEAR tells you that it acquired the Log package from the channel pear.php.net. In fact, I specified as much by installing pear/Log rather than just Log. I'll return to channels shortly.

Pyrus can also install the Log package:

```
php ./pyrus.phar install pear/Log
```

```
Pyrus version 2.0.0a1 SHA-1: 27EB8EB427EA50C05691185B41BBA0F0666058D0
Using PEAR installation found at /usr/share/pear2

Connected...

Installed pear.php.net/Log-1.12.0
Optional dependencies that will not be installed, use --optionaldeps:
pear.php.net/DB depended on by pear.php.net/Log
pear.php.net/MDB2 depended on by pear.php.net/Log
pear.php.net/Mail depended on by pear.php.net/Log
```

From here onward, I'll mention differences between the two systems rather than demonstrate them both in parallel.

If the package you wish to install has compulsory dependencies, the installation will fail with a warning message by default:

```
pear/dialekt requires package "pear/Fandango" (version >= 10.5.0)
No valid packages found
```

You can either install the required package before trying again, or you could run pear install with the -o flag.

```
pear install -o dialekt
```

The -o flag ensures that the PEAR installer will automatically install any required dependencies for you. Some PEAR packages specify optional dependencies, and these are ignored if -o is specified. To have all dependencies installed automatically, use the -a flag instead.

■**Note** Pyrus will attempt to install dependencies by default. It supports an -o flag, which will cause optional dependencies to be installed as well.

Although PEAR is designed to talk to a repository over a network online, you will find that some developers produce PEAR-compatible packages for ease of installation. You may be given the location of a tarball (a tarred and gzipped package). Installing this using PEAR is almost as easy as installing an official package:

```
$ pear install -o http://www.example.com/dialekt-1.2.1.tgz
downloading dialekt-1.2.1.tgz ...
Starting to download dialekt-1.2.1.tgz (1,783 bytes)
....done: 1,783 bytes
install ok: channel://pear.php.net/dialekt-1.2.1
```

You can also download a package and install it from the command line. Here, we use a Unix command called wget to fetch the dialekt package before installing it from the command line:

```
$ wget -nv http://127.0.1.2:8080/dialekt-1.2.1.tgz
20:21:40 URL:http://127.0.1.2:8080/dialekt-1.2.1.tgz [1783/1783]

    -> "dialekt-1.2.1.tgz.1" [1]
$ pear install dialekt-1.2.1.tgz
```

```
install ok: channel://pear.example.com/Dialekt-1.2.1
```

You can install a PEAR package by referencing an XML file (usually named package.xml), which provides information about what files are to be installed where.

```
$ pear install package.xml
install ok:  channel://pear.example.com/Dialekt-1.2.1
```

PEAR Channels

PEAR introduced channels in version 1.4. This powerful feature allows you to poll repositories other than pear.php.net for updates and dependencies. This means that you can build an application that requires packages from multiple repositories. PEAR can then handle acquiring dependencies on the user's behalf. Before the advent of channels, the application developer had to instruct his user to install dependencies or had to bundle them inside his own distribution.

Sebastian Bergmann's PHPUnit package is a real-world example. In order to install it, we first need PEAR to know about the channel in which it can be found:

```
$ pear channel-discover pear.phpunit.de
Adding Channel "pear.phpunit.de" succeeded
Discovery of channel "pear.phpunit.de" succeeded
```

Once you have established communication with this channel using discover, you can refer to a package within it by prefacing its name with phpunit/. In fact, phpunit is just an alias for pear.phpunit.de. You can find out about the alias for a channel by running channel-info:

```
$ pear channel-info pear.phpunit.de
Channel pear.phpunit.de Information:
======================================
Name and Server        pear.phpunit.de
Alias                  phpunit
Summary                PHPUnit channel server
...
```

Note Pyrus does not support the channel-info subcommand

So now I can install PHPUnit:

```
$ pear install -a phpunit/PHPUnit
```

```
Unknown remote channel: pear.symfony-project.com
phpunit/PHPUnit can optionally use package "channel://pear.symfony-project.com/YAML"
(version >= 1.0.2)
phpunit/PHPUnit can optionally use PHP extension "pdo_mysql"
phpunit/PHPUnit can optionally use PHP extension "soap"
phpunit/PHPUnit can optionally use PHP extension "xdebug" (version >= 2.0.5)
downloading PHPUnit-3.4.11.tgz ...
Starting to download PHPUnit-3.4.11.tgz (254,439 bytes)
..................................................done: 254,439 bytes
downloading Image_GraphViz-1.2.1.tgz ...
Starting to download Image_GraphViz-1.2.1.tgz (4,872 bytes)
...done: 4,872 bytes

install ok: channel://pear.phpunit.de/PHPUnit-3.4.11
install ok: channel://pear.php.net/Image_GraphViz-1.2.1
```

Notice that I used the -a flag, which asks PEAR to download all dependent packages. In this case, that means the Image_GraphViz package from channel pear.php.net. You may also notice that the command failed to install a package: YAML. That's because I have not yet run channel-discover on the channel pear.symfony-project.com. Pyrus sees this as a fatal error, so you would need to ensure that all relevant channels have been discovered before running channel-discover with the -o (optional dependencies) flag set.

Using a PEAR Package

Once you have installed a PEAR package, you should be able to use it in your projects immediately. Your PEAR directory should already be in your include path—there should be no problem including the package once it has been installed. Let's install PEAR_Config and any dependencies it might have:

```
$ pear install -a Config
downloading Config-1.10.11.tgz ...
Starting to download Config-1.10.11.tgz (27,718 bytes)
.........done: 27,718 bytes
downloading XML_Parser-1.2.8.tgz ...
Starting to download XML_Parser-1.2.8.tgz (13,476 bytes)
...done: 13,476 bytes
install ok: channel://pear.php.net/Config-1.10.11
install ok: channel://pear.php.net/XML_Parser-1.2.8
```

Here's how you would include the package:

```php
require_once("Config.php");

class MyConfig {
    private $rootObj;

    function __construct( $filename=null, $type='xml' ) {
        $this->type=$type;
        $conf = new Config();
        if ( ! is_null( $filename ) ) {
            $this->rootObj = $conf->parseConfig($filename, $type);
        } else {
            $this->rootObj = new Config_Container( 'section', 'config' );
            $conf->setroot($this->rootObj);
        }
    }

    function set( $secname, $key, $val ) {
        $section=$this->getOrCreate( $this->rootObj, $secname );
        $directive=$this->getOrCreate( $section, $key, $val );
        $directive->setContent( $val );
    }

    private function getOrCreate( Config_Container $cont, $name, $value=null ) {
        $itemtype=is_null( $value )?'section':'directive';
        if ( $child = $cont->searchPath( array($name) ) ) {
            return $child;
        }
        return $cont->createItem( $itemtype, $name, null );
    }

    function __toString() {
        return $this->rootObj->toString( $this->type );
```

```
    }
}
```

We begin by including `Config.php`. Most PEAR packages work in this way, providing a single top-level point of access. All further require statements are then made by the package itself.

The rest of the example simply works with the classes provided by the Config package: `Config` and `Config_Container`. The Config package lets you access and create configuration files in a variety of formats. This simple `MyConfig` class uses Config to work with configuration data. Here's a quick usage example:

```
$myconf = new MyConfig();
$myconf->set("directories", "prefs", "/tmp/myapp/prefs" );
$myconf->set("directories", "scratch", "/tmp/" );
$myconf->set("general", "version", "1.0" );
echo $myconf;
```

By default, this generates output in XML format:

```
<config>
  <directories>
    <prefs>/tmp/myapp/prefs</prefs>
    <scratch>/tmp/</scratch>
  </directories>
  <general>
    <version>1.0</version>
  </general>
</config>
```

As is often the case with sample code, this class is incomplete—it still requires additional error checking as well as methods for writing the configuration data to file. Still, it is pretty useful already, thanks to the power of the PEAR package. By passing different type strings to Config, we could have rendered the previous output in various configuration formats (like the INI format that the PHP application itself uses, for example).Of course, the details of the Config package are beyond the scope of this chapter. The good news is that for official PEAR packages, you will find API instructions on the web site at `http://pear.php.net/`. In all cases, you should expect to be able to add the functionality of a PEAR package to your script with minimal effort. The package should provide you with a clear, well-documented API.

■**Note** The bad news about PEAR packages is that the struggle to support older versions of PHP is extremely hard to square with the demands of later versions. Like many PEAR packages, Config now relies on deprecated language features, which cannot be easily discarded for the sake of backward compatibility. In order to turn off warnings about this, you can set an error_reporting directive like this:

```
error_reporting = E_ALL & ~E_DEPRECATED
```

in your php.ini file.

Handling PEAR Errors

Many, if not most, official PEAR packages use the standard PEAR error class PEAR_Error. This is often returned in place of the expected value if something goes wrong in an operation. This behavior should be documented, and you can test return values using the static PEAR::isError() method.

```
$this->rootObj = @$conf->parseConfig($filename, $type);
if ( PEAR::isError( $this->rootObj ) ) {
    print "message:    ". $this->rootObj->getMessage()   ."\n";
    print "code:       ". $this->rootObj->getCode()      ."\n\n";
    print "Backtrace:\n";

    foreach ( $this->rootObj->getBacktrace() as $caller ) {
        print $caller['class'].$caller['type'];
        print $caller['function']."() ";
        print "line ".$caller['line']."\n";
    }
    die;
}
```

Here, I test the return value from Config::parseConfig().

PEAR::isError($this->rootObj)

is the functional equivalent of

$this->rootObj instanceof PEAR_Error

So within my conditional block, I know that $this->rootObj is a PEAR_Error rather than a Config_Container object.

Once I am sure I have a PEAR_Error object, I can interrogate it for more information about the error. In my example, I have three of the most useful methods: getMessage() returns a message that describes the error; getCode() returns an integer corresponding to the error type (this is an arbitrary number that the package author will have declared as a constant and, we hope, documented); and finally, getBacktrace() returns an array of the methods and classes that lead to the error. This enables us to work our way back through our script's operation and locate the root cause of the error. As you can see, getBacktrace() is itself an array, which describes each method or function that led to the error. The elements are described in Table 15–1.

Table 15–1. *Fields Provided by PEAR_Error::getBacktrace()*

Field	Description
file	Full path to PHP file
args	The arguments passed to the method or function
class	The name of the class (if in class context)
function	The name of the function or method
type	If in class context, the nature of the method call (:: or ->)
line	The line number

The way that PEAR_Error pollutes a method's return value was an unfortunate necessity before the advent of PHP 5. With PHP 4 at or near the end of its life, it's no surprise that PEAR_Error has been deprecated.

Although many packages continue to use PEAR_Error and will probably do so for some time, more are beginning to use PEAR_Exception. If you were to use the XML_Feed_Parser package, for example you would be catching exceptions rather than testing return types:

```
$source="notthere";
try {
    $myfeed = new XML_Feed_Parser( $source );

} catch ( XML_Feed_Parser_Exception $e ) {
    print "message: ".      $e->getMessage()        ."\n";
    print "code: ".         $e->getCode()           ."\n";
    print "error class: ". $e->getErrorClass()    ."\n";
    print "error method: ".$e->getErrorMethod()  ."\n";
    print "trace: ".        $e->getTraceAsString()."\n";
    print "error data: ";
    print_r(                $e->getErrorData() );
}
```

Typically. a PEAR package will extend PEAR_Exception, partly so that it can add any functionality it needs, but mainly so that you can use your catch clause to distinguish between Exception types. PEAR_Exception, of course, itself extends Exception, so you get the standard methods I covered in Chapter 4. You also benefit from some additions. getErrorClass() and getErrorMethod(), for example, tell you the class and method from which the error originated. getErrorData() may include additional error information in an associative array, although this is left for extending classes to implement. Before being thrown to you, a PEAR_Exception object can be initialized with another Exception or with an array of Exception objects. In this way, PEAR packages can wrap Exception objects. You can get at wrapped exceptions by calling PEAR::getCause(). This will either return a wrapped Exception object, an array if there is more than one, or null if none are found.

PEAR_Exception also uses the Observer pattern, allowing you to register callback functions or methods that will be called whenever an exception is thrown. First, let's create some error conditions:

```
class MyPearException extends PEAR_Exception {
}


class MyFeedThing {
    function acquire( $source ) {
        try {
            $myfeed = @new XML_Feed_Parser( $source );
            return $myfeed;
        } catch ( XML_Feed_Parser_Exception $e ) {
            throw new MyPearException( "feed acquisition failed", $e );
        }
    }
}
```

I extend PEAR_Exception and create a simple class that wraps XML_Feed_Parser. If the XML_Feed_Parser constructor throws an exception, I catch it and pass it to the constructor of MyPearException, which I then rethrow. This trick allows me to raise my own error while bundling the root cause.

Here is a client class and a couple of lines of code to invoke it:

```
class MyFeedClient {
    function __construct() {
        PEAR_Exception::addObserver( array( $this, "notifyError") );
    }

    function process() {
        try {
            $feedt = new MyFeedThing();
            $parser = $feedt->acquire('wrong.xml');
        } catch ( Exception $e ) {
            print "an error occurred. See log for details\n";
        }
    }

    function notifyError( PEAR_Exception $e ) {
        print get_class( $e )."":";
        print $e->getMessage()."\n";
        $cause = $e->getCause();
        if ( is_object( $cause ) ) {
            print "[cause] ".get_class( $cause ).":";
            print $cause->getMessage()."\n";
        } else if ( is_array( $cause ) ) {
            foreach( $cause as $sub_e ) {
                print "[cause] ".get_class( $sub_e ).":";
                print $sub_e->getMessage()."\n";
            }
        }
        print "---------------------\n";
    }
}

$client = new MyFeedClient();
$client->process();
```

All the usual caveats about sample code apply here, of course—especially since this particular example is *designed* to fail. First of all, notice the constructor. PEAR_Exception::addObserver() is a static method that accepts a callback, either a function name or an array containing an object reference and a method name. The method or function will be invoked every time a PEAR_Exception is thrown. This trick allows us to design MyFeedClient so that it logs all exceptions.

The process() method passes a nonexistent file to MyFeedThing::acquire(), which passes it on to the XML_Feed_Parser constructor, thereby guaranteeing an error. We catch the inevitable exception and print a simple message. notifyError() is the callback method I referenced in the MyFeedClient constructor. Notice that it expects a PEAR_Exception object. In this case, I simply query the object and print out error information, although in a real-world situation, I would probably send this data to a log. Notice the call to PEAR_Exception::getCause(). Because this could return an array or a single Exception object, I handle both cases. If I run this toy code, this is what I get:

```
XML_Feed_Parser_Exception:Invalid input: this is not valid XML
----------------------
MyPearException:feed acquisition failed
[cause] XML_Feed_Parser_Exception:Invalid input: this is not valid XML
----------------------
an error occurred. See log for details
```

Our logger method is invoked for both the exceptions thrown by this sample (the first by XML_Feed_Parser, the second by MyFeedThing). The XML_Feed_Parser_Exception object makes a second appearance in the log output because we added it to the MyPearException object as a cause.

Creating Your Own PEAR Package

Packages from the PEAR repository are well documented and designed to be easy to use. How easy are they to create, though, and how do you go about creating your own? In this section, we will look at the anatomy of a PEAR package.

package.xml

The package.xml file is the heart of any PEAR package. It provides information about a package, determines where and how its participants should be installed, and defines its dependencies. Whether it operates on a URL, the local file system, or a tarred and gzipped archive, the PEAR installer needs the package.xml file to acquire its instructions.

No matter how well designed and structured your package is, if you omit the build file, the install will fail. Here's what happens if you attempt to install an archive that does not contain package.xml:

```
$ pear install baddialekt.tgz
could not extract the package.xml file from "baddialekt.tgz"
Cannot initialize 'baddialekt.tgz', invalid or missing package file
Package "baddialekt.tgz" is not valid
install failed
```

The PEAR installer first unpacks our archive to the temporary directory and then looks for package.xml. Here, it falls at the first hurdle. So if package.xml is so important, what does it consist of?

Package Elements

The package file must begin with an XML declaration. All elements are then enclosed by the root package element:

```
<?xml version="1.0" encoding="UTF-8"?>
<package packagerversion="1.4.11" version="2.0"
 xmlns="http://pear.php.net/dtd/package-2.0"
 xmlns:tasks="http://pear.php.net/dtd/tasks-1.0"
 xmlns:xsi="http://www.w3.org/2001/XMLSchema-instance"
 xsi:schemaLocation="http://pear.php.net/dtd/tasks-1.0
 http://pear.php.net/dtd/tasks-1.0.xsd
 http://pear.php.net/dtd/package-2.0
 http://pear.php.net/dtd/package-2.0.xsd">
```

```
<!-- additional elements here -->

</package>
```

This example would fail with an error. The PEAR installer requires a number of elements to work with. To start with, we must provide overview information:

```
<name>Dialekt</name>
<channel>pear.example.com</channel>
<summary>A package for translating text and web pages into silly tones
of voice</summary>
<description>Be the envy of your friends with this hilarious dialect
translator. Easy to extend and altogether delightful.
</description>

<!-- additional elements here -->
```

These new elements should be pretty self-explanatory. The `name` element defines the handle by which the user will refer to the package. The summary element contains a one-line overview of the package, and `description` provides a little more detail. All these elements are compulsory with the exception of `channel`. If you are not intending to add your package to a channel you can use the `uri` element instead of channel, and in the same part of the file.. This should contain a URI that points to your package file:

```
<uri>http://www.example.com/projects/Dialekt-1.2.1</uri>
```

The file name should not include an extension, even though the package file itself will likely end with a `.tgz` extension.

Next, you should provide information about the team behind your package. You should include at least one lead element:

```
<lead>
  <name>Matt Zandstra</name>
  <user>mattz</user>
  <email>matt@example.com</email>
  <active>yes</active>
</lead>
```

After this, you can define other projects participants in a similar way. Instead of lead, though, you can use developer, contributor, or helper elements. These are designations recognized by the PEAR community, but they should adequately cover most non-PEAR projects too. The user element refers to the contributor's user name with PEAR. Most teams use similar handles to allow users to log in to Subversion, a development server, or both.

Before you get to the files in your project, there are a few more details you must provide:

```
<date>2010-02-13</date>
<time>18:01:44</time>
<version>
  <release>1.2.1</release>
  <api>1.2.1</api>
</version>
<stability>
  <release>beta</release>
  <api>beta</api>
</stability>
<license uri="http://www.php.net/license">PHP License</license>
```

```
<notes>initial work
</notes>
```

Although this is mostly self-explanatory, it's worth pointing out a couple of features. Of the elements inside version, release is the one that really counts as far as your package is concerned. The release element is used by PEAR in dependency calculations. If another system claims to require Dialekt 1.0.0, and the installing user only has version 0.2.1 on her system, PEAR will halt its installation or attempt to fetch a later version, depending on the mode in which it was run. The api element, on the other hand, is there so that you can keep track of changes in your code's interface which may affect compatibility.

The stability element is similarly split between release and api. The value can be one of snapshot, devel, alpha, beta, or stable; you should choose the one that best describes your project.

If you are releasing your package according to specific license terms (such as GNU's GPL license, for example) you should add this information to the license element.

Unlike summary and description, the notes element will accept line breaks in the contents you add.

The contents Element

Now, we're finally ready to talk about the files and directories in the package. The contents element defines the files that will be included in the package archive (sometimes called a tarball, because it's archived with the tar and Gzip tools). You can describe the structure of your archive by combining dir and file elements.

Here's a simplified example:

```
<contents>
 <dir name="/">
  <dir name="data">
   <file name="alig.txt" role="data" />
   <file name="dalek.txt" role="data" />
  </dir> <!-- /data -->
  <dir name="Dialekt">
   <file name="AliG.php" role="php" />
   <file name="Dalek.php" role="php" />
  </dir>
</contents>
```

Every file in a PEAR package has a role. Every role is associated with a default (configurable) location. Table 15–2 describes the common roles.

Table 15–2. *Some Common PEAR File Roles*

Role	Description	PEAR Config Name	Example Location
php	PHP file	php_dir	/usr/local/lib/php
test	Unit test file	test_dir	/usr/local/lib/php/test/<package>
script	Command line script	bin_dir	/usr/local/bin
data	Resource file	data_dir	/usr/local/lib/php/data/<package>
doc	Documentation file	doc_dir	/usr/local/lib/php/doc/<package>

When installation takes place, files of role doc, data, and test are not dropped directly into their respective directories. Instead, a subdirectory named after the package is created in the test_dir and data_dir directories, and files are installed into this.

In a PEAR project, everything must have a role, and every role has its place. If you do not have the correct privileges to work with the default role locations, you can set your own locations using the pear command line tool:

```
$ pear config-set php_dir ~/php/lib/
```

```
$ pear config-set data_dir ~/php/lib/data/
$ pear config-set bin_dir ~/php/bin/
$ pear config-set doc_dir ~/php/lib/doc/
```

```
$ pear config-set test_dir ~/php/lib/test/
```

Note Pyrus uses set rather than config-set for the same purpose.

Now, PEAR will use your directories rather than those described in Table 15–2. Remember that if you do this, you should add the lib directory to your include path: either in the php.ini file, an .htaccess file, or using the ini_set() function in your scripts. You should also ensure that the bin directory is in your shell's path so that command line commands can be found.

My example revolves around a fictitious package called Dialekt. Here is the package's directory and file structure:

```
./package.xml
./data
    ./data/dalek.txt
    ./data/alig.txt
./script
    ./script/dialekt.sh
    ./script/dialekt.bat
./cli-dialekt.php
./Dialekt.php
./Dialekt
    ./Dialekt/AliG.php
    ./Dialekt/Dalek.php
```

As you can see, I have mirrored some of the standard PEAR roles in my data structure. So I include data and script directories. The top-level directory contains two PHP files. These should be installed in the PEAR directory (/usr/local/php/lib by default). Dialekt.php is designed to be the first port of call for client code. The user should be able to include Dialekt with

```
require_once("Dialekt.php");
```

Additional PHP files (Dalek.php and AliG.php) are stored in a Dialekt directory that will be added to the PEAR directory (these are responsible for the detailed process of translating web pages and text files into oh-so-funny versions of themselves). Dialekt.php will include these on behalf of client code. So that the installed Dialekt package will be callable from the command line, we have included a shell script that will be moved to PEAR's script directory. Dialekt uses configuration information stored in text files. These will be installed in PEAR's data directory.

Here's the full contents tag:

```xml
<contents>
  <dir name="/">
   <dir name="data">
    <file name="alig.txt" role="data" />
    <file name="dalek.txt" role="data" />
   </dir> <!-- /data -->
   <dir name="Dialekt">
    <file name="AliG.php" role="php" />
    <file name="Dalek.php" role="php" />
   </dir> <!-- /Dialekt -->
   <dir name="script">
    <file name="dialekt.bat" role="script">
     <tasks:replace from="@php_dir@" to="php_dir" type="pear-config" />
     <tasks:replace from="@bin_dir@" to="bin_dir" type="pear-config" />
     <tasks:replace from="@php_bin@" to="php_bin" type="pear-config" />
    </file>
    <file name="dialekt.sh" role="script">
     <tasks:replace from="@php_dir@" to="php_dir" type="pear-config" />
     <tasks:replace from="@bin_dir@" to="bin_dir" type="pear-config" />
     <tasks:replace from="@php_bin@" to="php_bin" type="pear-config" />
    </file>
   </dir> <!-- /script -->
   <file name="cli-dialekt.php" role="php" />
   <file name="Dialekt.php" role="php">
    <tasks:replace from="@bin_dir@" to="bin_dir" type="pear-config" />
   </file>
  </dir> <!-- / -->
</contents>
```

I have included a new element in this fragment. The tasks:replace element causes the PEAR installer to search the file for the trigger string given in the from attribute, replacing it with the pear-config setting in the to attribute. So the Dialekt.php file, for example, might start out looking like this:

```php
<?php
/*
 * Use this from PHP scripts, for a CLI implementation use
 * @bin_dir@/dialekt
 */
class Dialekt {
    const DIALEKT_ALIG=1;
    const DIALEKT_DALEK=2;
//...
}
```

After installation, the same class comment should look something like this:

```php
/*
 * Use this from PHP scripts, for a CLI implementation use
 * /home/mattz/php/bin/dialekt
 */
```

Dependencies

Although packages are generally stand-alone entities, they often make use of one another. Any use of another package introduces a dependency. If the used package is not present on the user's system, then the package that uses it will not run as expected.

The dependencies tag is a required element, and within it, you must specify at least the PHP, and PEAR installer versions.

```
<dependencies>
 <required>
  <php>
   <min>5.3.0</min>
  </php>
  <pearinstaller>
   <min>1.4.1</min>
  </pearinstaller>
  <!-- other dependencies here if required -->
 </required>
</dependencies>
```

Both php and pearinstall can contain min, max, and exclude elements. exlude defines a version which will be treated as incompatible with the package, and you can include as many of these as you need. The pearinstaller element can also contain a recommended element, in which you can set a preferred installer for the package.

If these or other dependencies within the required element are not satisfied, PEAR will refuse to install the package by default. A package can depend on another package, a PHP extension (such as zlib or GD) or a particular version of PHP. Here, I insist that Dialekt has access to the Fandango package at version 10.5.0 or greater (note, that I add this *within* the required element):

```
<package>
<name>Fandango</name>
<channel>pear.example.com</channel>
<min>10.5.0</min>
</package>
```

Notice the channel element; this specifies where pear should search for the package should it be invoked with the -a flag (which tells it to acquire all dependencies). You must specify either a channel or a uri element. The uri element should point to a package file:

```
<package>
<name>Fandango</name>
<uri>http://www.example.com/packages/fandango-10.5.0.tgz</uri>
</package>
```

The package element accepts the same dependency specifiers as pearinstaller, with the addition of conflicts in which you can define a version with which this package will *not* work.

In addition to package you could also specify extension, os, or arch. Table 15–3 summarizes these dependency elements.

Table 15–3. package.xml Dependency Types

Element	Description
php	The PHP application
package	A PEAR package
extension	A PHP extension (a capability compiled into PHP such as zlib or GD)
arch	Operating system and processor architecture
os	An operating system

Up until now I have specified mandatory dependencies. In fact, after `requires`, you can specify an `optional` element. This accepts the same dependency elements. When PEAR encounters an unfilled optional dependency, it will raise a warning but will continue to install nonetheless. You should add depencies to the `optional` element where your package can limp along adequately without the preferred package or extension.

If the user runs the `pear install` command with the -o flag

```
pear install -o package.xml
```

then PEAR will attempt to download and install all unmet *required* dependencies (remember, though that passing -o to pyrus means that it will install optional requirements). Running the command with the -a flag also automates the download of dependencies but will take in optional as well as required packages.

Tweaking Installation with `phprelease`

Although you define the files in a package archive with the contents element, you can use `phprelease` to fine tune the files that are actually installed onto the users system. Here are the two `phprelease` elements in our package:

```
<phprelease>
<installconditions>
 <os>
  <name>unix</name>
 </os>
</installconditions>
<filelist>
 <install as="dialekt" name="script/dialekt.sh" />
 <install as="dalek" name="data/dalek.txt" />
 <install as="alig" name="data/alig.txt" />
 <ignore name="script/dialekt.bat" />
</filelist>
</phprelease>
<phprelease>
<installconditions>
 <os>
  <name>windows</name>
 </os>
```

```
 </installconditions>
 <filelist>
  <install as="dialekt" name="script/dialekt.bat" />
  <install as="dalek" name="data/dalek.txt" />
  <install as="alig" name="data/alig.txt" />
  <ignore name="script/dialekt.sh" />
 </filelist>
</phprelease>
```

The installconditions element can be used to determine the phprelease element that is executed. It accepts the specifier elements os, extension, arch, and php. These elements work in the same way as their dependency namesakes. As well as providing phprelease elements qualified by installconditions, you can provide a default version to be executed if none of the others are matched.

Let's focus on the unix phprelease. The install element specifies that the file dialekt.sh should be renamed dialekt on installation.

I specify that my data files should be installed without the .txt suffix. I do not need to specify the dialekt subdirectory—this is automatically included for files with a data role. Note that the install element's as element also strips out the leading directory data that we specified in the contents element for these files. This means that they are installed as <data_dir>/dialekt/dalek and <data_dir>/dialekt/alig.

Note also that in Unix mode I don't want to install the dialekt.bat script file. The ignore element takes care of that. All being well our package is ready to install locally.

Preparing a Package for Shipment

Now that I have created my package and created a package.xml file,, it is time to generate an archived and compressed product.

There is a single PEAR command to achieve this. We ensure we are in the root directory of our project and run this subcommand:

```
$ pear package package.xml
Analyzing Dialekt/AliG.php
Analyzing Dialekt/Dalek.php
Analyzing cli-dialekt.php
Analyzing Dialekt.php
Package Dialekt-1.2.1.tgz done
```

This will generate a tarred and gzipped archive (including all referenced files as well as the package.xml file itself) suitable for distribution. You can make this available for straight download. If you have dependencies between packages, you can reference URIs in your package elements and use the uri element in place of channel. If you are offering many interdependent packages to your users, though, perhaps you should consider taking things to the next level.

Setting Up Your Own Channel

Why set up your own channel? Aside from the sheer coolness of such a thing, the main benefits lie in PEAR's automatic dependency management and the consequent ease of installation and upgrade for your users. It's easy enough for a user to install a single package using a full path to a tarball URL. If you have designed a library system in tiers working from low-level utility packages to high-level applications, things become more complicated. It can be a real pain for users to manage multiple interdependent packages on their systems, especially as they evolve.

For this section, I will focus on the Pyrus mechanism for creating and hosting channels. There are two reasons for this. First, Pyrus is the future. It is likely what we'll all be using in the coming years. It's written from the ground up, without the need for backward compatibility, which makes for cruft-free code and clean architecture. Second, the required packages are officially supported on the Pyrus site at http://pear2.php.net. Although a perfectly good PEAR-oriented solution for channel management has been available since 2006, it has somehow never made it from an external site (http://greg.chiaraquartet.net) onto the PEAR website. Whatever the reasons for this, it does not inspire confidence that the software will continue to be supported.

Still, with Pyrus so new, you may encounter some glitches along the way. Where I have to work around rough edges, I'll be sure to document it here.

If you're still using PEAR to build packages, don't worry. There's no reason why you can't use Pyrus channel management to serve PEAR packages. In order to create and host your own channel you will ideally have

- Root access to your web host computer

- Administrative access to a web server (probably Apache) and the ability to support a subdomain (pear.yourserver.com, for example)

If you do not have this kind of control over your server, don't worry, you can host your channel with a third-party provider such as Google Code (http://code.google.com). However you decide to host it, first of all you will need to define your channel and add some packages to it.

Defining a Channel with PEAR2_SimpleChannelServer

PEAR2_SimpleChannelServer is actually something of a misnomer. It is a tool for defining and channel and organizing your package files ready for serving, rather than a server or server component.

At the time of this writing, the Pyrus website claims that you should use Pyrus itself to install PEAR2_SimpleChannelServer. In fact, this currently causes an error. However, you can get the package in a phar file at http://pear2.php.net/get/PEAR2_SimpleChannelServer-0.1.0.phar

---

■**Note** You'll likely find that PEAR2_SimpleChannelServer installation will be improved. Check in at http://pear2.php.net/PEAR2_SimpleChannelServer to monitor progress.

Once you have phar file you can place it somewhere central, and rename it for convenience (I chose /usr/share/pearscs.phar). Then you can run it to set up your basic channel environment.

```
php /usr/share/pearscs.phar create pear.appulsus.com "Appulsus PHP repository" appulsus
```

```
Created pear.appulsus.com
      | ./channel.xml
      | ./rest/
      | ./get/
```

The create subcommand requires a channel name, which is usually a host and subdomain (I'll return to that), a summary, and, optionally, an alias. If you omit the alias, the system will suggest one taken from the name argument. As you can see I chose 'appulsus'. It then creates a file named channel.xml, which defines your channel. It also creates empty get/ and rest/ directories. I want these to be Web-accessible later, so I ran the command in a Web directory.

Now that I've created a channel, I can add some categories.

```
php /usr/share/pearscs.phar add-category productivity "things to help you work"
php /usr/share/pearscs.phar add-category fun "the fun never stops"
```

The add-category subcommand takes two arguments: the name of the category, and a description. It simply amends the channel.xml file.

Before I can add a package to the system, I must ensure that my new channel can be recognized or PEAR, or Pyrus will complain when the package is built. In order to do this I need another Pyrus package: PEAR2_SimpleChannelFrontend

Managing a PEAR Channel with PEAR2_SimpleChannelFrontend

Once again, the Pyrus site is not currently consistent about the best way to work with this package. The suggested installation method:

```
php pyrus.phar install PEAR2_SimpleChannelFrontend
```

results in an error at the time of this writing. By the time you read this, you may get more useful instructions on the package page at http://pear2.php.net/PEAR2_SimpleChannelServer. For now though, you can get a phar file from http://pear2.php.net/get/PEAR2_SimpleChannelFrontend-0.1.0.phar. You can also check http://pear2.php.net/get/ for more recent versions of the archive.

Now that I have the PEAR2_SimpleChannelFrontend phar file, I need to make it available via the Web. I can do this by renaming the file to index.php and placing it in the Web-accessible directory that houses channel.xml. This location should match up with the domain and subdomain that define the channel. So, earlier I chose the name pear.appulsus.com for my channel. I should configure Apache 2 so that pear.appulsus.com resolves to the directory in which I've placed index.php. Here's an extract from my httpd.conf file (that is the Apache Web server's configuration file):

```
<VirtualHost *:80>
ServerAdmin webmaster@appulsus.com
DocumentRoot /var/www/pear
ServerName pear.appulsus.com
ErrorLog logs/pear.appulsus.com-error_log
TransferLog logs/pear.appulsus.com-access_log
</VirtualHost>
```

This simply ensures that a request to http://pear.appulsus.com is routed to the DocumentRoot directory (/var/www/pear) in which I placed the newly renamed index.php. The SimpleChannelFrontend packages also requires that some mod_rewrite directives are applied to the channel directory:

```
<Directory "/var/www/pear">
<IfModule mod_rewrite.c>
RewriteEngine On
RewriteBase /
RewriteCond %{REQUEST_FILENAME} !-f
RewriteCond %{REQUEST_FILENAME} !-d
RewriteRule . index.php [L]
</IfModule>
</Directory>
```

There's enough in place now to for me to run a browser test. Figure 15.1 shows the default page that `PEAR2_SimpleChannelFrontend-0.1.0.phar` generates.

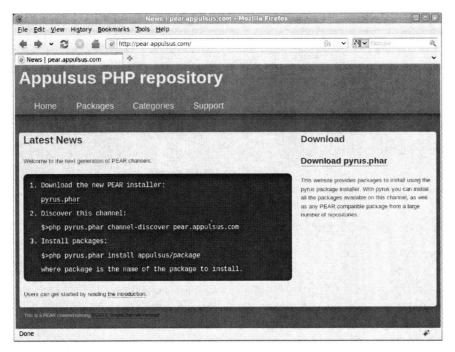

Figure 15–1. *The Channel Frontend Default Page*

This means I already have my own channel. I can confirm this on a remote command line.

```
pear channel-discover pear.appulsus.com
```

```
Adding Channel "pear.appulsus.com" succeeded
Discovery of channel "pear.appulsus.com" succeeded
```

Notice I'm using PEAR on the client side. I'm hoping to demonstrate that these Pyrus tools can provide service to a user running with a traditional PEAR setup. So far so good!

Managing a Package

Now that pear.appulsus.com can be recognized as a channel, I can alter the package.xml for Dialekt so that it belongs there:

```
<name>Dialekt</name>
<channel>pear.appulsus.com</channel>
<summary>A package for translating text and web pages into silly tones of voice</summary>
```

and regenerate the PEAR package

```
Analyzing Dialekt/AliG.php
Analyzing Dialekt/Dalek.php
Analyzing cli-dialekt.php
Analyzing Dialekt.php
Package Dialekt-1.2.1.tgz done
```

As before, I have a Dialekt-1.2.1.tgz package. This time, though, it's ready for the pear.appulsus.com channel. Now I can move or upload the package to my channel directory. Then, before I run the command to make the release, I must first check a setting in the php.ini file. If you don't know where that is, by the way, you can run

```
php --ini
```

from the command-line and PHP will tell you. Once I've looked up its location I can open up php.ini and look for a line like this:

```
phar.readonly = Off
```

If the line is not there, or if it differs, I must add or alter it. Without this setting, my release will likely fail. Now, at last I'm ready to make my release. I change to my channel directory and run.

```
php /usr/share/pearscs.phar release Dialekt-1.2.1.tgz mattz
```

```
Release successfully saved
```

Once again, I called the pearscs.phar file. Remember, that's the PEAR_SimpleChannelServer package. It requires a path to the package file, and a maintainer name. And that's it. I now have a channel, containing a package. I can also associate it with a category:

```
php /usr/share/pearscs.phar categorize Dialekt fun
```

```
Added  Dialekt to fun
```

Figure 15.2 shows how I can confirm my new package from the browser.
Of course, the proof of the pudding is in the installing. So, from a remote system I can try just that:

```
pear install appulsus/Dialekt
```

```
downloading Dialekt-1.2.1.tgz ...
Starting to download Dialekt-1.2.1.tgz (1,913 bytes)
....done: 1,913 bytes
install ok: channel://pear.appulsus.com/Dialekt-1.2.1
```

All that's left to do now is publicize the channel!

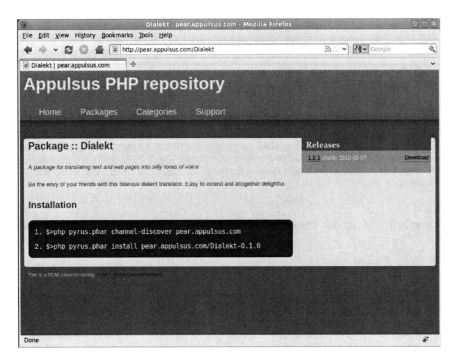

Figure 15–2. *A Channel Package Page*

Summary

PEAR is extensive almost by definition, and I have only had space to provide an introduction here. Nevertheless, you should leave this chapter with a sense of how easy it is to leverage PEAR packages to add power to your projects. Through the `package.xml` file, the PEAR installer (and Pyrus, its future replacement), you can also make your code accessible to other users. By setting up a channel, you can automate dependency downloads for your users and allow third-party packages to use yours without the need for bundling or complicated dependency management.

PEAR is best suited for relatively self-enclosed packages with well-defined functionality. For larger applications, other build solutions come into their own. We will be looking at Phing, a powerful tool for building applications, later in the book.

CHAPTER 16

Generating Documentation with phpDocumentor

Remember that tricky bit of code? The one in which you treated that method argument as a string, unless it was an integer? Or was it a Boolean? Would you recognize it if you saw it? Maybe you tidied it up already? Coding is a messy and complex business, and it's hard to keep track of the way your systems work and what needs doing. The problem becomes worse when you add more programmers to the project. Whether you need to signpost potential danger areas or fantastic features, documentation can help you. For a large codebase, documentation or its absence can make or break a project.

This chapter will cover

- *The phpDocumentor application*: Installing phpDocumentor and running it from the command line

- *Documentation syntax*: The DocBlock comment and documentation tags

- *Documenting your code*: Using DocBlock comments to provide information about classes, properties, and methods

- *Creating links in documentation*: Linking to web sites and to other documentation elements

Why Document?

Programmers love and loathe documentation in equal measure. When you are under pressure from deadlines, with managers or customers peering over your shoulders, documentation is often the first thing to be jettisoned. The overwhelming drive is to get results. Write elegant code, certainly (though that can be another sacrifice), but with a codebase undergoing rapid evolution, documentation can feel like a real waste of time. After all, you'll probably have to change your classes several times in as many days. Of course, everyone agrees that it's desirable to have good documentation. It's just that no one wants to undermine productivity in order to make it happen.

Imagine a very large project. The codebase is enormous, consisting of very clever code written by very clever people. The team members have been working on this single project (or set of related subprojects) for over five years. They know each other well, and they understand the code absolutely. Documentation is sparse, of course. Everyone has a map of the project in their heads, and a set of unofficial coding conventions that provide clues as to what is going on in any particular area. Then the team is extended. The two new coders are given a good basic introduction to the complex architecture and thrown in. This is the point at which the true cost of undocumented code begins to tell. What would otherwise have been a few weeks of acclimatization soon becomes months. Confronted with an undocumented class, the new programmers are forced to trace the arguments to every method, track down every referenced global, check all the methods in the inheritance hierarchy. And with each trail followed, the process begins again. If, like me, you have been one of those new team members, you soon learn to love documentation.

Lack of documentation costs. It costs in time, as new team members join a project, or existing colleagues shift beyond their area of specialization. It costs in errors as coders fall into the traps that all projects set. Code that should be marked private is called, argument variables are populated with the wrong types, functionality that already exists is needlessly re-created.

Documentation is a hard habit to get into because you don't feel the pain of neglecting it straightaway. Documentation needn't be difficult, though, if you work at it as you code. This process can be significantly eased if you add your documentation in the source itself as you code. You can then run a tool to extract the comments into neatly formatted web pages. This chapter is about just such a tool.

phpDocumentor is based on a Java tool called JavaDoc. Both systems extract special comments from source code, building sophisticated application programming interface (API) documentation from both the coder's comments and the code constructs they find in the source.

Installation

The easiest way to install phpDocumentor is by using the PEAR command line interface.

```
pear upgrade PhpDocumentor
```

■**Note** In order to install or upgrade a PEAR package on a Unix-like system, you usually need to run the `pear` command as the root user.

This will make a network connection (to http://pear.php.net) and automatically either install or update phpDocumentor on your system.

You can also download the package from SourceForge.net at http://sourceforge.net/projects/phpdocu/files/. You will find zipped and tarballed packages here. Once you have the package on your file system, you may be able to install it directly using PEAR if PHP was compiled with zlib support.

```
pear install PhpDocumentor-1.4.3.tgz
```

Alternatively, you can uncompress the archive and work with phpDocumentor directly from the distribution directory. The command line interface is handled by the file `phpdoc`, and you need to have the library directory `phpDocumentor` in your include path.

```
tar -xvzf PhpDocumentor-1.4.3.tgz
cd PhpDocumentor-1.4.3
chmod 755 phpdoc
./phpdoc -h
```

Here, I unpacked and entered the distribution directory. I made the `phpdoc` script executable and ran it with the -h flag, which calls up a usage message.

If you have any problems with installation, the phpDocumentor package includes a file named `INSTALL`, which contains extensive instructions and troubleshooting hints.

Generating Documentation

It might seem odd to generate documentation before we have even written any, but phpDocumentor parses the code structures in our source code, so it can gather information about your project before you even start.

I am going to document aspects of an imaginary project called "megaquiz." It consists of two directories, command and quiztools, which contain class files. These are also the names of packages in the project. phpDocumentor can be run as a command line tool or through a slick web GUI. I will concentrate on the command line, because it's easy then to embed documentation updates into build tools or shell scripts. The command to invoke phpDocumentor is phpdoc. You will need to run the command with a number of arguments in order to generate documentation. Here's an example:

```
phpdoc -d megaquiz/ \
        -t docs/megaquiz/ \
        -ti 'Mega Quiz' \
        -dn 'megaquiz'
```

The -d flag denotes the directory whose contents you intend to document. -t denotes your target directory (the directory to which you wish to write the documentation files). Use -ti to set a project title, and -dn to define the default package name.

If we run this command on our undocumented project, we get a surprising amount of detail. You can see the menu page of our output in Figure 16–1.

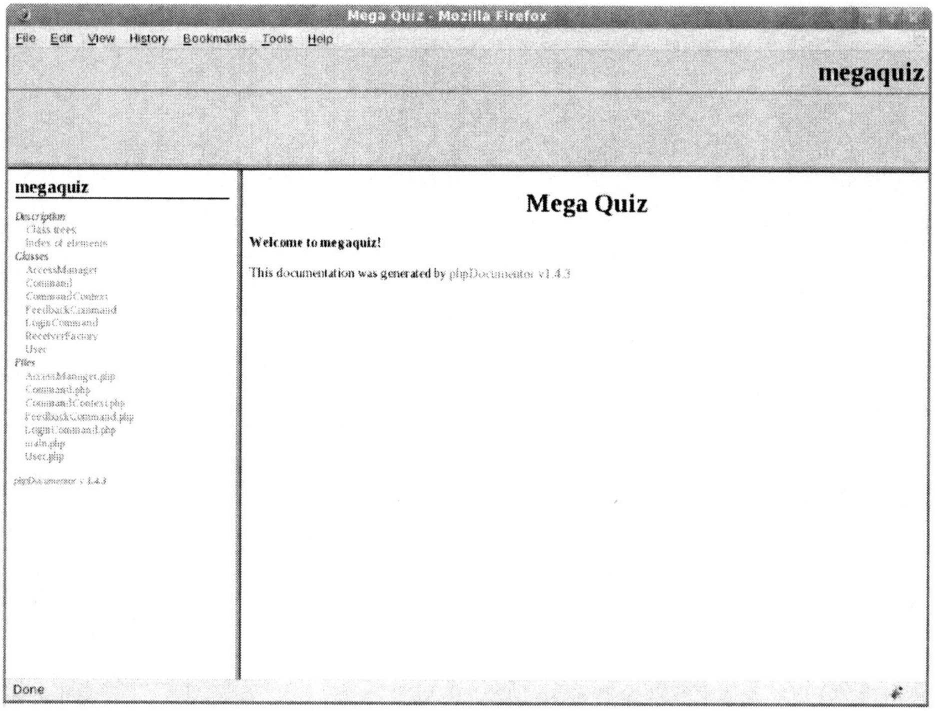

Figure 16–1. *A basic phpDocumentor output menu*

As you can see, all the classes and files in the project are listed in the left-hand frame. Both the project name and the package name are incorporated into the documentation. The class names are all hyperlinks. In Figure 16–2, you can see some of the documentation for the Command class I created in Chapter 11.

phpDocumentor is smart enough to recognize that Command is an abstract class, and that it is extended by FeedbackCommand and LoginCommand. Notice also that it has reported both the name and the type of the argument required by the execute() method.

Because this level of detail alone is enough to provide an easily navigable overview of a large project, it is a huge improvement over having no documentation at all. However, I can improve it significantly by adding comments to my source code.

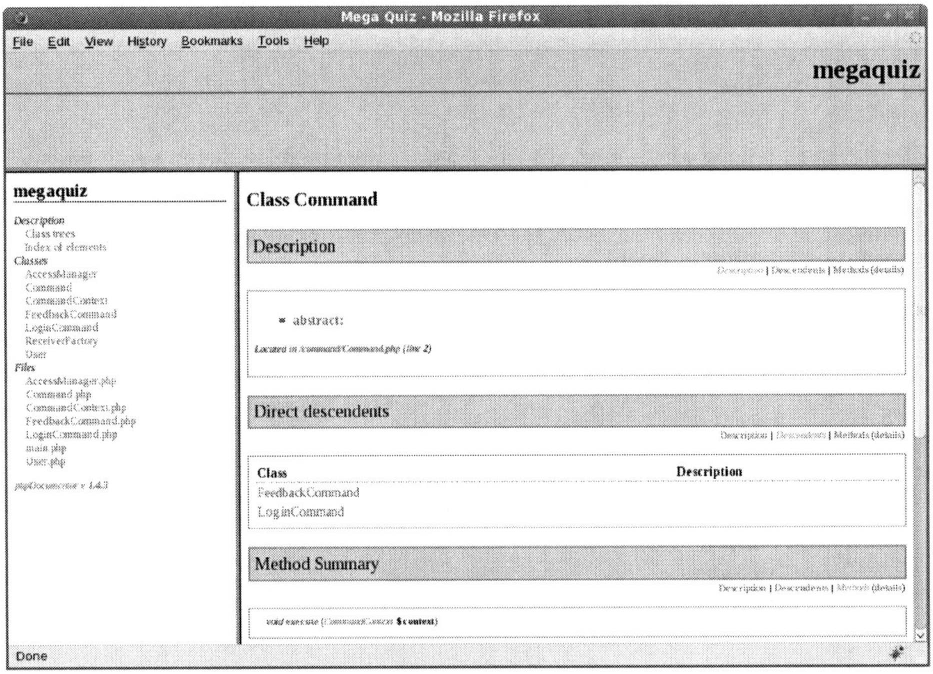

Figure 16–2. *Default documentation for the Command class*

DocBlock Comments

DocBlock comments are specially formatted to be recognized by a documentation application. They take the form of standard multiline comments. Standard, that is, with the single addition of an asterisk to each line within the comment:

```
/**
 * My DocBlock comment
 */
```

phpDocumentor is designed to expect special content within DocBlocks. This content includes normal text descriptive of the element to be documented (for our purposes, a file, class, method, or property). It also includes special keywords called tags. Tags are defined using the at sign (@) and may be associated with arguments. So the following DocBlock placed at the top of a class tells phpDocumentor the package to which it belongs:

```
/**
 * @package command
 */
```

If I add this comment to every class in my project (with the appropriate package name, of course), phpDocumentor will organize our classes for us. You can see phpDocumentor output that includes packages in Figure 16–3.

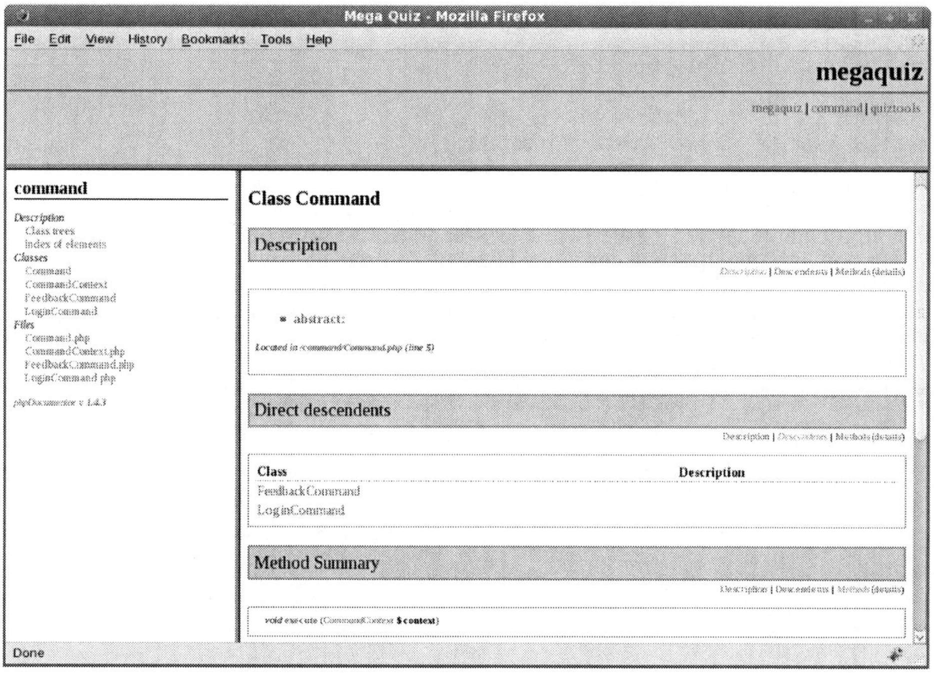

Figure 16–3. *Documentation output that recognizes the @package tag*

In Figure 16–3, notice that packages have been added to the navigation (top-right corner). In addition to the default megaquiz package I defined as a command line switch, I can now click command or quiztools. Because I am currently examining classes in the command package, the links that form the left-hand navigation list only those classes.

Generally, packages in documentation will mirror your directory structure. So the command package maps to a command directory. That isn't necessary, however. A third-party developer may wish to create a Command class that is part of the command package but lives in her own directory, for example. So the @package tag makes you take responsibility for associating classes with packages, but it also affords you flexibility that would not be available by using the file system to guess at package names.

Documenting Classes

Let's add some more tags and text that are useful in class- or file-level DocBlocks. I should identify the class, explain its uses, and add authorship and copyright information.

Here is the Command class in its entirety:

```
/**
 * Defines core functionality for commands.
 * Command classes perform specific tasks in a system via
 * the execute() method
 *
 * @package command
 * @author  Clarrie Grundie
 * @copyright 2004 Ambridge Technologies Ltd
 */
abstract class Command {
    abstract function execute( CommandContext $context );
}
```

The DocBlock comment has grown significantly. The first sentence is a one-line summary. This is emphasized in the output and extracted for use in overview listings. The subsequent lines of text contain more detailed description. It is here that you can provide detailed usage information for the programmers who come after you. As we will see, this section can contain links to other elements in the project and fragments of code in addition to descriptive text. I also include @author and @copyright tags, which should be self-explanatory. You can see the effect of my extended class comment in Figure 16–4.

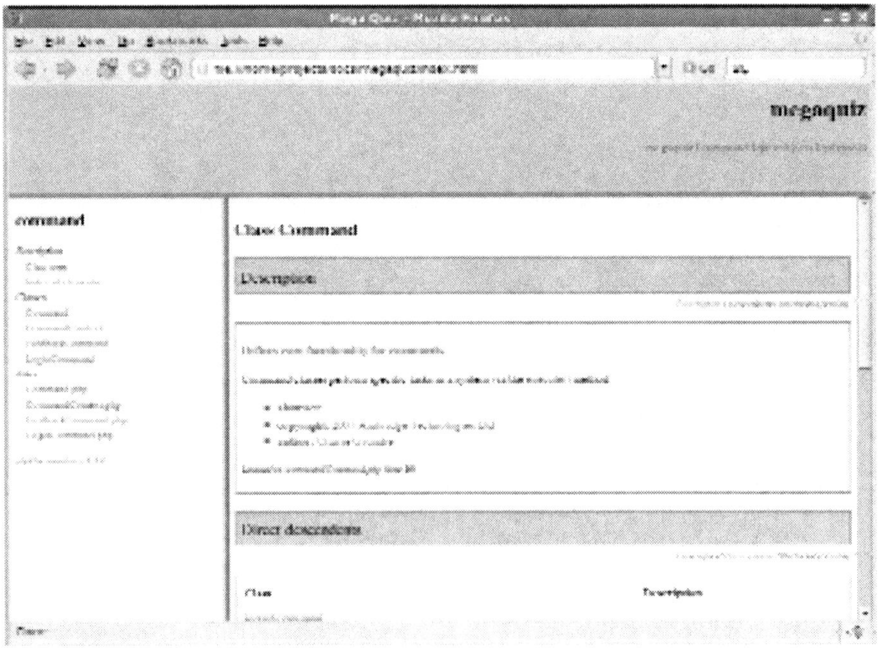

Figure 16–4. *Class details in documentation output*

Notice that I didn't need to tell phpDocumentor that the Command class is abstract. This confirms something that we already know, that phpDocmentor interrogates the classes with which it works even without our help. But it is also important to see that DocBlocks are contextual. phpDocumentor understands that we are documenting a class in the previous listing, because the DocBlock it encounters immediately precedes a class declaration.

Note At the time of this writing, phpDocumentor does not support namespaces. However, the project's maintainer, Greg Beaver, is on record as committed to provide this functionality (<http://lists.bluga.net/pipermail/phpdocumentor-devel/2008-September/000066.html>).

File-Level Documentation

Although I tend to think in terms of classes rather than of the files that contain them, there are good reasons in some projects for providing a layer of documentation at the file level.

First of all, phpDocumentor likes file comments. If you fail to include a DocBlock for a file in your project, a warning is raised that can clutter up the application's reporting, especially in large projects. A file comment should be the first DocBlock in a document. It should contain a @package tag, and it should not directly precede a coding construct. In other words, if you add a file-level DocBlock, you should ensure that you also add a class-level comment before the first class declaration.

Many open source projects require that every file includes a license notice or a link to one. Page-level DocBlock comments can be used, therefore, for including license information that you do not want to repeat on a class-by-class basis. You can use the @license tag for this. @license should be followed by a URL, pointing to a license document and a description:

```
/**
 * @license http://www.example.com/lic.html Borsetshire Open License
 * @package command
 */
```

The URL in the license tag will become clickable in the phpDocumentor output.

Documenting Properties

All properties are mixed in PHP. That is, a property can potentially contain a value of any type. There may be some situations in which you require this flexibility, but most of the time, you think of a property as containing a particular data type. phpDocmentor allows you to document this fact using the @var tag.

Here are some properties documented in the CommandContext class:

```
class CommandContext {
/**
 * The application name.
 * Used by various clients for error messages, etc.
 * @var string
 */
    public $applicationName;

/**
```

```
 * Encapsulated Keys/values.
 * This class is essentially a wrapper for this array
 * @var array
 */
    private $params = array();

/**
 * An error message.
 * @var string
 */
    private $error = "";
// ...
```

As you can see, I provide a summary sentence for each property and fuller information for the first two. We use the @var tag to define each property's type. If we were to use the same phpdoc command line arguments as usual to generate output at this point, you would only see documentation for the public $applicationName property. This is because private methods and properties do not appear in documentation by default.

Whether or not you choose to document private elements depends in large part on your intended audience. If you are writing for client coders, then you should probably hide your classes' internals. If, on the other hand, your project is under development, your team members may need more detailed documentation. You can make phpDocumentor include private elements by using the -pp (--parseprivate) command line argument when you invoke the script:

```
phpdoc -d /home/projects/megaquiz/ \
       -t /home/projects/docs/megaquiz/ \
       -ti 'Mega Quiz' \
       -dn 'megaquiz' \
       -pp on
```

Notice that you must explicitly set the -pp flag to on; it is not enough to include the flag on its own. You can see the documented properties in Figure 16–5.

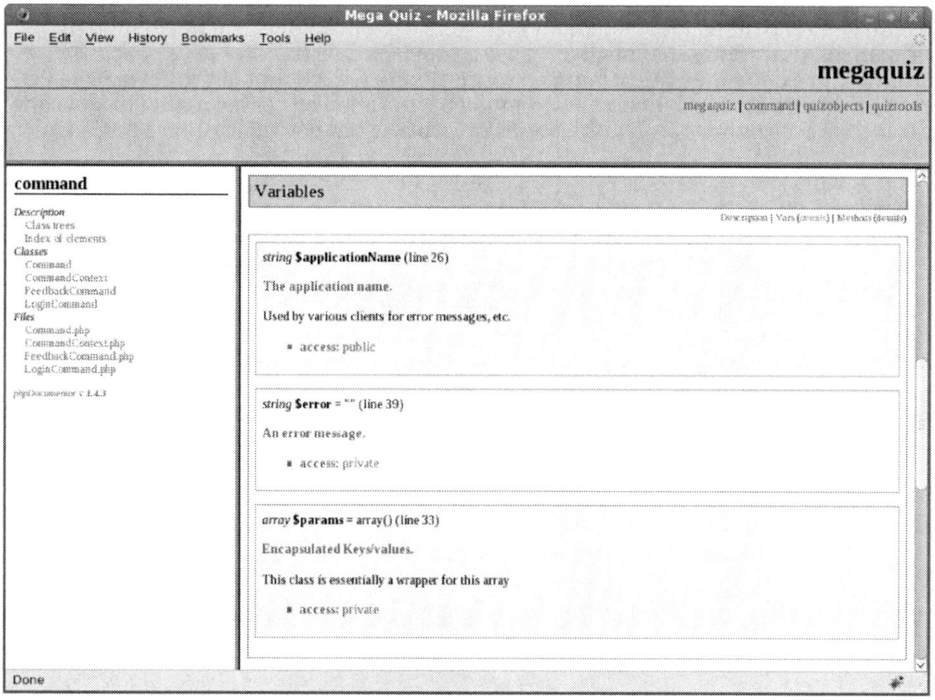

Figure 16–5. *Documenting properties*

Documenting Methods

Together with classes, methods lie at the heart of a documentation project. At the very least, readers need to understand the arguments to a method, the operation performed, and its return value.

As with class-level DocBlock comments, method documentation should consist of two blocks of text: a one-line summary and an optional description. You can provide information about each argument to the method with the @param tag. Each @param tag should begin a new line and should be followed by the argument name, its type, and a short description.

Because PHP does not constrain return types, it is particularly important to document the value a method returns. You can do this with the @return tag. @return should begin a new line and should be followed by the return value's type and a short description. I put these elements together here:

```
/**
 * Perform the key operation encapsulated by the class.
 * Command classes encapsulate a single operation. They
 * are easy to add to and remove from a project, can be
 * stored after instantiation and execute() invoked at
 * leisure.
 * @param  $context CommandContext Shared contextual data
 * @return bool     false on failure, true on success
 */
```

```
abstract function execute( CommandContext $context );
```

It may seem strange to add more documentation than code to a document. Documentation in abstract classes is particularly important, though, because it provides directions for developers who need to understand how to extend the class. If you are worried about the amount of dead space the PHP engine must parse and discard for a well-documented project, it is a relatively trivial matter to add code to your build tools to strip out comments on installation. You can see our documentation's output in Figure 16–6.

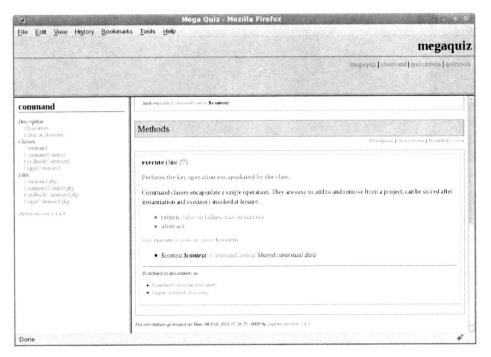

Figure 16–6. *Documenting methods*

Creating Links in Documentation

phpDocumentor generates a hyperlinked documentation environment for you. Sometimes, though, you will want to generate your own hyperlinks, either to other elements within documentation or to external sites. In this section, we will look at the tags for both of these and encounter a new syntax: the inline tag.

As you construct a DocBlock comment, you may want to talk about a related class, property, or method. To make it easy for the user to navigate to this feature, you can use the @see tag. @see requires a reference to an element in the following format:

```
class
class::method()
```

or like this:

```
class::$property
```

So in the following DocBlock comment, I document the CommandContext object and emphasize the fact that it is commonly used in the Command::execute() method:

```
/**
 * Encapsulates data for passing to, from and between Commands.
 * Commands require disparate data according to context. The
 * CommandContext object is passed to the Command::execute()
 * method and contains data in key/value format. The class
 * automatically extracts the contents of the $_REQUEST
 * superglobal.
 *
 * @package command
 * @author  Clarrie Grundie
 * @copyright 2004 Ambridge Technologies Ltd
 * @see Command::execute()
 */

class CommandContext {
// ...
```

As you can see in Figure 16–7, the @see tag resolves to a link. Clicking this will lead you to the execute() method.

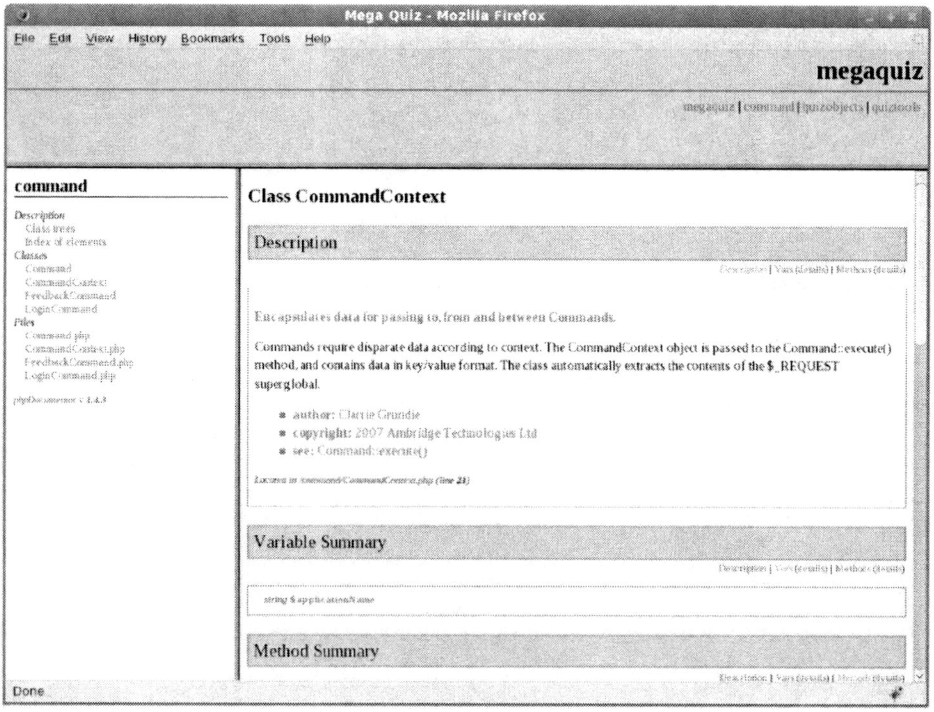

Figure 16–7. Creating a link with the @see tag

357

Notice, though, that we also embedded a reference to Command::execute() in the DocBlock description text. We can transform this into a live link by using the @link tag. @link can be added at the beginning of a line, as @see is, but it can also be used inline. In order to differentiate inline tags from their surroundings, you must surround them with curly brackets. So, to make my embedded reference to Command::execute() clickable, I would use the following syntax:

```
// ...
 * Commands require disparate data according to context. The
 * CommandContext object is passed to the {@link Command::execute()}
 * method and contains data in key/value format. The class
//...
```

Because the @link tag in the previous fragment includes only the element reference (Command::execute()), it is this string that becomes clickable. If I were to add some description here, it would become clickable instead.

@link can be used to refer to URLs as well. Simply replace the element reference with a URL:

```
@link http://www.example.com More info
```

Once again, the URL is the target, and the description that follows it is the clickable text.

You may want to make a reciprocal link. Command uses CommandContext objects, so I can create a link from Command::execute() to the CommandContext class and a reciprocal link in the opposite direction. I could, of course, do this with two @link or @see tags. @uses handles it all with a single tag, however:

```
/**
 * Perform the key operation encapsulated by the class.
 * ...
 * @param  $context {@link CommandContext} Shared contextual data
 * @return bool      false on failure, true on success
 * @link http://www.example.com More info
 * @uses CommandContext
 */
    abstract function execute( CommandContext $context );
```

In adding the @uses tag, I create a link in the Command::execute() documentation: "Uses: CommandContext". In the CommandContext class documentation, a new link will appear: "Used by: Command::execute()".

You can see the latest output in Figure 16–8. Note that I have not used @link inline, so it is output in list format.

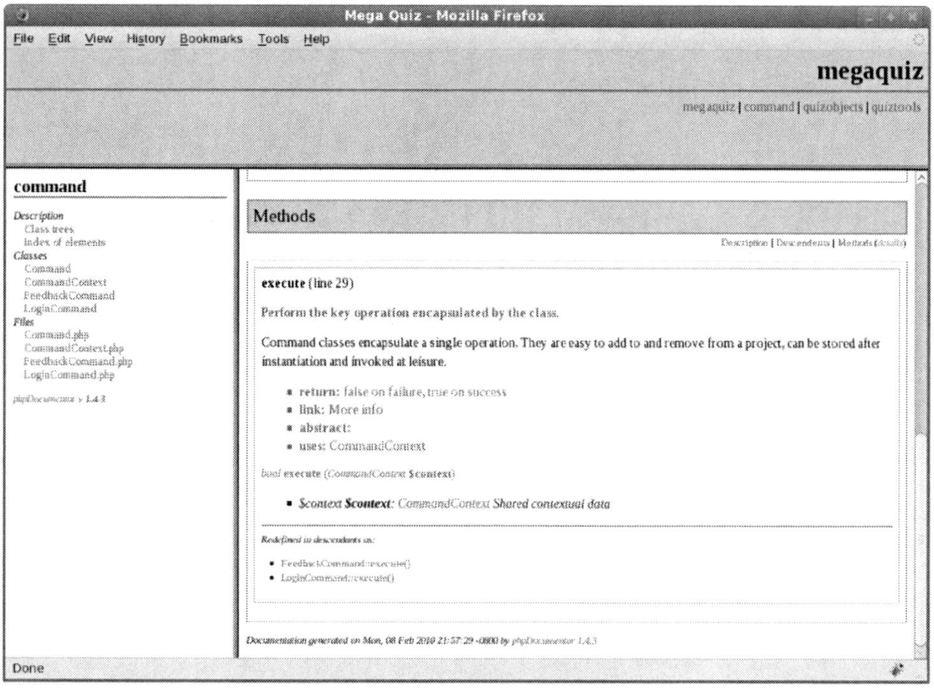

Figure 16–8. *Documentation including @link and @uses tags*

Summary

In this chapter, I covered the core features of phpDocumentor. You encountered the DocBlock comment syntax and the tags that can be used with it. I looked at approaches to documenting classes, properties, and methods, and you were provided with enough material to transform your documentation, and thus improve collaborative working immeasurably (especially when used in conjunction with build tools and version control). There is a lot more to this application than I have space to cover, though, so be sure to check the phpDocumentor homepage at http://www.phpdoc.org.

■ ■ ■

CHAPTER 17

Version Control with Subversion

All disasters have their tipping point, the moment at which order finally breaks down and events simply spiral out of control. Do you ever find yourself in projects like that? Are you able to spot that crucial moment? Perhaps it's when you make "just a couple of changes" and find that you have brought everything crashing down around you (and even worse, you're not quite sure how to get back to the point of stability you have just destroyed). It could be when you realize that three members of your team have been working on the same set of classes and merrily saving over each other's work. Or perhaps it's when you discover that a bug fix you have implemented twice has somehow disappeared from the codebase yet again. Wouldn't it be nice if there was a tool to help you manage collaborative working, allowing you to take snapshots of your projects and roll them back if necessary, and to merge multiple strands of development? In this chapter, we look at Subversion, a tool that does all that and more.

This chapter will cover

- *Basic configuration*: Some tips for setting up Subversion

- *Importing*: Starting a new project

- *Committing changes*: Saving your work to the repository

- *Updating*: Merging other people's work with your own

- *Branching*: Maintaining parallel strands of development

Why Use Version Control?

If it hasn't already, version control will change your life (if only your life as a developer). How many times have you reached a stable moment in a project, drawn a breath, and plunged onward into development chaos once again? How easy was it to revert to the stable version when it came time to demonstrate your work in progress? Of course, you may have saved a snapshot of your project when it reached a stable moment, probably by duplicating your development directory. Now, imagine that your colleague is working on the same codebase. Perhaps he has saved a stable copy of the code as you have. The difference is that his copy is a snapshot of his work, not yours. Of course, he has a messy development directory too. So you have four versions of your project to coordinate. Now imagine a project with four programmers and a web UI developer. You're looking pale. Perhaps you would like to lie down?

Subversion exists exclusively to address this problem. Using Subversion, all your developers check out their own copies of the codebase from a central repository. Whenever they reach a stable point in their code, they update their copies. This merges any changes in the shared code with their own recent work. After they fix any conflicts, they can check their new stable versions back into the shared repository. There is now only one authoritative source of code in your project. The fact that each developer merges her work into the central repository means that you no longer have to worry about reconciling multiple strands of development by hand. Even better, you can check out versions of your codebase based on a date or a label. So when your code reaches a stable point, suitable for showing to a client as work in progress, for example, you can tag that with an arbitrary label. You can then use that tag to check out the correct codebase when your client swoops into your office looking to impress an investor.

Wait! There's more! You can also manage multiple strands of development at the same time. If this sounds needlessly complicated, imagine a mature project. You have already shipped the first version, and you're well into development of version 2. Does version 1.n go away in the meantime? Of course not. Your users are spotting bugs and requesting enhancements all the time. You may be months away from shipping version 2, so where do you make and test the changes? Subversion lets you maintain distinct branches of the codebase. So you might create a bug-fix branch of your version 1.n for development on the current production code. At key points, this branch can be merged back into the version 2 code (the trunk), so that your new release can benefit from improvements to version 1.n.

■**Note** Subversion is not the only version control system available. You might also like to look into Git (http://git-scm.com/) or Mercurial (http://mercurial.selenic.com/). These are new and increasingly popular version control systems. Both use a decentralized model.

Let's get on and look at some of these features in practice.

Getting Subversion

If you are working with a Unix-like operating system (such as Linux or FreeBSD), you may already have a Subversion client installed and ready to use.

Try typing

```
$ svn help
```

from the command line. You should see some usage information that will confirm that you are ready to get started. If you do not already have Subversion, you should consult your distribution's documentation. You will almost certainly have access to a simple installation mechanism such as Yum or Apt.

■**Note** Throughout this chapter, I denote command line input by displaying it in bold text. A dollar sign ($) represents the command prompt.

If you get an error message, you may need to download and install Subversion yourself. You can acquire both source and binaries from http://subversion.apache.org/.

■**Note** If you'd rather work with a graphical user interface (GUI) instead of the command line, you might want to take a look at RapidSVN, a cross-platform front-end to Subversion. You can find it at http://rapidsvn.tigris.org/. If you're a Windows user, you should also evaluate TortoiseSVN (http://tortoisesvn.tigris.org/).

Configuring a Subversion Repository

Whether you are running Subversion locally or across multiple clients, you must have a repository in place before you can start work. What's more, every user's Subversion client must know where that repository is. In this section, I look at the steps necessary to get Subversion up and running, either on a single machine or over the Internet. I assume root access to a Linux machine. In order to create and manage a repository you need the svnadmin command.

Creating a Repository

You can create a Subversion repository with a simple svnadmin subcommand: create. This will create a properly configured Subversion repository directory.

Here, I create a repository in the directory /var/local/svn. Generally speaking, only the root user can create and modify directories in /var/local, so I run the following command as root:

```
$ svnadmin create --fs-type fsfs /var/local/svn
```

This command will execute silently, but you should find that it has created a directory called svn in the /var/local directory. The fs-type flag is not strictly necessary here, because fsfs is the default setting. This directive orders Subversion to use files to store version information. The alternative bdb specifies Berkeley DB to manage this data.

Let's assume that you have multiple users on this Linux machine, all of whom will need to commit to and update from this repository. You need to ensure that they can all write to the /var/local/svn directory. You can do this by adding these users to a common group and making the directory writable by this group.

You can create a new group (called svnusers) on the command line like this:

```
$ groupadd svnusers
```

You must run the groupadd command as root. You should now have this group on your system.

First, I'll add a user, bob, on the current host to the svnusers group. You can track this by monitoring a special file called /etc/group. In /etc/group, you should find a line that looks like this:

```
$ svnusers:x:504:
```

I add bob to the group with this command:

```
$ usermod -aG svnusers bob
```

Now, if you look at /etc/group, you should see that bob has been associated with the svnusers group.

```
$ svnusers:x:504:bob,
```

Next, I need to ensure that /var/local/svn is writable by anyone in the svnusers group. I can do this by changing the group of /var/local/svn to svnusers.

```
$ chgrp -R svnusers /var/local/svn/
$ chmod -R g+rws /var/local/svn/
```

The second line in the previous fragment causes all directories created here to take on the svnusers group. Accessing the Subversion Repository

In order to access a project within a subversion repository, you must use a URL to specify its location. I'm going to jump the gun now and pretend that I've already created a project named megaquiz. Another sneak peak is a subcommand called list (or ls for short), which lists the files at a location within a repository:

```
$ svn ls file:///var/local/svn/megaquiz
```

As you can see, a Subversion URL looks very much like the kind of thing you would type into a browser's location field. It consists of a scheme (the kind of connection you'd like to make), possibly a server name, then a path, which includes the repository location followed by any number of project directories. Because the fragment above specified the filesystem in its scheme, there was no need to provide a server.

Assuming the repository machine is running sshd, and that the firewall is properly configured, I could also access the same repository from a remote machine using ssh:

```
$ svn ls svn+ssh://localhost/var/local/svn/megaquiz
```

Subversion handles a number of other modes of communication. Depending on how the repository server is configured, you may also be able to use the WebDav protocol (the http or https schemes) or the svn network protocol (the svn scheme). Now that I've set up the Subversion repository on the server, I'll stick to ssh (more properly this is the svn protocol tunneled over ssh, hence the compound scheme svn+ssh), apart from some issues discussed below, is an easy and secure communication mechanism. Setting up Subversion for working with SSH is trivial. If your server is configured to accept ssh connections, then the repository is accessible as above. There are a couple of annoyances, however. It is hard, for example, to allow users full access to your repository without first giving them a shell account on the Subversion machine. If you are allowing nontrusted users, you could look into setting up a chroot jail, which supports an extremely restricted environment for user accounts. This strays too far into the realms of system administration for this chapter! A simpler solution is to disable login access for any users you don't want to have command line access. You can do this when you create the user's account. Check the man page for the adduser command for more details.

Also annoying for users is the requirement to continually type in their password or pass phrase for every Subversion command. I have already set up the user bob on the Subversion machine, so he has remote access to the repository using the svn+ssh scheme. How can I make it easier for him to authenticate himself, though? The finer details of SSH configuration are beyond the scope of this book.

■**Note** *Pro OpenSSH* by Michael Stahnke (Apress, 2005) covers SSH comprehensively.

In brief, though, Bob should generate a public key with a program called ssh-keygen on his client machine. He will be prompted to create a pass phrase. He should copy the generated public key, which he will find in .ssh/id_rsa.pub (where .ssh is in his client home directory), and append it to a file called .ssh/authorized_keys (where .ssh is in his home directory) on the Subversion server. He can now use a program called ssh-agent to handle the details of authentication for him.

Beginning a Project

To use Subversion on a project, you must add that project to the repository. You can do this by importing a project directory and any contents you might already have.

Before you start, take a good look at your files and directories, removing any temporary items you might find. Failure to do this is a common and annoying mistake. Temporary items to watch for include automatically generated files such as phpDocumentor output, build directories, installer logs, and so on.

Note You can specify files and patterns to ignore during import, commit, and update by editing the configuration file that the Subversion should have created in your home directory at `.subversion/config`. Look for an option called `global_ignores,` which will probably need to be uncommented. It should provide examples of filename wildcarding that you can amend to exclude the various lock files and temporary directories created by your build processes, editors, and IDEs.

Once your project is clean, it's time to think about how you're going to organize your versions. Subversion allows you to manage multiple versions of your project. You can easily branch the project to create new versions, and then merge your changes back from whence they came. Although there is nothing to stop you organizing your versions as you wish, there are some conventions that many developers observe. Typically, you will elect to keep a single 'main' line of development as the source and eventual destination of all branches. This branch is known as the *trunk*. In fact, thanks to Subversion's flexibility, this will simply be a directory named `trunk`. You also need a directory in which you can save your branches. If you're following the convention, you'll call this 'branches.' Finally, you might need a place to save snapshot branches. These are not different in nature from any other kind of branch, but their purpose is to provide a snapshot of a particular moment in a project's evolution, rather than a site for parallel development. These should be saved to a directory called `tags`.

You can move directories around the repository after import, but because I know what I want at import time, I might as well set up my directory structure first. If my directory structure looked like this:

```
megaquiz/
    quiztools/
    commands
    quizobjects/
```

I might add another layer of directories before import, so I end up with this:

```
megaquiz/
    branches/
    tags/
    trunk/
        quiztools/
        commands
        quizobjects/
```

As you can see, there's nothing magic about branches and tags. They are just regular directories. With everything in place, I can finally import my project:

```
$ svn import megaquiz svn+ssh://localhost/var/local/svn/megaquiz
```

Let's break down this use of the Subversion command. Subversion is a very big package consisting of many subcommands and switches. `import` requires a URL argument that points to the new directory on the server. The directory name is essentially the project name. As you can see, the `import` subcommand also accepts a path to the directory you wish to import. If you don't specify this, Subersion will import the current working directory.

When you run the `import` subcommand, you will be presented with an editor window and instructed to provide an import message. In Figure 17–1, you can see vi, my default editor, demanding just such input.

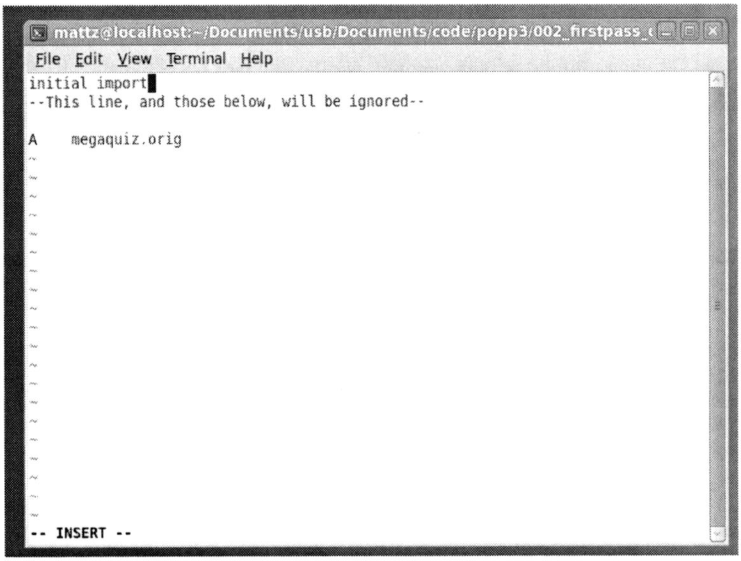

Figure 17–1. *Providing an import message*

When you attempt to import, you may get an error like this:

```
svn: Could not use external editor to fetch log message; consider setting the $SVN_EDITOR
environment variable or using the --message (-m) or --file (-F) options
svn: None of the environment variables SVN_EDITOR, VISUAL or EDITOR are set, and no 'editor-
cmd' run-time configuration option was found
```

That means that no editor is configured to work with Subversion. Depending on your preferred editor, something like

```
$ export SVN_EDITOR=/bin/vi
```

will quickly solve this problem. You can also pass a message argument to the import command (and to any command that requires a message) with the -m flag.

The import subcommand should generate output that looks something like this:

```
Adding         megaquiz/quizobjects
Adding         megaquiz/quizobjects/User.php
Adding         megaquiz/trunk
Adding         megaquiz/trunk/megaquiz.orig
Adding         megaquiz/trunk/megaquiz.orig/trunk
Adding         megaquiz/trunk/megaquiz.orig/trunk/pkg
```

```
Adding          megaquiz/trunk/megaquiz.orig/trunk/src
Adding          megaquiz/trunk/megaquiz.orig/branches
Adding          megaquiz/trunk/megaquiz.orig/tags
Adding          megaquiz/branches
Adding          megaquiz/quiztools
Adding          megaquiz/quiztools/AccessManager.php
Adding          megaquiz/main.php
Adding          megaquiz/command
Adding          megaquiz/command/Command.php
Adding          megaquiz/command/FeedbackCommand.php
Adding          megaquiz/command/CommandContext.php
Adding          megaquiz/command/LoginCommand.php
Adding          megaquiz/tags
Committed revision 1.
```

Now that you have imported your project, you should move your source directory out of the way. If you're feeling bold, you could delete it; otherwise rename it. I generally add the extension .orig to the directory name:

```
$ cd ..
$ mv megaquiz megaquiz.orig
```

An important point to remember here is that importing a project does not in any way transform the source directory. If you want to use version control, you must check out your project from the repository after you have imported it. You can check out a project with the checkout subcommand.

```
$ svn checkout svn+ssh://localhost/var/local/svn/megaquiz/trunk megaquiz-trunk
```

Remember, the dollar sign at the beginning of the line represents the shell prompt. The rest of the line is what a user might type. Subversion will re-create the trunk directory in a new directory named megaquiz-trunk, reporting as it does so:

```
A    megaquiz-trunk/megaquiz.orig
A    megaquiz-trunk/megaquiz.orig/trunk
A    megaquiz-trunk/megaquiz.orig/trunk/pkg
A    megaquiz-trunk/megaquiz.orig/trunk/src
A    megaquiz-trunk/megaquiz.orig/branches
A    megaquiz-trunk/megaquiz.orig/tags
Checked out revision 1.
```

If you look into the newly created megaquiz-trunk directory, you will see that it, and all of its subdirectories, contain a folder called .svn. This contains metadata about your project and its repository. You can pretty much ignore the .svn directories, but you should not delete any of them.

Now that you have a sandbox set up, it is time to start work. You can edit and save your files as normal, but remember, you are no longer alone! You need to keep your work synchronized with the central repository, or you will lose the benefits afforded by Subversion.

Updating and Committing

For the purposes of this chapter, I have invented a team member named Bob. Bob is working with me on the MegaQuiz project. Bob is, of course, a fine and talented fellow. Except, that is, for one common and highly annoying trait: he cannot leave other people's code alone.

Bob is smart and inquisitive, easily excited by shiny new avenues of development, and keen to help optimize new code. As a result, everywhere I turn, I seem to see the hand of Bob. Bob has added to my documentation; Bob has implemented an idea I mentioned over coffee. I may have to kill Bob. In the meantime, though, I must handle the fact that the code on which I am working needs to be merged with Bob's input.

Here's a file called `quizobjects/User.php`. At the moment, it contains nothing but the barest of bones:

```php
<?php
class User {}
?>
```

I have decided to add some documentation. As you know from the last chapter, I should add file and class comments. I begin by adding the file comment to my version of the file:

```php
<?php
/**
 * @license    http://www.example.com Borsetshire Open License
 * @package    quizobjects
 */

class User {}
?>
```

Meanwhile, working in his own sandbox, Bob is keen as ever, and he has created the class comment:

```php
<?php

/**
 * @package   quizobjects
 */
class User {}
?>
```

So we now have two distinct versions of `User.php`. At this time, the Subversion repository contains only the recently imported version of MegaQuiz. I decide to add my changes to the Subversion repository. This requires only one command, but two are advisable:

```
$ svn update quizobjects/User.php
```

```
At revision 1.
```

The `update` subcommand instructs Subversion to merge any changes stored in the repository into your local document or documents. Before you commit your own work, it is good practice to first see if anyone else's changes conflict with your own, resolving any such conflicts in your own sandbox. The command's output indicates that no third-party changes need be applied.

Running `update` will apply any changes from the repository version of a file to your local copy. If you omit the filepath, it will perform this operation on all files below your current location.

You may wish to know which files have changed *before* you incorporate differences locally. You can do this with the status subcommand.

```
$ svn status --show-updates
```

That gives you a list of files that an update would touch locally.

Whichever subcommand I chose, I can now go ahead and commit my changes:

```
$ svn commit quizobjects/User.php  -m 'added doc level comment'
```

```
Sending        quizobjects/User.php
Transmitting file data .
```

I use the commit subcommand to check new data into the Subversion repository. Notice that I used the -m switch to add a message on the command line, rather than via an editor.

Now it's Bob's turn to update and commit:

```
$ svn update quizobjects/User.php
```

```
Conflict discovered in 'quizobjects/User.php'.
Select: (p) postpone, (df) diff-full, (e) edit,
        (mc) mine-conflict, (tc) theirs-conflict,
        (s) show all options:
```

Subversion will happily merge data from two sources into to the same file so long as the changes don't overlap. Subversion has no means of handling changes that affect the same lines. How can it decide what is to have priority? Should the repository overwrite Bob's changes, or the other way around? Should both changes coexist? Which should go first? Subversion has no choice but to report a conflict and let Bob sort out the problem. When a conflict is encountered, Bob is presented with a bewildering seeming array of options. In Subversion itself explains the choices. If Bob hits 's'

```
        (s) show all options: s
  (e)  edit             - change merged file in an editor
  (df) diff-full        - show all changes made to merged file
  (r)  resolved         - accept merged version of file
  (dc) display-conflict - show all conflicts (ignoring merged version)
  (mc) mine-conflict    - accept my version for all conflicts (same)
  (tc) theirs-conflict  - accept their version for all conflicts (same)
  (mf) mine-full        - accept my version of entire file (even non-conflicts)
  (tf) theirs-full      - accept their version of entire file (same)
  (p)  postpone         - mark the conflict to be resolved later
  (l)  launch           - launch external tool to resolve conflict
  (s)  show all         - show this list
```

When you get a conflict, probably the first thing you'll want to do is to find out what's happened. The dc option will tell you. It shows the conflicting portions of the file in question. Here's what Bob sees when he selects dc: <?php

```
<<<<<<< MINE (select with 'mc') (2,4)
/**
 * @package  quizobjects
 */
||||||| ORIGINAL (2,0)
=======
/**
 * @license   http://www.example.com Borsetshire Open License
 * @package  quizobjects
 */

>>>>>>> THEIRS (select with 'tc') (2,5)
class User {}
?>
```

Subversion includes both Bob's comment and the conflicting changes, together with metadata that tells him which part originates where. The conflicting information is separated by a line of equals signs. Bob's input is signaled by a line of less-than signs followed by "MINE". Data pulled from the repository is delineated by a line of greater-than signs followed by "THEIRS".

Now that Bob has identified the conflict, he can choose an action to take in response to it. As you can see from the previous output, he can accept the repository version. That's rc for just conflicts, leaving his non-controversial changes in place, or rf to override his entire version of the document with that on the server. He can override the repository version. That's mc to impose his version of only conflicts or mf to override the entire repository version of the document with his own. He can choose to postpone action, which will leave the document tagged locally as a conflict until he runs svn resolve on the file. Most likely, though, he'll choose the e option, and resolve the conflict by hand. In this case, he deletes the metadata and arranges the content in the right order:

```
<?php
/**
 * @license   http://www.example.com Borsetshire Open License
 * @package  quizobjects
 */

/**
 * @package  quizobjects
 */
class User {}
?>
```

Having saved changes and closed the editor window, Bob must still confirm his edit by choosing the r option, which finally resolves the conflict. Even then, the changes are not committed. Bob must explicitly commit the changed file for his resolution to make it to the repository. There is an important principle at work here. Update works from the repository down to the local version. It would not do to change that flow just because a conflict was detected.

```
$ svn commit -m 'added class comment' quizobjects/User.php
```

```
bob@localhost's password:
Sending        quizobjects/User.php
Transmitting file data .
```

```
Committed revision 3.
```

So far, Bob and I have updated and committed a single file only. By omitting the file argument altogether, we can apply these commands to every file and directory in the project. Here I run update from the root directory of the project:

$ svn update

```
U    quizobjects/User.php
Updated to revision 3.
```

Subversion visits every directory in the project, finding nothing to update until it encounters the document User.php. Bob's changes are then incorporated into my version of the document.

You can commit globally in the same way. In this example, I have made minor changes to two documents, command/Command.php and quiztools/AccessManager.php:

$ svn commit -m'documentation amendments'

```
Sending          command/Command.php
Sending          quiztools/AccessManager.php
Transmitting file data ..
Committed revision 4.
```

Once again, Subversion works through every directory below the current working directory. It takes no action until it encounters a changed file. At this point, it checks the changes in to the repository.

Adding and Removing Files and Directories

Projects change shape as they develop. Version control software must take account of this, allowing users to add new files and remove deadwood that would otherwise get in the way.

Adding a File

You can add a new document to Subversion with the add subcommand. Here I add a document called Question.php to the project:

$ touch quizobjects/Question.php

$ svn add quizobjects/Question.php

```
A         quizobjects/Question.php
```

In a real-world situation, I would probably start out by adding some content to Question.php. Here, I confine myself to creating an empty file using the standard touch command. Once I have added a document, I must still invoke the commit subcommand to complete the addition.

```
$ svn commit -m'initial checkin'
```

```
Adding          quizobjects/Question.php
Transmitting file data .
Committed revision 5.
```

Question.php is now in the repository.

Removing a File

Should I discover that I have been too hasty and need to remove the document, it should come as no surprise to learn that you can use a subcommand called remove.

```
$ svn remove quizobjects/Question.php
```

```
D          quizobjects/Question.php
```

Once again, a commit is required to finish the job.

```
$ svn commit -m'removed Question'
```

```
Deleting          quizobjects/Question.php
Committed revision 6.
```

Adding a Directory

You can also add and remove directories with add and remove. Let's say Bob wants to make a new directory available:

```
$ mkdir resources
$ touch resources/blah.gif
$ svn add resources/
```

```
A          resources
A          resources/blah.gif
```

Notice how the contents of resources are added automatically to the repository.
findme

Removing Directories

As you might expect, you can remove directories with the remove subcommand. Here, I profoundly disagree with Bob's decision to add a resources directory.

```
$ svn remove resources/
```

```
D          resources/blah.gif
D          resources
```

Notice again that the subcommand works recursively. You'll need to run commit in order for the changes to be applied, though.

Tagging and Exporting a Release

All being well, a project will eventually reach a state of readiness, and you will want to ship it or deploy it. Subversion can help you here in two ways. First, you can generate a version of the project that does not contain Subversion metadata. Second, you can freeze this moment in your project's development so that you can always return to it later on.

Tagging a Project

Other version control systems have the concept of a tag built in at the command level. For Subversion though, a tag is really just a copy. It doesn't have any special qualities. Its status as a snapshot, a reference copy, is a purely a matter of user convention. Remember the directories I created when I first imported my project? There was trunk, which is where I've been working. There were also branch and tags. To create a tag, I simply ask Subversion to copy my current project into the tags directory.

How do I do that though? I checked out the trunk directory, so I don't have the other directories available locally right now. In fact I can order Subversion to make the copy within the repository.

```
$ svn copy svn+ssh://localhost/var/local/svn/megaquiz/trunk  \
    svn+ssh://localhost/var/local/svn/megaquiz/tags/megaquiz-release1.0.0 \
    -m'release branch'
```

```
Committed revision 9.
```

Because I'm dealing solely in URLs here, this is strictly a server operation, so you need to be sure you've committed everything you want included before running the copy command in this way. You can also run copy within a working copy, and supply file paths rather than URLs. This is a somewhat more expensive operation though, and it requires you to maintain your tags and branches locally.

Notice that I named my tag as part of the copy operation. I copied trunk to tags/megaquiz-release1.0.0. I can double-check this with the list command:

```
$ svn list svn+ssh://localhost/var/local/svn/megaquiz/tags/
```

```
megaquiz-release1.0.0/
```

I can now acquire this snapshot at anytime with the checkout command. However, a tag is not usually intended to form the basis of parallel development (see the section on branches later in this chapter for that). You may, however, want to export a tagged copy, ready for packaging.

Exporting a Project

As you have seen, a checked-out project includes administrative directories (named .svn). Depending upon how you have configured your build and packaging tools these may clutter up an official release of your project. Subversion provides the export subcommand to generate clean release versions of your codebase.

```
$ svn export svn+ssh://localhost/var/local/svn/megaquiz/tags/megaquiz-release1.0.0 \
    megaquiz1.0.0
```

```
A    megaquiz1.0.0
A    megaquiz1.0.0/quizobjects
A    megaquiz1.0.0/quizobjects/User.php
A    megaquiz1.0.0/quiztools
A    megaquiz1.0.0/quiztools/AccessManager.php
A    megaquiz1.0.0/main.php
A    megaquiz1.0.0/command
A    megaquiz1.0.0/command/Command.php
A    megaquiz1.0.0/command/CommandContext.php
A    megaquiz1.0.0/command/FeedbackCommand.php
A    megaquiz1.0.0/command/LoginCommand.php
```

Exported revision 9.The first argument to export specifies the source. In this case, the tag I created in the last section. The second argument specifies a destination directory which Subversion will create if necessary.

Branching a Project

Now that my project has been released, I can pack it away and wander off to do something new, right? After all, it was so elegantly written that bugs are an impossibility and so thoroughly specified that no user could possibly require any new features!

Meanwhile, back in the real world, I must continue to work with the codebase on at least two levels. Bug reports should be trickling in right about now, and the wish list for version 1.2.0 swelling with demands for fantastic new features. How do I reconcile these forces? I need to fix the bugs as they are reported, and I need to push on with primary development. I could fix the bugs as part of development and release in one go when the next version is stable. But then users may have a long wait before they see any problems addressed. This is plainly unacceptable. On the other hand, I could release as I go. Here, I risk shipping broken code. Clearly, I need two strands to my development.

Subversion allows you to maintain parallel strands of development in a project. I can continue working on as before in the trunk. It is here that I add new and experimental code. Let's use a particular file, command/FeedbackCommand.php, as an example.

```
class FeedbackCommand extends Command {
    function execute( CommandContext $context ) {
        // new and risky development
        // goes here
```

```
        $msgSystem = ReceiverFactory::getMessageSystem();
        $email = $context->get( 'email' );
        $msg = $context->get( 'pass' );
        $topic = $context->get( 'topic' );
        $result = $msgSystem->dispatch( $email, $msg, $topic );
        if ( ! $user ) {
            $this->context->setError( $msgSystem->getError() );
            return false;
        }
        $context->addParam( "user", $user );
        return true;
    }
}
```

All I have done here is to add a comment to simulate an addition to the code. Meanwhile, users begin to report that they are unable to use the feedback mechanism in the system. I locate the bug in the same file:

```
        //...
        $result = $msgSystem->dispatch( $email, $msg, $topic );
        if ( ! $user ) {
            $this->context->setError( $msgSystem->getError() );
        //...
```

I should, in fact, be testing $result, and not $user. I could fix this here, of course, but the users would not see the fix until my experimental code is stable. Instead, I can create a branch of the project.

In fact, I would do this at the same time as creating the release tag.

```
$ svn copy svn+ssh://localhost/var/local/svn/megaquiz/trunk  \
 svn+ssh://localhost/var/local/svn/megaquiz/branches/megaquiz-branch1.0.0
-m'release branch'
```

Committed revision 10.

What's the difference between this use of copy and the tag example from earlier? As far as Subversion is concerned, absolutely nothing. I'm simply copying into the branches directory rather than the tags directory. It's my intention that makes the difference. I intend to commit to this copy, rather than just to use it as a snapshot.

In order to work with my new branch I'll have to check it out first. I need to fix the code as it stood at the point of last release. I move out of the development project directory (so that my current working directory does not contain a Subversion administration directory), and then check out the project.

```
$ cd ..
$ svn checkout svn+ssh://localhost/var/local/svn/megaquiz/➥
branches/megaquiz-branch1.0.0
 \
megaquiz-branch1.0.0
```

```
A    megaquiz-branch1.0.0/quizobjects
A    megaquiz-branch1.0.0/quizobjects/User.php
A    megaquiz-branch1.0.0/quiztools
A    megaquiz-branch1.0.0/quiztools/AccessManager.php
A    megaquiz-branch1.0.0/main.php
```

```
A    megaquiz-branch1.0.0/command
A    megaquiz-branch1.0.0/command/Command.php
A    megaquiz-branch1.0.0/command/CommandContext.php
A    megaquiz-branch1.0.0/command/FeedbackCommand.php
A    megaquiz-branch1.0.0/command/LoginCommand.php
Checked out revision 10.
```

I moved out of the megaquiz-trunk directory before checking out the branch. Now I have two directories at the same level: megaquiz-trunk contains the trunk, and I'll commit my risky but useful new features here. In fact I'll do that now:

```
$ cd megaquiz-trunk/
$ svn commit -m'added new risky dev on trunk'
```

```
Sending         command/FeedbackCommand.php
Transmitting file data .
Committed revision 11.
```

megaquiz-branch1.0.0, on the other hand, is my bugfix branch. I'll only commit defect fixes here. Here's my fix:

```
class FeedbackCommand extends Command {

    function execute( CommandContext $context ) {
        $msgSystem = ReceiverFactory::getMessageSystem();
        $email = $context->get( 'email' );
        $msg = $context->get( 'pass' );
        $topic = $context->get( 'topic' );
        $result = $msgSystem->dispatch( $email, $msg, $topic );
        if ( ! $result ) {
            $this->context->setError( $msgSystem->getError() );
            return false;
        }
        $context->addParam( "user", $user );
        return true;
    }
}
```

I have changed

```
 if ( ! $user ) {
```

to

```
 if ( ! $result ) {
```

Now to commit

```
$ cd ../megaquiz-branch1.0.0/
$ svn commit -m'fixed bug'
```

```
Sending         command/FeedbackCommand.php
```

```
Transmitting file data .
```

Committed revision 12. I have edited this in the meagquiz-branch1.0.0 directory. By editing and committing here I ensure that my changes end up on the branch and not the trunk. I could tag, export and distribute this now as a point release.

It doesn't end there, though. Now that I have fixed the bug, I need to apply the change to my main development strand (the trunk).

Note To merge or not to merge? The choice is not always as straightforward as it might seem. In some cases, for example, your bug fix may be the kind of temporary work that is supplanted by a more thorough refactoring on the trunk, or it may no longer apply due to a change in specification. This is necessarily a judgment call. Most teams I have worked in, however, tend to merge to the trunk where possible while keeping work on the branch to the bare minimum. New features, for us, generally appear on the trunk and find their way quickly to users through a "release early and often" policy.

Subversion provides the merge command for this purpose. Change your working directory to the local destination, and invoke merge, passing it the source URL.

```
$ svn merge svn+ssh://localhost/var/local/svn/megaquiz/branches/megaquiz-branch1.0.0
```

```
--- Merging r12 into '.':
U    command/FeedbackCommand.php
```

Now, when I look at the version of FeedbackCommand in the trunk, I confirm that all changes have been merged.

```
function execute( CommandContext $context ) {
    // new and risky development
    // goes here
    $msgSystem = ReceiverFactory::getMessageSystem();
    $email = $context->get( 'email' );
    $msg = $context->get( 'pass' );
    $topic = $context->get( 'topic' );
    $result = $msgSystem->dispatch( $email, $msg, $topic );
    if ( ! $result ) {
        $this->context->setError( $msgSystem->getError() );
        return false;
    }
    $context->addParam( "user", $user );
    return true;
}
```

The execute() method now includes both my simulated trunk development and the bugfix.

Branches are often seen as an advanced Subversion topic, largely because of the difficulty of some of the concepts involved. For large or long-lived projects, though, branching soon becomes an essential technique.

Summary

Subversion comprises an enormous number of tools, each with a daunting range of options and capabilities. I can only hope to provide a brief introduction in the space available. Nonetheless, if you only use the features I have covered in this chapter, you should see the benefit in your own work, whether through protection against data loss or improvements in collaborative working.

In this chapter, we took a tour through the basics of Subversion. I looked briefly at configuration before importing a project. I checked out, committed, and updated code, finally tagging and exporting a release. I ended the chapter with a brief look at branches, demonstrating their usefulness in maintaining concurrent development and bug-fix strands in a project.

There is one issue that I have glossed over here to some extent. We established the principle that developers should check out their own versions of a project. On the whole, though, projects will not run in place. In order to test their changes, developers need to deploy code locally. Sometimes, this is as simple as copying over a few directories. More often, though, deployment must address a whole range of configuration issues. In the next chapter, we will look at some techniques for automating this process.

CHAPTER 18

Testing with PHPUnit

Every component in a system depends, for its continued smooth running, on the consistency of operation and interface of its peers. By definition, then, development breaks systems. As you improve your classes and packages, you must remember to amend any code that works with them. For some changes, this can create a ripple effect, affecting components far away from the code you originally changed. Eagle-eyed vigilance and an encyclopedic knowledge of a system's dependencies can help to address this problem. Of course, while these are excellent virtues, systems soon grow too complex for every unwanted effect to be easily predicted, not least because systems often combine the work of many developers. To address this problem, it is a good idea to test every component regularly. This, of course, is a repetitive and complex task and as such it lends itself well to automation.

Among the test solutions available to PHP programmers, PHPUnit is perhaps the most ubiquitous and certainly the most fully featured tool. In this chapter, you will learn the following about PHPUnit:

- *Installation*: Using PEAR to install PHPUnit

- *Writing Tests*: Creating test cases and using assertion methods

- *Handling Exceptions*: Strategies for confirming failure

- *Running multiple tests*: Collecting tests into suites

- Constructing assertion logic: Using constraints

- *Faking components*: Mocks and stubs

- Testing web applications: With and without additional tools.

Functional Tests and Unit Tests

Testing is essential in any project. Even if you don't formalize the process, you must have found yourself developing informal lists of actions that put your system through its paces. This process soon becomes wearisome, and that can lead to a fingers-crossed attitude to your projects.

One approach to testing starts at the interface of a project, modeling the various ways in which a user might negotiate the system. This is probably the way you would go when testing by hand, although there are various frameworks for automating the process. These functional tests are sometimes called acceptance tests, because a list of actions performed successfully can be used as criteria for signing off a project phase. Using this approach, you typically treat the system as a black box—your tests remaining willfully ignorant of the hidden components that collaborate to form the system under test.

Whereas functional tests operate from without, unit tests (the subject of this chapter) work from the inside out. Unit testing tends to focus on classes, with test methods grouped together in test cases. Each test case puts one class through a rigorous workout, checking that each method performs as advertised and fails as it should. The objective, as far as possible, is to test each component in isolation from its wider context. This often supplies you with a sobering verdict on the success of your mission to decouple the parts of your system.

Tests can be run as part of the build process, directly from the command line, or even via a web page. In this chapter, I'll concentrate on the command line.

Unit testing is a good way of ensuring the quality of design in a system. Tests reveal the responsibilities of classes and functions. Some programmers even advocate a test-first approach. You should, they say, write the tests before you even begin work on a class. This lays down a class's purpose, ensuring a clean interface and short, focused methods. Personally, I have never aspired to this level of purity—it just doesn't suit my style of coding. Nevertheless, I attempt to write tests as I go. Maintaining a test harness provides me with the security I need to refactor my code. I can pull down and replace entire packages with the knowledge that I have a good chance of catching unexpected errors elsewhere in the system.

Testing by Hand

In the last section, I said that testing was essential in every project. I could have said instead that testing is *inevitable* in every project. We all test. The tragedy is that we often throw away this good work.

So, let's create some classes to test. Here is a class that stores and retrieves user information. For the sake of demonstration, it generates arrays, rather than the User objects you'd normally expect to use:

```php
class UserStore {
    private $users = array();

    function addUser( $name, $mail, $pass ) {
        if ( isset( $this->users[$mail] ) ) {
            throw new Exception(
                "User {$mail} already in the system");
        }

        if ( strlen( $pass ) < 5 ) {
            throw new Exception(
                "Password must have 5 or more letters");
        }

        $this->users[$mail] = array( 'pass' => $pass,
                                     'mail' => $mail,
                                     'name' => $name );
        return true;
    }

    function notifyPasswordFailure( $mail ) {
        if ( isset( $this->users[$mail] ) ) {
            $this->users[$mail]['failed']=time();
        }
    }

    function getUser( $mail ) {
        return ( $this->users[$mail] );
    }
}
```

This class accepts user data with the addUser() method and retrieves it via getUser(). The user's e-mail address is used as the key for retrieval. If you're like me, you'll write some sample implementation as you develop, just to check that things are behaving as you designed them—something like this:

```
$store=new UserStore();
$store->addUser(  "bob williams",
                  "bob@example.com",
                  "12345" );
$user = $store->getUser(  "bob@example.com" );
print_r( $user );
```

This is the sort of thing I might add to the foot of a file as I work on the class it contains. The test validation is performed manually, of course; it's up to me to eyeball the results and confirm that the data returned by UserStore::getUser() corresponds with the information I added initially. It's a test of sorts, nevertheless.

Here is a client class that uses UserStore to confirm that a user has provided the correct authentication information:

```
class Validator {
    private $store;

    public function __construct( UserStore $store ) {
        $this->store = $store;
    }

    public function validateUser( $mail, $pass ) {
        if ( ! is_array($user = $this->store->getUser( $mail )) ) {
            return false;
        }
        if ( $user['pass'] == $pass ) {
            return true;
        }
        $this->store->notifyPasswordFailure( $mail );
        return false;
    }
}
```

The class requires a UserStore object, which it saves in the $store property. This property is used by the validateUser() method to ensure first of all that the user referenced by the given e-mail address exists in the store and secondly that the user's password matches the provided argument. If both these conditions are fulfilled, the method returns true. Once again, I might test this as I go along:

```
$store = new UserStore();
$store->addUser(  "bob williams", "bob@example.com", "12345" );
$validator = new Validator( $store );
if ( $validator->validateUser( "bob@example.com", "12345" ) ) {
    print "pass, friend!\n";
}
```

I instantiate a UserStore object, which I prime with data and pass to a newly instantiated Validator object. I can then confirm a user name and password combination.

Once I'm finally satisfied with my work, I could delete these sanity checks altogether or comment them out. This is a terrible waste of a valuable resource. These tests could form the basis of a harness to scrutinize the system as I develop. One of the tools that might help me to do this is PHPUnit.

Introducing PHPUnit

PHPUnit is a member of the xUnit family of testing tools. The ancestor of these is SUnit, a framework invented by Kent Beck to test systems built with the Smalltalk language. The xUnit framework was probably established as a popular tool, though, by the Java implementation, jUnit, and by the rise to prominence of agile methodologies like Extreme Programming (XP) and Scrum, all of which place great emphasis on testing.

The current incarnation of PHPUnit was created by Sebastian Bergmann, who changed its name from PHPUnit2 (which he also authored) early in 2007 and shifted its home from the pear.php.net channel to pear.phpunit.de. For this reason, you must tell the pear application where to search for the framework when you install:

```
$ pear channel-discover pear.phpunit.de
$ pear channel-discover pear.symfony-project.com
$ pear install phpunit
```

■**Note** I show commands that are input at the command line in bold to distinguish them from any output they may produce.

Notice I added another channel, pear.symfony-project.com. This may be needed to satisfy a dependency of PHPUnit that is hosted there.

Creating a Test Case

Armed with PHPUnit, I can write tests for the UserStore class. Tests for each target component should be collected in a single class that extends PHPUnit_Framework_TestCase, one of the classes made available by the PHPUnit package. Here's how to create a minimal test case class:

```
require_once 'PHPUnit/Framework/TestCase.php';

class UserStoreTest extends PHPUnit_Framework_TestCase {

    public function setUp() {
    }

    public function  tearDown() {
    }

    //...
}
```

I named the test case class UserStoreTest. You are not obliged to use the name of the class you are testing in the test's name, though that is what many developers do. Naming conventions of this kind can greatly improve the accessibility of a test harness, especially as the number of components and tests in the system begins to increase. It is also common to group tests in package directories that directly mirror those that house the system's classes. With a logical structure like this, you can often open up a test from the command line without even looking to see if it exists! Each test in a test case class is run in isolation from its siblings. The setUp() method is automatically invoked for each test method, allowing us to set up a stable and suitably primed environment for the test. tearDown() is invoked after each test method is run. If your tests change the wider environment of your system, you can use this method to reset state. The common platform managed by setUp() and tearDown() is known as a *fixture*.

In order to test the UserStore class, I need an instance of it. I can instantiate this in setUp() and assign it to a property. Let's create a test method as well:

```php
require_once('UserStore.php');
require_once('PHPUnit/Framework/TestCase.php');


class UserStoreTest extends PHPUnit_Framework_TestCase {
    private $store;

    public function setUp() {
        $this->store = new UserStore();
    }

    public function tearDown() {
    }

    public function testGetUser() {
        $this->store->addUser( "bob williams", "a@b.com", "12345" );
        $user = $this->store->getUser( "a@b.com" );
        $this->assertEquals( $user['mail'], "a@b.com" );
        $this->assertEquals( $user['name'], "bob williams" );
        $this->assertEquals( $user['pass'], "12345" );
    }
}
```

Test methods should be named to begin with the word "test" and should require no arguments. This is because the test case class is manipulated using reflection.

■**Note** Reflection is covered in detail in Chapter 5.

The object that runs the tests looks at all the methods in the class and invokes only those that match this pattern (that is, methods that begin with "test").

In the example, I tested the retrieval of user information. I don't need to instantiate UserStore for each test, because I handled that in setUp(). Because setUp() is invoked for each test, the $store property is guaranteed to contain a newly instantiated object.

Within the testGetUser() method, I first provide UserStore::addUser() with dummy data, then I retrieve that data and test each of its elements.

Assertion Methods

An assertion in programming is a statement or method that allows you to check your assumptions about an aspect of your system. In using an assertion you typically define an expectation that something is the case, that $cheese is "blue" or $pie is "apple". If your expectation is confounded, a warning of some kind will be generated. Assertions are such a good way of adding safety to a system that some programming languages support them natively and inline and allow you to turn them off in a production context (Java is an example). PHPUnit supports assertions though a set of static methods.

In the previous example, I used an inherited static method: assertEquals(). This compares its two provided arguments and checks them for equivalence. If they do not match, the test method will be chalked up as a failed test. Having subclassed PHPUnit_Framework_TestCase, I have access to a set of assertion methods. Some of these methods are listed in Table 18–1.

Table 18–1. *PHPUnit_Framework_TestCase Assert Methods*

Method	Description
assertEquals($val1, $val2, $delta, $message)	Fail if $val1 is not equivalent to $val2. ($delta represents an allowable margin of error.)
assertFalse($expression, $message)	Evaluate $expression. Fail if it does *not* resolve to false.
assertTrue($expression, $message)	Evaluate $expression. Fail if it does *not* resolve to true.
assertNotNull($val, $message)	Fail if $val is null.
assertNull($val, $message)	Fail if $val is anything other than null.
assertSame($val1, $val2, $message)	Fail if $val1 and $val2 are *not* references to the same object or if they are variables of different types or values.
assertNotSame($val1, $val2, $message)	Fail if $val1 and $val2 are references to the same object or variables of the same type and value.
assertRegExp($regexp, $val, $message)	Fail if $val is not matched by regular expression $regexp.
assertType($typestring, $val, $message)	Fail if $val is not the type described in $type.
assertAttributeSame($val, $attribute, $classname, $message)	Fail if $val is not the same type and value as $classname::$attribute.
fail()	Fail.

Testing Exceptions

Your focus as a coder is usually to make stuff *work* and work well. Often, that mentality carries through to testing, especially if you are testing your own code. The temptation is test that a method behaves as advertised. It's easy to forget how important it is to test for failure. How good is a method's error checking? Does it throw an exception when it should? Does it throw the right exception? Does it clean up after an error if for example an operation is half complete before the problem occurs? It is your role as a tester to check all of this. Luckily, PHPUnit can help.

Here is a test that checks the behavior of the UserStore class when an operation fails:

```
//...
public function  testAddUser_ShortPass() {
    try {
        $this->store->addUser(  "bob williams", "bob@example.com", "ff" );
    } catch ( Exception $e ) { return; }
    $this->fail("Short password exception expected");
}
//...
```

If you look back at the UserStore::addUser() method, you will see that I throw an exception if the user's password is less than five characters long. My test attempts to confirm this. I add a user with an illegal password in a try clause. If the expected exception is thrown, then all is well, and I return silently. The final line of the method should never be reached, so I invoke the fail() method there. If the addUser() method does not throw an exception as expected, the catch clause is not invoked, and the fail() method is called.

Another way to test that an exception is thrown is to use an assertion method called setExpectedException(), which requires the name of the exception type you expect to be thrown (either Exception or a subclass). If the test method exits without the correct exception having been thrown, the test will fail.

Here's a quick reimplementation of the previous test:

```
require_once('PHPUnit/Framework/TestCase.php');
require_once('UserStore.php');

class UserStoreTest extends PHPUnit_Framework_TestCase {
    private $store;

    public function setUp() {
        $this->store = new UserStore();
    }

    public function testAddUser_ShortPass() {
        $this->setExpectedException('Exception');
        $this->store->addUser(  "bob williams", "bob@example.com", "ff" );
    }
}
```

Running Test Suites

If I am testing the UserStore class, I should also test Validator. Here is a cut-down version of a class called ValidateTest that tests the Validator::validateUser() method:

```
require_once('UserStore.php');
require_once('Validator.php');
require_once('PHPUnit/Framework/TestCase.php');


class ValidatorTest extends PHPUnit_Framework_TestCase {
    private $validator;
```

```
    public function setUp() {
        $store = new UserStore();
        $store->addUser(  "bob williams", "bob@example.com", "12345" );
        $this->validator = new Validator( $store );
    }

    public function tearDown() {
    }

    public function testValidate_CorrectPass() {
        $this->assertTrue(
            $this->validator->validateUser( "bob@example.com", "12345" ),
            "Expecting successful validation"
            );
    }
}
```

So now that I have more than one test case, how do I go about running them together? The best way is to place your test classes in a directory called test. You can then specify this directory and PHPUnit will run all the tests beneath it.

$ phpunit test/

```
PHPUnit 3.4.11 by Sebastian Bergmann.
.....

Time: 1 second, Memory: 3.75Mb

OK (5 tests, 10 assertions)
```

For a larger project you may want to further organize tests in subdirectories preferably in the same structure as your packages. Then you can specify indivisual packages when required.

Constraints

In most circumstances, you will use off-the-peg assertions in your tests. In fact, at a stretch you can achieve an awful lot with AssertTrue() alone. As of PHPUnit 3.0, however, PHPUnit_Framework_TestCase includes a set of factory methods that return PHPUnit_Framework_Constraint objects. You can combine these and pass them to PHPUnit_Framework_TestCase::AssertThat() in order to construct your own assertions.

It's time for a quick example. The UserStore object should not allow duplicate e-mail addresses to be added. Here's a test that confirms this:

```
class UserStoreTest extends PHPUnit_Framework_TestCase {
    //....

    public function  testAddUser_duplicate() {
        try {
            $ret = $this->store->addUser(  "bob williams", "a@b.com", "123456" );
            $ret = $this->store->addUser(  "bob stevens", "a@b.com", "123456" );
```

```
            self::fail( "Exception should have been thrown" );
        } catch ( Exception $e ) {
            $const = $this->logicalAnd(
                        $this->logicalNot( $this->contains("bob stevens")),
                        $this->isType('array')
                    );
            self::AssertThat( $this->store->getUser( "a@b.com"), $const );
        }
    }
}
```

This test adds a user to the UserStore object and then adds a second user with the same e-mail address. The test thereby confirms that an exception is thrown with the second call to addUser(). In the catch clause, I build a constraint object using the convenience methods available to us. These return corresponding instances of PHPUnit_Framework_Constraint. Let's break down the composite constraint in the previous example:

```
$this->contains("bob stevens")
```

This returns a PHPUnit_Framework_Constraint_TraversableContains object. When passed to AssertThat, this object will generate an error if the test subject does not contain an element matching the given value ("bob stevens"). I negate this, though, by passing this constraint to another: PHPUnit_Framework_Constraint_Not. Once again, I use a convenience method, available though the TestCase class (actually through a superclass, Assert).

```
$this->logicalNot( $this->contains("bob stevens"))
```

Now, the AssertThat assertion will fail if the test value (which must be traversable) contains an element that matches the string "bob stevens". In this way, you can build up quite complex logical structures. By the time I have finished, my constraint can be summarized as follows: "Do not fail if the test value is an array and does not contain the string "bob stevens"." You could build much more involved constraints in this way. The constraint is run against a value by passing both to AssertThat().

You could achieve all this with standard assertion methods, of course, but constraints have a couple of virtues. First, they form nice logical blocks with clear relationships among components (although good use of formatting may be necessary to support clarity). Second, and more importantly, a constraint is reusable. You can set up a library of complex constraints and use them in different tests. You can even combine complex constraints with one another:

```
$const = $this->logicalAnd(
    $a_complex_constraint,
    $another_complex_constraint );
```

Table 18–2 shows the some of the constraint methods available in a TestCase class.

Table 18–2. *Some Constraint Methods*

TestCase Method	Constraint Fails Unless . . .
greaterThan($num)	Test value is greater than $num.
contains($val)	Test value (traversable) contains an element that matches $val.
identicalTo($val)	Test value is a reference to the same object as $val or, for non-objects, is of the same type and value.
greaterThanOrEqual($num)	Test value is greater than or equal to $num.
lessThan($num)	Test value is less than $num.
lessThanOrEqual($num)	Test value is less than or equal to $num.
equalTo($value, $delta=0, $depth=10)	Test value equals $val. If specified, $delta defines a margin of error for numeric comparisons, and $depth determines how recursive a comparison should be for arrays or objects.
stringContains($str, $casesensitive=true)	Test value contains $str. This is case sensitive by default.
matchesRegularExpression($pattern)	Test value matches the regular expression in $pattern.
logicalAnd(PHPUnit_Framework_Constraint $const, [, $const..])	All provided constraints pass.
logicalOr(PHPUnit_Framework_Constraint $const, [, $const..])	At least one of the provided constraints match.
logicalNot(PHPUnit_Framework_Constraint $const)	The provided constraint does not pass.

Mocks and Stubs

Unit tests aim to test a component in isolation of the system that contains it to the greatest possible extent. Few components exist in a vacuum, however. Even nicely decoupled classes require access to other objects as methods arguments. Many classes also work directly with databases or the filesystem.

You have already seen one way of dealing with this. The setUp() and tearDown() methods can be used to manage a fixture, that is, a common set of resources for your tests, which might include database connections, configured objects, a scratch area on the file system, and so on.

Another approach is to fake the context of the class you are testing. This involves creating objects that pretend to be the objects that do real stuff. For example, you might pass a fake database mapper to your test object's constructor. Because this fake object shares a type with the real mapper class (extends from a common abstract base or even overrides the genuine class itself), your subject is none the wiser. You can prime the fake object with valid data. Objects that provide a sandbox of this sort for unit tests are known as *stubs*. They can be useful because they allow you to focus in on the class you want to test without inadvertently testing the entire edifice of your system at the same time.

Fake objects can be taken a stage further than this, however. Since the object you are testing is likely to call a fake object in some way, you can prime it to confirm the invocations you are expecting. Using a fake object as a spy in this way is known as *behavior verification*, and it is what distinguishes a mock object from a stub.

You can build mocks yourself by creating classes hard-coded to return certain values and to report on method invocations. This is a simple process, but it can be time consuming.

PHPUnit provides access to an easier and more dynamic solution. It will generate mock objects on the fly for you. It does this by examining the class you wish to mock and building a child class that overrides its methods. Once you have this mock instance, you can call methods on it to prime it with data and to set the conditions for success.

Let's build an example. The UserStore class contains a method called notifyPasswordFailure(), which sets a field for a given user. This should be called by Validator when an attempt to set a password fails. Here, I mock up the UserStore class so that it both provides data to the Validator object and confirms that its notifyPasswordFailure() method was called as expected:

```
class ValidatorTest extends PHPUnit_Framework_TestCase {
    //...

    public function testValidate_FalsePass() {
        $store = $this->getMock("UserStore");
        $this->validator = new Validator( $store );

        $store->expects($this->once() )
            ->method('notifyPasswordFailure')
            ->with( $this->equalTo('bob@example.com') );

        $store->expects( $this->any() )
            ->method("getUser")
            ->will( $this->returnValue(array("name"=>"bob@example.com",
              "pass"=>"right")));

        $this->validator->validateUser("bob@example.com", "wrong");

    }
}
```

Mock objects use a *fluent interface*, that is, a language-like structure. These are much easier to use than to describe. Such constructs work from left to right, each invocation returning an object reference, which can then be invoked with a further modifying method call (itself returning an object). This can make for easy use but painful debugging.

In the previous example, I called the PHPUnit_Framework_TestCase method: getMock(), passing it "UserStore", the name of the class I wish to mock. This dynamically generates a class and instantiates an object from it. I store this mock object in $store and pass it to Validator. This causes no error, because the object's newly minted class extends UserStore. I have fooled Validator into accepting a spy into its midst.

Mock objects generated by PHPUnit have an expects() method. This method requires a matcher object (actually it's of type PHPUnit_Framework_MockObject_Matcher_Invocation, but don't worry; you can use the convenience methods in TestCase to generate your matcher). The matcher defines the cardinality of the expectation, that is, the number of times a method should be called.

Table 18–3 shows the matcher methods available in a TestCase class.

Table 18–3. *Some Matcher Methods*

TestCase Method	Match Fails Unless . . .
any( )	Zero or more calls are made to corresponding method (useful for stub objects that return values but don't test invocations).
never( )	No calls are made to corresponding method.
atLeastOnce( )	One or more calls are made to corresponding method.
once( )	A single call is made to corresponding method.
exactly($num)	$num calls are made to corresponding method.
at($num)	A call to corresponding method made at $num index (each method call to a mock is recorded and indexed).

Having set up the match requirement, I need to specify a method to which it applies. For instance, expects() returns an object (PHPUnit_Framework_MockObject_Builder_InvocationMocker, if you must know) that has a method called method(). I can simply call that with a method name. This is enough to get some real mocking done:

```
$store = $this->getMock("UserStore");
$store->expects( $this->once() )
            ->method('notifyPasswordFailure');
```

I need to go further, though, and check the parameters that are passed to notifyPasswordFailure(). The InvocationMocker::method() returns an instance of the object it was called on. InvocationMocker includes a method name with(), which accepts a variable list of parameters to match. It also accepts constraint objects, so you can test ranges and so on. Armed with this, you can complete the statement and ensure the expected parameter is passed to notifyPasswordFailure().

```
        $store->expects($this->once() )
            ->method('notifyPasswordFailure')
            ->with( $this->equalTo('bob@example.com') );
```

You can see why this is known as a fluent interface. It reads a bit like a sentence: "The $store object *expects* a single call to the notifyPasswordFailure() method with parameter bob@example.com."

Notice that I passed a constraint to with(). Actually, that's redundant—any bare arguments are converted to constraints internally, so I could write the statement like this:

```
        $store->expects($this->once() )
            ->method('notifyPasswordFailure')
            ->with( 'bob@example.com' );
```

Sometimes, you only want to use PHPUnit's mocks as stubs, that is, as objects that return values to allow your tests to run. In such cases you can invoke InvocationMocker::will() from the call to method(). The will() method requires the return value (or values if the method is to be called repeatedly) that the associated method should be primed to return. You can pass in this return value by calling either TestCase::returnValue() or TestCase::onConsecutiveCalls(). Once again, this is much easier to do than to describe. Here's the fragment from my earlier example in which I prime UserStore to return a value:

```
$store->expects( $this->any() )
->method("getUser")
->will( $this->returnValue(
        array(  "name"=>"bob williams",
                "mail"=>"bob@example.com",
                "pass"=>"right")));
```

I prime the UserStore mock to expect any number of calls to getUser()—right now, I'm concerned with providing data and not with testing calls. Next, I call will() with the result of invoking TestCase::returnValue() with the data I want returned (this happens to be a PHPUnit_Framework_MockObject_Stub_Return object, though if I were you, I'd just remember the convenience method you use to get it).

You can alternatively pass the result of a call to TestCase::onConsecutiveCalls() to will(). This accepts any number of parameters, each one of which will be returned by your mocked method as it is called repeatedly.

Tests Succeed When They Fail

While most agree that testing is a fine thing, you grow to really love it generally only after it has saved your bacon a few times. Let's simulate a situation where a change in one part of a system has an unexpected effect elsewhere.

The UserStore class has been running for a while when, during a code review, it is agreed that it would be neater for the class to generate User objects rather than associative arrays. Here is the new version:

```
class UserStore {
    private $users = array();

    function addUser( $name, $mail, $pass ) {

        if ( isset( $this->users[$mail] ) ) {
            throw new Exception(
                "User {$mail} already in the system");
        }

        $this->users[$mail] = new User( $name, $mail, $pass );
        return true;
    }

    function notifyPasswordFailure( $mail ) {
        if ( isset( $this->users[$mail] ) ) {
            $this->users[$mail]->failed(time());
        }
    }

    function getUser( $mail ) {
        if ( isset( $this->users[$mail] ) ) {
            return ( $this->users[$mail] );
```

```
        }
        return null;
    }
}
```

Here is the simple User class:

```
class User {
    private $name;
    private $mail;
    private $pass;
    private $failed;

    function __construct( $name, $mail, $pass ) {

        if ( strlen( $pass ) < 5 ) {
            throw new Exception(
                "Password must have 5 or more letters");
        }

        $this->name      = $name;
        $this->mail      = $mail;
        $this->pass      = $pass;
    }

    function getName() {
        return $this->name;
    }

    function getMail() {
        return $this->mail;
    }

    function getPass() {
        return $this->pass;
    }

    function failed( $time ) {
        $this->failed = $time;
    }
}
```

Of course, I amend the UserStoreTest class to account for these changes. So code designed to work with an array like this:

```
public function testGetUser() {
    $this->store->addUser( "bob williams", "a@b.com", "12345" );
    $user = $this->store->getUser( "a@b.com" );
    $this->assertEquals( $user['mail'], "a@b.com" );
    //...
```

is converted into code designed to work with an object like this:

```
public function testGetUser() {
    $this->store->addUser( "bob williams", "a@b.com", "12345" );
    $user = $this->store->getUser( "a@b.com" );
```

```
        $this->assertEquals( $user->getMail(), "a@b.com" );
    // ...
```

When I come to run my test suite, however, I am rewarded with a warning that my work is not yet done:

$ php AppTests.php

```
PHPUnit 3.0.6 by Sebastian Bergmann.

...FF

Time: 00:00

There were 2 failures:

1) testValidate_CorrectPass(ValidatorTest)
Expecting successful validation
Failed asserting that <boolean:false> is identical to <boolean:true>.
/project/wibble/ValidatorTest.php:22

2) testValidate_FalsePass(ValidatorTest)
Expectation failed for method name is equal to <string:notifyPasswordFailure> ➥
when invoked 1 time(s).
Expected invocation count is wrong.

FAILURES!
Tests: 5, Failures: 2.
```

There is a problem with ValidatorTest. Let's take another look at the Validator::validateUser() method:

```
public function validateUser( $mail, $pass ) {

    if ( ! is_array($user = $this->store->getUser( $mail )) ) {
        return false;
    }
    if ( $user['pass'] == $pass ) {
        return true;
    }
    $this->store->notifyPasswordFailure( $mail );
    return false;
}
```

I invoke getUser(). Although getUser() now returns an object and not an array, my method does not generate a warning. getUser() originally returned the requested user array on success or null on failure, so I validated users by checking for an array using the is_array() function. Now, of course, getUser() returns an object, and the validateUser() method will always return false. Without the test framework, the Validator would have simply rejected all users as invalid without fuss or warning.

Now, imagine making this neat little change on a Friday night without a test framework in place. Think about the frantic text messages that would drag you out of your pub, armchair, or restaurant, "What have you done? All our customers are locked out!"

The most insidious bugs don't cause the interpreter to report that something is wrong. They hide in perfectly legal code, and they silently break the logic of your system. Many bugs don't manifest where you are working; they are caused there, but the effects pop up elsewhere, days or even weeks later. A test framework can help you catch at least some of these, preventing rather than discovering problems in your systems.

Write tests as you code, and run them often. If someone reports a bug, first add a test to your framework to confirm it; then fix the bug so that the test is passed—bugs have a funny habit of recurring in the same area. Writing tests to prove bugs and then to guard the fix against subsequent problems is known as *regression testing*. Incidentally, if you keep a separate directory of regression tests, remember to name your files descriptively. On one project, our team decided to name our regression tests after Bugzilla bug numbers. We ended up with a directory containing 400 test files, each with a name like `test_973892.php`. Finding an individual test became a tedious chore!

Writing Web Tests

You should engineer your web systems in such a way that they can be invoked easily from the command line or an API call. In Chapter 12, you saw some tricks that might help you with this. In particular, if you create a `Request` class to encapsulate an HTTP request, you can just as easily populate an instance from the command line or method argument lists as from request parameters. The system can then run in ignorance of its context.

If you find a system hard to run in different contexts, that may indicate a design issue. If, for example, you have numerous filepaths hardcoded into components, it's likely you are suffering from tight coupling. You should consider moving elements that tie your components to their context into encapsulating objects that can be acquired from a central repository. The registry pattern, also covered in Chapter 12, will likely help you with this.

Once your system can be run directly from a method call, you'll find that high level web tests are relatively easy to write without any additional tools.

You may find, however, that even the most well thought-out project will need some refactoring to get things ready for testing. In my experience, this almost always results in design improvements. I'm going to demonstrate this by retrofitting one aspect the WOO example from Chapters 12 and 13 for unit testing.

Refactoring a Web Application for Testing

We actually left the WOO example in a reasonable state from a tester's point of view. Because the system uses a single Front Controller, there's a simple API interface. This is a simple class called Runner.php.

```
require_once( "woo/controller/Controller.php");
\woo\controller\Controller::run();
```

That would be easy enough to add to a unit test, right? But what about command line arguments? To some extent, this is already handled in the Request class:

```
// \woo\controller\Request
    function init() {
        if ( isset( $_SERVER['REQUEST_METHOD'] ) ) {
            $this->properties = $_REQUEST;
            return;
        }

        foreach( $_SERVER['argv'] as $arg ) {
            if ( strpos( $arg, '=' ) ) {
```

```
                list( $key, $val )=explode( "=", $arg );
                $this->setProperty( $key, $val );
            }
        }
    }
```

The init() method detects whether it is running in a server context, and populates the $properties array accordingly (either directly or via setProperty()). This works fine for command line invocation. It means I can run something like:

$ php runner.php cmd=AddVenue venue_name=bob

and get this response:

```
<html>
<head>
<title>Add a Space for venue bob</title>
</head>
<body>
<h1>Add a Space for Venue 'bob'</h1>
<table>
<tr>
<td>
'bob' added (5)</td></tr><tr><td>please add name for the space</td>
</tr>
</table>
[add space]
<form method="post">
    <input type="text" value="" name="space_name"/>
    <input type="hidden" name="cmd" value="AddSpace" />
    <input type="hidden" name="venue_id" value="5" />
    <input type="submit" value="submit" />
</form>
</body>
</html>
```

Although this works for the command line, it remains a little tricky to pass in arguments via a method call. One inelegant solution would be to manually set the $argv array before calling the controller's run() method. I don't much like this, though. Playing directly with magic arrays feels plain wrong, and the string manipulation involved at each end would compound the sin. Looking at the controller class more closely, I see an opportunity to improve both design and testability. Here's an extract from the handleRequest() method:

```
// \woo\controller\Controller
    function handleRequest() {

        $request = new Request();

        $app_c = \woo\base\ApplicationRegistry::appController();
        while( $cmd = $app_c->getCommand( $request ) ) {
            $cmd->execute( $request );
        }
```

```
        \woo\domain\ObjectWatcher::instance()->performOperations();
        $this->invokeView( $app_c->getView( $request ) );
    }
```

This method is designed to be invoked by the static run() method. The first thing I notice is a very definite code smell. The Request object is directly instantiated here. That means I can't swap in a stub should I want to. Time to pull on the thread. What's going on in Request? This is the constructor:

```
// \woo\controller\Request
    function __construct() {
        $this->init();
        \woo\base\RequestRegistry::setRequest($this );
    }
```

That smell's getting worse. The Request class refers itself to the RequestRegistry so that other components can get it. There are two things I don't like about this on reflection. First, the code implies a direct invocation must take place before the Registry is used to access the Request object. And second, there's a bit of unnecessary coupling going on. The Request class doesn't really need to know about the RequestRegistry.

So how can I improve my design and make the system more amenable to testing at the same time? I prefer to push instantiations back to the RequestRegistry where possible. That way later I can extend the implementation of RequestRegistry::instance() to return a MockRequestRegistry populated with fake components if I want to. I love to fool my systems. So first off I remove that setRequest() line from the Request object. Now I push my Request instantiation back to the RequestRegistry object:

```
namespace woo/controller;

//...

class RequestRegistry extends Registry {
    private $request;

// ...

    static function getRequest() {
        $that = self::instance();
        if ( ! isset( $that->request ) ) {
            $that->request = new \woo\controller\Request();
        }
        return $that->request;
    }
}
```

Finally, I must replace that direct instantiation in the Controller:

```
// \woo\controller\Controller
    function handleRequest() {

        $request = \woo\base\RequestRegistry::getRequest();
        $app_c = \woo\base\ApplicationRegistry::appController();
        while( $cmd = $app_c->getCommand( $request ) ) {
            $cmd->execute( $request );
        }
        \woo\domain\ObjectWatcher::instance()->performOperations();
        $this->invokeView( $app_c->getView( $request ) );
    }
```

With those refactorings out the way, my system is more amenable to testing. It's no accident that my design has improved at the same time. Now it's to begin writing tests.

Simple Web Testing

Here's a test case that performs a very basic test on the WOO system:

```
class AddVenueTest extends PHPUnit_Framework_TestCase {

    function testAddVenueVanilla() {
        $this->runCommand("AddVenue", array("venue_name"=>"bob") );
    }

    function runCommand( $command=null, array $args=null ) {
        $request = \woo\base\RequestRegistry::getRequest();
        if ( ! is_null( $args ) ) {
            foreach( $args as $key=>$val ) {
                $request->setProperty( $key, $val );
            }
        }
        if ( ! is_null( $command ) ) {
            $request->setProperty( 'cmd', $command );
        }
        woo\controller\Controller::run();
    }
}
```

In fact, it does not so much test anything as prove that the system can be invoked. The real work is done in the runCommand() method. There is nothing terribly clever here. I get a Request object from the RequestRegistry, and I populate it with the keys and values provided in the method call. Because the Controller will go to the same source for its Request object, I know that it will work the values I have set.

Running this test confirms that all is well. I see the output I expect. The problem is that this output is printed by the view, and is therefore hard to test. I can fix that quite easily by buffering the output:

```
class AddVenueTest extends PHPUnit_Framework_TestCase {
    function testAddVenueVanilla() {
        $output = $this->runCommand("AddVenue", array("venue_name"=>"bob") );

        self::AssertRegexp( "/added/", $output );

    }

    function runCommand( $command=null, array $args=null ) {

        ob_start();

        $request = \woo\base\RequestRegistry::getRequest();
        if ( ! is_null( $args ) ) {
            foreach( $args as $key=>$val ) {
                $request->setProperty( $key, $val );
            }
        }
        if ( ! is_null( $command ) ) {
            $request->setProperty( 'cmd', $command );
        }
```

```
        woo\controller\Controller::run();

        $ret = ob_get_contents();
        ob_end_clean();
        return $ret;

    }
}
```

By catching the system's output in a buffer, I'm able to return it from the runCommand() method. I apply a simple assertion to the return value to demonstrate.

Here is the view from the command line:

$ phpunit test/AddVenueTest.php

```
PHPUnit 3.4.11 by Sebastian Bergmann.
.
Time: 0 seconds, Memory: 4.00Mb
OK (1 test, 1 assertion)
```

If you are going to be running lots of tests on a system in this way, it would make sense to create a Web UI superclass to hold runCommand().

I am glossing over some details here that you will face in your own tests. You will need to ensure that the system works with configurable storage locations. You don't want your tests going to the same datastore that you use for your development environment. This is another opportunity for design improvement. Look for hardcoded filepaths, and DSN values, push them back to the Registry, and then ensure your tests work within a sandbox, but setting these values in your test case's setUp() method. Look into swapping in a MockRequestRegistry, which you can charge up with stubs, mocks, and various other sneaky fakes.

Approaches like this are great for testing the inputs and output of a web application. There are some distinct limitations, however. This method won't capture the browser experience. Where a web application uses JavaScript, Ajax, and other client-side cleverness, testing the text generated by your system, won't tell you whether the user is seeing a sane interface.

Luckily, there is a solution.

Introducing Selenium

Selenium (http://seleniumhq.org/) consists of a set of commands (sometimes called selenese) for defining web tests. It also provides tools for authoring and running browser tests, as well as for binding tests to existing test platforms. Luckily for us, one of these platforms is PHPUnit.

In this brief introduction, I'll author a quick WOO test using the Selenium IDE. Then I'll export the results, and run it as a PHPUnit test case.

Getting Selenium

You can download Selenium components at http://seleniumhq.org/download/. For the purposes of this example, you will want Selenium IDE. And Selenium RC.

If you're running Firefox as your browser (and you need to be in order to run the IDE) you should find that the Selenium IDE installs directly on download (after you've OK'd a prompt or two) and becomes available in the Tools menu.

Selenium RC requires a more manual approach. Once you've downloaded the package, you should find an archive called `selenium-remote-control-1.0.3.zip` (though, of course, your version number will probably be different). You should unzip this archive and look for a jar (Java ARchive) file somewhere like `selenium-server-1.0.3/selenium-server.jar`. Copy this file somewhere central. To proceed further, you'll need need Java installed on your system. Once you've confirmed this, you can start the Selenium Server.

Here, I copy the server to a directory named lib in my home directory. Then I start the server:

```
$ cp selenium-server-1.0.3/selenium-server.jar ~/lib/
$ java -jar ~/lib/selenium-server.jar
```

```
13:03:28.713 INFO - Java: Sun Microsystems Inc. 14.0-b16
13:03:28.745 INFO - OS: Linux 2.6.31.5-127.fc12.i686 i386
13:03:28.787 INFO - v2.0 [a2], with Core v2.0 [a2]
13:03:29.273 INFO - RemoteWebDriver instances should connect to:
http://192.168.1.65:4444/wd/hub
13:03:29.276 INFO - Version Jetty/5.1.x
13:03:29.284 INFO - Started HttpContext[/selenium-server/driver,/selenium-server/driver]
13:03:29.286 INFO - Started HttpContext[/selenium-server,/selenium-server]
13:03:29.286 INFO - Started HttpContext[/,/]
13:03:29.383 INFO - Started org.openqa.jetty.jetty.servlet.ServletHandler@b0ce8f
13:03:29.383 INFO - Started HttpContext[/wd,/wd]
13:03:29.404 INFO - Started SocketListener on 0.0.0.0:4444
13:03:29.405 INFO - Started org.openqa.jetty.jetty.Server@192b996
```

Now I'm ready to proceed.

Creating a Test

Selenese, the Selenium language, is simple but powerful. There's nothing to prevent you from authoring tests in the traditional manner, with a text editor. However, the Selenium IDE is by far the easiest way into testing. You can launch it from the Tools window.

Once you have the control panel up, you should add an address to the Base URL field. This should be the address against which relative links will work in the system under test. You should see a red dot on a button in the right-hand corner of the IDE control panel. It should be depressed, which means the tool is already in record mode.

Figure 18–1 shows the IDE as it should be at this point.

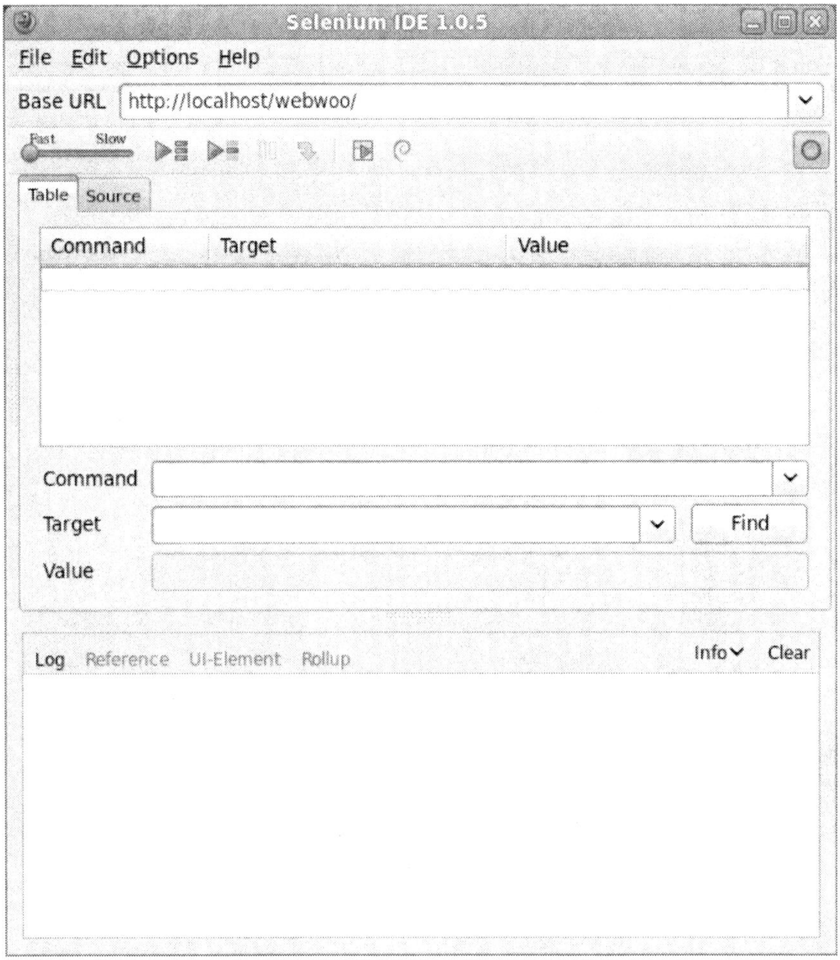

Figure 18–1. The Selenium IDE control panel

As you can see, I have used the base URL http://localhost/webwoo/. This is the address of an installed instance of the WOO application. I'm going to begin my test at http://localhost/webwoo/?cmd=AddVenue, so I point my browser to that URL. Having arrived there, I want to begin with a sanity test. The AddVenue page includes the string "no name provided." I'd like my test to verify this. So I right-click on the text in the browser. I'm given the option to select a Selenium command 'verifyWebText'. You can see this in Figure 18–2.

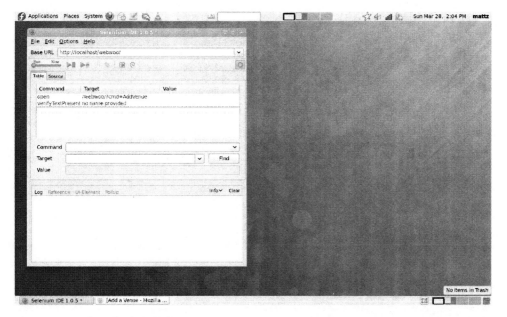

Figure 18–2. Verifying Text on a web page

Meanwhile, Selenium has recorded both of my visits to the page, and my requirement that text be verified. You can see this in Figure 18–3.

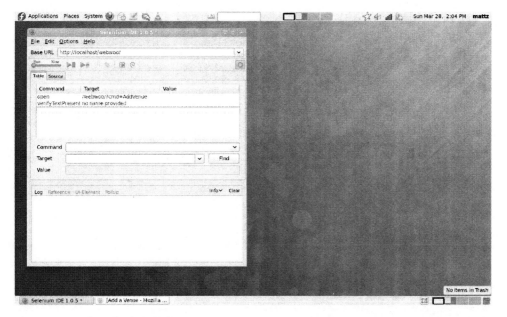

Figure 18–3. The Selenium IDE generates tests

Notice that each command is divided into three parts: *command*, *target*, and *value*. These subdivisions are also known as *actions, accessors,* and *assertions*. Essentially, a command then instructs the test engine to perform something (an action), somewhere (accessor), and then to confirm a result (assertion).

Now I can return to my WOO web interface, add a venue, confirm some text, add a space, and confirm again. Ultimately, I will end up with a runable test case. I can run it in the IDE itself by hitting one of the green "play" buttons at the stop of the IDE control panel. Failed test commands will be flagged red, and passes flagged green.

You can save your test case from the File menu, and rerun it at a later date. Or you can export your test as a PHPUnit class. To do this, choose Format from the Options menu and select PHPUnit. You can see the menu in Figure 18–4.

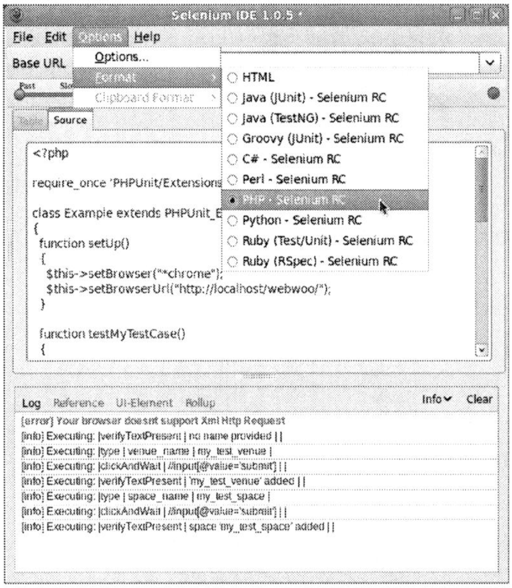

Figure 18–4. *Changing the format*

Note the log pane at the bottom of the panel. You can see a report there from a successful run of the test case. Now that I've set the correct format, it's a matter of saving the file. As you might expect, you can choose Save As from the File menu. Here's the contents of the saved file:

```php
class Example extends PHPUnit_Extensions_SeleniumTestCase
{
  function setUp()
  {
    $this->setBrowser("*firefox");
    $this->setBrowserUrl("http://localhost/webwoo/");
  }

  function testMyTestCase()
  {
    $this->open("/webwoo/?cmd=AddVenue");
    try {
```

```
        $this->assertTrue($this->isTextPresent("no name provided"));
    } catch (PHPUnit_Framework_AssertionFailedError $e) {
        array_push($this->verificationErrors, $e->toString());
    }
    $this->type("venue_name", "my_test_venue");
    $this->click("//input[@value='submit']");
    $this->waitForPageToLoad("30000");
    try {
        $this->assertTrue($this->isTextPresent("'my_test_venue' added"));
    } catch (PHPUnit_Framework_AssertionFailedError $e) {
        array_push($this->verificationErrors, $e->toString());
    }
    $this->type("space_name", "my_test_space");
    $this->click("//input[@value='submit']");
    $this->waitForPageToLoad("30000");
    try {
        $this->assertTrue($this->isTextPresent("space 'my_test_space' added"));
    } catch (PHPUnit_Framework_AssertionFailedError $e) {
        array_push($this->verificationErrors, $e->toString());
    }
  }
 }
}
```

I changed the default browser from 'chrome' to 'firefox.' Apart from that, I have made no changes at all to this test. Remember that I started the Selenium Server a while back. This must be running, or PHPUnit tests that use Selenium will fail. It is the server that launches the browser (Firefox in this case, though most modern browsers are supported for running tests).

With the test saved and the server running I can execute my test case:

$ phpunit seleniumtest.php

```
PHPUnit 3.4.11 by Sebastian Bergmann.
.
Time: 11 seconds, Memory: 4.00Mb
OK (1 test, 3 assertions)
```

If you run the test, not only will you see this output, you'll see a browser window pop up, invoked by the server, and the actions executed at lightning speed. The sort of point and click grunt work that we used to have to do by hand, neatly automated.

Of course I've only just scratched the surface of Selenium here. But hopefully it's enough to give you an idea of the possibilities. If you want to learn more, there is a complete Selenium manual at http://seleniumhq.org/docs/index.html. You should also take a look at the Selenium documentation on the PHPUnit site at http://www.phpunit.de/manual/current/en/selenium.html.

A Note of Caution

It's easy to get carried away with the benefits that automated tests can offer. I add unit tests to my projects, and I use PHPUnit for functional tests as well. That is, I test at the level of the system as well as that of the class. I have seen real and observable benefits, but I believe that these come at a price.

Tests add a number of costs to your development. As you build safety into the project, for example, you are also adding a time penalty into the build process that can impact releases. The time it takes to write tests is part of this but so is the time it takes to run them. On one system, we may have suites of functional tests that run against more than one database and more than one version control system. Add a few more contextual variables like that, and we face a real barrier to running the test suite. Of course, tests that aren't run are not useful. One answer to this is to fully automate your tests, so runs are kicked off by a scheduling application like cron. Another is to maintain a subset of your tests that can be easily run by developers as they commit code. These should sit alongside your longer, slower test run.

Another issue to consider is the brittle nature of many test harnesses. Your tests may give you confidence to make changes, but as your test coverage increases along with the complexity of your system, it becomes easier to break multiple tests. Of course, this is often what you want. You want to know when expected behavior does not occur or when unexpected behavior does.

Oftentimes, though, a test harness can break because of a relatively trivial change, such as the wording of a feedback string. Every broken test is an urgent matter, but it can be frustrating to have to change 30 test cases to address a minor alteration in architecture or output. Unit tests are less prone to problems of this sort, because by and large, they focus on each component in isolation.

The cost involved in keeping tests in step with an evolving system is a trade-off you simply have to factor in. On the whole, I believe the benefits justify the costs.

You can also do some things to reduce the fragility of a test harness. It's a good idea to write tests with the expectation of change built in to some extent. I tend to use regular expressions to test output rather than direct equality tests, for example. Testing for a few key words is less likely to make my test fail when I remove a newline character from an output string. Of course, making your tests too forgiving is also a danger, so it is a matter of using your judgment.

Another issue is the extent to which you should use mocks and stubs to fake the system beyond the component you wish to test. Some insist that you should isolate your component as much as possible and mock everything around it. This works for me in some projects. In others, though, I have found that maintaining a system of mocks can become a time sink. Not only do you have the cost of keeping your tests in line with your system but you must keep your mocks up to date. Imagine changing the return type of a method. If you fail to update the method of the corresponding stub object to return the new type, client tests may pass in error. With a complex fake system, there is a real danger of bugs creeping into mocks. Debugging tests is frustrating work, especially when the system itself is not at fault.

I tend to play this by ear. I use mocks and stubs by default, but I'm unapologetic about moving to real components if the costs begin to mount up. You may lose some focus on the test subject, but this comes with the bonus that errors originating in the component's context are at least real problems with the system. You can, of course, use a combination of real and fake elements. I routinely use an in-memory database in test mode, for example. This is particularly easy if you are using PDO. Here's a simplified class that uses PDO to speak to a database:

```
class DBFace {
    private $pdo;
    function __construct( $dsn, $user=null, $pass=null ) {
        $this->pdo = new PDO( $dsn, $user, $pass );
        $this->pdo->setAttribute(PDO::ATTR_ERRMODE, PDO::ERRMODE_EXCEPTION);
    }

    function query( $query ) {
        $stmt = $this->pdo->query( $query );
        return $stmt;
    }
}
```

If DBFace is passed around our system and used by mappers, then it's a simple matter to prime it to use SQLite in memory mode:

```
public function setUp() {
```

```
        $face = new DBFace("sqlite::memory:");
        $face->query("create table user ( id INTEGER PRIMARY KEY, name TEXT )");
        $face->query("insert into user (name) values('bob')");
        $face->query("insert into user (name) values('harry')");
        $this->mapper = new ToolMapper( $face );
    }
```

As you may have gathered, I am not an ideologue when it comes to testing. I routinely "cheat" by combining real and mocked components, and because priming data is repetitive, I often centralize test fixtures into what Martin Fowler calls Object Mothers. These classes are simple factories that generate primed objects for the purpose of testing. Shared fixtures of this sort are anathema to some.

Having pointed out some of the problems that testing may force you to confront, it is worth reiterating a few points that for my money trump all objections. Testing

- Helps you prevent bugs (to the extent that you find them during development and refactoring)

- Helps you discover bugs (as you extend test coverage)

- Encourages you to focus on the design of your system

- Lets you improve code design with less fear that changes will cause more problems than they solve

- Gives you confidence when you ship code

In every project for which I've written tests, I've had occasion to be grateful for the fact sooner or later.

Summary

In this chapter, I revisited the kinds of tests we all write as developers but all too often thoughtlessly discard. From there, I introduced PHPUnit, which lets you write the same kind of throw-away tests during development but then keep them and feel the lasting benefit! I created a test case implementation, and I covered the available assertion methods. I , examined constraints, and explored the devious world of mock objects. I showed how refactoring for testing can improve design, and demonstrated some techniques for testing web applications, first using just PHPUnit, and then using Selenium. Finally, I risked the ire of some by warning of the costs that tests incur and discussing the trade-offs involved.

∎∎∎

CHAPTER 19

Automated Build with Phing

If version control is one side of the coin, then automated build is the other. Version control allows multiple developers to work collaboratively on a single project. With many coders each deploying a project in her own space, automated build soon becomes essential. One developer may have her Web-facing directory in /usr/local/apache/htdocs; another might use /home/bibble/public_html. Developers may use different database passwords, library directories, or mail mechanisms. A flexible codebase might easily accommodate all of these differences, but the effort of changing settings and manually copying directories around your file system to get things working would soon become tiresome—especially if you need to install code in progress several times a day (or several times an hour).

You have already seen that PEAR handles installation. You'll almost certainly want to deliver a project to an end user via a PEAR package, because that mechanism provides the lowest barrier to installation (users will likely already have PEAR present on their systems, and PEAR supports network installation). PEAR handles the last stages of installation admirably, but there's a lot of work that might need automating before a package has been created. You may want to extract files from a version control repository, for example. You should run tests and compile files together into a build directory. Finally, you'll want to automate the creation of the PEAR package itself. In this chapter, I introduce you to Phing, which handles just such jobs. This chapter will cover

- Getting and installing Phing: Who builds the builder?

- Properties: Setting and getting data.

- Types: Describing complex parts of a project.

- Targets: Breaking a build into callable, interdependent sets of functionality.

- Tasks: The things that get stuff done.

What Is Phing?

Phing is a PHP tool for building projects. It is very closely modeled on the hugely popular (and very powerful) Java tool called Ant. Ant was so named because it is small but capable of constructing things that are very large indeed. Both Phing and Ant use an XML file (usually named build.xml) to determine what to do in order to install or otherwise work with a project.

The PHP world *really* needs a good build solution. Serious developers have had a number of options in the past. First, it is possible to use make, the ubiquitous Unix build tool that is still used for most C and Perl projects. However, make is extremely picky about syntax and requires quite a lot of shell knowledge, up to and including scripting—this can be challenging for some PHP programmers who have not come to programming via the Unix or Linux command line. What's more, make provides very few built-in tools for common build operations such as transforming file names and contents. It is really just a glue for shell commands. This makes it hard to write programs that will install across platforms. Not all environments will have the same version of make, or even have it at all. Even if you have make, you may not have all the commands the makefile (the configuration file that drives make) requires.

Phing's relationship with make is illustrated in its name: Phing stands for PHing Is Not Gnu make. This playful recursion is a common coder's joke (for example, GNU itself stands for Gnu is Not Unix).

Phing is a native PHP application that interprets a user-created XML file in order to perform operations on a project. Such operations would typically involve the copying of files from a distribution directory to various destination directories, but there is much more to Phing. Phing can be used to generate documentation, run tests, invoke commands, run arbitrary PHP code, create PEAR packages, replace keywords in files, strip comments, and generate tar/gzipped package releases. Even if Phing does not yet do what you need, it is designed to be easily extensible.

Because Phing is itself a PHP application, all you need to run it is a recent PHP engine. Since Phing is an application for installing PHP applications, the presence of a PHP executable is a reasonably safe bet.

You have seen that PEAR packages are breathtakingly easy to install. PEAR supports its own automated build mechanism. Since PEAR is bundled with PHP, should you not use the PEAR mechanism to install your own projects? Ultimately the answer to this is yes. PEAR makes installation easy, and supports dependencies well (so that you can ensure your packages are compatible with one another). There's a lot of tough work that must be automated during development, up to and including package creation. This technique, to use Phing for project development but to have it generate a PEAR package upon release, is used to produce the Phing application itself.

Getting and Installing Phing

If it is difficult to install an install tool, then something is surely wrong! However, assuming that you have PHP 5 or better on your system (and if you haven't, this isn't the book for you!), installation of Phing could not be easier.

You can acquire and install Phing with two simple commands.

```
$ pear channel-discover pear.phing.info
$ pear install phing/phing
```

This will install Phing as a PEAR package. You should have write permission for your PEAR directories, which, on most Unix or Linux systems, will mean running the command as the root user.

If you run into any installation problems, you should visit the download page at http://phing.info/trac/wiki/Users/Download. You will find plenty of installation instructions there.

Composing the Build Document

You should now be ready to get cracking with Phing! Let's test things out:

```
$ phing -v
Phing version 2.4.0
```

The -v flag to the phing command causes the script to return version information. By the time you read this, the version number may have changed, but you should see a similar message when you run the command on your system.

Now I'll run the phing command without arguments:

```
$ phing
Buildfile: build.xml does not exist!
```

As you can see, Phing is lost without instructions. By default, it will look for a file called `build.xml`. Let's build a minimal document so that we can at least make that error message go away:

```
<?xml version="1.0"?>
<!-- build xml -->

<project name="megaquiz" default="main">
    <target name="main"/>
</project>
```

This is the bare minimum you can get away with in a build file. If we save the previous example as `build.xml` and run `phing` again, we should get some more interesting output:

```
$ phing
Buildfile: /home/bob/working/megaquiz/build.xml


megaquiz > main:

BUILD FINISHED

Total time: 0.1107 seconds
```

A lot of effort to achieve precisely nothing, you may think, but we have to start somewhere! Look again at that build file. Because we are dealing with XML, I include an XML declaration. As you probably know, XML comments look like this:

```
<!-- Anything here is ignored. Because it's a comment. OK? -->
```

The second line in my build file is ignored. You can put as many comments as you like in your build files, and as they grow, you should make full use of this fact. Large build files can be hard to follow without suitable comments.

The real start of any build file is the `project` element. The `project` element can include up to four attributes. Of these, `name` and `default` are compulsory. The `name` attribute establishes the project's name; `default` defines a target to run if none are specified on the command line. An optional `description` attribute can provide summary information. You can specify the context directory for the build using a `basedir` attribute. If this is omitted, the current working directory will be assumed. You can see these attributes summarized in Table 19–1.

Table 19–1. *The Attributes of the project Element*

Attribute	Required	Description	Default Value
Name	Yes	The name of the project	None
Description	No	A brief project summary	None
Default	Yes	The default target to run	None
Basedir	No	The file system context in which build will run	Current directory (.)

Once I have defined a `project` element, I must create at least one target—the one I reference in the `default` attribute.

Targets

Targets are similar, in some senses, to functions. A target is a set of actions grouped together to achieve an objective: to copy a directory from one place another, for example, or to generate documentation.

In my previous example, I included a bare-minimum implementation for a target:

```
<target name="main"/>
```

As you can see, a target must define at least a name attribute. I have made use of this in the project element. Because the default element points to the main target, this target will be invoked whenever Phing is run without command-line arguments. This was confirmed by the output:

```
megaquiz > main:
```

Targets can be organized to depend on one another. By setting up a dependency between one target and another, you tell Phing that the first target should not run before the target it depends on has been run. Now to add a dependency to my build file:

```
<?xml version="1.0"?>
<!-- build xml -->

<project name="megaquiz"
        default="main"
>
    <target name="runfirst" />
    <target name="runsecond" depends="runfirst"/>
    <target name="main" depends="runsecond"/>
</project>
```

As you can see, I have introduced a new attribute for the target element. depends tells Phing that the referenced target should be executed before the current one, so I might want a target that copies certain files to a directory to be invoked before one that runs a transformation on all files in that directory. I added two new targets in the example: runsecond, on which main depends, and runfirst, on which runsecond depends. Here's what happens when I run Phing with this build file:

```
$ phing
Buildfile: /home/bob/working/megaquiz/build.xml

megaquiz > runfirst:

megaquiz > runsecond:

megaquiz > main:

BUILD FINISHED

Total time: 0.3029 seconds
```

As you can see, the dependencies are honored. Phing encounters the main target, sees its dependency, and moves back to runsecond. runsecond has its own dependency, and Phing invokes runfirst. Having satisfied its dependency, Phing can invoke runsecond. Finally, main is invoked. The depends attribute can reference more than one target at a time. A comma-separated list of dependencies can be provided, and each will be honored in turn.

Now that I have more than one target to play with, I can override the project element's default attribute from the command line:

```
$ phing runsecond
Buildfile: /home/bob/working/megaquiz/build.xml

megaquiz > runfirst:

megaquiz > runsecond:

BUILD FINISHED

Total time: 0.2671 seconds
```

By passing in a target name, I cause the default attribute to be ignored. The target matching my argument is invoked instead (as well as the target on which it depends). This is useful for invoking specialized tasks, such as cleaning up a build directory or running post-install scripts.

The target element also supports an optional description attribute, to which you can assign a brief description of the target's purpose:

```
<?xml version="1.0"?>
<!-- build xml -->

<project name="megaquiz"
        default="main"
        description="A quiz engine">
    <target name="runfirst"
            description="The first target" />
    <target name="runsecond"
            depends="runfirst"
            description="The second target" />
    <target name="main"
            depends="runsecond"
            description="The main target" />
</project>
```

Adding a description to your targets makes no difference to the normal build process. If the user runs Phing with a -projecthelp flag, however, the descriptions will be used to summarize the project:

```
$ phing -projecthelp
Buildfile: /home/bob/working/megaquiz/build.xml
A quiz engine
Default target:
-----------------------------------------------------------------------------
 main      The main target

Main targets:
-----------------------------------------------------------------------------
 main      The main target
 runfirst  The first target
 runsecond The second target
```

Notice that I added the description attribute to the project element too.

Properties

Phing allows you to set such values using the property element.

Properties are similar to global variables in a script. As such, they are often declared toward the top of a project to make it easy for developers to work out what's what in the build file. Here I create a build file that works with database information:

```xml
<?xml version="1.0"?>
<!-- build xml -->

<project name="megaquiz"
        default="main"
>

    <property name="dbname"  value="megaquiz" />
    <property name="dbpass"  value="default" />
    <property name="dbhost" value="localhost" />

    <target name="main">
        <echo>database: ${dbname}</echo>
        <echo>pass:     ${dbpass}</echo>
        <echo>host:     ${dbhost}</echo>
    </target>
</project>
```

I introduced a new element: property. property requires name and value attributes. Notice also that I have added to the main target. echo is an example of a task. I will explore tasks more fully in the next section. For now, though, it's enough to know that echo does exactly what you would expect—it causes its contents to be output. Notice the syntax I use to reference the value of a property here: by using a dollar sign, and wrapping the property name in curly brackets, you tell Phing to replace the string with the property value.

```
${propertyname}
```

All this build file achieves is to declare three properties and to print them to standard output. Here it is in action:

```
$ phing
Buildfile: /home/bob/working/megaquiz/build.xml

megaquiz > main:

    [echo] database: megaquiz
    [echo] pass:     default
    [echo] host:     localhost

BUILD FINISHED

Total time: 0.4402 seconds
```

Now that I have introduced properties, I can wrap up my exploration of targets. The target element accepts two additional attributes: if and unless. Each of these should be set with the name of a property. When you use if with a property name, the target will only be executed if the given property is set. If the property is not set, the target will exit silently. Here, I comment out the dbpass property and make the main task require it using the if attribute:

```
<property name="dbname"  value="megaquiz" />
<!--<property name="dbpass"  value="default" />-->
<property name="dbhost" value="localhost" />

<target name="main" if="dbpass">
    <echo>database: ${dbname}</echo>
    <echo>pass:     ${dbpass}</echo>
    <echo>host:     ${dbhost}</echo>
</target>
```

Let's run phing again:

```
$ phing
Buildfile: /home/bob/working/megaquiz/build.xml

megaquiz > main:

BUILD FINISHED

Total time: 0.2628 seconds
```

As you can see, I have raised no error, but the main task did not run. Why might I want to do this? There is another way of setting properties in a project. They can be specified on the command line. You tell Phing that you are passing it a property with the -D flag followed by a property assignment. So the argument should look like this:

```
-Dname=value
```

In my example, I want the dbname property to be made available via the command line:

```
$ phing -Ddbpass=userset
Buildfile: /home/bob/working/megaquiz/build.xml

megaquiz > main:

    [echo] database: megaquiz
    [echo] pass:     userset
    [echo] host:     localhost

BUILD FINISHED

Total time: 0.4611 seconds
```

The if attribute of the main target is satisfied that the dbpass property is present, and the target is allowed to execute.

As you might expect, the unless attribute is the opposite of if. If a property is set and it is referenced in a target's unless attribute, then the target will not run. This is useful if you want to make it possible to suppress a particular target from the command line. So I might add something like this to the main target:

```
<target name="main" unless="suppressmain">
```

main will be executed unless a suppressmain property is present:

```
$ phing -Dsuppressmain=yes
```

Now that I have wrapped up the target element, table 19–2 shows a summary of its attributes.

Table 19–2. *The Attributes of the target Element*

Attribute	Required	Description
Name	Yes	The name of the target
Depends	No	Targets on which the current depends
If	No	Execute target only if given property is present
Unless	No	Execute target only if given property is not present
Description	No	A short summary of the target's purpose

When a property is set on the command line, it overrides any and all property declarations within the build file. There is another condition in which a property value can be overwritten. By default, if a property is declared twice, the original value will have primacy. You can alter this behavior by setting an attribute called override in the second property element. Here's an example:

```xml
<?xml version="1.0"?>
<!-- build xml -->

<project name="megaquiz"
        default="main"
>

    <property name="dbpass" value="default" />

    <target name="main">
        <property name="dbpass" override="yes" value="specific" />
        <echo>pass:    ${dbpass}</echo>
    </target>

</project>
```

I set a property called dbpass, giving it the initial value "default". In the main target I set the property once again, adding an override attribute set to "yes" and providing a new value. The new value is reflected in the output:

```
$ phing
Buildfile: /home/bob/working/megaquiz/build.xml

megaquiz > main:

    [echo] pass:    specific

BUILD FINISHED

Total time: 0.3802 seconds
```

If I had not set the override element in the second property element, the original value of "default" would have stayed in place. It is important to note that targets are not functions: there is no concept of local scope. If you override a property within a task, it remains overridden for all other tasks throughout the build file. You could get around this, of course, by storing a property value in a temporary property before overriding, and then resetting it when you have finished working locally.

So far, I have dealt with properties that you define yourself. Phing also provides built-in properties. You reference these in exactly the same way that you would reference properties you have declared yourself. Here's an example:

```xml
<?xml version="1.0"?>
<!-- build xml -->

<project name="megaquiz"
         default="main"
>

    <target name="main">
        <echo>name:      ${phing.project.name}</echo>
        <echo>base:      ${project.basedir}</echo>
        <echo>home:      ${user.home}</echo>
        <echo>pass:      ${env.DBPASS}</echo>
    </target>

</project>
```

I reference just a few of the built-in Phing properties. phing.project.name resolves to the name of the project as defined in the name attribute of the project element; project.basedir gives the starting directory; user.home provides the executing user's home directory (this is useful for providing default install locations).

Finally, the env prefix in a property reference indicates an operating system environment variable. So by specifying ${env.DBPASS}, I am looking for an environment variable called DBPASS. Here I run Phing on this file:

```
$ phing
Buildfile: /home/bob/working/megaquiz/build.xml

megaquiz > main:

    [echo] name:      megaquiz
    [echo] base:      /home/bob/working/megaquiz
    [echo] home:      /home/bob
    [echo] pass:      ${env.DBPASS}

BUILD FINISHED

Total time: 0.1120 seconds
```

Notice that the final property has not been translated. This is the default behavior when a property is not found—the string referencing the property is left untransformed. If I set the DBPASS environment variable and run again, I should see the variable reflected in the output:

```
$ export DBPASS=wooshpoppow
$ phing
Buildfile: /home/bob/working/megaquiz/build.xml
```

```
megaquiz > main:
    ...
    [echo] pass:      whooshpoppow

BUILD FINISHED

Total time: 0.2852 seconds
```

So now you have seen three ways of setting a property: the property element, a command line argument, and an environment variable.

You can use targets to ensure that properties are populated. Let's say, for example, that my project requires a dbpass property. I would like the user to set dbpass on the command line (this always has priority over other property assignment methods). Failing that, I should look for an environment variable. Finally, I should give up and go for a default value:

```xml
<?xml version="1.0"?>
<!-- build xml -->

<project name="megaquiz"
        default="main"
>

    <target name="setenvpass" if="env.DBPASS" unless="dbpass">
        <property name="dbpass" override="yes" value="${env.DBPASS}" />
    </target>

    <target name="setpass" unless="dbpass" depends="setenvpass">
        <property name="dbpass" override="yes" value="default" />
    </target>

    <target name="main" depends="setpass">
        <echo>pass:      ${dbpass}</echo>
    </target>

</project>
```

So, as usual, the default target main is invoked first. This has a dependency set, so Phing goes back to the setpass target. setpass, though, depends on setenvpass, so I start there. setenvpass is configured to run only if dbpass has not been set and if env.DBPASS is present. If these conditions are met, then I set the dbpass property using the property element. At this stage then, dbpass is populated either by a command-line argument or by an environment variable. If neither of these were present, then the property remains unset at this stage. The setpass target is now executed, but only if dbpass is not yet present. In this case, it sets the property to the default string: "default".

Types

You may think that having looked at properties, you are now through with data. In fact, Phing supports a set of special elements called types that encapsulate different kinds of information useful to the build process.

FileSet

Let's say that you need to represent a directory in your build file, a common situation as you might imagine. You could use a property to represent this directory, certainly, but you'd run into problems straightaway if your developers use different platforms that support distinct directory separators. The answer is the FileSet data type. FileSet is platform independent, so if you represent a directory with forward slashes in the path, they will be automatically translated behind the scenes into backslashes when the build is run on a Windows machine. You can define a minimal fileset element like this:

```
<fileset dir="src/lib" />
```

As you can see, I use the dir attribute to set the directory I wish to represent. You can optionally add an id attribute, so that you can refer to the fileset later on:

```
<fileset dir="src/lib" id="srclib">
```

The FileSet data type is particularly useful in specifying types of documents to include or exclude. When installing a set of files, you may not wish those that match a certain pattern to be included. You can handle conditions like this in an excludes attribute:

```
<fileset dir="src/lib" id="srclib"
        excludes="**/*_test.php **/*Test.php" />
```

Notice the syntax I have used in the excludes attribute. Double asterisks represent any directory or subdirectory within src/lib. A single asterisk represents zero or more characters. So I am specifying that I would like to exclude files that end in _test.php or Test.php in all directories below the starting point defined in the dir attribute. The excludes attribute accepts multiple patterns separated by white space.

I can apply the same syntax to an includes attribute. Perhaps my src/lib directories contain many non-PHP files that are useful to developers but should not find their way into an installation. I could exclude those files, of course, but it might be simpler just to define the kinds of files I *can* include. In this case, if a file doesn't end in .php, it isn't going to be installed:

```
<fileset dir="src/lib" id="srclib"
        excludes="**/*_test.php **/*Test.php"
        includes="**/*.php" />
```

As you build up include and exclude rules, your fileset element is likely to become overly long. Luckily, you can pull out individual exclude rules and place each one in its own exclude subelement. You can do the same for include rules. I can now rewrite my FileSet like this:

```
<fileset dir="src/lib" id="srclib">
    <exclude name="**/*_test.php" />
    <exclude name="**/*Test.php" />
    <include name="**/*.php" />
</fileset>
```

You can see some of the attributes of the fileset element in Table 19–3.

Table 19–3. *Some Attributes of the fileset Element*

Attribute	Required	Description
Id	No	A unique handle for referring to the element
Dir	No	The fileset directory
Excludes	No	A list of patterns for exclusion
Includes	No	A list of patterns for inclusion
Refid	No	Current fileset is a reference to fileset of given ID

PatternSet

As you build up patterns in your fileset elements (and in others), there is a danger that you will begin to repeat groups of exclude and include elements. In my previous example, I defined patterns for test files and regular code files. I may add to these over time (perhaps I wish to include .conf and .inc extensions to my definition of code files). If I define other fileset elements that also use these patterns, I will be forced to make any adjustments across all relevant fileset elements.

You can overcome this problem by grouping patterns into patternset elements. The patternset element groups include and exclude elements so that they can be referenced later from within other types. Here I extract the include and exclude elements from my fileset example and add them to patternset elements:

```
<patternset id="inc_code">
    <include name="**/*.php" />
    <include name="**/*.inc" />
    <include name="**/*.conf" />
</patternset>

<patternset id="exc_test">
    <exclude name="**/*_test.php" />
    <exclude name="**/*Test.php" />
</patternset>
```

I create two patternset elements, setting their id attributes to inc_code and exc_test respectively. inc_code contains the include elements for including code files, and exc_test contains the exclude files for excluding test files. I can now reference these patternset elements within a fileset:

```
<fileset dir="src/lib" id="srclib">
    <patternset refid="inc_code" />
    <patternset refid="exc_test" />
</fileset>
```

To reference an existing patternset, you must use another patternset element. The second element must set a single attribute: refid. The refid attribute should refer to the id of the patternset element you wish to use in the current context. In this way, I can reuse patternset elements:

```
<fileset dir="src/views" id="srcviews">
    <patternset refid="inc_code" />
</fileset>
```

Any changes I make to the inc_code patternset will automatically update any types that use it. As with FileSet, you can place exclude rules either in an excludes attribute or a set of exclude subelements. The same is true of include rules.

Some patternset element attributes are summarized in Table 19–4.

Table 19–4. *Some Attributes of the patternset Element*

Attribute	Required	Description
Id	No	A unique handle for referring to the element
Excludes	No	A list of patterns for exclusion
Includes	No	A list of patterns for inclusion
Refid	No	Current patternset is a reference to patternset of given ID

FilterChain

The types that I have encountered so far have provided mechanisms for selecting sets of files. FilterChain, by contrast, provides a flexible mechanism for transforming the contents of text files.

In common with all types, defining a filterchain element does not in itself cause any changes to take place. The element and its children must first be associated with a task—that is, an element that tells Phing to take a course of action. I will return to tasks a little later.

A filterchain element groups any number of filters together. Filters operate on files like a pipeline—the first alters its file and passes its results on to the second, which makes its own alterations, and so on. By combining multiple filters in a filterchain element, you can effect flexible transformations.

Here I dive straight in and create a filterchain that removes PHP comments from any text passed to it:

```
<filterchain>
    <stripphpcomments />
</filterchain>
```

The StripPhpComments task does just what the name suggests. If you have provided detailed API documentation in your source code, you may have made life easy for developers, but you have also added a lot of dead weight to your project. Since all the work that matters takes place within your source directories, there is no reason why you should not strip out comments on installation.

■**Note** If you use a build tool for your projects, ensure that no one makes changes in the installed code. The installer will copy over any altered files, and the changes will be lost. I have seen it happen.

Let's sneak a peek of the next section and place the `filterchain` element in a task:

```
<target name="main">
    <copy todir="build/lib">
        <fileset refid="srclib"/>
        <filterchain>
            <stripphpcomments />
        </filterchain>
    </copy>
</target>
```

The Copy task is probably the one you get most use out of. It copies files from place to place. As you can see, I define the destination directory in the `todir` attribute. The source of the files is defined by the `fileset` element I created in the previous section. Then comes the `filterchain` element. Any file copied by the Copy task will have this transformation applied to it.

Phing supports filters for many operations including stripping new lines (StripLineBreaks) and replacing tabs with spaces (TabToSpaces). There is even an XsltFilter for applying XSLT transformations to source files! Perhaps the most commonly used filter, though, is ReplaceTokens. This allows you to swap tokens in your source code for properties defined in your build file, pulled from environment variables, or passed in on the command line. This is very useful for customizing an installation. It's a good idea to centralize your tokens into a central configuration file for easy overview of the variable aspects of your project.

ReplaceTokens optionally accepts two attributes, `begintoken` and `endtoken`. You can use these to define the characters that delineate token boundaries. If you omit these, Phing will assume the default character of @. In order to recognize and replace tokens, you must add `token` elements to the `replacetokens` element. Now to add a `replacetokens` element to my example:

```
<copy todir="build/lib">
        <fileset refid="srclib"/>
        <filterchain>
            <stripphpcomments />
            <replacetokens>
                <token key="dbname" value="${dbname}" />
                <token key="dbhost" value="${dbhost}" />
                <token key="dbpass" value="${dbpass}" />
            </replacetokens>
        </filterchain>
    </copy>
```

As you can see, token elements require key and value attributes. Let's see the effect of running this task with its transformations on a file in my project. The original file lives in a source directory, `src/lib/Config.php`:

```
/**
 * Quick and dirty Conf class
**/
class Config {
    public $dbname ="@dbname@";
    public $dbpass ="@dbpass@";
    public $dbhost ="@dbhost@";
}
```

Running my main target containing the Copy task defined previously gives the following output:

```
$ phing
```

```
Buildfile: /home/bob/working/megaquiz/build.xml
```

```
megaquiz > main:
```

```
    [copy] Copying 8 files to /home/bob/working/megaquiz/build/lib
[filter:ReplaceTokens] Replaced "@dbname@" with "megaquiz"
[filter:ReplaceTokens] Replaced "@dbpass@" with "default"
[filter:ReplaceTokens] Replaced "@dbhost@" with "localhost"
```

```
BUILD FINISHED
```

```
Total time: 0.1413 seconds
```

The original file is untouched, of course, but thanks to the Copy task, it has been reproduced at build/lib/Config.php:

```
class Config {
    public $dbname ="megaquiz";
    public $dbpass ="default";
    public $dbhost ="localhost";
}
```

Not only has the comment been removed, but the tokens have been replaced with their property equivalents.

Tasks

Tasks are the elements in a build file that get things done. You won't achieve much without using a task, which is why I have cheated and used a couple already. I'll reintroduce these.

Echo

The Echo task is perfect for the obligatory "Hello World" example. In the real world, you can use it to tell the user what you are about to do or what you have done. You can also sanity-check your build process by displaying the values of properties. As you have seen, any text placed within the opening and closing tags of an echo element will be printed to the browser:

```
<echo>The pass is '${dbpass}', shhh!</echo>
```

Alternatively, you can add the output message to a msg attribute:

```
<echo msg="The pass is '${dbpass}', shhh!" />
```

This will have the identical effect of printing the following to standard output:

```
[echo] The pass is 'default', shhh!
```

Copy

Copying is really what installation is all about. Typically, you will create one target that copies files from your source directories and assembles them in a temporary build directory. You will then have another target that copies the assembled (and transformed) files to their output locations. Breaking the installation into separate build and install phases is not absolutely necessary, but it does mean that you can check the results of the initial build before committing to overwriting production code. You can also change a property and install again to a different location without the need to run a potentially expensive copy/replace phase again.

At its simplest, the Copy task allows you to specify a source file and a destination directory or file:

```
<copy file="src/lib/Config.php" todir="build/conf" />
```

As you can see, I specify the source file using the `file` attribute. You may be familiar already with the `todir` attribute, which is used to specify the target directory. If the target directory does not exist, Phing will create it for you.

If you need to specify a target file, rather than a containing directory, you can use the `tofile` attribute instead of `todir`.

```
<copy file="src/lib/Config.php" tofile="build/conf/myConfig.php" />
```

Once again, the `build/conf` directory is created if necessary, but this time, `Config.php` is renamed to `myConfig.php`.

As you have seen, to copy more than one file at a time, you need to add a `fileset` element to copy:

```
<copy todir="build/lib">
    <fileset refid="srclib"/>
</copy>
```

The source files are defined by the `srclib` `fileset` element, so all you have to set in `copy` is the `todir` attribute.

Phing is smart enough to test whether or not your source file has been changed since the target file was created. If no change has been made, then Phing will not copy. This means that you can build many times and only the files that have changed in the meantime will be installed. This is fine, as long as other things are not likely to change. If a file is transformed according to the configuration of a `replacetokens` element, for example, you may want to ensure that the file is transformed every time that the Copy task is invoked. You can do this by setting an `overwrite` attribute:

```
<copy todir="build/lib" overwrite="yes">
    <fileset refid="srclib"/>
    <filterchain>
        <stripphpcomments />
        <replacetokens>
            <token key="dbpass" value="${dbpass}" />
        </replacetokens>
    </filterchain>
</copy>
```

Now whenever copy is run, the files matched by the `fileset` element are replaced whether or not the source has been recently updated.

You can see the copy element summarized in Table 19–5.

Table 19–5. *The Attributes of the copy Element*

Attribute	Required	Description	Default Value
Todir	Yes (if tofile not present)	Directory to copy into.	None
Tofile	Yes (if todir not present)	The file to copy to.	None
File	No	Source file.	None
Tstamp	No	Match the timestamp of any file overwritten (it will appear unaltered).	false
includeemptydirs	No	Copy empty directories over.	FALSE
Mode	No	Set the (octal) mode	755
Overwrite	No	Overwrite target if it already exists.	no

Input

You have seen that the echo element is used to send output to the user. To gather input *from* the user, I have used separate methods involving the command line and an environment variable. These mechanisms are neither very structured nor interactive, however.

■**Note** One reason for allowing users to set values at build time is to allow for flexibility from build environment to build environment. In the case of database passwords, another benefit is that this sensitive data is not enshrined in the build file itself. Of course, once the build has been run, the password will be saved into a source file, so it is up to the developer to ensure the security of his system!

The input element allows you to output a prompt message. Phing then awaits user input and assigns it to a property. Here it is in action:

```
<target name="setpass" unless="dbpass">
    <input message="You don't seem to have set a db password"
           propertyName="dbpass"
           defaultValue="default"
           promptChar=" >" />
</target>
```

```
<target name="main" depends="setpass">
    <echo>pass:      ${dbpass}</echo>
</target>
```

Once again, I have a default target: main. This depends on another target, setpass, which is responsible for ensuring that the dbpass property is populated. To this end, I use the target element's unless attribute, which ensures that it will not run if dbpass is already set.

The setpass target consists of a single input task element. An input element can have a message attribute, which should contain a prompt for the user. The propertyName attribute is required and defines the property to be populated by user input. If the user presses Enter at the prompt without setting a value, the property is given a fallback value if the defaultValue attribute is set. Finally, you can customize the prompt character using the promptChar attribute— this provides a visual cue for the user to input data. Let's run Phing using the previous targets:

$ phing
```
Buildfile: /home/bob/working/megaquiz/build.xml

megaquiz > setpass:

You don't seem to have set a db password [default] > mypass

megaquiz > main:

    [echo] pass:      mypass

BUILD FINISHED

Total time: 6.0322 seconds
```

The input element is summarized in Table 19–6.

Table 19–6. *The Attributes of the input Element*

Attribute	Required	Description
propertyName	Yes	The property to populate with user input.
Message	No	The prompt message.
defaultValue	No	A value to assign to the property if the user does not provide input.
validArgs	No	A list of acceptable input values separated by commas. If the user inputs a value that is not on this list Phing will re-present the prompt.
promptChar	No	A visual cue that the user should provide input.

Delete

Installation is generally about creating, copying, and transforming files. Deletion has its place as well, though. This is particularly the case when you wish to perform a clean install. As I have already discussed, files are generally only copied from source to destination for source files that have changed since the last build. By deleting a build directory, you ensure that the full compilation process will take place.

Here I delete a directory:

```
<target name="clean">
    <delete dir="build" />
</target>
```

When I run phing with the argument clean (the name of the target), my delete task element is invoked. Here's Phing's output:

```
$ phing clean
Buildfile: /home/bob/working/megaquiz/build.xml

megaquiz > clean:
    [delete] Deleting directory /home/bob/working/megaquiz/build

BUILD FINISHED
```

The delete element accepts an attribute, file, which can be used to point to a particular file. Alternatively, you can fine-tune your deletions by adding a fileset subelement to delete.

Summary

Serious development rarely happens all in one place. A codebase needs to be separated from its installation, so that work in progress does not pollute production code that needs to remain functional at all times. Version control allows developers to check out a project and work on it in their own space. This requires that they should be able to configure the project easily for their environments. Finally, and perhaps most importantly, the customer (even if the customer is yourself in a year's time, when you've forgotten the ins and outs of your code) should be able to install your project after a glance at a Read Me file.

In this chapter, I have covered some of the basics of Phing, a fantastic tool, which brings much of the functionality of Apache Ant to the PHP world. I have only scratched the surface of Phing's capabilities. Nevertheless, once you are up and running with the targets, tasks, types, and properties discussed here, you'll find it easy to bolt on new elements for advanced features, like creating tar/gzipped distributions, automatically generating PEAR package installations, and running PHP code directly from the build file.

If Phing does not satisfy all your build needs, you will discover that, like Ant, it is designed to be extensible—get out there and build your own tasks! Even if you don't add to Phing, you should take some time out to examine the source code. Phing is written entirely in object-oriented PHP, and its code is chock full of design examples.

■ ■ ■

CHAPTER 20

Continuous Integration

In previous chapters, you've seen a plethora of tools that are designed to support a well-managed project. Unit testing, documentation, build, and version control are all fantastically useful. But tools, and testing in particular, can be bothersome.

Even if your tests only take a few minutes to run, you're often too focused on coding to bother with them. Not only that, but you have clients and colleagues waiting for new features. The temptation to keep on coding is always there. But bugs are much easier to fix close to the time they are hatched. That's because you're more likely to know which change caused the problem, and better able to come up with a quick fix.

In this chapter, I introduce Continuous Integration, a practice that automates test and build, and brings together the tools and techniques you've encountered in recent chapters.

This chapter will cover

- Defining Continuous Integration

- Preparing a project for CI

- Looking at CruiseControl: a CI server

- Specializing CruiseControl for PHP with phpUnderControl

- Customizing CruiseControl

What Is Continuous Integration?

In the bad old days, integration was something you did after you'd finished the fun stuff. It was also the stage at which you realized how much work you still had to do. Integration is the process by which all the parts of your project are bundled up into packages that can be shipped and deployed. It's not glamorous, and it's actually hard.

Integration is tied up also with QA. You can't ship a product if it isn't fit for purpose. That means tests. Lots of tests. If you haven't been testing much prior to the integration stage, it probably also means nasty surprises. Lots of them.

You know from Chapter 18 that it's best practice to test early and often. You know from Chapters 15 and 19 that you should design with deployment in mind right from the start. Most of us accept that this is the ideal, but how often does the reality match up?

If you practice test-oriented development (a term I prefer to test-first development, because it better reflects the reality of most good projects I've seen), then the writing of tests is less hard than you might think. After all, you write tests as you code anyway. Every time you develop a component, you create code fragments, perhaps at the bottom of the class file, that instantiate objects, call their methods. If you gather up those throwaway scraps of code, written to put your component through its paces during development, you've got yourself a test case. Stick them into a class and add them to your suite.

Oddly, it's often the *running* of tests that people avoid. Over time, tests take longer to run. Failures related to known issues creep in, making it hard to diagnose new problems. Also, you suspect someone else committed code that broke the tests, and you don't have time to hold up your own work while you fix issues that are someone else's fault. Better to run a couple of tests related to your work than the whole suite.

Failing to run tests, and therefore to fix the problems they could reveal, makes issues harder and harder to address. The biggest overhead in hunting for bugs is usually the diagnosis and not the cure. Very often, a fix can be applied in a matter of minutes, set against perhaps hours searching for the reason a test failed. If a test fails within minutes or hours of a commit, though, you're more likely to know where to look for the problem.

Software build suffers from a similar problem. If you don't install your project often, you're likely to find that, while everything runs fine on your development box, an installed instance falls over with an obscure error message. The longer you've gone between builds, the more obscure the reason for the failure will likely be to you.

It's often something simple: an undeclared dependency upon a library on your system, or some class files you failed to check in. Easy to fix if you're on hand. But what if a build failure occurs when you're out the office, though? Whichever unlucky team member gets the job of building and releasing the project won't know about your set up, and won't have easy access to those missing files.

Integration issues are magnified by the number of people involved in a project. You may like and respect all your team members, but we all know that they are much more likely than you are to leave tests unrun. And then they commit a week's work of development at 4 p.m. on Friday, just as you're about to declare the project good to go for a release.

Continuous Integration (CI) reduces some of these problems by automating the build and test process.

CI is both a set of practices and tools. As a practice, it requires frequent commits of project code (at least daily). With each commit, tests should be run and any packages should be built. You've already seen some of the tools required for CI, in particular PHPUnit and PEAR. Individual tools aren't enough, though. A higher-level system is required to coordinate and automate the process.

Without the higher system, a CI server, it's likely that the practice of CI will simply succumb to our natural tendency to skip the chores. After all, we'd rather be coding.

Having a system like this in place has three clear benefits. Firstly, your project gets built, and tested frequently. That's the ultimate aim and good of CI. That it's automated, though, adds two further dimensions. The test and build happens in a different thread to that of development. It happens behind the scenes, and doesn't require that you stop work to run tests. Also, as with testing, CI encourages good design. In order for it to be possible to automate installation in a remote location, you're forced to consider ease of installation from the start.

I don't know how many times I've come across projects where the installation procedure was an arcane secret known only to a few developers. "You mean you didn't set up the URL rewriting?" asks one old hand with barely concealed contempt. "Honestly, the rewrite rules *are* in the Wiki, you know. Just paste them into the Apache config file."

Developing with CI in mind means making systems easier to test and install. This might mean a little more work upfront, but it makes our lives easier down the line. Much easier.

So, to start off, I'm going to lay down some of that expensive groundwork. In fact, you'll find that in most of the sections to come, you've encountered these preparatory steps already.

Preparing a Project for CI

First of all, of course, I need a project to integrate continuously. Now, I'm a lazy soul, so I'll look for some code that comes with tests already written. The obvious candidate is the project I created in

Chapter 18 to illustrate PHPUnit. I'm going to name it userthing, because it's a *thing*, with a User object in it.

First of all, here is a breakdown of my project directory. See Figure 20–1.

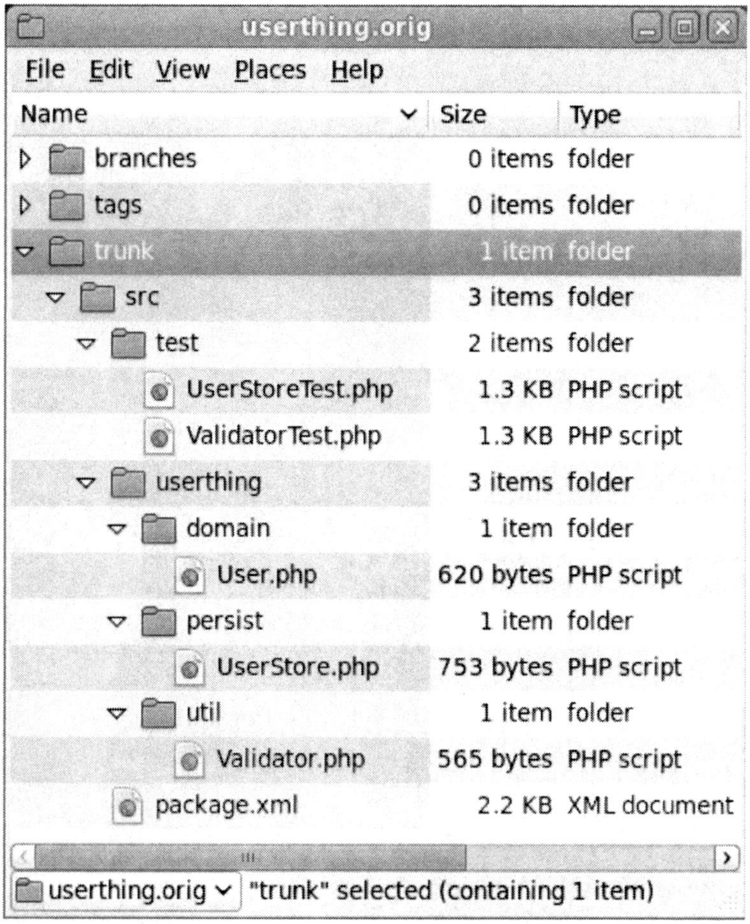

Figure 20–1. *Part of a sample project to illustrate CI*

As you can see, I've tidied up the structure a little, adding some package directories. Within the code, I've supported the package structure with the use of namespaces.

Now that I have a project, I should add it to a version control system.

CI and Version Control

Version control is essential for CI. A CI system needs to acquire the most recent version of a project without human intervention (at least once things have been set up).

You may have noticed that I moved the code for userthing into a directory named trunk. That's because I'm going to import the project into Subversion, and the branches, tags and trunk directories are a useful convention in that system.

Here's the import:

```
$ svn import userthing.orig/ file:///var/local/svn/userthing -m'first import'
```

And here's the checkout.

```
$ svn checkout file:///var/local/svn/userthing/trunk userthing
```

I covered Subversion in more detail in Chapter 17.

Now that I have the a local version of my project, I'm going to change my working directory to src/ in order to try out the various tools that my CI implementation will require.

```
$ cd userthing/src
```

Unit Tests

Unit tests are the key to continuous integration. It's no good successfully building a project that contains broken code. I covered unit testing with PHPUnit in Chapter 18. If you're reading out of order, though, you'll want to install this invaluable tool before proceeding.

```
$ pear channel-discover pear.phpunit.de
$ pear install phpunit
```

Also in Chapter 18 I wrote tests for a version of the userthing code I'll be working with in this chapter. Here I run them once again, to make sure my reorganization has not broken anything new.

```
$ phpunit test
```

```
PHPUnit 3.4.11 by Sebastian Bergmann.

.....
Time: 0 seconds, Memory: 4.50Mb
OK (5 tests, 6 assertions)
```

As you can see, I referenced the filesystem to invoke my tests. I passed the test directory as an argument to PHPUnit, and it automatically sought out my test files. However, one of the CI tools you'll encounter later, phpUnderControl, prefers that you reference a single class in order to run tests. To support this requirement, I can add a test suite class. Here is UserTests.php:

```php
require_once 'PHPUnit/Framework.php';
require_once 'test/UserStoreTest.php';
require_once 'test/ValidatorTest.php';


class UserTests {

    public static function suite() {
        $suite = new PHPUnit_Framework_TestSuite();
        $suite->addTestSuite('UserStoreTest');
        $suite->addTestSuite('ValidatorTest');
```

```
        return $suite;
    }
}
```

▓**Note** In in this case I've kept my test classes in the global namespace. Where tests have a close or one to one relationship to the components they test, however, it's often neater to place each test class in the same namespace as its target, and in a parallel directory structure. That way you can tell at a glance the relationship between a test and its subject both from the test's namespace and the location of its file.

The `PHPUnit_Framework_TestSuite` class allows you to collect individual test cases into a suite. Here's how I can call this from the command line:

```
$ phpunit test/UserTests
```

```
PHPUnit 3.4.11 by Sebastian Bergmann.
.....
Time: 1 second, Memory: 4.50Mb
OK (5 tests, 6 assertions)
```

Documentation

Transparency is one of the principles of CI. When you're looking at a build in a Continuous Integration environment, therefore, it's important to be able to check that the documentation is up to date, and covers the most recent classes and methods. I examined phpDocumentor in Chapter 16, so I've already run an install like this.

```
pear upgrade PhpDocumentor
```

I'd better run the tool just to be sure:

```
$ mkdir docs
$ phpdoc --directory userthing --target docs/
```

That generates some pretty bare documentation. Once that's published on a CI server, I'm sure to be shamed into writing some real inline documentation.

Code Coverage

It's no good relying on tests if they don't apply to the code you have written. PHPUnit includes the ability to report on code coverage. Here's an extract from PHPUnit's usage information.

```
--coverage-html <dir>    Generate code coverage report in HTML format.
--coverage-clover <file> Write code coverage data in Clover XML format.
--coverage-source <dir>  Write code coverage / source data in XML format.
```

In order to use this feature you must have the Xdebug extension installed. You can find more about this at `http://pecl.php.net/package/Xdebug` (installation information at `http://xdebug.org/docs/install`). You may also be able to install directly using your Linux distribution's package management system. This should work for you in Fedora 12, for example:

```
$ yum install php-pecl-xdebug
```

Here I run PHPUnit with code coverage enabled.

```
$ mkdir /tmp/coverage
$ phpunit --coverage-html /tmp/coverage test
```

```
PHPUnit 3.4.11 by Sebastian Bergmann.
.....
Time: 0 seconds, Memory: 5.25Mb
OK (5 tests, 6 assertions)
Generating code coverage report, this may take a moment.
```

Now you can see the report in your browser. See Figure 20–2.

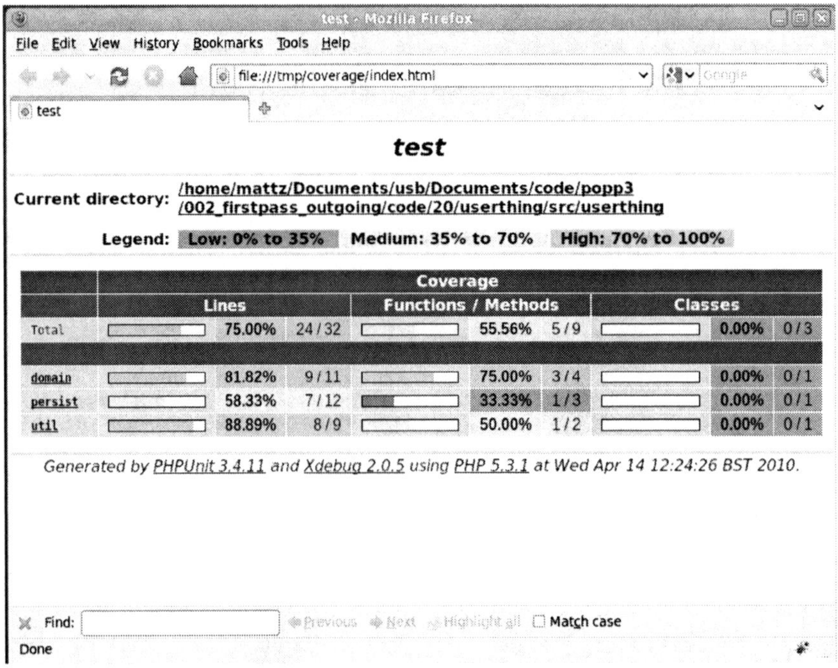

Figure 20–2. *The code coverage report*

It's important to note that achieving full coverage is not the same as adequately testing a system. On the other hand, it's good to know about any gaps in your tests. As you can see from Figure 20–2, I've still got some work to do.

Coding Standards

I can argue all day about the best place to put a brace, whether to indent with tabs or spaces, how to name a private property variable. Wouldn't it be nice if I could enforce my prejudices with a tool? Thanks to PHP_CodeSniffer I can. CodeSniffer can apply one of a set of coding standards to a project and generate a report, telling you just how bad your style is.

That might sound like a massive pain in the rear end. In fact, it can be just that. But there are sensible non-passive aggressive uses for a tool like this. I'll get to these, but first I'll put the tool through its paces. Installation first:

```
$ sudo pear install PHP_CodeSniffer
```

Now I'm going to apply the Zend coding standard to my code:

```
$ phpcs --standard=Zend userthing/persist/UserStore.php
```

```
FILE: ...userthing/src/userthing/persist/UserStore.php
--------------------------------------------------------------------------------
FOUND 10 ERROR(S) AND 0 WARNING(S) AFFECTING 8 LINE(S)
--------------------------------------------------------------------------------
  6 | ERROR | Opening brace of a class must be on the line after the definition
  7 | ERROR | Private member variable "users" must contain a leading underscore
  9 | ERROR | Opening brace should be on a new line
 13 | ERROR | Multi-line function call not indented correctly; expected 12
    |       | spaces but found 16
 ...
```

Clearly, I'd have to adjust my style to submit code to Zend!

It makes sense however, for a team to define coding guidelines. In fact, the decision as to *which* set of rules you choose is probably less important than the decision to abide by a common standard in the first place. If a codebase is consistent, then it's easier to read, and therefore easier to work with. Naming conventions, for example, can help to clarify the purpose of variables or properties.

Coding conventions can play a role in reducing risky or bug-prone code as well.

This is a dangerous area, though. Some style decisions are highly subjective, and people can be disproportionately defensive about their way of doing things. CodeSniffer allows you to define your own rules, so I suggest that you get buy in from your team on a set of rules so that no one feels that their coding life has become a coding nightmare.

Another benefit of an automated tool is its impersonal nature. If your team does decide to impose a set of coding conventions, it's arguably better having a humorless script correcting your style, than a humorless co-worker doing the same thing.

PHP Code Browser

You may be wedded to your exciting IDE or, like me, you might prefer to edit with vi. Either way, when you're looking at a report that tells you your style is lousy, or, more important, trying to understand a failed test, it's good to be able to pull up the code right away. The PHP_CodeBrowser package lets you do just that.

This is bleeding-edge code, so to install you need to tell PEAR that you're ready to accept an alpha release.

```
$ sudo pear config-set preferred_state alpha
```

```
config-set succeeded
```

Then you can install.

```
$ pear install --alldeps phpunit/PHP_CodeBrowser
```

```
downloading PHP_CodeBrowser-0.1.2.tgz ...
Starting to download PHP_CodeBrowser-0.1.2.tgz (76,125 bytes)
.................done: 76,125 bytes
install ok: channel://pear.phpunit.de/PHP_CodeBrowser-0.1.2
```

If all goes well, you'll have a command line tool called phpcb available. I'm going to point it at my source code. phpcb likes to have access to log files generated by PHPUnit, so first I'll run the tests first.

```
$ mkdir log
$ phpunit --log-junit log/log.xml test/
```

Now I can run phpcb:

```
$ mkdir output
$ phpcb --log log --output output/ --source userthing/
```

This writes files to the output directory. Figure 20–3 shows the output, which you can get by opening the generated index.html file in a browser.

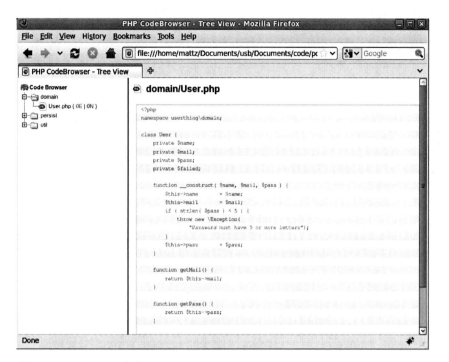

Figure 20–3. PHP code browser

Build

While it's possible to assess code in place, you should all also check that you can build and deploy a package. To that end, I've included a package.xml file in my package. Here I test the build and install stages.

```
$ pear package
```

```
Analyzing userthing/domain/User.php
Analyzing userthing/util/Validator.php
Analyzing userthing/persist/UserStore.php
Warning: in UserStore.php: class "UserStore" not prefixed with package name "userthing"
Warning: in Validator.php: class "Validator" not prefixed with package name "userthing"
Warning: in User.php: class "User" not prefixed with package name "userthing"
Warning: Channel validator warning: field "date" - Release Date "2010-03-07" is not today
Package userthing-1.2.1.tgz done
Tag the released code with `pear svntag package.xml'
(or set the SVN tag userthing-1.2.1 by hand)
```

Some of those warnings are a little out of date, since my classes use namespaces rather than the package underscore convention. Nevertheless, I have a successful build. Now to deploy.

```
$ pear install --force userthing-1.2.1.tgz
```

```
install ok: channel://pear.appulsus.com/userthing-1.2.1
```

So I have a lot of useful tools I can use to monitor my project. Of course, left to myself I'd soon lose interest in running them. In fact, I'd probably revert to the old idea of an integration phase, and pull out the tools only when I'm close to a release, by which time their effectiveness as early warning systems will be irrelevant. What I need is a CI server to run the tools for me.

CruiseControl and phpUnderControl

CruiseControl is a Continuous Integration server written in Java. It was released by ThoughtWorks (the company that employs Martin Fowler) in 2001. Version 2.0, a complete rewrite was released in late 2002.

According to directives in a configuration file (config.xml) CruiseControl kicks off a build loop for the projects it manages. For each project this involves any number of steps, which are defined in an Ant build file (remember, Ant is the original Java tool upon which Phing is based). Once the build has been run, CruiseControl, again according to configuration, can invoke tools to build reports.

The results of a build are made available in a Web application, which is the public face of CruiseControl.

We could configure CruiseControl to run any tools we want, and to generate reports for us, after all CruiseControl is designed to glue any number of test and build systems together. It would take a fair amount of work though. I'm sure you'd like something off the peg that already integrates some of the PHP tools you've already seen. phpUnderControl provides exactly that functionality. It customizes CruiseControl so that tools like PHPUnit and CodeSniffer are run, and their reports integrated into the Web interface.

Before I can use phpUnderControl, though, I must install CruiseControl.

■**Note** Why CruiseControl? CruiseControl is well established, and it has an excellent pedigree having been developed by ThoughtWorks. It's free and open source. Tools that support integration with PHP are under active development. The fact that many of these are hosted at phpunit.de bodes well for continuing support and interoperability. There are many CI server solutions out there, however. If you're looking for a native PHP implementation, you should definitely take a look at Xinc (http://code.google.com/p/xinc/).

Installing CruiseControl

CruiseControl is a Java system, so you will need to have Java installed. How you go about this will vary from system to system. On a Fedora distribution you might do something like

```
yum install java-1.6.0-openjdk-devel
```

In a Debian system this should do the job

```
sudo apt-get install sun-java6-jdk
```

Otherwise, you can get Java directly from www.java.com.

Once you've confirmed that you have java (the java website will tell you if you haven't), you need to acquire CruiseControl. You can download the latest version at http://cruisecontrol.sourceforge.net/download.html. You should end up with an archive named something like `cruisecontrol-bin-2.8.3.zip`. Now you can move the directory somewhere central, and launch the CruiseControl script.

```
$ unzip cruisecontrol-bin-2.8.3.zip
$ mv cruisecontrol-bin-2.8.3 /usr/local/cruisecontrol

$ cd /usr/local/cruisecontrol/
$ export JAVA_HOME=/usr/lib/jvm/java-1.6.0-openjdk/
$ ./cruisecontrol.sh
```

Notice that export line. Like many Java applications CruiseControl needs to know where your java executable resides. You can see where that is on my system. Your system may differ. You can try something like

```
ls -al `which java`
```

or

```
locate javac | grep bin
```

to find the directory you should use for JAVA_HOME. The java and javac (that's the java compiler) binaries will usually be found in a directory named bin. You should include the parent directory, and not bin itself, in JAVA_HOME.

■**Note** Once you've got your proof of concept up and running, you may want ensure that CruiseControl starts up automatically when you boot your integration server. An excellent blog entry by Felix De Vliegher at http://felix.phpbelgium.be/blog/2009/02/07/setting-up-phpundercontrol/ includes a start-up script for CruiseControl.

If all goes well, you should see some text scroll by, but that's about all. Once you've recovered from the sense of anti-climax, you can really find out whether you're ready to proceed by firing up your browser and visiting http://localhost:8080/dashboard. You should see something like the screen in Figure 20–4.

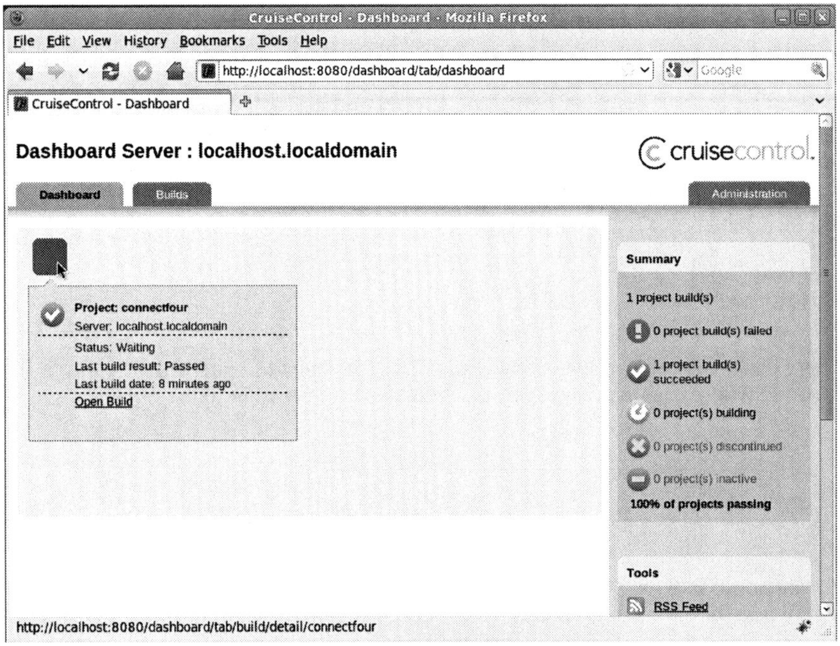

Figure 20–4. *The CruiseControl Dashboard screen*

■**Note** I'm running CruiseControl locally on my development box, so my URLs all point to localhost. You can, of course, use a different host for your CI Server.

Installing phpUnderControl

Like CruiseControl, phpUnderControl exists to marshal other tools. So you need to make sure that you have some prerequisites in place. I've already set up some of the tools this chapter. There's one more to install though:

```
$ pear channel-discover components.ez.no
$ pear install -a ezc/Graph
```

The ezcGraph package is used to generate useful status information. Now that it's in place, I can install phpUnderControl itself.

```
$ pear config-set preferred_state beta
$ pear channel-discover pear.phpunit.de
$ pear install --alldeps phpunit/phpUnderControl
```

As you can see, phpUnderControl remains beta software at the time of this writing. Once I have it installed, I should have access to a command line tool: phpuc. You can check this, with the usage flag:

```
$ phpuc --usage
```

```
Usage: phpuc.php <command> <options> <arguments>
For single command help type:
    phpuc.php <command> --help
Available commands:
  * clean          Removes old build artifacts and logs for a specified project.
  * delete         Deletes a CruiseControl project with all logs and artifacts.
  * example        Creates a small CruiseControl example.
  * graph          Generates the metric graphs with ezcGraph
  * install        Installs the CruiseControl patches.
  * merge-phpunit  Merges a set of PHPUnit logs into a single new file.
  * project        Creates a new CruiseControl project.
```

So, I've already installed the package onto my system. Now I need to amend the CruiseControl environment to support phpUnderControl. As you can see, phpuc provides a second installation step: a command named install.

■Note This two-part installation mechanism is a useful one. PEAR is good at getting library code, runnable scripts, and supporting data files in place. When it comes to complex installation for things like Web applications and database driven systems, it's often a good idea to provide a configurable installation command *as part of* your application. Of course, Phing would be a good choice for this secondary installation. Most users won't have Phing to hand though, so it can be better to build the installation logic into an application command.

```
$ phpuc install /usr/local/cruisecontrol/
```

Now to restart CruiseControl

```
$ cd /usr/local/cruisecontrol/
$ kill `cat cc.pid`
$ ./cruisecontrol.sh
```

CruiseControl stores its process id in a file called cc.pid. I use that to kill the current process, then I run the cruisecontrol.sh script to restart. Now, I can visit http://localhost:8080/cruisecontrol/ to confirm that CruiseControl had been rebranded. You can see the new interface in Figure 20–5.

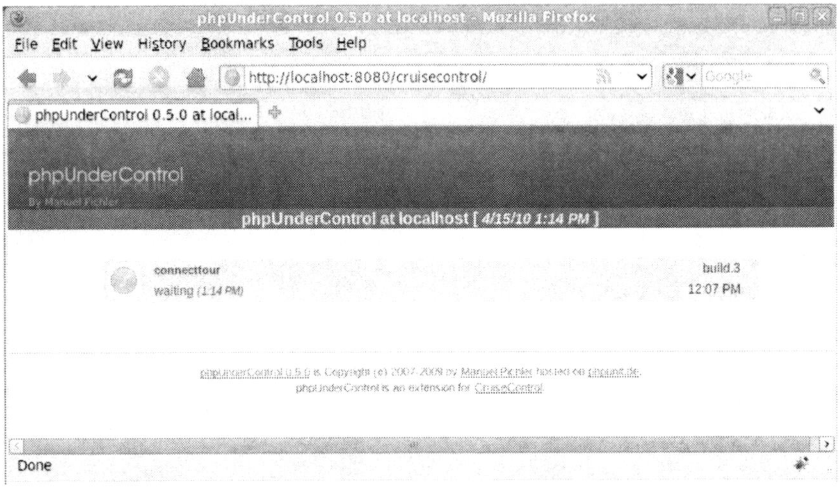

Figure 20–5. phpUnderControl

Now that I have phpUnderControl in place, somehow I need to get CruiseControl to acquire and build the userthing project.

Installing Your Project

I'm a coder. I love fiddling around with text editors. But, like many, I hate writing configuration files. So I'm lucky that phpuc provides me with a tool to generate the directories and configuration for my project.

■**Note** Remember I installed CruiseControl at /usr/local/cruisecontrol. All files and directories discussed in this section are relative to that location.

If I were to add userthing to CruiseControl manually, I'd start by editing a configuration file called config.xml, which can be found at the top level of the CruiseControl directory. In that file I'd tell CruiseControl that it should recognize the project, as well as telling it about some key locations, the build schedule. I'd set up some publishers that help to build reports.

Then I'd create a working directory called userthing within the projects directory. Probably the most important file within the userthing project directory is named build.xml. You encountered files with this name in Chapter 19. Phing is based on Ant, and Ant is the tool that CruiseControl uses to build its projects and to run any assessment tools. The syntax for Ant and Phing build files is identical.

There's quite a learning curve to setting up CruiseControl. There's an excellent reference to the config.xml file at http://cruisecontrol.sourceforge.net/main/configxml.html which documents 123 XML elements at the time of this writing. You'll likely use it when you start to delve deeper into CI. As useful as the documentation is, it might give you the impression that you won't be up and running with a build and test cycle any time soon.

phpuc comes to the rescue, though, with the project command. This creates the required files and directories, and amends any configuration files.

```
phpuc project --source-dir src \
--version-control svn \
--version-control-url file:///var/local/svn/userthing/trunk \
--test-dir test \
--test-case UserTests \
--test-file UserTests.php \
--coding-guideline Zend \
--project-name userthing \
/usr/local/cruisecontrol/
```

■**Note** If I were running CruiseControl on system remote from my version control repository, I'd also want to set the user and password options.

Much of this should be self-explanatory. CruiseControl will need access to the userthing source, so, through phpuc, I need to tell it I'm using Subversion, and provide it with the URL for the code. Then I tell it where to find the tests, the coding standard I wish to apply. To set things up, phpUnderControl needs to know where to find the cruisecontrol directory, so I provide the path. The output of the phpuc project command gives you a good idea of the work that needs to be done in order to pass on this information.

```
Performing project task.
    1. Creating project directory: projects/userthing
    2. Creating source directory:   projects/userthing/source
    3. Creating build directory:    projects/userthing/build
    4. Creating log directory:      projects/userthing/build/logs
    5. Creating build file:         projects/userthing/build.xml
    6. Creating backup of file:     config.xml.orig
    7. Searching ant directory
    8. Modifying project file:      config.xml
Performing checkout task.
    1. Checking out project.
    2. Preparing config.xml file.
    3. Preparing build.xml checkout target.
Performing PhpDocumentor task.
    1. Creating apidoc dir:  project/userthing/build/api
    2. Modifying build file: project/userthing/build.xml
    3. Modifying config file:          config.xml
Performing PHP_CodeSniffer task.
    1. Modifying build file: project/userthing/build.xml
Performing PHPUnit task.
    1. Creating coverage dir: project/userthing/build/coverage
    2. Modifying build file:  project/userthing/build.xml
    3. Modifying config file: config.xml
```

```
Performing PHP_CodeBrowser task.
   1. Creating browser dir: project/userthing/build/php-code-browser
   2. Modifying config file: config.xml
Performing ezcGraph task.
   1. Modifying config file: config.xml
```

phpuc helpfully tells you exactly what it's up to. As you can see it amends one or both of config.xml and build.xml for each of the tasks I want CruiseControl to run.

By the time you read this, running phpuc in this way might be enough to get you up and running. At the time of this writing though, there are a few issues that must first be addressed. phpUnderControl is a beta product, after all.

First of all phpuc writes an element to the config.xml file that CruiseControl 2.8.3 chokes on. If you find this line in config.xml:

```
<currentbuildstatuspublisher file="logs/${project.name}/buildstatus.txt"/>
```

and either comment it out, or delete it, you should avoid a fatal error.

Secondly, phpuc writes a call to itself into the main configuration file at config.xml. Here's the relevant section:

```
<project name="userthing" buildafterfailed="false">
  <!-- ... -->

  <publishers>
    <!-- ... -->

    <execute command="/usr/bin/phpuc graph logs/${project.name}
      artifacts/${project.name}"/>
  </publishers>

</project>
```

CruiseControl allows you to add your own publishers to provide custom reports for the user. Unfortunately, there is a bug with the phpuc graph command that, at the time of this writing, prevents the command from running. The workaround is to remove a file from the PEAR repository:

```
$ rm /usr/share/pear/phpUnderControl/Graph/Input/ClassComplexityInput.php
```

where /usr/share/pear is my PEAR directory. You can find yours with the command:

```
$ pear config-get php_dir
```

Since this problem may be fixed by now, you might skip this step, but bear it mind if the project metrics reports are not generated.

Lastly, I must make a change that is related to my setup, rather than to a problem with the phpuc command. I like to keep my source code in a subdirectory (named src/) within my project. That way I can add housekeeping scripts, documentation, and other miscellanea at the top level. phpuc asks me to specify the test directory in my command line arguments, but it will construct a call from the root of my source directory. So if I tell phpuc that my test directory is to be found at src/test/ and that my test suite is in UserTests.php, it will construct a call to src/test/UserTest.php.

Because my tests are designed to be run *from* the src/ directory, this will fail. All my require statements use paths that are relative to src/ as a starting point, and not its parent directory. Showing you how to change this also gives us the opportunity to take a quick look at the build.xml file.

■**Note** A reminder of the CruiseControl environment: `config.xml` sits at the top level and handles application wide configuration. Project specific build targets live in an Ant file at `projects/userthing/build.xml`. phpUnderControl created the `userthing` directory and the build file on my behalf when I ran the `phpuc project` command.

Here's the phpunit task, and some context.

```xml
<?xml version="1.0" encoding="UTF-8"?>

<project name="userthing" default="build" basedir=".">

  <target name="build" depends="checkout,php-documentor,php-codesniffer,phpunit"/>
  <!-- ... -->

  <target name="phpunit">

    <exec executable="phpunit" dir="${basedir}/source" failonerror="on">

      <arg line=" --log-junit ${basedir}/build/logs/phpunit.xml
                  --coverage-clover ${basedir}/build/logs/phpunit.coverage.xml
                  --coverage-html ${basedir}/build/coverage UserTests test/UserTests.php"/>
    </exec>
  </target>

</project>
```

As you can see, this is just the same as a Phing document. It's divided into `target` elements, which relate to one another via their `depends` attributes. The phpunit task would fail as it stands. It's calling `test/UserTest.php`, but from the context of `${basedir}/source`. In order to make this work, all I need do is amend the exec element, so that it runs from `${basedir}/source/src`.

```xml
<exec executable="phpunit" dir="${basedir}/source/src" failonerror="on">
```

Now, I'm about ready to run my project.

Running phpUnderControl / CruiseControl

First of all I need to restart CruiseControl:

```
$ kill `cat cc.pid`
$ ./cruisecontrol.sh
```

Now, I can see the results of my initial build by visiting `http://localhost:8080/cruisecontrol`. The control panel should show that the `userthing` project has been added, and indicate the outcome of the build. Clicking on the project name will call up the Overview screen.

You can see this screen in Figure 20–6.

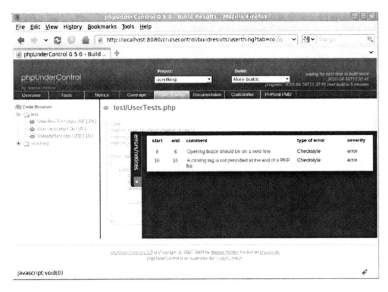

Figure 20–6. *The Overview screen*

As you can see, the build went well, although CodeSniffer is complaining about my style. I can get the full whine by clicking on the `CodeSniffer` tab, or I can see the complaints in the context of the code itself by clicking on `Code Browser`. Figure 20–7 shows the code browser with the contextual `errors/notices` tab open.

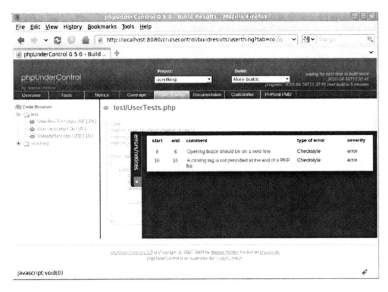

Figure 20–7. *The code browser showing "Errors"*

Most of the tools I tested earlier are available inline through these tabs. I can check code coverage, examine test results, and browse documentation. And I can be secure that CruiseControl will regularly update the project and run a build (every five minutes by default). I can see an overview by clicking on the `Metrics` tab. You can see this screen in Figure 20–8.

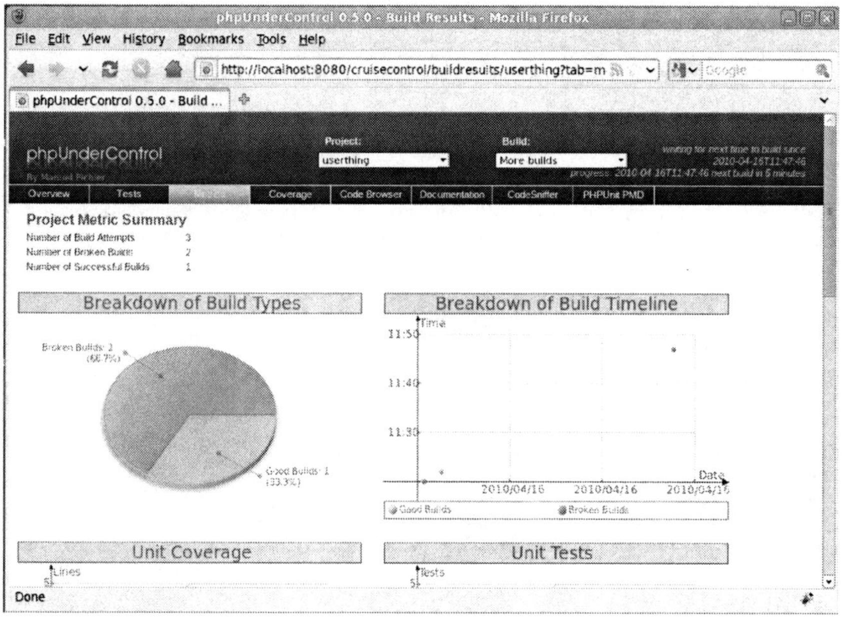

Figure 20–8. *The Metrics screen*

Test Failures

So far everything seems to be going well, even if userthing won't be finding its way into the Zend codebase any time soon. But tests succeed when they fail, so I'd better break something to make sure that CruiseControl reports on it.

Here is a part of a class named `Validate` in the namespace `userthing\util`:

```php
public function validateUser( $mail, $pass ) {
    // make it always fail!
    return false;

    $user = $this->store->getUser( $mail );
    if ( is_null( $user ) ) {
        return null;
    }

    if ( $user->getPass() == $pass ) {
        return true;
    }
}
```

```
        $this->store->notifyPasswordFailure( $mail );
        return false;
}
```

See how I've sabotaged the method? As it now stands validateUser() will always return false. Here's the test that should choke on that. It's in test/ValidatorTest.php:

```
public function testValidate_CorrectPass() {
    $this->assertTrue(
        $this->validator->validateUser( "bob@example.com", "12345" ),
        "Expecting successful validation"
        );
}
```

Having made my change, all I need do is commit, and wait. Sure enough, before long, my status page highlights userthing in an alarming orangey red. Once I've clicked on the project name, I select the Tests tab. You can see the error report in Figure 20–9

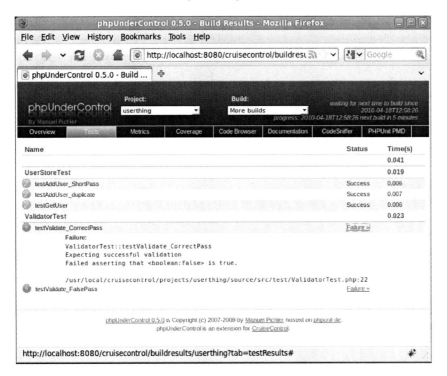

Figure 20–9. *Failed tests*

Failure Notification

It's very well having errors reported on the CruiseControl web interface, so long as people visit frequently. There is a danger that the system's quiet efficiency might cause it to be forgotten. You can change that by making CruiseControl a nag. In order to do this you can use a built-in publisher: `email`, which you should add to the `publishers` element in your project's section of the `config.xml` file:

```
<email mailhost="smtp.somemail.com"
    mailport="465"
    username="some.user@somemail.com"
    password="somepass"
    usessl="true"
    returnaddress="ci_guy@getinstance.com"
    buildresultsurl="http://localhost:8080/cruisecontrol/buildresults/${project.name}"
    returnname="CruiseControl">

        <always address="builds@userthing-team.com" />
        <failure address="panic@userthing-team.com" reportWhenFixed="true" />

</email>
```

The email element contains all the information needed to connect to a mail server. I've assumed that an SSL connection is required, but you could omit the `mailport` and and `usessl` elements otherwise. The `always` element defines an address to which a message should be sent for all builds whether successful or not. The `failure` element defines an address to which failure notifications should be sent. As a bonus, with `reportWhenFixed` set to `true`, the failure recipient will also get an all clear message when a builds are once again successful.

The failure message is very short, consisting of a subject line, which gives the build status and a URL for the full report.

■Note If you want more verbose messages you should look at the `htmlemail` publisher, which shares a common set of attributes and child elements with the `email` publisher, but also provides additional options to help you format an inline message. You can find more information about `htmlemail` at http://cruisecontrol.sourceforge.net/main/configxml.html#htmlemail.

Adding Your Own Build Targets

So far I have stuck to the toolset supported by phpUnderControl. That gets us a long way, after all. However you should know that you can quite easily add your own checks to CruiseControl.

The biggest omission so far has been a test of for creating and installing a package. This is significant, because CI is about build as well as testing. One approach would be to create a PHPUnit test case which attempts to build and install a package.

In order to illustrate some of CruiseControl's features, though, I propose to perform the build and install from within the product build file. I've already shown you the `build` target. It invokes the other targets in the file through its `depends` attribute. Here I add a new dependency.

```
<target name="build"
    depends="checkout,php-documentor,php-codesniffer,phpunit,install-package"/>
```

The `install-package` target does not exist yet. Time to add it.

```
<target name="make-package">
  <exec executable="pear" dir="${basedir}/source/src"
```

```
        failonerror="on"
        output="${basedir}/build/builderror/index.txt">
      <arg line=" package" />
    </exec>
  </target>

  <target name="install-package" depends="make-package">
  </target>
```

In fact install-package is currently empty. That's because it depends on another new target, make-package, which must be run first. There I use an Ant task called exec to invoke the command pear package. This looks for a file called package.xml in the ${basedir}/source/src directory. How do I know that this will be there? That's thanks to the checkout target in the same file that calls Subversion and updates userthing under ${basedir}/source.

I send any error messages to a file in a directory at build/builderror using the output attribute. Other tasks use the build directory so it's already in place, but builderror is new, so I need to create it from the command line.

Once I restart CruiseControl I should see no difference. Once again, I'll only see the benefit when things change. So, it's time to create an error. Here I poison my package.xml file:

```
<summary>A sample package that demo's aspects of CI</summary>
<wrong />
<description>Consisting of tests, code coverage, Subversion, etc
</description>
```

Once I've committed this, the pear package command will choke that wrong element there. It should refuse to build the package. Because the exec element has a failonerror attribute set, the build will fail, and CruiseControl should then alert the team.

Figure 20–10 shows the failed build in the CruiseControl Web interface.

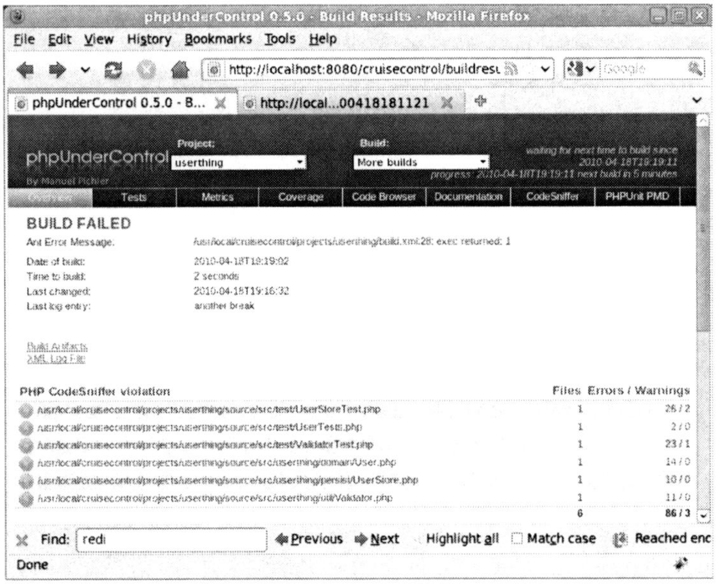

Figure 20–10. The build fails

You can see that an error has occurred, but the details aren't entirely clear. The error message just tells me that the build failed. In fact if I hit the XML Log File link I'll eventually find the error, buried under an avalanche of XML. There are a couple of ways I could make this error more obvious. One way would be to influence the failure messages generated by Ant. Another is to use a publisher to create an artifact directory.

Artifacts are arbitrary outputs that can be incorporated into CruiseControl interface. All the reports you have seen so far this chapter are actually acquired from artifact directories. CruiseControl provides the `artifactspublisher` element, which belongs in `config.xml` under a project's publishers element. You've already seen email, a sibling element from this section. `artifactspublisher` simply takes output generated either during a build or by post processing, and moves it into the artifacts directory. So here I add an `artifactspublisher` element to my `config.xml` directory.

```
<artifactspublisher dir="projects/${project.name}/build/builderror"
    dest="artifacts/${project.name}"
    subdirectory="builderror"/>
```

This copies the builderror directory from projects/userthing/build to artifacts/userthing/<datestamp>/builderror. Next time CruiseControl encounters a build error, I can click on the Build Artifacts link you saw in Figure 20.10, and then click through artifact directory links to arrive at the page you can see in Figure 20–11.

Figure 20–11. *A simple artifact report*

Now that I've set up a basic report for the make-package target, I can go ahead and do the same for install-package. I'd better implement it at the same time.

```
<target name="install-package" depends="make-package">
    <fileset id="package.ref"
        dir="${basedir}/source/src/"
        includes="userthing*.tgz" />
    <pathconvert property="package.file" refid="package.ref" />

    <exec executable="pear" dir="${basedir}/source/src"
        failonerror="on"
        output="${basedir}/build/builderror/index.txt">
      <arg value="install" />
      <arg value="--force" />
      <arg value="--installroot=${basedir}/build/install" />
      <arg file="${package.file}" />
```

```
    </exec>

    <delete>
    <fileset refid="package.ref" />
    </delete>
    </target>
```

Once again, this target consists primarily of a call to the exec task. First, though, I create a fileset that matches the userthing package file (userthing-1.2.1.tgz), and I convert this to an expanded path using a new task: pathconvert. Now I have something I can pass to the command invoked by exec which is pear install. Because the output attribute is set in this exec element, a failure will be accessible as before. Finally, I delete the package file. It's important to clean this up, because I'm making an assumption that there's only one file in the directory that matches userthing*.tgz. If I let the old package files remain in my src directory, I would likely suffer unexpected results when I next increment the version number.

Summary

In this chapter I brought together many of the tools you have seen in previous chapters, and glued them in place with CruiseControl. I demonstrated that this Continuous Integration server is well suited to PHP projects thanks to phpUnderControl. I prepared a small project for CI, applying a range of tools including PHPUnit (both for testing and code coverage), PHP_CodeSniffer, PHP_CodeBrowser, phpDocumentor and Subversion. Then I set up CruiseControl with phpUnderControl and showed you how to add a project to the system. I put the system through its paces and, finally, showed you how to extend CruiseControl so that it can bug you with emails, and test both build and installation.

PART 5

Conclusion

CHAPTER 21

Objects, Patterns, Practice

From object basics through design pattern principles, and on to tools and techniques, this book has has focused on a single objective: the successful PHP project.

In this chapter, I recap some of the topics I have covered and points made throughout the book:

- *PHP and objects*: How PHP continues to increase its support for object-oriented programming, and how to leverage these features.

- *Objects and design*: Summarizing some OO design principles.

- *Patterns*: What makes them cool.

- *Pattern principles*: A recap of the guiding object-oriented principles that underlie many patterns.

- *The tools for the job*: Revisiting the tools I have described, and checking out a few I haven't.

Objects

As you saw in Chapter 2, for a long time, objects were something of an afterthought in the PHP world. Support was rudimentary to say the least in PHP 3, with objects barely more than associative arrays in fancy dress. Although things improved radically for the object enthusiast with PHP 4, there were still significant problems. Not the least of these was that by default, objects were assigned and passed by reference.

The introduction of PHP 5 finally dragged objects center stage. You can still program in PHP without ever declaring a class, of course, but there can be no doubt that the language is optimized for object-oriented design.

In Chapters 3, 4, and 5, I looked at PHP's object-oriented support in detail. Here are some of the new features PHP has introduced since version 5: reflection, exceptions, private and protected methods and properties, the __toString() method, the static modifier, abstract classes and methods, final methods and properties, interfaces, iterators, interceptor methods, type hinting, the const modifier, passing by reference, __clone(), the __construct() method, late static binding, and namespaces. The extensive length of this incomplete list reveals the degree to which the future of PHP is bound up with object-oriented programming.

I would still like to see a few features that are not yet planned, such as hinting for primitive types. I would also like to see support for return type hinting—in which a method declaration can include the return type the method must yield. The engine would then enforce this commitment, both for the current and overriding methods (at the time of writing, this feature is slated for a future release).

These are quibbles, though. The Zend Engine 2 and PHP 5 have made object-oriented design central to the PHP project, opening up the language to a new set of developers and opening up new possibilities for existing devotees.

In Chapter 6, I looked at the benefits that objects can bring to the design of your projects. Since objects and design are one of the central themes of this book, it is worth recapping some conclusions in detail.

Choice

There is no law that says you have to develop with classes and objects only. Well-designed object-oriented code provides a clean interface that can be accessed from any client code, whether procedural or object oriented. Even if you have no interest in writing objects (unlikely if you are still reading this book), you will probably find yourself using them, if only as a client of PEAR packages.

Encapsulation and Delegation

Objects mind their own business and get on with their allotted tasks behind closed doors. They provide an interface through which requests and results can be passed. Any data that need not be exposed, and the dirty details of implementation, are hidden behind this front.

This gives object-oriented and procedural projects different shapes. The controller in an object-oriented project is often surprisingly sparse, consisting of a handful of instantiations that acquire objects and invocations that call up data from one set and pass it on to another.

A procedural project, on the other hand, tends to be much more interventionist. The controlling logic descends into implementation to a greater extent, referring to variables, measuring return values, and taking turns along different pathways of operation according to circumstance.

Decoupling

To decouple is to remove interdependence between components, so that making a change to one component does not necessitate changes to others. Well-designed objects are self-enclosed. That is, they do not need to refer outside of themselves to recall a detail they learned in a previous invocation.

By maintaining an internal representation of state, objects reduce the need for global variables—a notorious cause of tight coupling. In using a global variable, you bind one part of a system to another. If a component (whether a function, a class, or a block of code) refers to a global variable, there is a risk that another component will accidentally use the same variable name and substitute its value for the first. There is a chance that a third component will come to rely on the value in the variable as set by the first. Change the way that the first component works, and you may cause the third to stop working. The aim of object-oriented design is to reduce such interdependence, making each component as self-sufficient as possible.

Another cause of tight coupling is code duplication. When you must repeat an algorithm in different parts of your project, you will find tight coupling. What happens when you come to change the algorithm? Clearly you must remember to change it everywhere it occurs. Forget to do this, and your system is in trouble.

A common cause of code duplication is the parallel conditional. If your project needs to do things in one way according to a particular circumstance (running on Linux, for example), and another according to an alternative circumstance (running on Windows), you will often find the same if/else clauses popping up in different parts of your system. If you add a new circumstance together with strategies for handling it (MacOS), you must ensure that all conditionals are updated.

Object-oriented programming provides a technique for handling this problem. You can replace conditionals with *polymorphism*. Polymorphism, also known as *class switching*, is the transparent use of different subclasses according to circumstance. Because each subclass supports the same interface as the common superclass, the client code neither knows nor cares which particular implementation it is using.

Conditional code is not banished from object-oriented systems; it is merely minimized and centralized. Conditional code of some kind must be used to determine which particular subtypes are to be served up to clients. This test, though, generally takes place once, and in one place, thus reducing coupling.

Reusability

Encapsulation promotes decoupling, which promotes reuse. Components that are self-sufficient and communicate with wider systems only through their public interface can often be moved from one system and used in another without change.

In fact, this is rarer than you might think. Even nicely orthogonal code can be project-specific. When creating a set of classes for managing the content of a particular web site, for example, it is worth taking some time in the planning stage to look at those features that are specific to your client, and those that might form the foundation for future projects with content management at their heart.

Another tip for reuse: centralize those classes that might be used in multiple projects. Do not, in other words, copy a nicely reusable class into a new project. This will cause tight coupling on a macro level, as you will inevitably end up changing the class in one project and forgetting to do so in another. You would do better to manage common classes in a central repository that can be shared by your projects.

Aesthetics

This is not going to convince anyone who is not already convinced, but to me, object-oriented code is aesthetically pleasing. The messiness of implementation is hidden away behind clean interfaces, making an object a thing of apparent simplicity to its client.

I love the neatness and elegance of polymorphism, so that an API allows you to manipulate vastly different objects that nonetheless perform interchangeably and transparently—the way that objects can be stacked up neatly or slotted into one another like children's blocks.

Of course, there are those who argue that the converse is true. Object-oriented code can lead to tortuous class names that must be combined with method names to form even more labored invocations. This is especially true of PEAR, where class names include their package names to make up for PHP's lack of support for namespaces. There is an end in sight to this now that namespaces are poised part of the language. PEAR developers prize backward compatibility, though, so it will be some time before the old naming conventions fall by the wayside.

It is also worth mentioning that a beautiful solution is not always the best, or most efficient. It is tempting to use a full-blown object-oriented solution where a quick script or a few system calls might have got the job done.

Another fair criticism is that object-oriented code can dissolve into a babel of classes and objects that can be very hard to read. There is no denying that this can be the case, although matters can be eased considerably through careful documentation containing usage examples.

Patterns

Recently a Java programmer applied for a job in a company with which I have some involvement. In his cover letter, he apologized for only having used patterns for a couple of years. This assumption that design patterns are a recent discovery—a transformative advance—is testament to the excitement they have generated. In fact, it is likely that this experienced coder has been using patterns for a lot longer than he thinks.

Patterns describe common problems and tested solutions. Patterns name, codify, and organize real-world best practice. They are not components of an invention or clauses in a doctrine. A pattern would not be valid if it did not describe practices that are already common at the time of hatching.

Remember that the concept of a pattern language originated in the field of architecture. People were building courtyards and arches for thousands of years before patterns were proposed as a means of describing solutions to problems of space and function.

Having said that, it is true that design patterns often provoke the kind of emotions associated with religious or political disputes. Devotees roam the corridors with an evangelistic gleam in their eye and a copy of the Gang of Four book under their arm. They accost the uninitiated and reel off pattern names like articles of faith. It is little wonder that some critics see design patterns as hype.

In languages such as Perl and PHP, patterns are also controversial because of their firm association with object-oriented programming. In a context in which objects are a design decision and not a given, associating oneself with design patterns amounts to a declaration of preference, not least because patterns beget more patterns, and objects beget more objects.

What Patterns Buy Us

I introduced patterns in Chapter 7. Let's reiterate some of the benefits that patterns can buy us.

Tried and Tested

First of all, as I've noted, patterns are proven solutions to particular problems. Drawing an analogy between patterns and recipes is dangerous: recipes can be followed blindly, whereas patterns are "half-baked" (Martin Fowler) by nature and need more thoughtful handling. Nevertheless, both recipes and patterns share one important characteristic: they have been tried out and tested thoroughly before inscription.

Patterns Suggest Other Patterns

Patterns have grooves and curves that fit one another. Certain patterns slot together with a satisfying click. Solving a problem using a pattern will inevitably have ramifications. These consequences can become the conditions that suggest complementary patterns. It is important, of course, to be careful that you are addressing real needs and problems when you choose related patterns, and not just building elegant but useless towers of interlocking code. It is tempting to build the programming equivalent of an architectural folly.

A Common Vocabulary

Patterns are a means of developing a common vocabulary for describing problems and solutions. Naming is important—it stands in for describing, and therefore lets us cover lots of ground very quickly. Naming, of course, also obscures meaning for those who do not yet share the vocabulary, which is one reason why patterns can be so infuriating at times.

Patterns Promote Design

As discussed in the next section, patterns can encourage good design when used properly. There is an important caveat, of course. Patterns are not fairy dust.

Patterns and Principles of Design

Design patterns are, by their nature, concerned with good design. Used well, they can help you build loosely coupled and flexible code. Pattern critics have a point, though, when they say that patterns can be overused by the newly infected. Because pattern implementations form pretty and elegant structures, it can be tempting to forget that good design always lies in fitness for purpose. Remember that patterns exist to address problems.

When I first started working with patterns, I found myself creating Abstract Factories all over my code. I needed to generate objects, and Abstract Factory certainly helped me to do that.

In fact, though, I was thinking lazily and making unnecessary work for myself. The sets of objects I needed to produce were indeed related, but they did not yet have alternative implementations. The classic Abstract Factory pattern is ideal for situations in which you have alternative sets of objects to generate according to circumstance. To make Abstract Factory work, you need to create factory classes for each type of object and a class to serve up the factory class. It's exhausting just describing the process.

My code would have been much cleaner had I created a basic factory class, only refactoring to implement Abstract Factory if I found myself needing to generate a parallel set of objects.

The fact that you are using patterns does not guarantee good design. When developing, it is a good idea to bear in mind two expressions of the same principle: KISS ("Keep it simple, stupid") and "Do the simplest thing that works." eXtreme programmers also give us another, related, acronym: YAGNI. "You aren't going to need it," meaning that you should not implement a feature unless it is truly required.

With the warnings out of the way, I can resume my tone of breathless enthusiasm. As I laid out in Chapter 9, patterns tend to embody a set of principles that can be generalized and applied to all code.

Favor Composition over Inheritance

Inheritance relationships are powerful. We use inheritance to support runtime class switching (polymorphism), which lies at the heart of many of the patterns and techniques I explored in this book. By relying on solely on inheritance in design, though, you can produce inflexible structures that are prone to duplication.

Avoid Tight Coupling

I have already talked about this issue in this chapter, but it is worth mentioning here for the sake of completeness. You can never escape the fact that change in one component may require changes in other parts of your project. You can, however, minimize this by avoiding both duplication (typified in our examples by parallel conditionals) and the overuse of global variables (or Singletons). You should also minimize the use of concrete subclasses when abstract types can be used to promote polymorphism. This last point leads us to another principle:

Code to an Interface, Not an Implementation

Design your software components with clearly defined public interfaces that make the responsibility of each transparent. If you define your interface in an abstract superclass and have client classes demand and work with this abstract type, you then decouple clients from specific implementations.

Having said that, remember the YAGNI principle. If you start out with the need for only one implementation for a type, there is no immediate reason to create an abstract superclass. You can just as well define a clear interface in a single concrete class. As soon as you find that your single implementation is trying to do more than one thing at the same time, you can redesignate your concrete class as the abstract parent of two subclasses. Client code will be none the wiser, since it continues to work with a single type.

A classic sign that you may need to split an implementation and hide the resultant classes behind an abstract parent is the emergence of conditional statements in the implementation.

Encapsulate the Concept That Varies

If you find that you are drowning in subclasses, it may be that you should be extracting the reason for all this subclassing into its own type. This is particularly the case if the reason is to achieve an end that is incidental to your type's main purpose.

Given a type UpdatableThing, for example, you may find yourself creating FtpUpdatableThing, HttpUpdatableThing, and FileSystemUpdatableThing subtypes. The responsibility of your type, though, is to be a *thing* that is *updatable*—the mechanism for storage and retrieval are incidental to this purpose. Ftp, Http, and FileSystem are the things that vary here, and they belong in their own type—let's call it UpdateMechanism. UpdateMechanism will have subclasses for the different implementations. You can then add as many update mechanisms as you want without disturbing the UpdatableThing type, which remains focused on its core responsibility.

Notice also that I have replaced a static compile-time structure with a dynamic runtime arrangement here, bringing us (as if by accident) back to our first principle: "Favor composition over inheritance."

Practice

The issues that I covered in this section of the book (and introduced in Chapter 14) are often ignored by texts and coders alike. In my own life as a programmer, I discovered that these tools and techniques were at least as relevant to the success of a project as design. There is little doubt that issues such as documentation and automated build are less revelatory in nature than wonders such as the Composite pattern.

■**Note** Let's just remind ourselves of the beauty of Composite: a simple inheritance tree whose objects can be joined at runtime to form structures that are also trees, but are orders of magnitude more flexible and complex. Multiple objects that share a single interface by which they are presented to the outside world. The interplay between simple and complex, multiple and singular, has got to get your pulse racing—that's not just software design, it's poetry.

Even if issues such as documentation and build, testing, and version control are more prosaic than patterns, they are no less important. In the real world, a fantastic design will not survive if multiple developers cannot easily contribute to it or understand the source. Systems become hard to maintain and extend without automated testing. Without build tools, no one is going to bother to deploy your work. As PHP's user base widens, so does our responsibility as developers to ensure quality and ease of deployment.

A project exists in two modes. A project is its structures of code and functionality, and it is also set of files and directories, a ground for cooperation, a set of sources and targets, a subject for transformation. In this sense, a project is a system from the outside as much as it is within its code. Mechanisms for build, testing, documentation, and version control require the same attention to detail as the code such mechanisms support. Focus on the metasystem with as much fervor as you do on the system itself.

Testing

Although testing is part of the framework that one applies to a project from the outside, it is intimately integrated into the code itself. Because total decoupling is not possible, or even desirable, test frameworks are a powerful way of monitoring the ramifications of change. Altering the return type of a method could influence client code elsewhere, causing bugs to emerge weeks or months after the change is made. A test framework gives you half a chance of catching errors of this kind (the better the tests, the better the odds here).

Testing is also a tool for improving object-oriented design. Testing first (or at least concurrently) helps you to focus on a class's interface and think carefully about the responsibility and behavior of every method. I introduced the PHPUnit2 package, which is used for testing, in Chapter 18.

Documentation

Your code is not as clear as you think it is. A stranger visiting a codebase for the first time can be faced with a daunting task. Even you, as author of the code, will eventually forget how it all hangs together. In Chapter 16, I covered phpDocumentor, which allows you to document as you go, and automatically generates hyperlinked output.

The output from phpDocumentor is particularly useful in an object-oriented context, as it allows the user to click around from class to class. As classes are often contained in their own files, reading the source directly can involve following complex trails from source file to source file.

Version Control

Collaboration is hard. Let's face it: people are awkward. Programmers are even worse. Once you've sorted out the roles and tasks on your team, the last thing you want to deal with is clashes in the source code itself. As you saw in Chapter 17, Subversion (and similar tools such as CVS and Git) enable you to merge the work of multiple programmers into a single repository. Where clashes are unavoidable, Subversion flags the fact and points you to the source to fix the problem.

Even if you are a solo programmer, version control is a necessity. Subversion supports branching, so that you can maintain a software release and develop the next version at the same time, merging bug fixes from the stable release to the development branch.

Subversion also provides a record of every commit ever made on your project. This means that you can roll back by date or tag to any moment. This will save your project someday—believe me.

Automated Build

Version control without automated build is of limited use. A project of any complexity takes work to deploy. Various files need to be moved to different places on a system, configuration files need to be transformed to have the right values for the current platform and database, database tables need to be set up or transformed. I covered two tools designed for installation. The first, PEAR (see Chapter 15), is ideal for standalone packages and small applications. The second build tool I covered was Phing (see Chapter 19), which is a tool with enough power and flexibility to automate the installation of the largest and most labyrinthine project.

Automated build transforms deployment from a chore to a matter of a line or two at the command line. With little effort, you can invoke your test framework and your documentation output from your build tool. If the needs of your developers do not sway you, bear in mind the pathetically grateful cries of your users as they discover that they need no longer spend an entire afternoon copying files and changing configuration fields every time you release a new version of your project.

Continuous Integration

It is not enough to be able to test and build a project; you have do it *all the time*. This becomes increasingly important as a project grows in complexity and you manage multiple branches. You should build and test the stable branch from which you make minor bug fix releases, an experimental development branch or two, and your main trunk. If you were to try to do all that manually, even with the aid of build and test tools, you'd never get around to any coding. Of course, all coders hate that, so build and testing inevitably get skimped on.

In chapter 20 I looked at Continuous Integration, a practice and a set of tools that automate the build and test processes as much as possible.

What I Missed

A few tools I have had to omit from this book due to time and space constraints are, nonetheless, supremely useful for any project.

Perhaps foremost among these is Bugzilla. Its name should suggest two things to you. First, it is a tool concerned with bug tracking. Second, it is part of the Mozilla project.

Like Subversion, Bugzilla is one of those productivity tools that, once you have tried it on a project, you cannot imagine not using. Bugzilla is available for download from http://www.bugzilla.org.

It is designed to allow users to report problems with a project, but in my experience it is just as often used as a means of describing required features and allocating their implementation to team members.

You can get a snapshot of open bugs at any time, narrowing the search according to product, bug owner, version number, and priority. Each bug has its own page, in which you can discuss any ongoing issues. Discussion entries and changes in bug status can be copied by mail to team members, so it's easy to keep an eye on things without going to the Bugzilla URL all the time.

Trust me. You want Bugzilla in your life.

Every serious project needs at least one mailing list so that users can be kept informed of changes and usage issues, and developers can discuss architecture and allocation of resources. My favorite mailing list software is Mailman (http://www.gnu.org/software/mailman/), which is free, relatively easy to install, and highly configurable. If you don't want to install your own mailing list software, however, there are plenty of sites that allow you to run mailing lists or newsgroups for free.

Although inline documentation is important, projects also generate a broiling heap of written material. This includes usage instructions, consultation on future directions, client assets, meeting minutes, and party announcements. During the lifetime of a project, such materials are very fluid, and a mechanism is often needed to allow people to collaborate in their evolution.

A wiki (wiki is apparently Hawaiian for "very fast") is the perfect tool for creating collaborative webs of hyperlinked documents. Pages can be created or edited at the click of a button, and hyperlinks are automatically generated for words that match page names. Wiki is another one of those tools that seems so simple, essential, and obvious that you are sure you probably had the idea first but just didn't get around to doing anything about it. There are a number of wikis to choose from. I have had good experience with one called Foswiki, which is available for download from http://foswiki.org/. Foswiki is written in Perl. Naturally, there are wiki applications written in PHP. Notable among them are PhpWiki, which can be downloaded from http://phpwiki.sourceforge.net, and DokuWiki, which you can find at http://wiki.splitbrain.org/wiki:dokuwiki.

Summary

In this chapter I wrapped things up, revisiting the core topics that make up the book. Although I haven't tackled any concrete issues such as individual patterns or object functions here, this chapter should serve as a reasonable summary of this book's concerns.

There is never enough room or time to cover all the material that one would like. Nevertheless, I hope that this book has served to make one argument: PHP is growing up. It is now one of the most popular programming languages in the world. I hope that PHP remains the hobbyist's favorite language, and that many new PHP programmers are delighted to discover how far they can get with just a little code. At the same time, though, more and more professional teams are building large systems with PHP. Such projects deserve more than a just-do-it approach. Through its extension layer, PHP has always been a versatile language, providing a gateway to hundreds of applications and libraries. Its object-oriented support, on the other hand, gains you access to a different set of tools. Once you begin to think in objects, you can chart the hard-won experience of other programmers. You can navigate and deploy pattern languages developed with reference not just to PHP but to Smalltalk, C++, C#, or Java, too. It is our responsibility to meet this challenge with careful design and good practice. The future is reusable.

APPENDIX A

■ ■ ■

Bibliography

Books

Alexander, Christopher, Sara Ishikawa, Murray Silverstein, Max Jacobson, Ingrid Fiksdahl-King, and Shlomo Angel. *A Pattern Language: Towns, Buildings, Construction*. Oxford, UK: Oxford University Press, 1977.

Alur, Deepak, John Crupi, and Dan Malks. *Core J2EE Patterns: Best Practices and Design Strategies*. Englewood Cliffs, NJ: Prentice Hall PTR, 2001.

Beck, Kent. *Extreme Programming Explained: Embrace Change*. Reading, MA: Addison-Wesley, 1999.

Fogel, Karl, and Moshe Bar., *Open Source Development with CVS, Third Edition*. Scottsdale, AZ: Paraglyph Press, 2003.

Fowler, Martin, and Kendall Scott. *UML Distilled, Second Edition: A Brief Guide to the Standard Object Modeling Language*. Reading, MA: Addison-Wesley, 1999.

Fowler, Martin, Kent Beck, John Brant, William Opdyke, and Don Roberts. *Refactoring: Improving the Design of Existing Code*. Reading, MA: Addison-Wesley, 1999.

Fowler, Martin. *Patterns of Enterprise Application Architecture*. Reading, MA: Addison-Wesley, 2003.

Gamma, Erich, Richard Helm, Ralph Johnson, and John Vlissides. *Design Patterns: Elements of Reusable Object-Oriented Software*. Reading, MA: Addison-Wesley, 1995.

Hunt, Andrew, and David Thomas. *The Pragmatic Programmer: From Journeyman to Master*. Reading, MA: Addison-Wesley, 2000.

Kerievsky, Joshua. *Refactoring to Patterns*. Reading, MA: Addison-Wesley, 2004.

Metsker, Steven John. *Building Parsers with Java*. Reading, MA: Addison-Wesley, 2001.

Nock, Clifton. *Data Access Patterns: Database Interactions in Object-Oriented Applications*. Reading, MA: Addison-Wesley, 2004.

Shalloway, Alan, and James R Trott. *Design Patterns Explained: A New Perspective on Object-Oriented Design.* Reading, MA: Addison Wesley, 2002.

Stelting, Stephen, and Olav Maasen. *Applied Java Patterns.* Palo Alto, CA: Sun Microsystems Press, 2002.

Articles

Beaver, Greg. "Setting Up Your Own PEAR Channel with Chiara_Pear_Server—The Official Way." http://greg.chiaraquartet.net/archives/123-Setting-up-your-own-PEAR-channel-the-official-way.html

Beck, Kent, and Erich Gamma. "Test Infected: Programmers Love Writing Tests." http://junit.sourceforge.net/doc/testinfected/testing.htm

Collins-Sussman, Ben, Brian W. Fitzpatrick, C. Michael Pilato. "Version Control with Subversion"

http://svnbook.red-bean.com/

Lerdorf, Rasmus. "PHP/FI Brief History." http://www.php.net//manual/phpfi2.php#history

Suraski, Zeev. "The Object-Oriented Evolution of PHP." http://www.devx.com/webdev/Article/10007/0/page/1

Sites

Bugzilla: http://www.bugzilla.org

CruiseControl: http://cruisecontrol.sourceforge.net/

CVS: http://www.cvshome.org/

CvsGui: http://www.wincvs.org/

CVSNT: http://www.cvsnt.org/wiki

DokuWiki: http://wiki.splitbrain.org/wiki:dokuwiki

Foswiki: http://foswiki.org/

Eclipse: http://www.eclipse.org/

Java: http://www.java.com

GNU: http://www.gnu.org/

Git: http://git-scm.com/

Google Code: http://code.google.com

Mailman: http://www.gnu.org/software/mailman/

Martin Fowler: http://www.martinfowler.com/

Memcached: http://danga.com/memcached/

Phing: http://phing.info/trac/

PHPUnit: http://www.phpunit.de

PhpWiki: http://phpwiki.sourceforge.net

PEAR: http://pear.php.net

PECL: http://pecl.php.net/

Phing: http://phing.info/

PHP: http://www.php.net

PhpWiki: http://phpwiki.sourceforge.net

PHPDocumentor: http://www.phpdoc.org/

Portland Pattern Repository's Wiki (Ward Cunningham): http://www.c2.com/cgi/wiki

Pyrus: http://pear2.php.net

RapidSVN: http://rapidsvn.tigris.org/

QDB: http://www.bash.org

Selenium: http://seleniumhq.org/

SPL: http://www.php.net/spl

Subversion: http://subversion.apache.org/

Ximbiot—CVS Wiki: http://ximbiot.com/cvs/wiki/

Xdebug: http://xdebug.org/

Zend: http://www.zend.com

■ ■ ■

A Simple Parser

The Interpreter pattern discussed in Chapter 11 does not cover parsing. An interpreter without a parser is pretty incomplete, unless you persuade your users to write PHP code to invoke the interpreter! Third-party parsers are available that could be deployed to work with the Interpreter pattern, and that would probably be the best choice in a real-world project. This appendix, however, presents a simple object-oriented parser designed to work with the MarkLogic interpreter built in Chapter 11. Be aware that these examples are no more than a proof of concept. They are not designed for use in real-world situations.

■Note The interface and broad structure of this parser code are based on Steven Metsker's *Building Parsers with Java* (Addison-Wesley, 2001). The brutally simplified implementation is my fault, however, and any mistakes should be laid at my door. Steven has given kind permission for the use of his original concept.

The Scanner

In order to parse a statement, you must first break it down into a set of words and characters (known as tokens). The following class uses a number of regular expressions to define tokens. It also provides a convenient result stack that I will be using later in this section. Here is the Scanner class:

```
namespace gi\parse;

class Scanner {

    // token types
    const WORD       = 1;
    const QUOTE      = 2;
    const APOS       = 3;
    const WHITESPACE = 6;
    const EOL        = 8;
    const CHAR       = 9;
    const EOF        = 0;
    const SOF        = -1;

    protected $line_no = 1;
    protected $char_no = 0;
```

```
protected $token = null;
protected $token_type = -1;
// Reader provides access to the raw character data. Context stores
// result data
function __construct( Reader $r, Context $context ) {
    $this->r = $r;
    $this->context = $context;
}

function getContext() {
    return $this->context;
}

// read through all whitespace characters
function eatWhiteSpace( ) {
    $ret = 0;
    if ( $this->token_type != self::WHITESPACE &&
        $this->token_type != self::EOL ) {
        return $ret;
    }
    while ( $this->nextToken() == self::WHITESPACE ||
            $this->token_type == self::EOL ) {
        $ret++;
    }
    return $ret;
}

// get a string representation of a token
// either the current token, or that represented
// by the $int arg
function getTypeString( $int=-1 ) {
    if ( $int<0 ) { $int=$this->tokenType(); }
    if ( $int<0 ) { return null; }
    $resolve = array(
        self::WORD =>        'WORD',
        self::QUOTE =>       'QUOTE',
        self::APOS =>        'APOS',
        self::WHITESPACE =>  'WHITESPACE',
        self::EOL =>         'EOL',
        self::CHAR =>        'CHAR',
        self::EOF =>         'EOF' );
    return $resolve[$int];
}

// the current token type (represented by an integer)
function tokenType() {
    return $this->token_type;
}

// get the contents of the current token
function token() {
    return $this->token;
}
```

```php
// return true if the current token is a word
function isWord( ) {
    return ( $this->token_type == self::WORD );
}

// return true if the current token is a quote character
function isQuote( ) {
    return ( $this->token_type == self::APOS ||
             $this->token_type == self::QUOTE );
}

// current line number in source
function line_no() {
    return $this->line_no;
}

// current character number in source
function char_no() {
    return $this->char_no;
}

// clone this object
function __clone() {
    $this->r = clone($this->r);
}

// move on to the next token in the source. Set the current
// token and track the line and character numbers
function nextToken() {
    $this->token = null;
    $type;
    while ( ! is_bool($char=$this->getChar())   ) {
        if ( $this->isEolChar( $char ) ) {
            $this->token = $this->manageEolChars( $char );
            $this->line_no++;
            $this->char_no = 0;
            $type = self::EOL;
            return ( $this->token_type = self::EOL );

        } else if ( $this->isWordChar( $char ) ) {
            $this->token = $this->eatWordChars( $char );
            $type = self::WORD;

        } else if ( $this->isSpaceChar( $char ) ) {
            $this->token = $char;
            $type = self::WHITESPACE;

        } else if ( $char == "'" ) {
            $this->token = $char;
            $type = self::APOS;

        } else if ( $char == '"' ) {
```

```
                $this->token = $char;
                $type = self::QUOTE;

            } else {
                $type = self::CHAR;
                $this->token = $char;
            }

            $this->char_no += strlen( $this->token() );
            return ( $this->token_type = $type );
        }
        return ( $this->token_type = self::EOF );
    }

    // return an array of token type and token content for the NEXT token
    function peekToken() {
        $state = $this->getState();
        $type = $this->nextToken();
        $token = $this->token();
        $this->setState( $state );
        return array( $type, $token );
    }

    // get a ScannerState object that stores the parser's current
    // position in the source, and data about the current token
    function getState() {
        $state = new ScannerState();
        $state->line_no       = $this->line_no;
        $state->char_no       = $this->char_no;
        $state->token         = $this->token;
        $state->token_type    = $this->token_type;
        $state->r             = clone($this->r);
        $state->context       = clone($this->context);
        return $state;
    }

    // use a ScannerState object to restore the scanner's
    // state
    function setState( ScannerState $state ) {
        $this->line_no       = $state->line_no;
        $this->char_no       = $state->char_no;
        $this->token         = $state->token;
        $this->token_type    = $state->token_type;
        $this->r             = $state->r;
        $this->context       = $state->context;
    }

    // get the next character from source
    private function getChar() {
        return $this->r->getChar();
    }

    // get all characters until they stop being
```

```
// word characters
private function eatWordChars( $char ) {
    $val = $char;
    while ( $this->isWordChar( $char=$this->getChar() )) {
        $val .= $char;
    }
    if ( $char ) {
        $this->pushBackChar( );
    }
    return $val;
}

// get all characters until they stop being space
// characters
private function eatSpaceChars( $char ) {
    $val = $char;
    while ( $this->isSpaceChar( $char=$this->getChar() )) {
        $val .= $char;
    }
    $this->pushBackChar( );
    return $val;
}

// move back one character in source
private function pushBackChar( ) {
    $this->r->pushBackChar();
}

// argument is a word character
private function isWordChar( $char ) {
    return preg_match( "/[A-Za-z0-9_\-]/", $char );
}

// argument is a space character
private function isSpaceChar( $char ) {
    return preg_match( "/\t| /", $char );
}

// argument is an end of line character
private function isEolChar( $char ) {
    return preg_match( "/\n|\r/", $char );
}

// swallow either \n, \r or \r\n
private function manageEolChars( $char ) {
    if ( $char == "\r" ) {
        $next_char=$this->getChar();
        if ( $next_char == "\n" ) {
            return "{$char}{$next_char}";
        } else {
            $this->pushBackChar();
        }
    }
```

```
            return $char;
    }
    function getPos() {
        return $this->r->getPos();
    }

}

class ScannerState {
    public $line_no;
    public $char_no;
    public $token;
    public $token_type;
    public $r;
}
```

First off, I set up constants for the tokens that interest me. I am going to match characters, words, whitespace, and quote characters. I test for these types in methods dedicated to each token: isWordChar(), isSpaceChar(), and so on. The heart of the class is the nextToken() method. This attempts to match the next token in a given string. The Scanner stores a Context object. Parser objects use this to share results as they work through the target text.

Note also a second class: ScannerState. The Scanner is designed so that Parser objects can save state, try stuff out, and restore if they've gone down a blind alley. The getState() method populates and returns a ScannerState object. setState() uses a ScannerState object to revert state if required.

Here is the Context class:

```
namespace gi\parse;
//...

class Context {
    public $resultstack = array();

    function pushResult( $mixed ) {
        array_push( $this->resultstack, $mixed );
    }

    function popResult( ) {
        return array_pop( $this->resultstack );
    }

    function resultCount() {
        return count( $this->resultstack );
    }

    function peekResult( ) {
        if ( empty( $this->resultstack ) ) {
            throw new Exception( "empty resultstack" );
        }
        return $this->resultstack[count( $this->resultstack ) -1 ];
    }
}
```

As you can see, this is just a simple stack, a convenient noticeboard for parsers to work with. It performs a similar job to that of the context class used in the Interpreter pattern, but it is not the same class.

Notice that the Scanner does not itself work with a file or string. Instead it requires a Reader object. This would allow me to easily to swap in different sources of data. Here is the Reader interface and an implementation: StringReader:

```php
namespace gi\parse;

abstract class Reader {

    abstract function getChar();
    abstract function getPos();
    abstract function pushBackChar();
}

class StringReader extends Reader {
    private $in;
    private $pos;

    function __construct( $in ) {
        $this->in = $in;
        $this->pos = 0;
    }

    function getChar() {
        if ( $this->pos >= strlen( $this->in ) ) {
            return false;
        }
        $char = substr( $this->in, $this->pos, 1 );
        $this->pos++;
        return $char;
    }

    function getPos() {
        return $this->pos;
    }

    function pushBackChar() {
        $this->pos--;
    }

    function string() {
        return $this->in;
    }
}
```

This simply reads from a string one character at a time. I could easily provide a file-based version, of course.

Perhaps the best way to see how the Scanner might be used is to use it. Here is some code to break up the example statement into tokens:

```php
$context = new \gi\parse\Context();
$user_in = "\$input equals '4' or \$input equals 'four'";
```

```
$reader = new \gi\parse\StringReader( $user_in );
$scanner = new \gi\parse\Scanner( $reader, $context );

while ( $scanner->nextToken() != \gi\parse\Scanner::EOF ) {
    print $scanner->token();
    print "\t{$scanner->char_no()}";
    print "\t{$scanner->getTypeString()}\n";
}
```

I initialize a Scanner object and then loop through the tokens in the given string by repeatedly calling nextToken(). The token() method returns the current portion of the input matched. char_no() tells me where I am in the string, and getTypeString() returns a string version of the constant flag representing the current token. This is what the output should look like:

```
$        1       CHAR
input    6       WORD
         7       WHITESPACE
equals   13      WORD
         14      WHITESPACE
'        15      APOS
4        16      WORD
'        17      APOS
         18      WHITESPACE
or       20      WORD
         21      WHITESPACE
$        22      CHAR
input    27      WORD
         28      WHITESPACE
equals   34      WORD
         35      WHITESPACE
'        36      APOS
four     40      WORD
'        41      APOS
```

I could, of course, match finer-grained tokens than this, but this is good enough for my purposes. Breaking up the string is the easy part. How do I build up a grammar in code?

The Parser

One approach is to build a tree of Parser objects. Here is the abstract Parser class that I will be using:

```
namespace gi\parse;
abstract class Parser {

    const GIP_RESPECTSPACE = 1;
    protected $respectSpace = false;
    protected static $debug = false;
    protected    $discard = false;
    protected $name;
    private static $count=0;

    function __construct( $name=null, $options=null ) {
        if ( is_null( $name ) ) {
            self::$count++;
            $this->name = get_class( $this )." (".self::$count.")";
```

```
        } else {
            $this->name = $name;
        }
        if ( is_array( $options ) ) {
            if ( isset( $options[self::GIP_RESPECTSPACE] ) ) {
                $this->respectSpace=true;
            }
        }
    }

    protected function next( Scanner $scanner ) {
        $scanner->nextToken();
        if ( ! $this->respectSpace ) {
            $scanner->eatWhiteSpace();
        }
    }

    function spaceSignificant( $bool ) {
        $this->respectSpace = $bool;
    }

    static function setDebug( $bool ) {
        self::$debug = $bool;
    }

    function setHandler( Handler $handler ) {
        $this->handler = $handler;
    }

    final function scan( Scanner $scanner ) {
        if ( $scanner->tokenType() == Scanner::SOF ) {
            $scanner->nextToken();
        }
        $ret = $this->doScan( $scanner );
        if ( $ret && ! $this->discard && $this->term() ) {
            $this->push( $scanner );
        }
        if ( $ret ) {
            $this->invokeHandler( $scanner );
        }

        if ( $this->term() && $ret ) {
            $this->next( $scanner );
        }
        $this->report("::scan returning $ret");
        return $ret;
    }

    function discard() {
        $this->discard = true;
    }

    abstract function trigger( Scanner $scanner );
```

```
    function term() {
        return true;
    }

// private/protected

    protected function invokeHandler(
            Scanner $scanner ) {
        if ( ! empty( $this->handler ) ) {
            $this->report( "calling handler: ".get_class( $this->handler ) );
            $this->handler->handleMatch( $this, $scanner );
        }
    }

    protected function report( $msg ) {
        if ( self::$debug ) {
            print "<{$this->name}> ".get_class( $this )."': $msg\n";
        }
    }

    protected function push( Scanner $scanner ) {
        $context = $scanner->getContext();
        $context->pushResult( $scanner->token() );
    }

    abstract protected function doScan( Scanner $scan );
}
```

The place to start with this class is the scan() method. It is here that most of the logic resides. scan() is given a Scanner object to work with. The first thing that the Parser does is defer to a concrete child class, calling the abstract doScan() method. doScan() returns true or false; you will see a concrete example later in the section.

If doScan() reports success, and a couple of other conditions are fulfilled, then the results of the parse are pushed to the Context object's result stack. The Scanner object holds the Context that is used by Parser objects to communicate results. The actual pushing of the successful parse takes place in the Parser::push() method.

```
    protected function push( Scanner $scanner ) {
        $context = $scanner->getContext();
        $context->pushResult( $scanner->token() );
    }
```

In addition to a parse failure, there are two conditions that might prevent the result from being pushed to the scanner's stack. First, client code can ask a parser to discard a successful match by calling the discard() method. This toggles a property called $discard to true. Second, only terminal parsers (that is, parsers that are not composed of other parsers) should push their result to the stack. Composite parsers (instances of CollectionParser, often referred to in the following text as *collection parsers*) will instead let their successful children push their results. I test whether or not a parser is terminal using the term() method, which is overridden to return false by collection parsers.

If the concrete parser has been successful in its matching then I call another method: invokeHandler(). This is passed the Scanner object. If a Handler (that is, an object that implements the Handler interface) has been attached to Parser (using the setHandler() method), then its handleMatch()

method is invoked here. I use handlers to make a successful grammar actually do something, as you will see shortly.

Back in the scan() method, I call on the Scanner object (via the next() method) to advance its position by calling its nextToken() and eatWhiteSpace() methods. Finally, I return the value that was provided by doScan().

In addition to doScan(), notice the abstract trigger() method. This is used to determine whether a parser should bother to attempt a match. If trigger() returns false then the conditions are not right for parsing. Let's take a look at a concrete terminal Parser. CharacterParse is designed to match a particular character:

```
namespace gi\parse;

class CharacterParse extends Parser {
    private $char;

    function __construct( $char, $name=null, $options=null ) {
        parent::__construct( $name, $options );
        $this->char = $char;
    }

    function trigger( Scanner $scanner ) {
        return ( $scanner->token() == $this->char );
    }

    protected function doScan( Scanner $scanner ) {
        return ( $this->trigger( $scanner ) );
    }
}
```

The constructor accepts a character to match and an optional parser name for debugging purposes. The trigger() method simply checks whether the scanner is pointing to a character token that matches the sought character. Because no further scanning than this is required, the doScan() method simply invokes trigger().

Terminal matching is a reasonably simple affair, as you can see. Let's look now at a collection parser. First I'll define a common superclass, and then go on to create a concrete example.

```
namespace gi/parse;

// This abstract class holds subparsers
abstract class CollectionParse extends Parser {
    protected $parsers = array();

    function add( Parser $p ) {
        if ( is_null( $p ) ) {
            throw new Exception( "argument is null" );
        }
        $this->parsers[]= $p;
        return $p;
    }

    function term() {
        return false;
    }
}
```

```
class SequenceParse extends CollectionParse {

    function trigger( Scanner $scanner ) {
        if ( empty( $this->parsers ) ) {
            return false;
        }
        return $this->parsers[0]->trigger( $scanner );
    }

    protected function doScan( Scanner $scanner ) {
        $start_state = $scanner->getState();
        foreach( $this->parsers as $parser ) {
            if ( ! ( $parser->trigger( $scanner ) &&
                    $scan=$parser->scan( $scanner )) ) {
                $scanner->setState( $start_state );
                return false;
            }
        }
        return true;
    }
}
```

The abstract CollectionParse class simply implements an add() method that aggregates Parsers and overrides term() to return false.

The SequenceParse::trigger() method tests only the first child Parser it contains, invoking its trigger() method. The calling Parser will first call CollectionParse::trigger() to see if it is worth calling CollectionParse::scan(). If CollectionParse::scan() is called, then doScan() is invoked and the trigger() and scan() methods of all Parser children are called in turn. A single failure results in CollectionParse::doScan() reporting failure.

One of the problems with parsing is the need to try stuff out. A SequenceParse object may contain an entire tree of parsers within each of its aggregated parsers. These will push the Scanner on by a token or more and cause results to be registered with the Context object. If the final child in the Parser list returns false, what should SequenceParse do about the results lodged in Context by the child's more successful siblings? A sequence is all or nothing, so I have no choice but to roll back both the Context object and the Scanner. I do this by saving state at the start of doScan() and calling setState() just before returning false on failure. Of course, if I return true then there's no need to roll back.

For the sake of completeness, here are all the remaining Parser classes:

```
namespace gi\parse;

// This matches if one or more subparsers match
class RepetitionParse extends CollectionParse {
    private $min;
    private $max;

    function __construct( $min=0, $max=0, $name=null, $options=null ) {
        parent::__construct( $name, $options );
        if ( $max < $min && $max > 0 ) {
            throw new Exception(
                "maximum ( $max ) larger than minimum ( $min )");
        }
        $this->min = $min;
        $this->max = $max;
```

```php
    }

    function trigger( Scanner $scanner ) {
        return true;
    }

    protected function doScan( Scanner $scanner ) {
        $start_state = $scanner->getState();
        if ( empty( $this->parsers ) ) {
            return true;
        }
        $parser = $this->parsers[0];
        $count = 0;

        while ( true ) {
            if ( $this->max > 0 && $count >= $this->max ) {
                return true;
            }

            if ( ! $parser->trigger( $scanner ) ) {
                if ( $this->min == 0 || $count >= $this->min ) {
                    return true;
                } else {
                    $scanner->setState( $start_state );
                    return false;
                }
            }
            if ( ! $parser->scan( $scanner ) ) {
                if ( $this->min == 0 || $count >= $this->min ) {
                    return true;
                } else {
                    $scanner->setState( $start_state );
                    return false;
                }
            }
            $count++;
        }
        return true;
    }
}

// This matches if one or other of two subparsers match
class AlternationParse extends CollectionParse {

    function trigger( Scanner $scanner ) {
        foreach ( $this->parsers as $parser ) {
            if ( $parser->trigger( $scanner ) ) {
                return true;
            }
        }
        return false;
    }
```

```php
    protected function doScan( Scanner $scanner ) {
        $type = $scanner->tokenType();
        foreach ( $this->parsers as $parser ) {
            $start_state = $scanner->getState();
            if ( $type == $parser->trigger( $scanner ) &&
                    $parser->scan( $scanner ) ) {
                return true;
            }
        }
        $scanner->setState( $start_state );
        return false;
    }
}

// this terminal parser matches a string literal
class StringLiteralParse extends Parser {

    function trigger( Scanner $scanner ) {
        return ( $scanner->tokenType() == Scanner::APOS ||
                    $scanner->tokenType() == Scanner::QUOTE );
    }

    protected function push( Scanner $scanner ) {
        return;
    }

    protected function doScan( Scanner $scanner ) {
        $quotechar = $scanner->tokenType();
        $ret = false;
        $string = "";
        while ( $token = $scanner->nextToken() ) {
            if ( $token == $quotechar ) {
                $ret = true;
                break;
            }
            $string .= $scanner->token();
        }

        if ( $string && ! $this->discard ) {
            $scanner->getContext()->pushResult( $string );
        }

        return $ret;
    }
}

// this terminal parser matches a word token
class WordParse extends Parser {

    function __construct( $word=null, $name=null, $options=null ) {
        parent::__construct( $name, $options );
        $this->word = $word;
    }
```

```
    function trigger( Scanner $scanner ) {
        if ( $scanner->tokenType() != Scanner::WORD ) {
            return false;
        }
        if ( is_null( $this->word ) ) {
            return true;
        }
        return ( $this->word == $scanner->token() );
    }

    protected function doScan( Scanner $scanner ) {
        $ret = ( $this->trigger( $scanner ) );
        return $ret;
    }
}
```

By combining terminal and nonterminal Parser objects, I can build a reasonably sophisticated parser. You can see all the Parser classes I use for this example in Figure B–1.

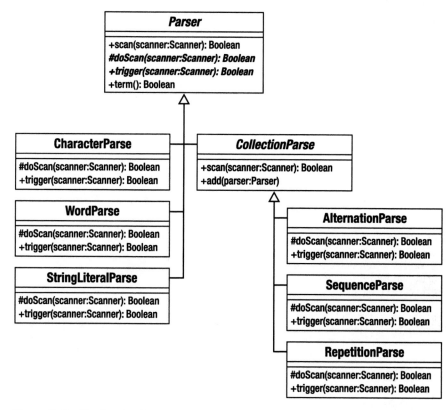

Figure B–1. *The Parser classes*

The idea behind this use of the Composite pattern is that a client can build up a grammar in code that closely matches EBNF notation. Table B–1 shows the parallels between these classes and EBNF fragments.

Table B–1. *Composite Parsers and EBNF*

Class	EBNF Example	Description
AlternationParse	orExpr | andExpr	Either one or another
SequenceParse	'and' operand	A list (all required in order)
RepetitionParse	(eqExpr)*	Zero or more required

Now to build some client code to implement the mini-language. As a reminder, here is the EBNF fragment I presented in Chapter 11:

```
expr      ::= operand (orExpr | andExpr )*
operand   ::= ( '(' expr ')' | <stringLiteral> | variable ) ( eqExpr )*
orExpr    ::= 'or' operand
andExpr   ::= 'and' operand
eqExpr    ::= 'equals' operand
variable  ::= '$' <word>
```

This simple class builds up a grammar based on this fragment and runs it:

```php
class MarkParse {
    private $expression;
    private $operand;
    private $interpreter;
    private $context;

    function __construct( $statement ) {
        $this->compile( $statement );
    }

    function evaluate( $input ) {
        $icontext = new InterpreterContext();
        $prefab = new VariableExpression('input', $input );
        // add the input variable to Context
        $prefaB->interpret( $icontext );

        $this->interpreter->interpret( $icontext );
        $result = $icontext->lookup( $this->interpreter );
        return $result;
    }

    function compile( $statement_str ) {
        // build parse tree
        $context = new \gi\parse\Context();
        $scanner = new \gi\parse\Scanner(
            new \gi\parse\StringReader($statement_str), $context );
        $statement = $this->expression();
```

```php
    $scanresult = $statement->scan( $scanner );

    if ( ! $scanresult || $scanner->tokenType() != \gi\parse\Scanner::EOF ) {
        $msg  = "";
        $msg .= " line: {$scanner->line_no()} ";
        $msg .= " char: {$scanner->char_no()}";
        $msg .= " token: {$scanner->token()}\n";
        throw new Exception( $msg );
    }

    $this->interpreter = $scanner->getContext()->popResult();
}

function expression() {
    if ( ! isset( $this->expression ) ) {
        $this->expression = new \gi\parse\SequenceParse();
        $this->expression->add( $this->operand() );
        $bools = new \gi\parse\RepetitionParse( );
        $whichbool = new \gi\parse\AlternationParse();
        $whichbool->add( $this->orExpr() );
        $whichbool->add( $this->andExpr() );
        $bools->add( $whichbool );
        $this->expression->add( $bools );
    }
    return $this->expression;
}

function orExpr() {
    $or = new \gi\parse\SequenceParse( );
    $or->add( new \gi\parse\WordParse('or') )->discard();
    $or->add( $this->operand() );
    $or->setHandler( new BooleanOrHandler() );
    return $or;
}

function andExpr() {
    $and = new \gi\parse\SequenceParse();
    $and->add( new \gi\parse\WordParse('and') )->discard();
    $and->add( $this->operand() );
    $and->setHandler( new BooleanAndHandler() );
    return $and;
}

function operand() {
    if ( ! isset( $this->operand ) ) {
        $this->operand = new \gi\parse\SequenceParse( );
        $comp = new \gi\parse\AlternationParse( );
        $exp = new \gi\parse\SequenceParse( );
        $exp->add( new \gi\parse\CharacterParse( '(' ))->discard();
        $exp->add( $this->expression() );
        $exp->add( new \gi\parse\CharacterParse( ')' ))->discard();
        $comp->add( $exp );
        $comp->add( new \gi\parse\StringLiteralParse() )
```

```
                ->setHandler( new StringLiteralHandler() );
        $comp->add( $this->variable() );
        $this->operand->add( $comp );
        $this->operand->add( new \gi\parse\RepetitionParse( ) )
            ->add($this->eqExpr());
    }
    return $this->operand;
}

function eqExpr() {
    $equals = new \gi\parse\SequenceParse();
    $equals->add( new \gi\parse\WordParse('equals') )->discard();
    $equals->add( $this->operand() );
    $equals->setHandler( new EqualsHandler() );
    return $equals;
}

function variable() {
    $variable = new \gi\parse\SequenceParse();
    $variable->add( new \gi\parse\CharacterParse( '$' ))->discard();
    $variable->add( new \gi\parse\WordParse());
    $variable->setHandler( new VariableHandler() );
    return $variable;
}
}
```

This may seem like a complicated class, but all it is doing is building up the grammar I have already defined. Most of the methods are analogous to production names (that is, the names that begin each production line in EBNF, such as eqExpr and andExpr). If you look at the expression() method, you should see that I am building up the same rule as I defined in EBNF earlier:

```
// expr      ::= operand (orExpr | andExpr )*
    function expression() {
        if ( ! isset( $this->expression ) ) {
            $this->expression = new \gi\parse\SequenceParse();
            $this->expression->add( $this->operand() );
            $bools = new \gi\parse\RepetitionParse( );
            $whichbool = new \gi\parse\AlternationParse();
            $whichbool->add( $this->orExpr() );
            $whichbool->add( $this->andExpr() );
            $bools->add( $whichbool );
            $this->expression->add( $bools );
        }
        return $this->expression;
    }
```

In both the code and the EBNF notation, I define a sequence that consists of a reference to an operand, followed by zero or more instances of an alternation between orExpr and andExpr. Notice that I am storing the Parser returned by this method in a property variable. This is to prevent infinite loops, as methods invoked from expression() themselves reference expression().

The only methods that are doing more than just building the grammar are compile() and evaluate(). compile() can be called directly or automatically via the constructor, which accepts a statement string and uses it to create a Scanner object. It calls the expression() method, which returns a tree of Parser objects that make up the grammar. It then calls Parser::scan(), passing it the Scanner object. If the raw code does not parse, the compile() method throws an exception. Otherwise, it retrieves the result of compilation as left on the Scanner object's Context. As you will see shortly, this should be an Expression object. This result is stored in a property called $interpreter.

The evaluate() method makes a value available to the Expression tree. It does this by predefining a VariableExpression object named input and registering it with the Context object that is then passed to the main Expression object. As with variables such as $_REQUEST in PHP, this $input variable is always available to MarkLogic coders.

Note See Chapter 11 for more about the VariableExpression class that is part of the Interpreter pattern example.

The evaluate() method calls the Expression::interpret() method to generate a final result. Remember, you need to retrieve interpreter results from the Context object.

So far, you have seen how to parse text and how to build a grammar. You also saw in Chapter 11 how to use the Interpreter pattern to combine Expression objects and process a query. You have not yet seen, though, how to relate the two processes. How do you get from a parse tree to the interpreter? The answer lies in the Handler objects that can be associated with Parser objects using Parser::setHandler(). Let's take a look at the way to manage variables. I associate a VariableHandler with the Parser in the variable() method:

```
$variable->setHandler( new VariableHandler() );
```

Here is the Handler interface:

```
namespace gi\parse;

interface Handler {
    function handleMatch(    Parser $parser,
                             Scanner $scanner );
}
```

And here is VariableHandler:

```
class VariableHandler implements \gi\parse\Handler {
    function handleMatch( \gi\parse\Parser $parser, \gi\parse\Scanner $scanner ) {
        $varname = $scanner->getContext()->popResult();
        $scanner->getContext()->pushResult( new VariableExpression( $varname ) );
    }
}
```

If the Parser with which VariableHandler is associated matches on a scan operation, then handleMatch() is called. By definition, the last item on the stack will be the name of the variable. I remove this and replace it with a new VariableExpression object with the correct name. Similar principles are used to create EqualsExpression objects, LiteralExpression objects, and so on.

Here are the remaining handlers:

```
class StringLiteralHandler implements \gi\parse\Handler {
    function handleMatch( \gi\parse\Parser $parser, \gi\parse\Scanner $scanner ) {
        $value = $scanner->getContext()->popResult();
        $scanner->getContext()->pushResult( new LiteralExpression( $value ) );
    }
```

```
}

class EqualsHandler implements \gi\parse\Handler {
    function handleMatch( \gi\parse\Parser $parser, \gi\parse\Scanner $scanner ) {
        $comp1 = $scanner->getContext()->popResult();
        $comp2 = $scanner->getContext()->popResult();
        $scanner->getContext()->pushResult(
            new EqualsExpression( $comp1, $comp2 ) );
    }
}

class BooleanOrHandler implements \gi\parse\Handler {
    function handleMatch( \gi\parse\Parser $parser, \gi\parse\Scanner $scanner ) {
        $comp1 = $scanner->getContext()->popResult();
        $comp2 = $scanner->getContext()->popResult();
        $scanner->getContext()->pushResult(
            new BooleanOrExpression( $comp1, $comp2 ) );
    }
}

class BooleanAndHandler implements \gi\parse\Handler {
    function handleMatch( \gi\parse\Parser $parser, \gi\parse\Scanner $scanner ) {
        $comp1 = $scanner->getContext()->popResult();
        $comp2 = $scanner->getContext()->popResult();
        $scanner->getContext()->pushResult(
            new BooleanAndExpression( $comp1, $comp2 ) );
    }
}
```

Bearing in mind that you also need the Interpreter example from Chapter 11 at hand, you can work with the MarkParse class like this:

```
$input     = 'five';
$statement = "( \$input equals 'five')";

$engine = new MarkParse( $statement );
$result = $engine->evaluate( $input );
print "input: $input evaluating: $statement\n";
if ( $result ) {
    print "true!\n";
} else {
    print "false!\n";
}
```

This should produce the following results:

```
input: five evaluating: ( $input equals 'five')
true!
```

Index

■ ■ ■

■ T

■ U

CPSIA information can be obtained at www.ICGtesting.com
Printed in the USA
LVOW112123191011

251300LV00006B/1/P